STREET HOMELESSNESS AND
CATHOLIC THEOLOGICAL ETHICS

CATHOLIC THEOLOGICAL ETHICS IN THE WORLD CHURCH

James F. Keenan, Series Editor

The book series of Catholic Theological Ethics in the World Church (CTEWC) responds to the challenge of pluralism, the call to dialogue from and beyond local culture, and the need to interconnect within a world church. While pursuing critical and emerging issues in theological ethics, CTEWC engages in cross-cultural, interdisciplinary conversations motivated by mercy and care and shaped by shared visions of hope.

Volumes in the series to date, published by Orbis Books:

Catholic Theological Ethics Past, Present, and Future:
The Trento Conference
James F. Keenan, editor

Feminist Catholic Theological Ethics: Conversations in the World Church
Linda Hogan and A. E. Orobator, editors

Just Sustainability: Technology, Ecology, and Resource Extraction
Christiana Z. Peppard and Andrea Vicini, editors

Living with(out) Borders:
Catholic Theological Ethics on the Migrations of Peoples
Agnes M. Brazal and María Teresa Dávila, editors

The Bible and Catholic Theological Ethics
Yiu Sing Lúcás Chan, James F. Keenan, and Ronaldo Zacharias, editors

The Catholic Ethicist in the Local Church
Antonio Autiero and Laurenti Magesa, editors

Building Bridges in Sarajevo: The Plenary Papers from CTEWC 2018
Kristin E. Heyer, James F. Keenan, and Andrea Vicini, editors

Street Homelessness and Catholic Theological Ethics
James F. Keenan and Mark McGreevy, editors

STREET HOMELESSNESS AND CATHOLIC THEOLOGICAL ETHICS

Edited by

JAMES F. KEENAN, SJ

MARK MCGREEVY

ORBIS BOOKS
Maryknoll, New York 10545

ORBIS BOOKS
Maryknoll, New York 10545

Fathers and Brothers
MARYKNOLL.

Founded in 1970, Orbis Books endeavors to publish works that enlighten the mind, nourish the spirit, and challenge the conscience. The publishing arm of the Maryknoll Fathers and Brothers, Orbis seeks to explore the global dimensions of the Christian faith and mission, to invite dialogue with diverse cultures and religious traditions, and to serve the cause of reconciliation and peace. The books published reflect the views of their authors and do not represent the official position of the Maryknoll Society. To learn more about Maryknoll and Orbis Books, please visit our website at www.maryknollsociety.org.

Library of Congress Cataloging-in-Publication Data

Names: Keenan, James F., editor.
Title: Street homelessness and Catholic theological ethics / edited by James F. Keenan, SJ, Mark McGreevy, OBE.
Description: Maryknoll : Orbis Books, 2019. | Series: Catholic theological ethics in the world church series | Includes bibliographical references and index.
Identifiers: LCCN 2019014950 (print) | LCCN 2019981444 (ebook) | ISBN 9781626983441 (print) | ISBN 9781608338085 (ebook)
Subjects: LCSH: Church work with the homeless. | Church work—Catholic Church. | Homelessness—Religious aspects—Christianity. | Christian ethics—Catholic authors.
Classification: LCC BV4456 .S76 2019 (print) | LCC BV4456 (ebook) | DDC 261.8/32592—dc23
LC record available at https://lccn.loc.gov/2019014950
LC ebook record available at https://lccn.loc.gov/2019981444

To every homeless brother and sister of Christ

sleeping on our streets tonight.

Contents

FOREWORD

Street Homelessness in the Time of Pope Francis

Cardinal Peter Turkson

The homeless, "those who lack access to minimally adequate housing," have been for too long a part of modern urban living.[1] Either because of mental illness or substance misuse, or because of simple insolvency; or because lawsuits and courts have thrown fathers out on the streets as part of divorce settlements; or because the presence of some parents in homes are considered by courts to be harmful, indeed, a threat to families' security; or because wars and conflicts have driven people from their homes, adults and children alike, as in Afghanistan, Syria, Iraq, Ukraine, South Sudan, or the Democratic Republic of Congo; or because of intolerable government policies as in Eritrea, Venezuela, and El Salvador; or because a natural disaster has struck as in Haiti, the Philippines, Colombia, and Bangladesh; or because wildfire has chased people out of their homes as in Australia, Chile, and the Pacific and Mountain States of the United States of America; or because a disease, like HIV-AIDS or Ebola, has ravaged a home, taking away parents and turning the children onto the streets; homes and families are broken, and a spate of refuge-seeking people are set on the move, making homelessness common, global, and worldwide.

As one can see, the causes of homelessness are many and varied. A 2015 Habitat for Humanity report estimates that 1.6 billion people around the world are living in inadequate shelter. It is about a quarter of the world's population. Even in the United States, the figures are alarming. In 2016, a survey found that over half a million people were living in this great and good nation on streets, in cars, and in homeless shelters. Just under half of these were from broken families—so they were not just lone wanderers—and a quarter of the entire group were children.

In a 2017 report from *Caritas Berlin,* an organization in Germany that stages yearly "cold aid campaigns" at the onset of the winter, director Ulrike Kostka observed that "Germany cannot only benefit from the open markets and the EU citizens' free movement, it must also take responsibility for immigrants." And this was because, with six thousand poor people in the streets of Berlin (with some in illegal camps like the one in Tiergarten Park), Ulrike deplored, "the homeless are now at the centre of society."[2]

Not only are popular public areas of cities being taken over by the homeless, as in Berlin; there has been a proposal that the European Union facilities themselves in Brussels be open as shelters in the night for the homeless. It is reported that the Vice President of the European Parliament, Mr. David Sassoli, has written to the President of the European Parliament, Mr. Antonio Tajani: "The poor cannot wait, and we cannot remain indifferent to those people in situations of real difficulty who sleep rough every night, trying to shelter themselves from the cold outside the Parliament. . . . You just need to take a walk outside to realize how many people need help and assistance. I think it would be an act of great humanity to open some rooms of the European Parliament overnight, without compromising its functioning and safety, to ensure these people have an appropriate shelter."[3]

One of the early results of Great Britain joining the European Union (European Economic Community) in January 1973 was the arrival in London and other cities of Great Britain some non-English-speaking Europeans from Eastern Europe. These constituted the major component of homeless "boozers" on the streets of London, a situation that the Bishops' Conference of England and Wales decided to study at the dawn of the third millennium. The problem of homelessness has persisted in Great Britain, reaching crisis levels in several cities, according to BBC News reports on international and home radio channels. These are the "rough sleepers" on Great Britain's streets; the Catholic Bishops revisited the issue in their Plenary Assembly in November 2018. The bishops directed that Catholic Charities in the UK are to make the construction of new homes and the homeless their top priority up to 2030, in line with the UN's Sustainable Development Goals.[4]

A year earlier and as a result of the increasing number of deaths of persons "sleeping rough," the Irish bishops, at their Plenary Assembly in December 2017, appealed to all people and in particular to their policy makers, to recommit to building a society that enables all people to live in a decent home. Then they added: "In an Ireland which is approaching full employment, we have the choice whether to respect the dignity of all or to ignore this suffering."[5]

So homelessness is a global phenomenon, which is indeed a tragedy. And it is a *tragedy,* not just because it is a phenomenon that has become global on account of a pervasive culture and an attitude of indifference that is quickly replacing our sense of neighborliness, solidarity, and belongingness as members of a human family. It is a tragedy most importantly because it is incompatible with our sense of *human dignity*.

Our incontrovertible belief in the dignity of every human person is fast waning and ceding its place to an emerging ugly attitude that every life is dispensable, except our own. We are increasingly acquiring the attitude of observing people and things from *balconies* (an expression of Pope Francis), without getting involved, and of being unaffected and untouched by the situations and sufferings of others. In this sense, the Irish bishops had reason to remind the readers in their pastoral letter, *A Room in the Inn?* that "Recognizing the dignity of all in our society is not an empty formula of words, nor is it a mere charitable posture. . . . The Catholic Church teaches that each person, regardless of his or her economic or social position, racial or faith background, must be treated in a manner which fully respects their dignity."

Similarly, during his visit to a Capuchin Day Centre for homeless people in his visit to Ireland last August (2018), Pope Francis is reported to have said to the homeless visitors to the day centre: "Do you know why you come here with trust? Because they help you without detracting from your dignity. For them, each of you is Jesus Christ. We must always strive to honor and uphold the dignity of every human person, created in God's image."[6]

Indeed, the dignity each person has by reason of his or her creation by God is the basis of all the rights a person has, and the right to shelter is one of them. Having adequate shelter is a basic human right—a key part of respecting and recognizing our dignity as persons. Accordingly, as Pope Francis said during his visit to a shelter in Washington, DC, during his 2015 visit to the United States of America, "We can find no social or moral justification, no justification whatsoever, for lack of housing."[7] A house is much more than a roof over one's head. It's a place where a person creates and lives out his or her life. Accordingly, a society ensures social justice when it provides the conditions that allow individuals to obtain what is their due.[8] So we have a collective responsibility to work together as individuals and in concert with other bodies—including state and local governments, the private sector, and community groups—to ensure the *justice of housing* and other forms of justice in society.

Where the justice of housing and other forms of justice are wanting, the church shares the "light of the Gospel" to defend and to promote the right and need of every person to be helped to live with dignity. For example, the Archdiocese of Cape Coast, Ghana, supports a state-owned leprosarium with chaplaincy and health care service. In the 1990s, the archdiocese, recognizing the great difficulty that healed and discharged leprosy patients had finding accommodation on account of prejudice and stigma, and how, invariably, they ended up on the streets, "courting still worse diseases," developed a small township with houses, tarred streets, and street lights for these cured leprosy patients. The patients called the township, "dream (the unexpected) town," and quickly developed handwork outposts and a mission post.

This is a real-life application of St. Pope John Paul II's teaching on *solidarity as a virtue*. Recognizing how deeply the Scriptures root human life in coexistence and in relationship with others, the *Compendium of the Social Teaching of the Church* teaches that *relationships* are not incidental to the human person. Relationships are not something we happen to be in by chance, just as dignity is not something we may or may not have. Relationships and dignity are what we are and have as human beings, and no one else and nothing else in heaven or on earth is so constituted. As creatures with inalienable rights, we exist in relationships with others; outside these relationships, we are less than human. Accordingly, for John Paul II, *solidarity* meant "a firm and persevering determination to commit oneself to the common good: our good and the good of others"[9]—the common good is the sum total of all the conditions that allow people, either as groups or individuals, to reach their fulfillment more fully and more easily.

Pope Francis takes up John Paul II's call for solidarity and prescribes for it the creation of a new mentality that thinks in terms of community and the priority of the life of the whole over and above the appropriation of property by a few. Solidarity, thus practiced, allows people to become artisans of their destiny, since each person is called to self-fulfillment.[10]

Pope Francis and the Homeless

Now, let me tell you what Pope Francis is doing in the face of global homelessness.

Remember the story of the Good Samaritan? (Lk 10:25–37). A man on a journey from Jerusalem to Jericho was attacked and left half-dead. While some ignored his plight, a "good Samaritan" had compassion, pouring oil and wine onto his wounds. It strikes me that in the parable, the Good Samaritan gives up his place on his mule to bring that injured man to safety at a shelter, promising to return and pay for his keep. Pope Francis tells us that the Samaritan's concrete, personal actions teach us that "compassion, love, is not a vague feeling. It means to take care of the other even to paying in person. . . . It means to commit oneself, taking all the necessary steps to 'come close' to the other, to the point of identifying oneself with him; for the commandment says: 'you shall love your neighbor as yourself.' This parable is a stupendous gift for all of us, and also a commitment," the Holy Father concludes. "Jesus repeats to each one of us what He said to the Doctor of the Law: 'Go and do likewise.'"[11]

Pope Francis has done just that for the homeless and those living on the margins—seeing in them the dignity of children of God:

- In 2013, on his seventy-seventh birthday, he invited homeless people to his residence for breakfast to listen to their concerns and what the church could do for them. The homeless brought even their dogs!
- The following year, again on his birthday, he bought four hundred sleeping bags for those living on the streets around the Vatican.
- Also in 2014, Pope Francis ordered showers to be built for the homeless in St. Peter's Square, as well as a barber shop that would be open on a weekly basis.
- In 2015, he opened a homeless shelter near St. Peter's Basilica. Joey, a homeless man, said this: "Everyone else spits on the homeless. Not here!"
- In the very hot Roman summer of 2016, he treated the homeless to an outing to the beach and bought them pizza on the way back.
- Most recently, he has opened a free laundromat (2017) and a free medical center (2018) for the poor and homeless near the Vatican.
- He has also given shelter in apartments in the Vatican to refugees forced to flee war-torn regions such as Syria and Iraq.

Pope Francis shows that each of us can contribute something toward the creation of social justice in the face of the forces that create global homelessness and global indifference. As Saint Teresa of Kolkata tells us: "If I had not begun picking up the first man whom I saw lying on the street, together with my Sisters, we would never have picked up the other thousands." So, as Jesus concludes the Parable of the Good Samaritan, "Let us go and do the same"!

Notes

1. In villages, where dwellers usually know one another, either as relatives or as acquaintances, homelessness is a rarity.

2. Servizio Informazione Religiosa (November 2, 2017), https://www.agensir.it/quotidiano/2017/11/2/germany-kostka-caritas-berlin-the-homeless-are-now-at-the-centre-of-society-6-thousand-poor-people-in-the-streets-of-berlin/.

3. https://www.agensir.it/quotidiano/2019/1/25/cold-snap-emergency-mr-sassoli-vice-president-ep-in-brussels-should-shelter-the-homeless-overnight/.

4. https://agensir.it/quotidiano/2018/11/20/england-and-wales-plenary-assembly-sends-message-to-catholic-charities-take-care-of-the-homeless-and-address-the-housing-crisis/.

5. Cf. also *A Room at the Inn? A Pastoral Letter on Housing and Homelessness* (The Irish Catholic Bishops' Conference, 2018).

6. https://www.catholicnewsagency.com/news/irish-bishops-call-on-government-to-address-homelessness-75955.

7. Pope Francis, address at Washington, DC, homeless shelter, September 24, 2015.

8. *Catechism of the Catholic Church,* no. 1928.

9. Pope John Paul II, 1987 encyclical, *Sollicitudo Rei Socialis* (On Social Concern), no. 38.

10. Pope Francis, 2013 Apostolic Exhortation, *Evangelii Gaudium* (The Joy of the Gospel), no. 190.

11. Pope Francis, General Audience, April 27, 2016.

INTRODUCTION

James F. Keenan, SJ

Most of the contributors to this volume, theologians, practitioners, and social scientists, came to Rome for a symposium titled "Street Homelessness and Catholic Social Teaching" that took place from November 30 to December 2, 2017. The event was sponsored by the Institute for Global Homelessness at DePaul University in coordination with the Dicastery for Promoting Integral Human Development, with other support coming from St. John's University, Niagara University, the Center for Catholic Studies at the University of Durham, and Depaul International.

We had been invited by Mark McGreevy, OBE, Group Chief Executive of Depaul International and Founder of the Institute of Global Homelessness. He, together with Anna Rowlands and Pat Jones at Durham University, William Cavanaugh at Chicago's DePaul University, Meghan Clark from St. John's University, and Ethna Regan of Dublin City University, organized the symposium.

Their aim was to bring the tradition of Catholic social thought into dialogue with the experience and analysis of global homelessness, in order to develop new theological resources and generate deeper Catholic engagement in practical responses. In short, this symposium was intended to promote global dialogue on street homelessness.

The conference had great effect, and one of the many resolutions to come out of it was the commitment that Catholic Theological Ethics in the World Church (CTEWC) would publish with Orbis Books a collection of essays that would further that global dialogue.

Yet would that it were that simple.

When we met in November, Mark reported that he and his team invited us to the symposium because one of his colleagues, Pat Jones, at that time, a doctoral student at Durham University, had lamented that for her dissertation on street homelessness she was unable to find any article or book by any theological ethicist anywhere in the world on the topic of street homelessness.*

This book responds ashamedly to that notice. Not only are those living on the streets "overlooked" by passersby, but we in the church and the academy have done the same as others in ignoring their situation. What's worse, our business is to critically reflect on and respond to the situations of those on the margins, but these margins we ignored like otherwise preoccupied passersby (Lk 10:31–32).

I believe that the contributors to this volume realized that we had to make amends for our neglect, and I think that anyone who reads this will sense how dedicated the contributors became to this project that brings street homelessness to the fore.

Moreover, in doing this book in our own CTEWC series, we want to note that as CTEWC enters into its second generation, this volume takes us in a slightly different direction than previous books in the series. In addition to the plenary papers at Trento in 2010 and those in Sarajevo in 2018, the five books between these two collections dealt with broad themes from multitudinous perspectives: feminism, sustainability, migration, the use of the Bible, and the ethicist's place in the church. But this is the first time that we are descending into the particularities of a very particular topic. We intend this volume to break the ground for other urgent issues so as to attend to their particularities and provide appropriate international investigation.

In order to do this, we divided the book into two parts: Accompanying the Homeless and Working to End Homelessness. The first part has two sections: the first gives voice to the homeless through a variety of ways: a dialogical sharing, an expression of prayer, papal witnesses, and ethnography. The first section is about listening, and the second is about meeting, and here we encounter the stateless migrant, the violated Indian woman, the African elder, the returning veteran, the Hong Kong worker, youth (and in particular members of the LBGT community driven from their homes), and finally the US drug user.

The second part is divided into three sections. The first of these is devoted to global and ecclesial strategies, and here we begin by taking aim at three of the United Nations' Sustainable Development Goals (1, 3, and 11), then two strategies from above (government and Caritas), and two from below (subsidiarity and *The Catholic Worker*). The second section turns to theological-ethical foundations: the spiritual works of mercy, the Matthean Beatitudes, Catholic Social Teaching, Human Rights, and the virtues of Solidarity and Hospitality. The last section takes us to three locations to witness actual strategies for ending homelessness in Cameroon, India, and Jamaica.

We hope that we have provided here a work that can be used in a variety of ways to grow in competency about street homelessness, both by understanding and meeting the people directly affected by it and by working to end something that is so commonly overlooked. The structure hopefully leads readers to see, judge, and act. For that reason, the work can then be used for individuals or collectives, in classes or in study groups, in urban or rural areas, in churches or schools. We think we have given readers, individually and collectively, a foundational and comprehensive introduction to Street Homelessness.

We thank our benefactors and our contributors and we particularly thank Msgr. Bruno Marie Duffé, the Secretary of the Dicastery for Promoting Integral Human, and Cardinal Peter Kodwo Appiah Turkson, the Dicastery's first Prefect, for their support of our project and their participation in our symposium. Finally, we thank Sara Samir for her excellent assistance in editing this volume and Jill O'Brien at Orbis Books who has accompanied us throughout this project.

* An exception to this claim is Kelly Johnson's *The Fear of Beggars: Stewardship and Poverty in Christian Ethics* (Grand Rapids, MI: Eerdmans, 2007).

Preface

The Summons to End Global Homelessness

Mark McGreevy and Molly Seeley

In 1991, the charity I (Mark) work for, Depaul International, published its first full-year annual report. The front cover carried an image that we hoped would explain, in simple terms, the reasons why people become homeless and the routes out of it. It was a hand-drawn sketch of a person descending a ladder leading to homelessness and a life on the street in the UK. Each rung of the descent represented a particular problem an individual might have faced along their journey—poverty, unemployment, lack of housing options, personal debt, family breakdown, physical or mental ill health, addiction or abuse, and circumstances leading to their becoming a refugee or asylum seeker—which, either in isolation or, more likely, in combination, would have contributed to their situation.

It is an image that is as relevant today as it was then. Most of us will slip down a ladder from time to time, and most of us will experience at least one, if not several, of the problems listed above leading to homelessness over the course of our lifetimes. We are all vulnerable to personal tragedy and the failings of others—it is part of our shared human experience. Most of us survive and thrive because we have the support of family and friends, or we have access to enough resources to compensate when things go wrong. There is usually someone, or something, there to catch us before we hit the bottom rung. However, this is not true for all of us. Millions of people are not so fortunate. They do not have the support and safety net that we take for granted, and it is those who represent a growing population of homeless people on the streets of our cities around the world.

Luckily, ladders work both ways. If you can climb down, then you can also climb up, and the same sketch from 1991 had another set of steps with each rung being an intervention that would lead someone out of homelessness. Experience shows that it is absolutely possible for anyone to escape homelessness if we take the right approach. You just need to construct a ladder that personally addresses each individual's needs and then be there for them, holding that ladder steady as they climb away from the street. Ending street homelessness worldwide, meaningfully and sustainably, is as simple, and as complicated, as that.

Ending homelessness is not a pipe dream, nor an idealist's fantasy. It is a reality that is already happening, and can spread. There is an ever-growing body of evidence to prove that, like any complex problem, with the right mix of coordinated efforts, street homelessness is a completely solvable issue. Moreover, the interventions and policy implementations required to reduce the number of people sleeping rough benefit the broader community in a variety of ways—economically, environmentally, and socially. We know this because we have already seen street homelessness reduced and even resolved in cities and nations around the world.

This is not to suggest that ending street homelessness is *easy*, nor that it can be done overnight, but rather that even the tallest walls may be scaled with the right ladder. In this essay, we examine some of the current debates related to street homelessness and the challenges we face. It is a problem best tackled locally, but to put that in perspective, let us begin by examining the issues from a global perspective.

We can think about the metaphorical ladder out of homelessness as having four rungs: consistent vocabulary; data collection and analysis; intersectional thinking; and systemic, coordinated policy. We will address each of these in turn.

Vocabulary

It is impossible to solve a problem that you cannot discuss with adequate precision. Globally, street homelessness has varied and sometimes conflicting definitions, which can lead to ambiguous policy, difficulty understanding scope, and lack of analogous data. We have tried to address this question in relation to many other critical global development issues: for example, extreme poverty is described in the first of the United Nations' Sustainable Development Goals[1] as living below US $1.90 per day. Although this definition may be debatable—for example, the World Bank also looks at poverty lines of $3.20 and $5.50[2]—it is nevertheless a basis for understanding what the benchmark is when discussing something as complex and multifaceted as "extreme poverty." There is no globally accepted equivalent of this baseline definition in street homelessness.

Part of the problem is that conceptions of appropriate housing vary wildly from context to context, and the delineations between forms of homelessness and various types of displacement are not straightforward. This lack of clarity, among other obstacles, has made data collection complex and difficult to verify or analyze, particularly in developing contexts. For example, the 2011 Indian national census considered anyone homeless who lived anywhere other than a "census house," defined simply as a "structure with a roof." But some Indian states use more nuanced definitions; the state of Karnataka uses a definition with five categories and includes families and individuals spending the night in their workplaces.[3] These differing ideas of what makes someone homeless renders the numbers from both surveys functionally incomparable; after all, we do not know whether they were even surveying the same populations. This is not to say that these surveys were not accurate as reflections of their methodologies, only that we cannot use one to comment on the other—to say nothing of using one to comment on homelessness in similar (or even differing) contexts.

To confront this issue, in 2015 the Institute of Global Homelessness (IGH) commissioned the IGH Global Framework for Understanding Homelessness,[4] which offers shared vocabulary for comparison and discussion even when countries may be concerned with different types, levels, or subsets of homelessness. Rather than prescribe one strict definition to be adopted everywhere, the Framework captures three broad categories of people who may be understood to be experiencing homelessness, defined as "lacking access to minimally adequate housing." These categories are: (1) People without accommodation (e.g., street sleepers); (2) people living in temporary or crisis accommodation (e.g., shelters or refugee encampments); and (3) people living in severely inadequate and insecure accommodation (e.g., slum dwellers). The IGH has chosen to focus on the street sleepers (in category 1) and the sheltered homeless (in category 2), because these types of "literal homelessness" are prevalent across most countries and continents, and despite being at the most extreme end of the housing deprivation spectrum, these groups are often neglected in discussion at global and local levels. However, this does not suggest that other categories cannot or should not be considered homelessness in local contexts. In fact, in many places these categories may not present as necessarily distinct; they frequently overlap and blur together. For this reason, each of these categories breaks down further to describe the multiplicity of ways in which they can manifest on the ground—internally displaced people in Ukraine, for example, have very different needs from individuals newly released from prison unable to secure housing due to a criminal record, but they may be sleeping on the same stretch of pavement. Even within categories 1 and 2, then, there are diverse manifestations.

For this reason, the Framework is designed to be flexible enough for countries and regions with unique sociocultural and economic contexts to choose what is applicable to them and discard what is not; the precision around what each place finds relevant to their measurement processes will then allow for better and broader comparison. In some cases, we may see that countries are measuring very different types of street homelessness, but even if we understand that their numbers do not represent the same types of populations, this specificity will establish parameters around what each place is dealing with, and what the scope of their problem is. Therefore, while no amount of nuanced vocabulary could enable universal measurement comparisons, the Framework will allow for a global understanding of the scope of homelessness in every region, as it applies to that region. This, then, is the first rung on our ladder.

Data Collection and Analysis

It is only once we have answered the question, "What is street homelessness?" that we can begin to measure it. First we define our problem; then we seek to understand its dimensions. This is the second rung on the ladder: data collection and analysis. Unfortunately, homelessness lags behind other global development and health issues in this regard. The United Nations Human Settlements Program estimates that 1.1 billion people globally live in inadequate housing, and the best data available suggest that more than 100 million people have no housing at all.[5] But this data is incomplete and based largely on estimates; there is no standardized system of counting, nor any database for global statistical analysis, and nations with regular, reliable measurement processes tend to be concentrated in "developed" nations. This is not to say that there are no developing contexts with adequate measures, nor that all developed nations have perfected the art of enumeration; only that a pattern has emerged wherein wealthier nations tend to have more precise data. In many developing contexts, data is collected infrequently or irregularly, if at all.

This is a problem we must solve if we want to end homelessness globally. We know from other global health initiatives that measurement of problems is a core piece to solving those problems—meaningful improvements do not happen by accident. Setting a clear goal, with a deadline, and tracking progress acts as a motor for campaigns seeking to address inequality of any kind. For example, we cannot definitively say whether we are reducing the number of people sleeping rough if we do not have data that accurately enumerates how many people are without shelter every night to begin with.

Data performs three key functions: primarily, it enables coordination bodies to set goals, measure progress, and hold communities accountable; secondarily, it provides critical insight into how systems are functioning, and where they are failing; and finally, it offers insight into who is living on the streets, why, and for how long. Shared local and national data enables local bodies to problem-solve, assess progress, and make the case for resources and political support, while setting targets with deadlines and tracking progress can change a system that manages homelessness into a system that ends it.

Even a minimum standard for data collection, which may neglect this third function, would generate a simple measure of how many people are sleeping rough on any given night. Sophisticated data systems can dig far deeper into local realities, but regularly collected snapshot pictures of what is happening on the street can provide valuable guidance with regard to understanding trends, size, and geographical scope of the problem.

The street is an incredibly dynamic place, with people entering and exiting every day in a variety of ways and for a variety of reasons. Some families and individuals self-resolve their homelessness and find homes, with very little intervention from homelessness service providers. Others, typically those with more complex needs, require a heavier investment of time and resources. The more sophisticated our data systems get, the better we can mobilize numbers into more efficient service delivery, focusing on areas where need is greatest. The key to any efficient and effective service system is to match interventions to need—be it something light-touch, such as preventive rental assistance to stem inflow, or a heavy investment such as permanent supportive housing to help chronically homeless individuals adjust to life off the street. Data helps service providers understand who needs what, allowing communities to focus their resources and to guide effective policy.

Intersectional Thinking

This brings us to the third rung: intersectional thinking. We have defined our problem and begun to consider its nuances; now we must open it up to debate and stimulate action within the international community if we are to tackle its roots. Global homelessness, as previously discussed, has many causes but it also sits at the intersection of many ongoing development debates. In 2016, the United Nations released its seventeen Sustainable Development Goals (SDGs) with 232 measurable indicators, designed to guide the global community toward a future of equality, prosperity, and sustainability. It is clear that ending street homelessness is directly relevant to achieving a number of these goals, and yet there is not one indicator aimed at either reducing or ending homelessness in any part of the document.

Let us look first at SDG 11: "Make Cities and Human Settlements Inclusive, Safe, Resilient and Sustainable." Although rural homelessness exists, the problem is most prevalent in cities, where housing prices are rising far above wage averages, and where an increasing number of rural-to-urban migrants are congregating, pulled by economic opportunity and often pushed by decreasing agricultural viability. Rapid urbanization and city growth have drawn segments of the rural population inward to urban centers. The global population was split evenly between rural and urban areas for the first time in 2008; by 2050, it is expected that 70 percent of the global population will be concentrated in urban areas.[6] These population increases in urban areas may be accompanied by housing deficits and insufficient or overburdened social services, as the viable market for rural-urban migrants is typically limited to seasonal and low-paying work, which may not be enough to secure stable and adequate housing. For example, in Ghana the three most reported reasons for voluntary rural-urban migration are poverty, lack of employment opportunities, and family disruption, and the majority of these migrants are unable to secure accommodation.[7] SDG 11 has a subset goal, 11.1, which includes ensuring "access for all to adequate, safe and affordable housing"—however, there is no measurable indicator for those who are homeless as a consequence of urbanization. If we are to succeed in ending homelessness, then it is an issue best tackled—at least initially—at the city level, where policies and practice can be highly responsive to local challenges and resources. Federal and national-level interventions are an important component in on-the-ground practice, but homelessness is an issue that is concentrated in urban centers, and progress must be made there first if it is going to be significant and sustainable.

Inequality also plays a large role in who becomes homeless and who does not, and any attempts to achieve SDG 10, to "Reduce inequality within and among countries," will require an examination of that role. Homeless populations are typically made up of whichever local demographics are the most heavily stigmatized and disenfranchised, as they may be denied access to services or services may not be geared toward their specific needs. This usually plays out along racial, ethnic, gender, and sexuality lines—simply put, people who are the most affected by structural inequalities are also typically the most affected by homelessness.[8] This in turn can lead to worsening stereotypes about those very populations, decreasing public sympathy and establishing a holding pattern in which the most vulnerable populations become homeless, are not provided adequate supports, and are then blamed for remaining on the street.

Another intersection with the issue of street homelessness is SDG 3: "Ensure healthy lives and promote well-being for all at all ages." The more entrenched an individual becomes in street life, the more vulnerable they become. Homelessness itself is a health risk: regardless of borders, cultures, and geography, a chronically homeless individual is three to four times more likely to die than someone in the general population.[9] Simply put, life on the streets makes the healthy become sick and the sick become sicker.[10] Homelessness makes it difficult to manage chronic illness and adhere to treatment regimens; healthy, nutritional meals are few and far between; exercise and access to hygiene care are rare; exposure to harsh elements and violence are constant; and comorbidity of health issues is common. We cannot talk about public health without talking about the ways in which living without shelter contributes to the deterioration of one's physical and mental health, as likely to trigger an episode or illness as to be triggered by one.

Finally, homelessness is caused by and is an expression of poverty at its most extreme. If we, as a global community, are going to achieve SDG 1: "End Poverty in all its forms everywhere," homelessness *must* be on the agenda. Although poverty is rarely the *sole* cause of someone's experience of homelessness, it is almost always *a* cause. Poverty erodes an individual's safety net, making it harder for them to recover from a crisis, like sudden unemployment or unforeseen costs, rendering them vulnerable to homelessness and its associated trauma. Poverty is a driving force behind people becoming homelessness, and it is a primary barrier against a return to housing. A world without poverty must therefore also be a world without homelessness; as long as homelessness persists, we will know that poverty has not yet been resolved.

If we are to seriously tackle street homelessness globally, then it should be a key indicator for all of these goals. When poverty is rampant, homelessness numbers rise; when wages are low and housing prices are high, homelessness numbers rise; when health care is expensive or inaccessible and mental health stigmatized, homelessness numbers rise; when prejudice shuts out members of a population due to issues of gender, race, and sexuality, homelessness numbers rise. Any approach that seeks to measurably and sustainably reduce the number of people sleeping rough must include buy-in and coordination with all the sectors who operate on the periphery of the homelessness sector. In fact, those sectors must begin to view homelessness as an indicator of their *own* success or failure.

Policy

This is where the fourth rung of the ladder, policy, comes into play. Our problem is defined, its ebbs and flows understood, its genetic origins mapped; now we can begin to piece together the solution. Suggested frameworks to end homelessness vary across countries, but typically include the following elements: clear, shared goals; a well-coordinated system that plans for outcomes; citywide strategies that weave together prevention, emergency response, and housing and supports; and resources to support this work and to provide an adequate supply of safe, affordable accommodations. A system's balance of investment in prevention, emergency services, and housing will depend on context. In a system moving toward ending homelessness, fewer resources will go to emergency services, with the balance shifting toward housing and prevention.

Agencies seeking to end homelessness should support work across their cities and countries to address housing affordability; discrimination based on race or sexual orientation; stigma around mental health, substance abuse, and unemployment; and should build partnerships with those who are doing this work. Although homelessness may be triggered by a life event, a failure of a local social services system, or a personal or family conflict, structural factors make some people more vulnerable to homelessness than others, and must be addressed for any reductions to be sustainable over time.

Of course, many of the structural factors that are a cause of homelessness are not easy to solve outright, but places that have meaningfully reduced and even ended homelessness show we can do so in cities where other challenges exist. In *Exploring Effective Systems Responses to Homelessness*,[11] Doberstein and Nichols note that "a key problem is that most services and programs within [the homelessness sector] have been developed incrementally and have evolved in parallel: housing separate from social services which are separate from health services, corrections, mental health or employment and each has a separate funding stream, different set of rules and usually a separate service location." Cities or countries should leverage shared goals to bring city agencies, nonprofits, people who have experienced homelessness, and other stakeholders to the same table to align their work. This creates a more efficient system that better targets resources and fosters a less chaotic experience for people experiencing homelessness.

To get these systems right, homelessness care providers and policy makers should also engage people who have experienced homelessness to help clarify the experience of the housing process and inform solutions. This involvement should be substantive rather than symbolic. We must work with people to determine what route off the street is most appropriate to their goals and competencies, and to understand their pathway *to* the street in order to ensure that their feet do not find it again.

Finally, to enable a coordinated effort to move forward, communities must have the right policies and legal frameworks in place to provide support with funding and political will. Some communities have sought to create alternative justice systems, such as homeless courts, mental health courts, and drug courts, which aim to help connect individuals to appropriate services and reintegrate into society. Rights-based approaches to housing aim to create policies, laws, and regulations centered on what services rights-holders are entitled to, as well as what must be done to fulfill that duty and by whom.[12] The Right to the City[13] framework, which argues that cities are public spaces and must therefore be inclusive of the public and responsive to its needs, situates housing as a key component. In this framework, housing ought not be viewed as a commodity but as a fundamental right, enshrined in law and guaranteed by local and national governments. The outcomes of constitutionally enshrined rights may depend on legal, cultural, and enforcement contexts.

Key to the success of these types of strategies is coordination between public and private stakeholders at the local systems level. These collaborations allow for additional funding and resource streams, innovation, and wider community engagement. The support of public policies and federal funding allow local actors to improve service delivery systems, strengthen data management systems, and broaden continuums of care. We have seen this whole-system approach successfully reduce homelessness over and over again: Medicine Hat in Alberta, Canada, is widely recognized to be the first city to achieve functional zero;[14] the United States have seen a 46 percent reduction in veteran homelessness;[15] the UK's Rough Sleepers Initiative in 1999 reduced rough sleeping in England by at least two-thirds by 2002;[16] and Finland's National Programme to Reduce Long-Term Homelessness has so far reduced the number of people experiencing homelessness throughout the country from 20,000 to 8,000, a number that is still declining.[17] Simply put, we know that radically reducing and even ending rough sleeping is possible, because it has already been done.

There are numerous economic benefits to housing people sleeping on the street. Housing First is an intervention that posits that housing is the *first* step to resolving homelessness and addressing complex need, with services and supports built into that housing. Key to this perspective is the idea that clients are not bound by rules typically found in other housing placements, such as sobriety requirements. The housing they are assigned is permanent and includes the customized support of a caseworker. Studies have indicated that Housing First interventions for chronically homeless individuals saved American taxpayers an average of US $23,000 *per consumer* in cost offsets.[18] Even more cautious reviews of financial impact found that significant cost offsets, combined with the benefits for participants, make better use of existing resources than maintaining the status quo of homelessness management (as opposed to systems oriented toward homelessness reduction).[19] Estimates of money saved through prevention methods suggest a savings of $20,000 per person;[20] in New York City, versions of this number are between $8 million and $26.7 million overall per year.[21]

Targeted Housing First interventions have also been shown to correlate with reduced involvement between homeless individuals and the criminal justice system,[22] and helping newly released prisoners find housing upon reentry into the community has proven to reduce instances of recidivism, even above and beyond other variables, such as disadvantage and poverty.[23]

The needs of individuals experiencing homelessness are an enormous burden on local emergency services. Public hospitals are frequently the first and only point of call for people experiencing homelessness for any and all health care needs, increasing the burden on staff and demand for resources. People who are marginally or unstably housed visit emergency departments in the United States at a rate three times higher than the general public.[24] This trend is true also across the European Union, where homeless individuals have high rates of acute health care use, including emergency department visits and inpatient hospital admissions; this pattern is seen across many countries and health care systems, including in countries with and without universal health care insurance.[25]

Studies in South Africa suggest that public hospitals are the most commonly used health care institution for homeless individuals, despite receiving poor treatment as a result of their housing status.[26] A 2017 study in Turkey showed that homeless patients were exposed to higher rates of trauma and chronic disease, resulting in increased levels of hospitalization in comparison to their housed peers.[27] The complexity of need in homeless patients is a heavy drain on hospital time and resources; by lowering the risk factors that homelessness presents—exposure to bad weather, violence, and risky behavior, to name a few—that strain on public servants and institutions can be reduced.

Much has been written about the negative effect of housing instability on the social and educational development of children, both on its own and as an indicator of other factors, such as violence, hunger, and poverty. Children with experience of homelessness are typically more likely to be victims of exposure to environmental toxins, such as lead.[28] In turn, these interactions lower educational outcomes, including maintained attention on academic endeavors, lower academic achievement, and poor classroom social engagement. Homeless children living in doubled-up housing situations have been shown to earn lower grade point averages and are less likely to graduate on time.[29] Additionally, their attendance rates are consistently lower than their housed counterparts.[30] Some studies indicate that reading scores are lowered, others math; some studies suggest that homelessness alone does not account for either one of those things alone, but that as a co-occurring risk factor can contribute to both.[31]

Housing people saves money, but that is not why we should do it. Housing people reduces strain on public hospitals and services, but that is not why we should do it. Housing people improves educational and social development outcomes for children, but that is not why we should do it. We should end homelessness because we can.

In 1657, at a conference of the Daughters of Charity, St. Vincent DePaul said, "Charity leads us to God."[32] It is useful to consider the trouble that this notion, charity, has given us through the years; in the Bible's original Greek, the word sometimes translated to mean *charity* is "αγαπη (agape)." αγαπη has a swath of meanings and connotations; linguists and theologians alike have wrestled with its breadth for centuries. But, broadly, it is a word that we are given to understand means "love," not in a static sense, but as love expressed somehow. It is the love of God for man and man for God; the love that man extends as fellowship to fellow Christians and to strangers. This is perhaps why αγαπη is sometimes translated as "charity"; there is a sense of movement and action to it, love through action rather than word. But this interplay between modern notions of charity and love is interesting: yes, it was love that drew Christ to Earth, to save mankind; but it was also, fundamentally, a charitable act, giving salvation to mankind that we could not earn on our own merit. We are all charity cases before God.

This quote from Deuteronomy is particularly apt: "If among you, one of your brothers should become poor, in any of your towns within your land that the Lord your God is giving you, you shall not harden your heart or shut your hand against your poor brother, but you shall open your hand to him and lend him sufficient for his need, whatever it may be."[33]

God does not call us to help the poor when it is easy, or when it is economically responsible, or when it will benefit our public servants and improve our public spaces. We are summoned to help the poor whenever we have what is sufficient to meet the need. God loved and gave; we were made in God's image and are called to love and give in equal measure.

There will be debates over what it means to "end" homelessness, and conversations around whether it is possible to ever truly ensure that no one ever loses their housing again. These are important conversations well worth having, but at the end of the day, we cannot let them delay a beginning to the work. As keepers of the starting gate, questions of difficulty and of nuance are beside the point; the point is nothing more and nothing less than that there is human suffering in the world where there need not be. Our neighbor needs a ladder, and we have one; simply that.

Notes

1. *Sustainable Development Goals,* https://www.un.org/sustainabledevelopment/poverty/.

2. The World Bank, "Piecing Together the Poverty Puzzle," *World Bank,* https://www.worldbank.org/en/publication/poverty-and-shared-prosperity.

3. Motilal Mahamallik, "Why Re-defining Homelessness and Responding to Census Data Should Inform Homeless Policy in India," *India Homelessness Resource Network,"* July 13, 2016, http://www.ihrn.org.in/blog/Why-Re-defining-Homelessness-and-Responding-to-Census-Data-Should-Inform-Homeless-Policy-in-India.

4. Institute of Global Homelessness, "An Overview of Global Homelessness and Strategies for Systemic Change." *The IGH Hub.* February 2017. Accessed 10 17, 2018. https://ighhub.org/resource/overview-global-homelessness-and-strategies-systemic-change.

5. United Nations Centre for Human Settlements Office of the High Commissioner for Human Rights, "The Right to Adequate Housing: A Major Commitment of the Habitat Agenda." *United Nations,* May 2001. Accessed October 15, 2018. http://www.un.org/ga/Istanbul+5/hr.PDF.

6. Population Reference Bureau, *Population Reference Bureau,* July 1, 2009. https://www.prb.org/humanpopulation/.

7. Ama De-Graft Aikins and Angela Ofori-Atta, "Homelessness and Mental Health in Ghana," *Journal of Health Psychology* 12, no. 5 (2007): 761–78.

8. Arthur L. Whaley, "Brief Report: Demographic and Clinical Correlates of Homelessness Among African Americans with Severe Mental Illness," *Community Mental Health Journal* 38, no. 4 (August 2002): 327–38.

9. James J. O'Connell, "Premature Mortality in Homeless Populations: A Review of the Literature," *Literature Review, Nashville: National Health Care for the Homeless Council,* 2005. http://www.nhchc.org/wp-content/uploads/2011/09/Premature MortalityFinal.pdf.

10. Hayashi Seiji, "How Health and Homelessness Are Connected—Medically." *Atlantic Media Company,* January 25, 2016. http://www.theatlantic.com/politics/archive/2016/01/how-health-and-homelessness-are-connectedmedically/458871/.

11. Naomi Nichols & Carey Doberstein, eds., *Exploring Effective Systems Responses to Homelessness* (Toronto: The Canadian Observatory on Homelessness Press, 2016), 7.

12. Padraic Kenna and Guillem Fernandez Evangelista, "Applying a Human Rights-Based Approach to Homelessness: from Theory to Practice," *Mean Streets: A Report on the Criminalization of Homelessness in Europe* (Brussels: European Federation of National Associations Working with the Homeless AISBL, 2013), 33–52.

13. First named by Henri Lefebvre in his book *Le Droit à la ville* (Paris: Anthropos, 1968).

14. Medicine Hat Community Housing Society, "At Home In Medicine Hat: Our Plan to End Homelessness," *Homelessness & Housing Development,* January 2014. http://production.mhchs.ca/static/main-site/files/housing-development/Refocused-Plan-to-end-Homelessness.pdf.

15. United States Interagency Council on Homelessness, "Homelessness in America: Focus on Veterans," *United States Interagency Council on Homelessness,* June 7, 2018. https://www.usich.gov/tools-for-action/homelessness-in-america-focus-on-veterans/.

16. Wendy Wilson, "Rough Sleepers Initiative (RSI) 1990–1999." *House of Commons Library,* March 6, 2015. researchbriefings.files.parliament.uk/documents/SN07121/SN07121.pdf.

17. Nicholas Pleace, Marcus Knutagård, Dennis P. Culhane, and Riita Granfelt, "The Strategic Response to Homelessness in Finland: Exploring Innovation and Coordination within a National Plan to Reduce and Prevent Homelessness," *Government Report, Canadian Observatory on Homelessness* 60, no. 11 (November 2016).

18. National Alliance to End Homelessness, "Fact Sheet: Housing First." *National Alliance to End Homelessness,* April 2016. http://endhomelessness.org/wp-content/uploads/2016/04/housing-first-fact-sheet.pdf.

19. Angela Ly and Eric Latimer, "Housing First Impact on Costs and Associated Cost Offsets: A Review of the Literature," *Canadian Journal of Psychiatry* 60, no. 11 (2015): 475–87.

20. William N. Evans, James X. Sullivan, and Melanie Wallskog, "The Impact of Homelessness Prevention Programs on Homelessness," *Science* 353 (2016): 694–99.

21. "Eviction and Homeless Prevention: Curating Critically Timed Choice Sets to Prevent Homelessness," *European Observatory on Homelessness,* September 21, 2018. https://www.feantsaresearch.org/en/conference-presentations/2018/09/21/13th-european-research-conference-on-homelessness?bcParent=760.

22. Julian M. Somers, Stefanie N. Rezansoff, Akm Moniruzzaman, Anita Palepu, and Michelle Patterson, "Housing First Reduces Re-offending among Formerly Homeless Adults with Mental Disorders: Results of a Randomized Controlled Trial," *PLoS ONE* (9/4/2013). https://journals.plos.org/plosone/article?id=10.1371/journal.pone.0072946.

23. Jessica Reichert, Mark Powers, and Rebecca Skorek, "Housing and Services after Prison: Evaluation of the St. Leonard's House Reentry Program," *Chicago: Illinois Criminal Justice Information Authority* (12/18/2016), https://www.researchgate.net/publication/311949606_Housing_and_Services_After_Prison_Evaluation_of_the_St_Leonard's_House_Reentry_Program; David S. Kirk, Geoffret C. Barnes, Jordan M. Hyatt, and Brook W. Kearley, "The Impact of Residential Change and Housing Stability on Recidivism: Pilot Results from the Maryland Opportunities through Vouchers Experiment (MOVE)," *Journal of Experimental Criminology* 14, no. 2 (2017): 213–26; Valerie A. Clark, "The Effect of Community Context and Post-Release Housing Placements on Recidivism: Evidence from Minnesota," *St. Paul: Minnesota Department of Corrections* (2015). https://mn.gov/doc/assets/Ecology_Study_-_April_2015_tcm1089-272810.pdf.

24. Margot B. Kushel, Sharon Perry, David Bangsberg, Richard Clark, and Andrew R. Moss, "Emergency Department Use among the Homeless and Marginally Housed: Results From a Community-Based Study," *American Journal of Public Health* 92, no. 5 (2002): 778–84.

25. Seena Fazel, John R. Geddes, and Margot Kushel, "The Health of Homeless People in High-Income Countries: Descriptive Epidemiology, Health Consequences, and Clinical and Policy Recommendations," *The Lancet* 384, no. 9953 (October 25, 2014): 1529–40. https://www.ncbi.nlm.nih.gov/pmc/articles/PMC4520328/.

26. Unotida Moyo, Leila Patel, and Eleanor Ross, "Homelessness and Mental Illness in Hillbrow, South Africa: A Situation Analysis." *Social Work/Maatskaplike Werk* 51, no. 1 (2015). http://socialwork.journals.ac.za/pub/article/view/425.

27. Selman Yeniocak, Asim Kalkan, Ozgur Sogut, Gökce Akgül Karadana, and Mehmet Toptas, "Demographic and Clinical Characteristics among Turkish Homeless Patients Presenting to the Emergency Department," *Turkish Journal of Emergency Medicine* 17, no. 4 (2017): 136–40. https://www.ncbi.nlm.nih.gov/pmc/articles/PMC5812920/.

28. Benjamin Brumley, John Fantuzzo, Staci Perlman, and Margaret L. Zager, "The Unique Relations between Early Homelessness and Educational Well-Being: An Empirical Test of the Continuum of Risk Hypothesis," *Children and Youth Services Review* 48 (2015): 31–37.

29. Justin A. Low, Ronald E. Hallett, and Elaine Mo, "Doubled-Up Homeless: Comparing Educational Outcomes with Low-Income Students," *Education and Urban Society* 49, no. 9 (2017): 795–813.

30. J. J. Cutuli, and Janette E. Herbers, "Housing Interventions and the Chronic and Acute Risks of Family Homelessness: Experimental Evidence for Education," *Child Development* (February 2018). doi:10.1111/cdev.13041. https://www.ncbi.nlm.nih.gov/pubmed/29468670.

31. Ibid.

32. Vincent De Paul, Conferences to the Daughters of Charity, November 15, 1657, 3:310; CCD 10:286. https://vinformation.org/en/vincentian-spirituality/virtues-and-charism/quotations-2/#_edn23.

33. Deuteronomy 15:7–11, ESV.

Part I

Accompanying the Homeless

Hearing the Voices of the Homeless

ACCOMPANYING EACH OTHER ON THE JOURNEY HOME

Mary Scullion, RSM, and Christopher Williams

Since the beginning of his papacy, Pope Francis has made the struggles of persons on the margins, those experiencing poverty and oppression, a main priority in his public witness. He has concretely addressed the inequities and injustices in the global economic and political systems, and he has frequently proposed as a response what he terms "a revolution of tenderness."

We are writing this article as two persons whose lives have connected through the crisis of urban street homelessness. Chris has experienced street homelessness in the city of Philadelphia. He is now living in permanent supportive housing and is employed. He is a leader at Project HOME, where he contributes in numerous ways to the mission of ending homelessness. Sister Mary began working with chronically homeless persons on the streets of Philadelphia over forty years ago. She and Joan McConnon co-founded Project HOME in 1989. Both of us (Chris and Sr. Mary) are part of a community that seeks to live out Pope Francis's "revolution of tenderness." In this essay, we share our conviction that such a revolution—as a concrete response to the human, social, and spiritual crisis of street homelessness—is rooted in relationships and community that, through the power of grace, foster mutual transformation.

Even since its emergence as a widespread national crisis starting in the 1980s, homelessness in the United States, especially chronic street homelessness, gradually became a common feature of urban America. The almost iconic visuals of the person on the street vent or the panhandler were burned into our consciousness as inevitable parts of our national life. In numerous ways, homelessness evoked deep fears and insecurities about our own human lives; it manifested a complex blend of many strands of our cultural and societal history: a rugged individualism that asserts that each person is responsible for his or her own fate; a competitive system of winners and losers; a materialistic meritocracy of the worthy and unworthy. Homelessness had become an essential feature of the geographic and even moral landscape of the United States.

A predominant reaction for many Americans has largely been one of fear. Often it is a fear associated with deep-rooted public attitudes toward addiction and mental illness. (Though it is true that among persons who experience chronic homelessness on the streets, these behavioral health issues affect a large percentage; in fact, that is a relatively small portion of persons experiencing homelessness. The large majority are families, usually women with children, whose homelessness is primarily an economic issue.) This fear can even be embedded in our language,

3

such as when we use the dehumanizing label "the homeless," stripping individuals of even their fundamental personhood. We often see those experiencing homelessness as a separate breed, not like us, the other. The frequent battles over public space in municipalities that sought to criminalize homelessness is an expression of this us-versus-them mentality.

Chris's Story

The primary feeling I [Chris] experienced when I became homeless was disbelief. It was a culture shock. I felt like some kind of alien.

Many of the preconceived notions people have about being homeless—drugs, alcohol, mental illness—were not factors in my fall into homelessness. What I experienced was what I call a spiraling. It was already a rough time for me. I was grieving for my father, who had died recently. I felt his absence on a daily basis. I then suffered another loss—the woman I had been in a relationship with chose to move south, which I was not able to do. In an effort to distract myself from the pain, I immersed myself in work. I was employed at a social service agency, where I had worked for years. During a short vacation from my job, I suffered a severe heat stroke, which required weeks of hospitalization. When I tried to return to work, I was terminated.

What followed was a period of severe mental stress. I was used to being a financial anchor for both my family of origin and for myself and my lady. Now, in between jobs and living back at my childhood home, I tried to keep busy doing freelance work and neighborhood volunteering—anything to occupy my time. I was becoming more and more sleep-deprived, and I began making poor decisions, including excessive gambling and losing touch with my responsibilities. Compounding the financial insecurity was increasing criticism and even hostility from my family.

Lonely, lacking support, feeling disconnected and abandoned as I was going through this hard time, a day came when I felt I was no longer welcome in my home environment and I needed to endure a different path. I left, and ended up on a bench in Center City Philadelphia. Though I had spent much time as a child there, and I worked there as an adult, now it was a place to disappear in the anonymity, where I wouldn't have to encounter anyone I knew.

I didn't really embrace the idea that I was "homeless." I wasn't residing on the bench—I just went there to sit and think over the mistakes I made. I was mentally beating myself up, dealing with deep self-disappointment. I didn't want to be around people because of all the pain I experienced having been a giving person but experiencing no reciprocity. I wasn't experiencing paranoia, but I had a strong feel of people as takers, manipulators, and I had had enough of them.

During those months, I mostly stayed outside. I would brave the cold weather rather than go to a drop-in center or shelter, mainly because I wanted to stay away from people, but also because I was in denial of my situation.

Gradually, really out of the need to survive, I began going to drop-in centers, churches, and feeding sites. Soon I found people who genuinely wanted to help me. Staff at St. John's Hospice especially cared for me. They gave me shelter, but in the lobby areas, which worked for me, because that lessened the culture shock of it all. When we are used to a level of independence, it's completely different to have to live in a dormitory-style setting, where all the noise and activity of many people all trying to survive are intensified. I didn't want to deal with that.

As I began to trust persons who treated me with dignity, I also began to understand that I was clearly going through a deep depression for the first time in my life, and I was experiencing medical issues, namely gout flares, so it became necessary and more feasible to accept help and get connected to the right resources.

Empathy, Humanity, and Hospitality

In the early years of the homelessness exploding in Center City Philadelphia, I [Mary] began to do street outreach to the men and women who were out there. One of my earliest insights was that our work did not constitute acts of generosity to "the less fortunate." These were powerful human encounters. The women and men who lived on our streets were a prophetic presence calling us to personal and societal transformation.

I began to understand that, rather than the platitude often used when we encounter those who are poor or homeless, "There but by the grace of God go I," the deeper truth was, "There go I."

As Chris learned from his powerful experience, others need to understand: People end up on the homeless path for unique reasons. Sometimes it is the loss of a job, sickness, and/or eviction. Sometimes it's a tragic, traumatic loss, but most often it is a combination of many closed doors that contributes to a growing sense of marginalization along with crippling poverty that leads gradually to the streets.

We all have a picture of living a stable life that's visible to society. But when things go wrong, that visibility diminishes and then vanishes. Chris worked since he was twelve years old. But the perception of a working, contributing man is drastically different from that of a man who may appear able to work but given his circumstances or psyche is no longer in the flow of his role as a contributor to society. You go from being a productive member of society to a burdensome one.

There are penalties associated with that. When we commute to work, we see the man who is not in the flow of work, who stands idly by, loitering. He might be scurrying for heat and trying to stay warm, and we can see him as a public nuisance. But if it were a working person standing in the chill, he would be given leniency, not chased away. The person who is homeless is perceived as criminal, as burdensome rather than a productive member of society. Then there is the stereotypical homeless person who is assumed to be a drug addict or an alcoholic.

And yet many people face the same issues—family struggles, employment-related stresses. The issues homeless persons struggle with are the same issues we all do. Their needs are really no different from those of anyone else who goes through hard times. The reality is that a lot of working people lack a sense of financial literacy, and many people are just a paycheck or two away from being evicted. It costs so little to hold back a facial expression of condescension. It costs so little, instead of hurrying past the person on the street, to consider sharing a donut, a cup of coffee, or just a kind word, to try to encourage him or her. An investment of humanity and hospitality, can lift a person's spirit. Just saying hello or giving an affirming smile can ignite hope in another.

Accompaniment

In those early days of street outreach, we were blessed by a powerful revelation: Our role was not just to offer help, but to build relationships. Needless to say, this led us to a far different experience of men and women on the streets than anything we might read in the newspaper or see on television. Not only were we able to see beyond the external factors of a person's poverty, illness, or emotional and mental scarring to get to know him or her as a unique individual, we also experienced something deep within ourselves, which changed us forever.

This is a call to a deeper bond than simply a relationship—it is one of accompaniment. We recognize that, despite the radical differences in our experiences, we need each other, we are bound up with each other—we hold the key to a mutual transformation. This relationship of accompaniment is different from simply "charity" where there is a giver and receiver—in other words, there is still a distance, a separation between two persons. In true accompaniment, both persons are changed.

As we get to know men, women, and children who experience poverty and homelessness, we begin to recognize the distorted ways our society values persons based on their success and productivity, or the way human dignity is often bound up with material accomplishments and belongings. Poverty forces us to strip that veil away. Poverty makes us confront the stark truth that suffering is a universal and inescapable part of being human and that we cannot be fully human until we embrace the truth of suffering. But mysteriously, in seeing this truth of human vulnerability, we are also empowered to see more clearly the authentic worth of each person.

The men and women who experience homelessness have felt the dehumanization of a society that stigmatizes and marginalizes them because of their situations and their struggles. We have learned over the years that, in addition to providing effective and professional services, one of the most transformative aspects of our work is simply to affirm a person's dignity, to stress that whatever their situation, we see their gifts, worth, and potential, and that they, no less than anyone else, deserve the chance to flourish in life. We have also learned the amazing truth that in this process we are also affirming our own dignity and worth.

Through our experience of accompaniment, we have understood more deeply the wisdom of the African proverb: "A person becomes a person through other people." And as the Australian aboriginal activist Lilla Watson put it so powerfully, "If you have come to help me you are wasting your time. But if you have come because your liberation is bound up with mine, then let us work together."

Even in small ways, we can experience this mutual transformation. As we walk along life's path with another person, that connection or sense of community can help us get "unstuck." This is a common experience for staff, residents, and trustees at Project HOME. In the most unexpected situations with the most unlikely people, through an experience at an inspirational meeting or through a conversation or the smallest kind deed, we experience a mini-transformation of getting "unstuck." Certainly, persons who have been on the street can attest to the power of simple kindness in helping unlock some inner turmoil and motivating them to begin working for recovery, to reach out for help. But it is not a one-way street: In a genuine sharing of lives, we all receive this gift from each other.

The community we formed, Project HOME, has as its mission to empower persons to break the cycle of homelessness and poverty. But because the model of relationships, community, and accompaniment is at the heart of what we do, Project HOME is not a distribution of services but a process of transformation. It is not an "agency" serving "clients." We are a community where the process of transformation takes place.

One of our great friends and teachers in recent years has been Father Greg Boyle, who is nationally recognized for his work and ministry with gang members in Los Angeles through the Homeboys program. His immersion of many decades into deeply broken lives and communities, marred by poverty, violence, drugs, anger, despair, and drugs has illuminated for him the overwhelming mystery of divine compassion. He speaks of

> kinship, inching ourselves closer to creating a community of kinship such that God might recognize it. Soon we imagine, with God, this circle of compassion. Then we imagine no one standing outside of it moving closer to those margins so that the margins themselves will be erased. We stand there with those whose dignity has been denied. We locate ourselves with the poor and the powerless and the voiceless. At the edges we join the despised and the readily left out. We stand with the demonized so the demonizing will stop. We situate ourselves right next to the disposable so that the day will come when we will stop throwing people away.[1]

In Father Greg Boyle's beautiful words with which we so deeply resonate: "Our common human hospitality longs to find room for those who are left out. It's just who we are if allowed to foster something different, something more greatly resembling what God had in mind. Perhaps, together, we can teach each other how to bear the beams of love, persons becoming persons, right before our eyes. Returned to ourselves."[2]

Others on the Journey

After years of surviving on the streets, Hyacinth King described the first day she came to Project HOME to move into permanent housing. Patrick, the receptionist at the front desk, offered the simple words, "Welcome home." Hyacinth, who had developed deep distrust from trauma on the streets, felt an abounding warm welcome of hospitality. In time, this same spirit of hospitality that exuded from Patrick was present in her, as she generously and caringly welcomed newer residents, as well as staff and visitors. The gift she had received from Patrick—deep hospitality and a sense that she was indeed home—was a gift she would offer others for many years after that, until her untimely passing in 2016.

Reginald Young, another member of the Project HOME community who lives as a powerful model of recovery, captures this miracle in these beautiful words: "It is that delicacy of kindness and respect that sees every other life as another gift, another reflection of Divine Generosity." We move from encounter to relationship to true accompaniment through grace, which empower us to be present to another, to be grateful for another, and to be touched by the divine generosity of another. It is in the little things that we learn great lessons if we are able to truly be present to another.

Alfonso Geiger would certainly vouch for the importance of the housing and services that helped him get off the streets. But far more importantly, he describes (echoing Father Greg Boyle) how "Project HOME returned me to myself. I didn't like who I was or what I had become. I know I needed to change. At Project HOME the change began. I became more refined. I developed through the relationships with good people. I am a miracle."

David Brown, who spent twenty years on the streets, always attributes his decision to come home to the relentless and persistent care of outreach workers who treated him as a human being. David, who had minimal formal education prior to his homelessness, also says that the best teacher is someone who loves you. A volunteer teacher empowered him to learn, he recounts; she believed in him, and with her care and concern he soon developed literacy and math skills.

As another community member reminds us, it is in accepting ourselves, our own story, that we truly learn to love ourselves. This takes humility and courage. The special gift we receive from those who have had to survive on the margins is that it is often in our pain and failure where the openings of grace is found. Adversity is often our greatest teacher.

"None of Us Are Home until All of Us Are Home"

At Project HOME, we seek to capture this notion of accompaniment as our core vision, "None of us are home until all of us are home." Again, although we are not a religious organization, this idea echoes the words of the late Jesuit Superior General Pedro Arrupe, who said, "If there is hunger anywhere in the world, then our celebration of the Eucharist is somehow incomplete everywhere in the world."[3] As people of faith, we do not respond charitably to those who are poor and oppressed because it gives us a good feeling or it lets us feel especially holy. We do not do it out of a sense of moral duty or to fulfill any ecclesial obligations. We are drawn toward mercy, compassion, and justice, because, in the mystery of the Gospel, we recognize that our common humanity is at stake. We become most fully human when we enter the mystery of suffering and, with God's grace, tap into the miracles of healing and transformation.

We learn the power of the words of Martin Luther King Jr.: "We are caught in an inescapable network of mutuality; tied in a single garment of destiny. Whatever affects one directly, affects all indirectly."[4] This recognition moves us to work together for what Dr. King called the Beloved Community.

The transformation we experience in relationships of true accompaniment also contains the seeds of societal transformation. The communities we build with persons on the margins help us realize the profound truth that we are one human community, one human family—and we are compelled to act. When we truly feel each other's pain and struggles, we cannot help but work toward both personal healing and structural change. As we learn the depths of the inviolable dignity of each person, we will not be content with a social order that upholds the dignity of some and denies the dignity of others. The deepest human connections we make show us clearly that homelessness and poverty are not only spiritual scandals—but also are economic and political crises. Compassion and justice spring from the same root.

Even in our earliest days, we believed that the men, women, and children who sleep on our streets and live in communities devastated by poverty were and still are a prophetic presence that something is radically wrong in our society. We are far from the vision of a just social order and economy envisioned in Catholic Social Teaching or in Dr. King's vision of the Beloved Community. But we also believe that these same men, women, and children are inviting us to new possibilities. Their suffering cries out for transformation—and when we hear these cries, we take the first hopeful steps toward personal and social liberation. In Project HOME, numerous members of our community who experienced homelessness firsthand have taken the lead in organizing, meeting with legislators, registering voters, marching, and demonstrating. They remind us that it isn't enough to simply critique unjust systems—the human reality of suffering and of transformation moves us to activism, advocacy, civic, and political action. Pope Francis's "revolution of tenderness" is not just a spiritual idea. "The future of humankind," he said, "is in the hands of those people who recognize the other as a 'you' and themselves as part of an 'us.'"[5]

Our experiences of accompaniment and community also are powerful channels to embody Pope Francis's challenge to not be regulators of faith but transmitters of faith. As those who are poor, homeless, addicted, and marginalized evoke in us a spirit of mercy and a commitment to justice, they also reveal to us a new depth of understanding of our God, who is a God of mercy and justice, whose very being is compassion. As Pope Francis has put it, "We need to look at our cities with a contemplative gaze, a gaze of faith which sees God dwelling in their homes, in their streets and squares. God's presence accompanies the sincere efforts of individuals and groups to find encouragement and meaning in their lives. He dwells among them, fostering solidarity, fraternity, and the desire for goodness, truth and justice."[6]

Revolution of Tenderness

In 2015, Project HOME was very involved in Pope Francis's visit to Philadelphia. In the months prior to his arrival, we developed a Mercy and Justice Campaign, with the goal of finding concrete ways to manifest the Holy Father's global witness. The campaign included a "Francis Fund," through which $1.4 million was raised to support groups working with persons on the margins—those who were homeless, addicted, imprisoned, trapped in sex trafficking, and others. We also generated over 20,000 letters to Congress from around the country, calling for a new national commitment to justice and the common good.

But the most powerful part of the campaign was a public art installation by Meg Saligman that Project HOME sponsored entitled the Knotted Grotto, inspired by the painting "Our Lady Undoer of Knots," which is beloved by Pope Francis. The grotto, installed next to the cathedral during the pope's visit, contained almost 150,000 ribbons of white paper on which people had written their own personal "knots"—struggles, prayers, hopes, or needs. Many of these knots were collected at soup kitchens, homeless shelters, recovery residences, prisons, and food pantries—as evidence of the need to undo the knots of poverty, hunger, and homelessness. But in the end, the knots represented the struggles of people from all walks of life. The huge crowds at the grotto during the week of the papal visit indicated that this art project touched a deep chord in people—we all have our struggles, we all ultimately need to give expression to those struggles and share them with others. And only when we do this, can we truly tap into the grace of God and the spirit of community that strengthens us to heal each other.

By accompanying those who have suffered through homelessness, we are returned to ourselves. We discover the miracle of our shared humanity, with its gifts, flaws, beauty, and failures. We discover the grace that empowers us to live more authentically, with mercy and compassion. We experience the power of mutual transformation—and we plant the seeds for a broader social transformation, a revolution of tenderness, a political agenda that is grounded in the Beloved Community that fosters economic, political, and societal structures rooted in the dignity of each person. In doing so, we accompany each other on the journey home.

Notes

1. Gregory Boyle, *Tattoos on the Heart: The Power of Boundless Compassion* (New York: Free Press, 2011), 190.

2. Ibid., xiv.

3. Pedro Arrupe, Address at Eucharistic Congress, Philadelphia, August 2, 1976. See https://theeucharist.wordpress.com/index/chapter-7-the-post-eucharist-mission.

4. Martin Luther King Jr., "Letter from a Birmingham Jail," April 16, 1963, https://www.africa.upenn.edu/Articles_Gen/Letter_Birmingham.html.

5. Pope Francis, TED Talk: "Why the Only Future Worth Building Includes Everyone," April 2017, https://www.ted.com/talks/pope_francis_why_the_only_future_worth_building_includes_everyone?language=en.

6. Pope Francis, *Evangelii Gaudium* (November 24, 2013), no. 71, http://w2.vatican.va/content/francesco/en/apost_exhortations/documents/papa-francesco_esortazione-ap_20131124_evangelii-gaudium.html.

THE PRAYERS OF THE HOMELESS

Carol Elizabeth Thomas

I write this essay during the season of Advent, with Christmas approaching. I can only ponder that in celebrating the birth of Jesus Christ, we are also paying homage to those families and individuals whose reality is homelessness, just what Joseph and Mary faced centuries ago. The fear, desperation, and heaviness of reaching out for help, being rejected, or worse, being ignored and invisible in the eyes of our brothers and sisters, is against all principles of Catholic Social Teaching and more importantly against humanity. However, the triumph of Joseph and Mary speaks of more than survival. They overcame hardships and persecution to raise a son who subsequently influenced our worldview. Jesus's words and examples are more relevant today because homelessness has not been eradicated. Instead, it seems to spread like locusts throughout the global community. It beseeches us to look at how some who have no place to call home survive each day and night on the streets. How do they hold on in the midst of the trauma that is homelessness? How are the voices of people who are often deemed invisible or unworthy of human kindness heard by each of us? How do we project those voices to be the light that chases the darkness away? How do we keep our faith amid such suffering?

Simply, with prayer. Prayer is defined and expressed in diverse ways, but the common thread of all faiths is that prayer is communication with God. It requires us to act in some way. "Prayer is not only a means of asking God to act, it is also a means of asking God to give us the opportunities to act. . . . We pray as we move into action."[1] This essay will recount some of the encounters and experiences that led me to move into action, working with broken people because of their lack of shelter and possessions. It will highlight the depth of my feelings about doing this work for more than twenty years with individuals who have experienced street homelessness and giving a voice to their prayers. And in doing so, I cannot help but realize that I have been blessed with the gift of hearing prayers of joy, despair, hope, sadness, successes, and struggles. I have been profoundly affected by the celebrations of life, the tears of struggle, and the veracity of death.

> There are difficult moments in life but with hope
> the soul goes forward and looks ahead to what awaits us.[2]

Working among people living on the streets has always been a privilege. When you approach someone who may be at their most vulnerable, a warm hello is often your first opportunity to connect with a person who is probably very guarded. The elements greatly influence the interaction and the response. The absence of shelter from the cold, heat, rain, and snow usually results in open communication. The offering of food, water, or cigarettes can create a bond. The comfort they provide are pathways to a positive exchange, but no matter what the tenor of that exchange is, the contact is paramount to letting someone know that he or she is acknowledged, that he or she is seen.

It has not always been easy to hear the voices of persons experiencing homelessness. Prior to becoming an outreach worker to the homeless, I was employed in social services for about five years. I primarily worked with people with mental illness who lived in residential settings. I had limited experience working with homeless people and often did not really see the impact of the problem in our city. But that changed when I took a position as a street outreach worker concentrating on an area of Philadelphia in which there were communities of homeless people who lived isolated from mainstream society. I asked my supervisor for guidance to get started and was pointed in the direction of Sister Mary Scullion, who had been coordinating outreach efforts in Philadelphia. She invited me to accompany her on outreach to encounter men and women on the streets. While watching her engage people, it became clear to me that we were conduits of a sort, and that this was more than a job.

When it came time for me to focus on doing "my job," I reflected on the grace and compassion that Sister Mary Scullion demonstrated as I started to perform outreach in West Philadelphia. I didn't have a partner and really struggled going out alone. My early outreach efforts were hit or miss, and I encountered very few people who seemed to have a mental health disability. After my first frustrating week on the street, I encountered a young lady, JJ, who said she had been watching me talking to people at night. She asked what I was doing and then asked me for a few dollars. People asking for money is a red flag in the outreach profession, but it was a great conversation starter. I asked what JJ needed it for, and she replied that I already knew and I did. Drugs. Crack cocaine, to be exact. I told her about my job and that I was looking for people who were mentally ill and homeless. She offered to show me where the "loonies" (as she dubbed them) were for five dollars. I bartered with her. We settled on a warm meal.

JJ then guided me to a three-story abandoned house in the Mantua section of Philadelphia. We entered through a plywood door haphazardly hinged to the rear of the house, which we accessed from an alleyway. She led me to a room on the second floor. I looked up, and I could see all the way up to the poorly maintained roof. It was unnerving. We went upstairs, and she left me on the second floor, pointing out a room in which I would find my targeted population, homeless mentally ill folks. After looking around in the dimly lit room, I began to speak to people. I engaged a few folks that night, and when JJ came down she rode along as I was able to convince one man to come with me and accept shelter placement.

After that experience, JJ would partner with me whenever we crossed paths, and together we would engage homeless folks. From that first encounter, we built a friendship. We would share meals, and I laughingly recall that she would make us pray before eating. We exchanged our stories of growing up Catholic and attending Stations of the Cross; it drew us closer. As JJ shared her story, she invited me to the abandoned house in which she slept. She was a striking young woman with a personality that seemed to put people at ease, myself included. Life had been a series of trials for her, including being born with a clubfoot, which gave her a very pronounced limp. Being homeless as a teen, she was raped and assaulted on the streets, and drugs became her way to ease the pain of being violated and mistreated. She was estranged from her mother, whom I learned was caring for JJ's daughter. Our work together transformed her and motivated her to accept services, shift her focus, and benefit from the intersection of seeing herself in others. The work also brought us together and helped me gain the courage to listen to people's stories with grace, in awe of their strength.

By the time she passed away, JJ was drug-free and housed, and she was able to reconnect with her mother and daughter. In looking back, I realized I saw so much pain and suffering that I could not alleviate. I prayed every day for people experiencing homelessness and for the strength to carry on.

> Miracles happen. But prayer is needed! Prayer that is courageous, struggling, and persevering, not prayer that is a mere formality.[3]

Capturing the voices of people living on the streets without a place to call home can only happen by recognizing and witnessing their daily struggles and being aware of the reality that before each day breaks, they wake from a restless sleep that fails to provide them with the restorative, rejuvenating sanctuary they need. For some people, waking up is a quiet prayer of gratitude to God that they have risen or for those who were terrorized during the night, a silent prayer that they survived to see another sunrise. For others, who are lost, hopeless souls with no connection to that which is greater than their circumstances, they walk around feeling unloved, unwanted, and unheard.

Therefore, it is essential for those who are blessed to work with homeless persons to make an effort to let their voices be heard. As outreach workers engaging people who are the street homeless, our goal is to make connections by building relationships no matter what the reaction is from the person. It is hard to speak and connect through pain, disappointment, and trauma, but it is our job to advocate for their basic human rights of food, clothing, and shelter. Working alongside our homeless brothers and sisters should be done in the spirit of instilling hope that no matter what the hardship, another human being cares. Instilling such hope can be hard given external challenges in our society, including public policies. However, there are times when pivotal events help address the lack of faith, reassuring us that things are not hopeless. One such event took place in the United States in 2015 during the World Meeting of Families (WMOF).

On September 26, 2015, Pope Francis came to Philadelphia to address the WMOF and say Mass on Benjamin Franklin Parkway. The parkway is a picturesque, green space with museums, fountains, statues, and our main public library. It is also a safe place where up to two hundred people slept every night. As the WMOF approached, many of us feared that people living on the parkway would be displaced. Philadelphia Archbishop Charles J. Chaput created a WMOF Hunger and Homelessness Committee to uphold the rights and dignity of those experiencing homelessness. This committee, working with the street outreach team, homeless advocates, providers from many social service city departments, local law enforcement agencies, and the Secret Service, collaborated to ensure that people experiencing homelessness would not be hidden, displaced, or disenfranchised. In the weeks prior to the pontiff's visit, street outreach workers and formerly homeless members of the committee worked together to survey unsheltered people on the parkway about what options they would be willing to take when the parkway was shut off for the WMOF. The results were surprising: people overwhelmingly wanted to see the pope. They felt that his visit was a recognition of their plight. He inspired hope in them, and many submitted their prayers at the public art installation called "The Knotted Grotto."[4] The grotto, which was located in front of the Cathedral Basilica SS. Peter and Paul, held over 150,000 white ribbons that had handwritten prayers, petitions, hopes, dreams, and cries of people all over North America. It represented a place where all people, regardless of their beliefs, posted their prayers. When Pope Francis blessed the grotto just prior to the Mass on the parkway, the crowd roared in admiration, representing an unbridled faith that their prayers would be acknowledged by God.

Two experiences stand out from the historic visit of Pope Francis, both of which give voice to the prayers of the homeless. RS was a Cuban man with ulcerated legs and a slow shuffling gait from severe edema in his feet from sleeping outside. He came to the United States in early 1980s and had lived on the street for twenty years. His excitement when he heard the news about "Papa's" upcoming visit touched our hearts. The archdiocese had agreed to provide outreach workers with tickets to give to homeless people who wanted to attend the Mass and other events where the pope was speaking. We searched for RS to give him a ticket, and when we found him and gave it to him, he cried, repeating over and over, "Dios te Bendiga! (God bless you)."[5] He accepted the offer to shower and change into new clothes, something he never did. But the possibility of seeing Papa, as he called Pope Francis, was an answer to all his prayers.

The other experience concerned SV, a formerly homeless outreach volunteer who was part of the Mercy and Justice Campaign. He worked tirelessly for weeks talking to the persons living on the parkway, helping them fill out the surveys and know their options during the WMOF. SV engaged them with dignity and grace, patiently listening to every person he encountered. He exuded an uninhibited joyfulness in sharing his story. He was raised Catholic but had converted to Islam some years before. Years of abuse from his father had left him with a deep sense of feeling unworthy. He witnessed his father terrorizing his mother and siblings. He overcame drug dependence, incarceration, and mental illness to start a career as an outreach worker. He loved the work—and it showed in his work on the parkway prior to the WMOF. SV collected more surveys than all of us combined and later shared with us the impact this had on strengthening his belief in God. He felt that the pope's visit was an answer to his own prayers. After all he had been through, SV longed to belong and make a difference. He loved the chance to let people know how much they mattered, and that with assistance they could change their circumstances. He let people know their voices were being heard. He exemplified prayer in action.

Hearing the Voices from the Living Room

"Silence is the source of my pain! In finding my voice I am Silent no More."[6]

Hearing the prayers of the homeless happens every day. The pain of seeing people lying on the dank floor next to urine and feces with no blanket to cover them cries out to the immorality of homelessness. But reaching out to someone who reaches back and accompanies you to take a shower or drink a cup of coffee is a prayer answered. Giving people the opportunity to participate at every level of their journey without any requirements builds a connection of the heart. It helps renew our faith to be that voice when someone cannot speak for themselves. The Hub of Hope is such a place.

The Hub of Hope is a year-round engagement center operated by Project HOME that was born out of listening to the voices of the homeless. It is located in the underground transportation concourse below Center City Philadelphia— where many persons living on the streets stay during the cold winter months. It was a vital point of access for many homeless persons, where they can come in to get a hot beverage and an array of hospitality services consisting of showers, laundry, and clean clothes. They are offered social services, medical care, behavioral health care, legal services for the homeless, clothes mending, and meals.

Continuing on this pathway to hear the prayers of the homeless leads us to the Living Room. It is a quiet, welcoming space nestled within the Hub of Hope. It can be described as a family bound not by blood but by community. A place where the most vulnerable people experiencing homelessness are called members. This sense of belonging is evident when you walk into the Living Room. It speaks of solidarity and reinforces that we are one human family regardless of our differences.

The Living Room is coordinated by Sister Eileen Sizer, who makes a point of letting everyone know that she is a member, too. Having been involved in God's work for over fifty years, Sister Eileen naturally embraces all the key principles of Catholic Social Teaching within the framework of unconditional love and hospitality. This is evident by the diversity and varied backgrounds of the living room members. But their commonality is the state of homelessness they have all shared at various stages in their life.

I was invited in by the members to have a discourse about their prayers, and in joining them, I agreed to project their voices through the written word. Upon entering the Living Room, there were at least a dozen members sitting in a circle. The conversation started with prayer. This is something that happens every day in the Living Room. Prayers both formal and informal are shared by different members but always from the heart. I realized that prayer is the anchor that provides security, stability, and comfort to each member. The prayer that was shared started the dialogue and what transpired was sacred. The complexity of emotion flowed like a river of magma, igniting pain that connected to centuries of the masses without a place to call home. Looking around through hot tears, awed by the brutal honesty of their lives on the street, I saw that the underlying theme was their connection to God. Although they spoke of being emotionally wounded and afraid of "dying on the streets,"[7] they did not feel alone or abandoned; God was there and prayer was their connection to God. One member vented with such anger about the treatment she received since being homeless, crying out, "No one should have to live like this! Lying on bare floors or sitting in a chair all night, is criminal."[8]

Everyone spoke, wanting the collective voices of the Living Room included in this essay to bring to light the inhumanity of homelessness. One of the youngest members spoke of the Common Good. It is derived, he explained, from the word Commonwealth, which means the good of the people, and I understood from him that the Common Good is an activity, not merely an ideology. Another member shared, "Being homeless is a perpetual struggle, but that struggle brings transition and transitions bring Hope."[9] Although the dialogue was heartbreaking to witness, the intersection of grace in the midst of their pain brought forth healing. Finally, the scripture verse read at the beginning and again at the end reinforced how each of us came full circle in the Living Room, acknowledging that each member "bears all things, believes all things, hopes all things, and endures all things."[10] This humbly speaks to the spirit of people experiencing homelessness worldwide, and their will to survive, persevere, and be heard.

Conclusion

Hearing the prayers of the homeless is bringing to light their needs, listening to what they need to resolve homelessness, and acting on that information. Sharing my limited experiences, encounters, and conversations through my work with people reinforces that prayer is a call to action. Seeing people lying on the floor of the train station huddled in a fetal position trying to get warm, or people living under the bridge burdened with mental health disabilities and afflicted with a voracious addiction, should compel us to act. That action takes many forms. Saying hello, offering a word of comfort, feeding the hungry, advocating for housing, or talking about the plight of the homeless in places of worship is to bear witness and act. These actions are their prayers. We have a responsibility to bear witness to the suffering of our brothers and sisters and to see ourselves in each and every one of them. Accepting that responsibility is the intersection of the homeless and God. We are an interactive fragment. Our prayers should instill hope as unspoken exchanges lead to action, which is God's work. The foundation of Catholic Social Teaching is the belief in the sanctity of human life and the inherent dignity of the human person. Finally, a thoughtful prayer to all the people experiencing homelessness is "None of us are Home, until all of us are Home."[11]

Notes

1. Tara Isabella Burton, "Nine Faith Leaders on Thought and Prayers," *Vox*, February 15, 2018, https://www.vox.com/identities/2017/10/3/16408658/9-faith-leaders-action-after-tragedy-florida-shooting-majory-stoneman-douglas.

2. Pope Francis, "Solemnity of All Saints," November 1, 2013, https://w2.vatican.va/content/francesco/en/homilies/2013/documents/papa-francesco_20131101_omelia-ognissanti.html.

3. Pope Francis, Tweet, @Pontifex, May 24, 2013, https://twitter.com/pontifex/status/337870587676487680?lang=en.

4. Elizabeth Fisher, "Grotto Highlights Homelessness and Mary as 'Untier of Knots,'" CatholicPhilly.com, September 3, 2015, http://www.catholicphilly.com.

5. Carol Thomas, conversation with outreach partner, September 26, 2015.

6. Wildflower, Living room member in discussion with Sister Eileen Sizer. December 13, 2018.

7. Anonymous. 2018. Discussion with Living room member by author. December 19, 2018.

8. Linda Costello, Living room member in discussion with author. December 19, 2018.

9. Anonymous. 2018. Discussion with Living room member by author. December 19, 2018.

10. 1 Cor 13:7.

11. Mary Scullion, "Vision Statement," Project Home, 2018. http://www.projecthome.org.

FRIENDS OF THE HOMELESS

Saint John Paul II, Pope Benedict XVI, and Pope Francis

Carlo Santoro

The Bible makes it very clear: there was no place for them in the inn. I can see Joseph, with his wife on the point of giving birth to her son, without a roof, without a house, without a place to stay. The Son of God entered into this world as a homeless person. The Son of God knew what it was to start life without a roof over his head.

—Pope Francis,
Charitable Center of Saint Patrick's Parish in Washington, DC,
meeting with the homeless, September 24, 2015

In November 2013, on Saint Peter's Square, Pope Francis blessed the statue "Homeless Jesus." It was then given a place in the Vatican, directly in front of the offices of the Vatican Almonry, the organization that assists the poor in the name of the pope.

The statue, which appears on the cover of this book, is a work of Canadian sculptor Timothy P. Schmalz, who wanted to depict one of the numerous homeless persons he encounters in the city.

A copy of the statue was placed in 2018 in front of the church of Sant'Egidio in Rome, on the fiftieth anniversary of the foundation of the community.

In the homeless man on the bench, exposed to all the bad weather, to the rain, to the sun, to the cold, and to the snow, one can recognize Jesus: his feet are marked by the nail of the crucifixion. There is a free seat alongside him, for anyone who wants to come close to those who are poor and alone.

Over the centuries, the relationship between the bishop of Rome, that is to say, the pope, and the poor beggars who crowded Saint Peter's Square and the surrounding district is described in intensive and important pages in church history that are full of mercy and compassion. It suffices here to mention Saint Callistus I, Saint Gregory the Great, and many other popes who were genuine friends of the poor.

In this short essay, I will discuss only the popes of the last forty years: Saint John Paul II, Pope Benedict, and Pope Francis, the popes whom I have known

19

personally in my activity as a helper of the homeless poor. In order to do so, I shall draw on a very limited amount of personal testimonies and memories.

One of the many Roman legends speaks of a pope who used to leave the Vatican at night dressed like a beggar and mingle with the poor people on the streets. We often read in newspapers and social media that Pope Francis also has a custom of going out at night to meet the poor, dressed like a simple priest.

Although one can imagine that that would make him really happy, it is not very credible, given the obvious security measures to which Pope Francis is subject. It is, however, true that he is a friend of the poor and that he never loses any opportunity to demonstrate this concretely. At the heart of his magisterium lies the objective of putting the poor at the center of the church, even if this requires overcoming resistance in some parts. And we must remember that Jorge Mario Bergoglio (Pope Francis's original name), a true son of the Second Vatican Council, is retracing the steps of his predecessors, whom I have mentioned above, who were also great friends of the poor. I shall relate briefly a few anecdotes of their encounters with the poor and quote from some of their most important speeches on the topic of the homeless.

I began to frequent Saint Peter's because my family used to live in that area, and the poor on the square were an everyday presence. When I was a kid, I even used to play football on the square. I could come and go from the Basilica without any control. There were very few policemen, unlike today. In 1984, I started to visit the homeless on the square with my friends from Sant'Egidio, and we have continued to do so up to the present day, visiting very frequently during the week.

Saint John Paul II

One year after the election of John Paul II, unknown persons set fire to the bedding of a poor Somalian refugee while he was sleeping in front of an ancient church in the center of Rome. The members of Sant'Egidio were deeply disturbed by his death and wrote to John Paul II, who said in his Angelus message on May 27, 1979: "At this moment, I cannot fail to recall with profound distress the young Somalian, Amhed Ali Giama, who was barbarously burnt alive very close to the church of Santa Maria della Pace. How can such atrocious actions take place here at Rome, the native country of law, the city of Saint Peter?"

On January 5, 1985, Rome was covered in a historic snowfall that blocked air and rail transport. The pope was obliged to return to the Vatican that evening from a pastoral visit in a car with chains. There were few of us on Saint Peter's Square that evening, a few poor people, including Arturo and Josef, and some voluntary workers who had accompanied me to try to convince those few poor persons who remained to come into a shelter. The pope stopped his car, opened the window, and greeted us.

On September 17, 1986, I saw John Paul II at the end of an audience he gave to the Community of Sant'Egidio. When I greeted him, I told him that I had for some years been a friend of the poor persons who slept on Saint Peter's Square. The Holy Father listened very attentively to my words and told me that he intended to open a hostel for the poor inside the Vatican. This news seemed really incredible, but the Casa Dono di Maria for homeless women was inaugurated in 1988 by two saints: John Paul and Mother Teresa of Calcutta.

On June 15, 2000, after passing through the Holy Door for the Jubilee, two hundred homeless persons had lunch at Santa Marta with John Paul II, who was ill and tired, but was always affectionate and attentive to the difficult stories that the poor told him. The pope spent a long time with John, a Scot who had once been a monk and had been sleeping for ten years in the Trastevere district.

Pope Francis told a very interesting story about John Paul II in an interview in 2017:

> There is a famous story in the Vatican about a homeless Pole who lived on the street in Rome. He was a shy man and didn't speak to anyone. But after some time, volunteers began to bring him a hot meal in the evening. It was only after a long time that they succeeded in getting him to tell his story: "I am a priest, and I know your Pope well. We studied together in the seminary!" The Pope was informed about this, and when he heard the name, he confirmed that he had been with him in the seminary, and he wanted to meet him. They embraced, after forty years, and then the Pope asked him to hear his confession. And so, the former seminary companion, a priest and now a homeless man, heard the Pope's confession—incredible!

This, according to Bergoglio, is how one ought to approach the poor on the street, like two friends who meet—indeed, as much more than friends.

On the day John Paul II died, the square was suddenly full of pilgrims. Hundreds of thousands came, filling up the entire district until the day of his funeral. But among the first to arrive were the innumerable poor persons who were already present in that area. Each of them held a souvenir, a photograph, a rosary, things that reminded them of an encounter they had had with that great pope, a friend of the poorest.

Pope Benedict XVI

In the course of his magisterium, Pope Benedict XVI said some very important things about the relationship between the poor and the church. It is good to remind ourselves of this, because of the great value of what he said. In his general audience on October 1, 2008, Pope Benedict said:

> Love for the poor and the divine liturgy are inseparable, love for the poor and liturgy. The two horizons are present in every liturgy that is

celebrated and lived in the Church, which by its very nature is opposed to the separation of worship and life, of faith and works, of prayer and charity towards one's brothers and sisters. And thus, the Council of Jerusalem is born of the need to resolve the question of how to act towards the pagans who joined the faith . . . and this question is resolved in the ecclesial and pastoral authoritative body that places at the center faith in Christ Jesus and love for the poor of Jerusalem and of the entire Church.

Pope Benedict expressed on various other occasions his thinking about the centrality and the importance that the poor have, and have had, in the life of the church. But perhaps the words that I cherish the most (also because I heard them with my own ears) are those that Pope Benedict spoke when he visited the food kitchen in the Community of Sant'Egidio in Rome on December 27, 2009, and ate lunch with a hundred poor people, homeless, Roma, and refugees. The pope said:

"As you did it to one of the least of these my brethren, you did it to me." Listening to these words, how is it possible not to feel truly friends of those in whom one recognizes the Lord? And not only friends but also relatives. I have come to you precisely on the Feast of the Holy Family because, in a certain way, you resemble it. . . . What happens at home is taking place here today: those who serve and help mingle with those who are helped and served and those in greatest need are given priority. . . . Like Saint Lawrence, a Deacon of the Church of Rome, when the Roman magistrates of the time sought to intimidate him, to make him hand over the Church's treasure, he pointed to the poor of Rome as the true treasure of the Church. We can make Saint Lawrence's gesture our own and say that you poor people really are the Church's treasure.

Benedict's thinking was clear. It can be summed up in three important concepts: the church is the family of the poor; friendship joins the one who serves with the one who is served in a true family; and the poor (as the martyr Saint Lawrence said long ago) are the true treasure of the church.

Pope Francis

Finally, we come to Pope Francis. As I said above, many people are justly surprised by the friendliness and attentiveness that Pope Francis displays toward everyone, but particularly toward the poor and to those who have no home. In the perspective of Pope Francis, we must first of all bear in mind the integral vision that every human being has dignity (every human being, with no one excluded), which is the antithesis of the "throwaway culture," a society of efficiency whatever the cost, a society that tends to violate human dignity. For Francis, no one may be thrown away or excluded from society; and for the church, the one who is thrown away is truly the "flesh of Christ." From the very beginning of his pontificate, the pope has shown an attitude that leaves no room for doubt about how the relationship with every poor person ought to be:

> When you give alms, do you look into the eyes of the man or woman to whom you are giving the alms?—"Ah, I don't know, I didn't notice." And when you give this person alms, do you touch the hand of the person to whom you are giving the alms, or do you throw the coin into the hand? This is the problem: the flesh of Christ, touching the flesh of Christ, taking on ourselves this suffering for the poor.[1]

In 2014, the pope expressed his great concern: "We get accustomed to brothers and sisters who sleep on the street, who have no roof to shelter them. We get accustomed to refugees in search of freedom and dignity, who are not welcomed as they ought to be. We get accustomed to living in a society that claims to be able to do without God."[2] For Francis, excluding the poor means doing without God.

But he notes that friendship with the poor cannot be merely an occasional matter:

> Let us not think of the poor only as recipients of a good voluntary action that is to be performed once a week, and still less, as the recipients of impromptu gestures of goodwill that aim to pacify our conscience. Such experiences, which are indeed valid and useful in making us aware of the needs of so many brothers and sisters, and of the injustices that are often the cause of this distress, ought to introduce us to a genuine encounter with the poor. And this encounter should lead to a sharing that becomes a lifestyle.[3]

The pope's words in his homily in Santa Marta in February 2015 before the distribution to the poor of three hundred umbrellas that pilgrims had forgotten, are even clearer: "The Church must announce the Gospel in poverty, because salvation is not a theology of prosperity. Accordingly, its sole objective is to bring Christ to the poor, to the blind, to the prisoners."[4]

It seems obvious that for Francis, the poor are not a societal category, but a theological dimension, and that the Word makes its passage via the poor. As he said at the Angelus on March 22, 2015, addressing the faithful who were present: "I offer today to you who are present on the Square a pocket Gospel that will be distributed to you free of charge by some homeless persons who live in Rome. We see this too as a very beautiful action that pleases Jesus: those who are most needy are the ones who give us the gift of the Word of God."[5]

The pope shows in concrete actions his closeness to those who are homeless. They are not extraneous to the life of the city. In the course of the Te Deum on December 31, 2018, he exhorted everyone to realize this:

And at this point, we must stop short, stop short in order to reflect with pain and repentance because, even during this year which is nearing its end, so many men and women have lived, and live, in conditions of slavery that are unworthy of human persons. Even in our city of Rome, there are brothers and sisters who for various reasons live like this. I am thinking in particular of how many homeless persons there are. There are more than ten thousand of them. Their situation is especially harsh in winter. They are all sons and daughters of God, but various forms of slavery, sometimes extremely complex, have brought them to a life at the limits of human dignity.[6]

The pope's words are very true. Those who are homeless experience various forms of slavery, which are very complex, and there are ten thousand of them in Rome, without a house, without a family—people who have nothing. We thus have to stop short, alongside every poor person. Pope Francis stops short before the poor every day, and he invited everyone to do this consistently, not just from time to time. It is difficult to give a summary of the important elements, the personal encounters, and the attention that the pope gives to the poor every day, beginning from December 17, 2013, when he wanted to celebrate his first birthday in the Vatican by welcoming into his house four homeless persons who slept on Saint Peter's Square. The four poor men, who were incredulous until the very last minute, were wakened early in the morning by Father Konrad and brought to the pope to have breakfast with him.

It seems clear that the pope wanted to express his own love for the poor by manifesting his own simple gestures of friendship toward them. He installed showers for them in the Vatican, as well as a medical clinic with a podiatrist, and a small dormitory for men. He gave a laundry to the hospitality center for the homeless at Sant'Egidio. All of these actions are an attempt to help every poor person to recover the dignity that has often been denied them. The pope fights against all the prejudices that often condemn the poor as strange people who do not wash, persons who are dirty, or who want at all costs to sleep on the streets, people who do not want to work, or at any rate, people who are responsible for their own situation, so that it is their own fault if they live in these conditions—or even persons whose very presence besmirches the beauty of a city like Rome (as we often read in the press). But not only this: for the pope, the poor are not different from other people. They do not only have material needs (as many people think); they also have a right to have access to cultural events and to spend time enjoyably with each other. This is why he invited a large group of down-and-out persons to join him in visiting the Sistine Chapel, and he often gives them tickets to the theater. The pope also intends to give another precise signal: we must fight against indifference. Everyone can help the poor, every parish, every church, and every Christian can do so. Huge structures are not required, in order to show the mercy of God.

In his homily in the Mass in Santa Marta on January 9, 2019, Francis said that many people are incapable of understanding the needs of others, and are therefore unable to feel compassion. In order to explain what he meant, he showed a photograph that had been taken by a boy in Rome one winter evening near Saint Peter's. Some very well-dressed people are coming out of a restaurant, satisfied after a good meal, while alongside them we see a homeless man stretching out his hand to ask for alms. This photograph catches the precise moment in which they look away, in order to avoid meeting the eyes of the poor man. For Pope Francis, the photograph describes well the culture of indifference. He says that the opposite of love is not hatred, but indifference. The love of God always takes priority: it is a love that consists of compassion and mercy. There is indifference—not "a conscious hatred"—in so many people. They think that they are satisfied, they think that they have everything, and that they have even made sure of having eternal life, because they are good Christians and go to Mass on Sunday. But when these Christians leave the restaurant, they turn their heads aside: and this is a true sickness. "Let us ask the Lord to cure humankind, beginning with our own selves! May he heal my heart of this sickness that is the culture of indifference." Indifference and inequality often prevail in our society, and the economics of exclusion wins the day. It is the poor who are the victims. He had already affirmed in the apostolic exhortation *Evangelii Gaudium* (2013): "Today we have to say 'thou shalt not' to an economy of exclusion and inequality. Such an economy kills. How can it be that it is not a news item when an elderly homeless person dies of exposure, but it is news when the stock market loses two points?"[7] A city in which the death of a poor person is not a scandal, and is not mentioned in the newspapers, is inhuman.

The pope is attentive to the life of every poor person, and he teaches us that life, every life, has an immense value—even the life of an old tramp who died alone of cold and hardship.

The story of Willy is very significant. He was eighty years old and had come from Antwerp in Belgium to Rome, where he spent thirty years of his life on the streets around Saint Peter's. Everyone in the Vatican knew him, including the gendarmes and the Swiss Guards at the Gate of Saint Anna, where he went to Mass every morning. He walked around, always dragging his trolley. He wore a long coat and had a cross around his neck. He said to everyone he met: "If you want to go to paradise, you have to go to confession and be reconciled to God." When he died in 2015 in the hospital beside Saint Peter's, he was given a huge funeral. But the most important thing is that he was buried inside the Vatican, in the cemetery of the German princes, among kings and noblemen. This is a very rare occurrence, and it happened at the express wish of the pope. In this way, the words of Psalm 113:7 are fulfilled: "He raises the poor from the dust, and lifts the needy from the ash heap, to make them sit with princes, with the princes of his people."

It is likewise in accordance with the wishes of Pope Francis that almost all the funerals of persons who live on the streets in Rome are celebrated by Cardinal

Konrad Krajewski, the Papal Almoner, who organizes the assistance of the poor in the name of the Holy Father himself.

For Bergoglio, the theology of the poor is expressed by means of closeness, that is to say, by the attempt to enter into his or her needs and to be friends with the one who is poor, without judging. The pope does this through concrete gestures and times of friendship and feast, but also through audiences and special liturgical moments, beginning with the Holy Year of Mercy (the Jubilee of the Poor and the World Day of the Poor, which has now become a tradition, as well as the so-called "Fridays of Mercy," when he makes surprise visits to places that give shelter to the poor).

During the encounter that took place on the occasion of the Jubilee of the Poor, the pope spoke words that were truly unforgettable, before he prayed intensely with a group of homeless persons who surrounded him: "Life becomes beautiful, and the fact that we succeed in seeing its beauty even in the worst situations that you are experiencing, this is what dignity means"[8] He went on to ask pardon both personally and in the name of the church:

> I ask you for pardon, if I have sometimes offended you with my words, and by not having said the things I ought to have said. I ask you for pardon in the name of the Christians who do not read the Gospel, which has poverty at its center; pardon for all those times in which the Christians, faced by a poor person or by a situation of poverty, turned aside. Your pardon is holy water for us, it is a clarity that allows us to understand that at the heart of the Gospel stands poverty, and that we Christians must build up a poor Church for the poor, and that every man and woman of every religion ought to see in every poor person a message of the God who becomes poor in order to accompany us in our life.[9]

I conclude by speaking of Pope Francis's friendship with the poor. As I said at the beginning, he walks in the footsteps of his predecessors. He loves to eat with the poor, to spend time talking and celebrating with them. This now happens regularly in the Vatican after the Mass for the World Day of the Poor (I myself had the privilege of taking part in these meals with my homeless friends), and it took place in the church of Saint Petronius in 2017, with two hundred poor persons and with Archbishop Zuppi of Bologna. This lunch is a part of the tradition of Christmas lunches that the Community of Sant'Egidio has organized since 1983.

I cannot fail to mention another lunch with two hundred homeless persons that took place in the Vatican in June 2018, when Father Konrad was designated a cardinal. He is a great friend of the poor. I was invited to the lunch, and it was a great honor for me to be there among the poor, as often happens. None of us expected the pope to arrive, and even less that he would eat with us and sit at our table. Nor could anyone have imagined that Francis would spend two hours in an atmosphere that was very much that of a family, talking to everyone and even joking with the poor, just as if we were at home in our own family. The pope was truly at his ease, and he succeeded in putting everyone at their ease, perhaps because there were no television cameras or official photographers present.

Before bidding farewell to everyone at the end of the celebration on that unique and unrepeatable day, the pope took the red skullcap from Father Konrad and put it on the head of a friend with a long beard . . . and he said: "I have just made a poor homeless man a cardinal." This is indeed the poor church that celebrates together with the poor.[10]

Notes

1. Vigil of Pentecost with the ecclesial movements, the new communities, and the lay associations and groups, Saint Peter's Square, Saturday, May 18, 2013, http://w2.vatican.va/content/francesco/en/speeches/2013/may/documents/papa-francesco_20130518_veglia-pentecoste.html.

2. General Audience on Ash Wednesday, Saint Peter's, March 5, 2014, http://w2.vatican.va/content/francesco/en/audiences/2014/documents/papa-francesco_20140305_udienza-generale.html.

3. Message of the Holy Father for the World Day of the Poor, November 19, 2017, http://w2.vatican.va/content/francesco/en/messages/poveri/documents/papa-francesco_20170613_messaggio-i-giornatamondiale-poveri-2017.html.

4. https://w2.vatican.va/content/francesco/en/cotidie/2015/documents/papa-francesco-cotidie_20150205_i-will-cure-you.html.

5. https://w2.vatican.va/content/francesco/en/angelus/2015/documents/papa-francesco_angelus_20150322.html.

6. http://w2.vatican.va/content/francesco/en/homilies/2018/documents/papa-francesco_20181231_te-deum.html.

7. Pope Francis, *Evangelii Gaudium*, 53, http://w2.vatican.va/content/francesco/en/apost_exhortations/documents/papa-francesco_esortazione-ap_20131124_evangelii-gaudium.html.

8. https://w2.vatican.va/content/francesco/en/speeches/2016/november/documents/papa-francesco_20161111_giubileo-senza-fissa-dimora.html.

9. Ibid.

10. [English translation: Brian McNeil.]

Eclipse

Paul Houston Blankenship

"Do you feel me?"

"I am little," he tells me, "but I become a monster when somebody fucks with me. That's why people on the streets call me Little Monster." His gray sneakers slap the ground. Abruptly, the bike he pushes up and down the sidewalk stops. Standing still, we splinter and slow the anonymous train of people walking toward us. With a penetrating look, he gathers my attention. "Do you feel me?"

"I feel you," I say. "I feel you."

In truth, I didn't feel him. Truer still: I was afraid to. I hurried past the uncomfortable emotion Little Monster's question evoked and focused instead on what I knew. I helped him fit confidently into a street name. I was fine with that. It is common for people who are homeless to use such techniques to distance themselves from the crushingly destructive conditions of street life.[1] "To be known," Howard Thurman wrote, "to be called by one's name, is to find one's place and hold it against all the hordes of hell."[2]

Little Monster ran away from home. It wasn't a home to him anyway. He said none of his foster homes have been. He said abuse and arbitrary rules don't make a home, so he left. The streets called out to him because he imagined he had no place else to go. In addition to living on the streets, Little Monster is addicted to several hard drugs. I am a novice ethnographer. I've never used hard drugs, run away from home, or been homeless. How could I feel him? His gray sneakers won't fit me.

The Pastoral Clinic is an ethnography by Stanford anthropologist Angela Garcia. It explores the relationship between placelessness and addiction in New Mexico's Española Valley, which has one of the highest rates of heroin addiction and fatal overdoses in the United States. Garcia proposes that heroin addiction in the Española Valley is a symptom of historic and ongoing oppression. that it is a mistake to view addiction outside the fraught cultural context in which it is experienced. Real bodies suffer from real historical wounds. Real cultural change is needed to heal this. During her research, Garcia became intimately acquainted with heroin addicts. She used the term "moments of incomprehensibility" to describe how much of the suffering she witnessed escaped her comprehension and remained unknowable to her.[3] Rather than abandon the incomprehensible, however, Garcia attended to it. It became a place she inhabited to discern how to render a presence that is good and caring for the people she got to know. Looking back, the time Little Monster asked if I could feel him appears as a moment of incomprehensibility. I am still learning how to inhabit it.

28

Cultivating Presence

This essay is about presence. More precisely, it is about how to become present to people who live on the streets in order to help render a presence that is good for them. Based on a narrative from the ethnographic research I conducted over a period of almost three years with people who live on the streets of Seattle, I make one central proposal. The proposal, I must say, is limited in scope; it is meant to evoke a dialogue rather than suggest a final, authoritative answer. God forbid it be read otherwise.

I propose that presence emerges from a distance that is cultivated and adored through spiritual practice. Let me explain. On the one hand, presence is about being close; being close involves respectful listening and careful attention. If the smell of the streets has permanently stained your skin and you struggle to wash it from your mind, it is possible that you have become present to people living on the streets.[4] On the other hand, however, presence is about being distant. Being distant involves recognizing that the Other is not reducible to the way you think or feel. If you have cultivated a field between yourself and the Other so that the Other can emerge to you in his or her freedom, it is possible that you have become distant. This is love. "To love purely is to consent to distance," Simone Weil wrote. "It is to adore the distance between ourselves and that which we love."[5]

Left to its own devices, knowledge can be a painkilling drug. Knowledge, Karl Rahner wrote, is meant to bloom into love.[6] This essay is written in the hope that a few seeds of knowledge will fall onto the ground of ethical reflection to help create real and lasting solutions to the global problem of homelessness.

The Stranger

Little Monster is pinching the filter of a cigarette between his right thumb and index finger. "Come on," he says, "follow me." He pushes his bike back down the street, hoping I'd tag along. "Sorry," I say. "It's not a good day."

My day started in a small urban park located in Pioneer Square, Seattle's most historic neighborhood. It took me half an hour to walk there from my downtown apartment. When I got there, a tour guide had just finished discussing the historical significance of the park. I stared at the totem pole he and the tourists were huddled around. In *Native Seattle*, Coll Thrush argues that totem poles help write Seattle's "place-story." Place-stories build the identity of a city and its people; they shape the stories we tell about the world and our place within it.[7] On the surface, totems seem to evoke respect for Indigenous history. We might pause, looking at them, and imagine in awe what it would have been like to live such a long time ago. On a deeper level, however, Thrush argues, totems can write Indigenous people out of the historical present. That is because Indigenous symbols are employed not just to remember but to forget. Totems announce Seattle's separateness from its past; they mark the present as a new frontier. In effect, people may come to believe that

Indigenous people used to populate Seattle, that now they're history, and that the evil of colonization is vindicated by technological progress. We might also overlook the fact that Indigenous people are still living in the city without adequate recognition and care.

Although tourists and business professionals do frequent the park, most of the people here are homeless. I went to speak with Sam and Eddie, two older homeless women who hang out there during the day, but they weren't there. I sat down on a park bench and waited for them to show up. There was a kind of peace to the steady movement of the cars driving behind me. I let this peace move through me and felt the sun rest gently on my forehead. I said a prayer.

Moments later, I hear distant yelling. It gets louder, closer. A man enters the park holding a large stack of newspapers. He has brown skin and is speaking in an Asian tongue. He is clearly homeless. He offers a newspaper to everyone he encounters. Some people accept a newspaper; others do not. If people do not accept one, he throws it at their feet. A white homeless individual, who is sitting on a bench across from me, stands up and yells back at him: "Nothing shall separate you from the love of God, motherfucker!" By the time he leaves, newspapers line the ground.

The newspaper is called *The Stranger*. It's a free, weekly paper held in dispensers throughout the city. On the front page is a large black circle. Light comes out from behind it. Beneath the rim of the light is this caption: "Total Eclipse of the Trump: astrologers predict doom for the president. P. 6." On page six there are seven yellow moons. In each moon, there is a sliver of president Trump's face. "If we're lucky," the article reads, wryly, "whatever shift Trump undergoes will be an improvement and not the start of a nuclear holocaust. Or a race war."[8]

The cover story is about the first total solar eclipse that will be visible from the United States in forty years—and the first to cross the entire country in a century. Since Seattle is close to the point of totality, the view is expected to be spectacular. The story is also about the relationship between astrology and presidential politics in the United States. A "Virgo astrologer," Margo Orr, points out that JFK's assassination, the attempted assassination of Ronald Reagan, and the impeachment of Bill Clinton all occurred on or near eclipses. The popular Susan Miller from Astrology Zone cautions that nothing is stronger than an eclipse. She predicts that it will bring a scandal in the Trump orbit to light. In a column titled "Free Will Astrology," *The Stranger*'s own astrologer is more reticent. He believes the eclipse will kill egos, not persons. "In a normal person," he writes, "that could be a good thing, because it would relieve that person of illusions and delusions that he has about himself. In Trump's case," however, he concludes, "there could be a shattering."[9]

The yelling of the man with the newspapers washes over me again, on the park bench I am sitting on. He—the man whose name I do not know—has come back to the park. I close the paper. A family from England is taking a picture by the totem pole. Evidently, he desires a conversation. He first tries to speak with the father. When the father ignores him, he moves toward the children. The mother steps in front of her children. In haste, the father tucks his camera under his coat. The mother throws out her hands in the air like they have magic power. In panic, the family frets aloud about what to do. "You're British are you?" He detects their accent. "Do you know the queen?"

He then puts his hand on the father's shoulder. "Please, leave us alone," the father pleads. "We just want to enjoy the park." Like a frightened puppy, the father comes up to me and asks what to do. I want to say "play it cool . . . you'll be alright . . . just walk away . . ." but I haven't the courage to speak. "Crackers! Crackers! Fuck the queen!" They are doused in racial expletives as they hurry out of the park.

A Tour of the Streets

"Well . . . are you coming?" Little Monster wants to give me a tour of the streets. He imagines that will help my research and, I believe, render a material good for him. Like cigarettes or cash, for example. Or a friend. Given the experience I had in the park earlier in the day, I am hesitant but ultimately decide to go.

Our first stop is an alley behind a homeless shelter. There, Little Monster introduces me to Jed. "Don't talk to him unless you want smokes or weed," he says. "Got it," I reply. Our second stop is behind Chief Seattle Club, an organization that provides care to Native Americans. Little Monster asks a volunteer on a cigarette break if he can have a smoke. "You're too young, kid." "Alright," Little Monster tells me, "Let's go. There's someone I want you to meet."

Little Monster pushes his bike out of the alley and into another one. Following closely behind him, I step in a large puddle. My right foot is soaking wet. I begin to imagine that the tour is a ruse and that he may not actually know who he is going to introduce me to next. Then, a white male comes up to him and demands his private attention. "Can't," Little Monster says. "It's an emergency," he protests. "Later."

Little Monster grabs two flattened cardboard boxes lying on the ground. He places the cardboard boxes next to a group of men standing in front of a dumpster. "Sit down," he tells me. I sit down. He calls out to one of the men— whom he calls "Knife"—and asks him to come over. "This is Paul," he says. "He's writing a book about spirituality."

Knife is intrigued. "What do you mean you're writing a book about spirituality?" I give the elevator speech I've rehearsed time and again in front of academic audiences: "I want to know what people pray about and how they think about God and what that has to do with life on the streets. Would you like to do an interview sometime?" "I don't mean any offense," Knife responds curtly, "but you don't know what you're talking about right now."

Knife brings me away from the group. He puts his hand on my shoulder. "Look, you're not one of those people who's going to tell me to read a Bible verse, are you? I don't talk to those people." I assure him I am not. "This is interesting then." He pauses and then goes on. "You see, I've been asking God to send me someone to talk about this with. Usually God sends me an attractive woman, though. You look good, but you're not a woman. I don't think you're the one I am supposed to talk to."

Knife looks me up and down and then deep in the eyes. He is searching for my soul, I think, for a place that will tell him who I am. He is upset. Our conversation woke rage. "God is nice and all," he tells me, "but he doesn't fuck around. Do you understand? He will take your life if you hurt one of his kids. That's in the Bible."

I tell Knife that perhaps I am not the person he is supposed to speak with. I gather myself to go. "Look," Knife responds, "what do you need to know?" I want to leave and no longer know what I need to know. "I talk to God and I talk to Satan, too. Okay? That is what you need to know. Jesus and Satan are not enemies— they're friends."

I thank him and Little Monster for their willingness to speak with me. I cut the rope Knife is using to pull me in and push me away. Before I could leave, however, he gathers my attention again. "Before you come back," Knife said, "you need to answer this question: Why is it that I can see God and Satan even though I am not dead?"

I left the alley in haste and rode a streetcar to what locals describe as "the Other Seattle." Homelessness is less visible in this Seattle; it is eclipsed by tower cranes, luxurious condominiums, and hipster coffee shops. I ordered coffee at one of those coffee shops, eased into a comfortable chair, and began to write.

Journaling

An ethnographer takes copious notes. The world he or she constructs comes to life from the words in his or her journal.[10] Sipping my coffee, I wrote down what had just happened: the trouble I had relating to Little Monster, the ins and outs of the tour he gave me, and especially what Knife said about Satan. A number of images ran through my mind. I wrote them down. Anton LaVey, the founder of the Church of Satan, who was also known as "The Black Pope," came to mind first. Like Anton, I imagined that Knife was drawn to the figure of Satan out of rebellion over Christian hypocrisy.[11] I judged Knife for glorifying rebellion. The image of the hapless victim of social circumstance came to mind next. I imagined Knife suffering from a serious mental illness caused by a life of unbearable pain. I judge there to be nothing actually real about his conversations with Satan; he is actually listening to the impersonal force of injustice when he thinks Satan speaks to him.

In addition to writing about the images that came to mind during my encounter with Knife, I also wrote about the emotions I felt. In *Emotions and Fieldwork,* Sherryl Kleinman and Martha Copp suggest that ethnographers often avoid exploring the emotions they experience in their research out of concern for being considered unscientific and solipsistic. In their view, emotions can actually be helpful companions on the journey toward robust and clear-eyed cultural understanding.[12] The practical theologian Elizabeth Liebert makes a similar point about the relationship between emotion and prayer. With careful discernment, she suggests, our emotions can help lead us closer to God.[13]

Fear was more salient than the various images that came to mind when I wrote about Knife. Certainly, the fear was related to the obvious fact that I was in a rough neighborhood and that I witnessed harassment earlier in the day. The center didn't seem to hold. The fear ran deeper than the immediate present, however. It was connected to the religious socialization I experienced as a child. In the religious world I grew up in, Satan roamed the world like a roaring lion, preying on the souls of sinners. He'd swallow you into a lake of eternal fire and brimstone if you got too close to his mouth. We kids were taught to be very afraid. Most of us still are.

Paradoxically, I discovered myself by journaling about my encounter with Knife. I did not in fact know whether Knife had a serious mental illness or if he befriends Satan because of Christian hypocrisy. My emotional experience of Knife, like the thoughts I had about him, were drawn mostly from my own story, not his. The point I am making is that he did not yet emerge to me; I did not yet know his name. He never told me, and I never asked. In reaching this place of unknowing, a presence beneath the surface became possible. I had questions rather than answers.

Swimming

Religion, the French theologian Simone Weil wrote, is nothing else but a looking. It is the sacred manner in which human persons learn to fix their soulful gaze upon the world.[14] Prayer, for Weil, consists principally in cultivating attention to what is actually present. This kind of attentiveness means "suspending our thought, leaving it detached, empty, and ready to be penetrated by the object."[15] Love also requires a peculiar looking. Weil writes: "This way of looking is first of all attentive. The soul empties itself of all its own contents in order to receive into itself the being it is looking at, just as he is, in all his truth."[16] Love, in Weil's analysis, means learning to free the Other from ourselves and, through God's grace, simply ask: "What are you going through?"[17]

Summers in Seattle are warm. The nights are long. Whenever I could, after a long day on the streets, I'd swim in Lake Washington. When I dunked my head under water, I'd image the people I got to know. Eyes closed and submerged, I held them gently in my mind. Breathing out in the water, I tried to release them from the grip of my emotion and understanding. I'd ask the water bubbles my breath created to carry them away. When I got out of the lake, and threw my towel around my body, I looked out at the water. I imagined that I left my thoughts and emotions in the lake. I'd thank God for another day to learn someone's story.

The practice does not work like magic. I still feel fear when I think about what Knife told me about Satan. Anton LaVey and the hapless victim of social circumstance still runs through my mind. The thoughts and feelings are not as salient, though. They have less grip on me. I do not empty my soul into Lake Washington. Really, it's an absurd proposition. Nonetheless, I found a way—my own way—of consenting to the distance between me and the people I began spending time with on the streets. As a result, I found it easier to look away from myself and ask the person in front of me: What are you going through?

The practices of journaling and swimming helped me expand the distance between me and the people I came to know. They helped me understand that presence can emerge through spiritual practices that prevent the Other from being reduced to the way I think and feel. Let me be clear, however. I am not proposing that we stop interpreting social reality, that we leave the world in a cryptic fog— that would be an irresponsible, grotesque failure. We need to see the global problem of homelessness clearly in order to respond to it effectively. What I am proposing, however, is that becoming present—to people and to social problems—requires actual practices that dip us regularly into the waters of unknowing.

Reality is not fixed; our capacity to grasp social problems is finite. Before the infinite presence of the incomprehensible, we must each find idiosyncratic ways to embody epistemological humility. I found it in water; you might find it in the sky.

The Eclipse

The eclipse came a few days after Little Monster's tour. I went back to the park and noticed that there weren't any newspapers on the ground. There were, however, a lot of tourists and business professionals standing on it. They were looking up at the sky with sunglasses on; they were taking pictures of the shadows on the ground. My grandmother always said staring at the sun will cause blindness. I stared at the sun until my vision got blurry and I become paranoid that there'd be irreparable damage to my eyes.

I saw Sam and Eddie sitting on a park bench. I asked what they made of the eclipse. They weren't even looking up at the sky. Over a can of beer, they were sharing a conversation. "Oh, is that today?"

Notes

1. David Snow and Leon Anderson, *Down on Their Luck* (Berkeley: University of California Press, 1993), 214.

2. Howard Thurman, *A Strange Freedom: The Best of Howard Thurman on Religious Experience and Public Life*, ed. Walter Earl Fluker and Catherine Tumber (Boston: Beacon Press, 1998).

3. Angela Garcia, *The Pastoral Clinic: Addiction and Dispossession along the Rio Grande* (Berkeley: University of California Press, 2010), 11.

4. I am inspired here by Pope Francis, who has encouraged priests to have the smell of sheep on them.

5. Simone Weil, *Gravity and Grace* (New York: Van Rees Press, 1952), 115.

6. Karl Rahner, *Encounters with Silence* (South Bend, IN: St. Augustine's Press, 1999), 29.

7. Coll Thrush, *Native Seattle: Histories from the Crossing-Over Place* (Seattle: University of Washington Press, 2017), 10.

8. Katie Herzog, "Astrologers Agree: The Eclipse Is Bad News for Trump. Astronomers Agree: Astrology is Bullshit," *Seattle Weekly,* August 16, 2017.

9. Ibid.

10. Robert Emerson, Rachel Fretz, and Linda Shaw, *Writing Ethnographic Fieldnotes* (Chicago: University of Chicago Press, 2011).

11. Lawrence Wright, "Sympathy for the Devil," *Rolling Stone,* September 5, 1991.

12. Sherryl Kleinman and Martha Copp, *Emotions and Fieldwork* (London: SAGE Publications, 1993).

13. Elizabeth Liebert, *The Way of Discernment: Spiritual Practices for Decision Making* (Louisville, KY: Westminster John Knox Press, 2008).

14. Simone Weil, *Waiting for God* (New York: Harper/Perennial, 2009), 57.

15. Ibid., 62.

16. Ibid., 65.

17. Ibid., 64.

Encountering Particular Populations

STATELESS-CUM-HOMELESS REFUGEES

Hard Choices for the Future

Elias Opongo, SJ

The stateless-cum-homeless refugees are hardly mentioned as a special category of displaced persons, despite the fact that they suffer the double tragedy of forced migration and lack of recognized citizenship. This often implies that this category of refugees without any physical or conceptual affiliation to a country becomes vulnerable to grave social, political, religious, and economic marginalization. According to the statistical yearbook of the United Nations High Commissioner for Refugees (UNHCR), there are 25.4 million refugees worldwide, 55 percent of which come from just three countries: South Sudan (1.4m); Afghanistan (2.5m); and Syria (5.5m).[1] Of the numerous host countries, the majority of these refugees are found in (in ascending order) Ethiopia, Uganda, Iran, Lebanon, Pakistan, and Turkey. Of the 25.4 million refugees globally, 10 million are said to be stateless persons.

In order to meet the definition of refugee by international conventions, a person must face persecution in his or her home state. This assumes that a home state exists to which the refugees can return, but legal questions arise as to whether allegations of persecution are sufficient and substantiated to merit protection and granting of refugee status. It also does not guarantee that the person has the right to remain in the host state beyond the period in which the persecution remains, unless they commence the formal naturalization process. What is often ignored is the fact that the blanket definition of refugees tends to include stateless persons within the refugee population as simply refugees. This category of refugees is often in a much more precarious situation that relates to displacement, homelessness, and statelessness.

Catholic Social Teaching (CST) emphasizes the need to take care of the displaced persons and immigrants who often find themselves in disadvantaged situations of neglect, abandonment, and homelessness. Empathy and respect for the dignity of the refugees and displaced persons is imperative and ought to be considered a fundamental human right. Stateless refugees are twice as vulnerable compared to other categories of refugees. This is particularly so given the double jeopardy of statelessness: stateless refugees have to live with the uncertainties of a future without citizenship and thus without a place to call their home. Not paying attention to stateless refugees and providing special care renders them vulnerable to abuses, frustrations, and desperation, while creating possible sociopolitical imbalances and threats to national cohesion. A stateless population can be instrumentalized for cheap labor, sexual abuse, and even recruitment to militia and terrorist groups. It is paramount that governments pay attention to the care of stateless persons and initiate legal and social processes for citizenship acquisition through comprehensive resettlement programs.

Conceptualizing Stateless-cum-Homeless Refugees

Stateless refugees can be defined as persons who have been denied citizenship by their own countries or asylum countries due to social, cultural, political, economic, or religious reasons. According to Aileen Thomson, statelessness has two main causes: *direct discrimination*, when a state deprives a minority of citizenship or when people are displaced and rejected by their country, and *structural inadequacies*, including unregistered births as well as gender discriminatory laws that do not allow mothers to pass on nationalities to their children.[2]

The Non-Traditional Security Studies (NTS) indicates that there are two types of stateless persons defined as *de jure* and *de facto* statelessness.[3] *De jure* stateless refugees are not recognized as nationals by laws of any country, and could be members of a repressed minority who may have been nationals of a state at some time, but had their citizenship removed due to some political or legal changes. *De facto* stateless refugees had hitherto had a nationality, but do not have convincing proof due either to insufficient or ineffective documentation. NTS suggests that it is often difficult to distinguish between the two.

Despite the 1948 Universal Declaration of Human Rights proclamation that everyone has the right to a nationality and should therefore not be deprived of citizenship, statelessness is a critical problem. There are in fact conventions that recognize the rights of stateless persons. These conventions and international treaties seek to prevent or reduce statelessness. They include, among others, the 1966 International Covenant on Civil and Political Rights; the 1979 Convention on the Elimination of All Forms of Discrimination against Women; the 1989 Convention on the Rights of the Child; the 1961 Convention on the Reduction of Statelessness; the 1954 Convention Relating to the Status of Stateless Persons; as well as the Universal Declaration itself. In order to decrease statelessness, the Convention on the Reduction of Statelessness obliged parties to offer citizenship to stateless persons or those born within their respective territories. Although most of the 1954 Convention relating to statelessness is devoted to protection, it does prescribe that "contracting states shall as far as possible facilitate the assimilation and naturalization of stateless persons."[4]

The purely legal description of the condition of being stateless known as de jure statelessness describes a person not considered a citizen by any state based on its legal framework. The characteristics and value of a person's nationality as realized in their particular home state is irrelevant to this definition. The definition should be extended to include de facto statelessness, particularly in relation to those with nationality by law but without proof or documentation. There are also instances when states withhold benefits of citizenship (protection and assistance) or when these benefits have been relinquished. For example, the Rohingya people with a population of 1.1 million have been denied citizenship by the Myanmar government since 1982 and are not recognized among the country's 135 ethnic groups. Their constant persecution as a minority Muslim community in a majority Buddhist country has meant that they are constantly on the move seeking a home, with refugee status as well as lack of citizenship. The neighboring nation of Bangladesh has persistently denied them entry into the country as well as recognition as refugees.

There is growing attention to refugees and migrants in the Western world; unfortunately, the reception of refugees and migrants has not been positive in recent years. Linda Kerber is of the opinion that attention to immigration, particularly from the Western world's perspective, was initially raised by reflections of the writings of Hannah Arendt in 1951 on the nature of political existence, but then receded until the 1960s when refugees from Vietnam and the contested territory of Palestine sparked interest.[5] The post–Arab spring conflict and subsequent migration to Europe, as well as perennial attempts by political and economic immigrants to get into Europe via the Mediterranean Sea, have put social, economic, and political pressure on Europe. Despite the immense human suffering of these immigrants and refugees, only a handful of European states have laws and policies in place to identify stateless refugees within its broader refugee population. There have been reactionary temporary measures marred by social and political debates that have made naturalization a distant reality.

Even as states work to create legislation that aims to deal with the challenge of statelessness, international conventions that speak to the status of refugees and stateless persons lay the foundation for the idea that human rights protections do not necessitate the acquisition of nationality.[6] In other words, in most cases, stateless refugees face violation of basic rights even before they are classified as stateless.

The Dynamics of Statelessness and Homelessness of Refugees

Political, economic, and social factors have contributed to the increased population of stateless refugees in the world. Conflicts and natural disaster displacements have led to multiple migrations of refugees into different countries. In some cases, refugees have not been recognized by host governments, and at the same time children born in countries of asylum have not necessarily acquired local citizenship. In a presentation at a workshop on the challenges of forced migration in the Middle East, Zahra Albarazi looked at three sets of groups within the displaced Syrian population: first, the *general refugee population*, including those born in exile, have Syrian nationality and have a minimal risk of statelessness (however, this is not the case for other refugee nationals); second, the *high-risk groups*, in which, due to legal frameworks of the host state and Syria, a minority of refugees increasingly face difficulties protecting their nationality.[7] These include children born in female-headed households; undocumented persons; children of Palestinian refugees formerly based in Syria; Syrian children in Lebanon who have turned fifteen and are eligible to receive a national identification card yet are not recognized as citizens; and refugees not registered with UNHCR. Third, there are the *stateless refugees* who are stateless prior to the crisis, including stateless Kurds, those born to Syrian mothers but without paternal links to Syria, and Syrian refugees who claim that the Syrian government rejected their document renewal attempts for political reasons. According to a survey in northern Iraq by UNHCR, 10 percent of Syrian Kurdish refugees are stateless, given that many fled Syria before they could get a chance to apply for nationality.[8]

In Lebanon, stateless persons are denied access to basic rights such as employment in the formal sector, social security, or the ability to take school exams. Being stateless and refugee at the same time comes with a myriad of other challenges such as perceptions of illegal entry into another country; restricted movements, given the many police checkpoints in countries of asylum; and challenges faced when attempting to return home, especially in relation to having to prove one's nationality.

As with many other social ills, it must be noted that women bear the disproportional weight of the human experience of statelessness. Although refugee numbers are evenly split between men and women, women are more likely to be accompanied by children and face a significant disparity in exposure to statelessness in various parts of the world. There is also a larger number of men who seek asylum, even though women and children represent 80 percent of refugees, and this is due to the fact that men have more access to formal and informal structures that can facilitate migration. According to Zahra Albarazi, Syrian laws do not allow its female citizens who give birth in exile to pass on their nationality to their offspring fathered by another national.[9]

Across all demographics and classifications, it must be noted that all stateless refugees are exposed to conditions likely to present challenges to their mental status. In their cross-sectional study, Riley, Varner, Ventevogel, and Hasan examined trauma history, daily environmental stressors, and mental health outcomes for 148 Rohingya adults in a refugee camp in Bangladesh.[10] Their findings revealed high levels of mental health problems including posttraumatic stress disorder, depression, and associated functional impairment. Respondents also validated local expressions of distress such as somatic complaints and concerns of spirit possession. When asked about their daily experiences and stressors within camps, refugees emphasized food insufficiency, lack of free movement, and concerns for personal safety.

Statelessness in itself is an important risk factor that increases exposure to human rights violations and inhumane living conditions, which make it difficult for the refugees to recover from the psychological and physical distress of being stateless. Avyanthi Azis, describing the plight of the Rohingya in greater Kuala Lumpur, states that the Rohingya are disqualified from an idealized citizenship based on a capitalistic Muslim subjectivity and are classified as low-skilled workers within the informal economy.[11] Given that an estimated 50 percent of the entire refugee population is made up of urban refugees, Kuala Lumpur has become one of the major

Asian cities hosting urban refugees, even though Malaysia is not a signatory to the 1951 Refugee Convention. Azis's study focused on the how the Rohingya negotiate belonging and on the strategies employed in the absence of effective citizenship. Although the refugees share Islamic religion with the locals and are generally welcomed, they still lack the desired economic and racial attributes that would make them feel much more at home. They are considered to be sources of cheap labor and are often exploited. Rohingya men are disadvantaged and are ineligible to marry locals, and have to marry among themselves, further increasing the stateless population in the country.[12]

The post-9/11 era has brought in new dimensions of the right to citizenship. A number of Western countries have threatened withdrawal of citizenship to individuals joining terrorist groups such as the Islamic State of Iraq (ISIS). Also, special location prisons, like America's Guantánamo Bay in Cuba, designated to hold suspected terrorists, denied individuals' basic rights. Often these prisoners have no right to legal counsel, visitation, or reconsideration of their cases. Their respective countries have also often not intervened to address their cases. The suspected person is not given a right to defend himself or herself in a court of law. In the meantime, such individuals are de jure stateless.

There are also borderline refugees or economic immigrants who are often rendered stateless by social circumstances. For example, persons who have escaped hardships in their home countries to search for better economic opportunities elsewhere sometimes find themselves in difficult situations in which they cannot ask for asylum for fear of repatriation. Such persons often have no documents to prove their nationalities, nor do they have the funds and legal means to rectify their status. In situations where such persons have been trafficked into forced labor or prostitution, they tend to be at the mercy of their recruiters.

Catholic Social Teaching and Stateless Refugees

Catholic Social Teaching (CST) emphasizes human dignity and the right of every individual to enjoy the satisfaction of the basic needs of human life. The Israelites lived as a homeless population in Egypt for many years, and learned what it meant to be a foreigner in another county. Thus, God ordered: "You shall treat the alien who resides with you no differently than the natives born among you; have the same love for him as for yourself; for you too were once aliens in the land of Egypt" (Lev 19:33–34). In the New Testament, Matthew narrates the story of Mary and Joseph fleeing to Egypt because they were afraid that King Herod would kill the newborn Jesus. Later, Matthew (25:35) quotes Jesus reiterating the importance of caring for the person in need: "For I was hungry and you gave me food, I was thirsty and you gave me drink, a stranger and you welcomed me" (Mt 25:35). Paul calls for the appreciation of every person regardless of race, color, nationality, or ethnic group, for we are all equal before God: "There is neither Jew nor Greek . . . for you are all one in Christ Jesus" (Gal 3:28).

The above emphasis on the care for the poor, marginalized, and displaced brings to our attention the need to take care of the most disadvantaged in our societies. Stateless and homeless refugees face two difficult challenges: displacement and homelessness. They rely on the goodwill of the church and plead their cases to those in positions of authority. Pope Francis has reiterated that governments, church, and society in general are obligated to take care of immigrants, homeless persons, and refugees, given their vulnerable status.

The recent sociopolitical hostilities against refugees and immigrants in Europe, the United States, and Australia demonstrate less tolerance for this category of vulnerable population. While recognizing the difficulties that a large influx of refugees can cause, there are, however, benefits that such a multicultural mix can bring. But even if that were not the case, the basic rights of the refugees ought to be respected anyway. William O'Neil reiterates the importance of solidarity with refugees, those near to us and those far away. He calls for "hospitable treatment of those seeking to change nationality, whether through local integration in the host country or resettlement in a third country; assistance in their integration to a new homeland; respect for their cultural heritage; and recognition of the benefits of hosting, and the contributions of migrants."[13]

The double jeopardy of stateless refugees who find themselves both away from home but at the same time with no place to call home, and hence no citizenship to claim as their own, heightens the level of vulnerability among such a population. However, in light of the respect for human dignity, the church puts the emphasis on recognition of global citizenship. Pope John XXIII states that loss of citizenship "does not detract in any way from (one's) membership in the human family as a whole, nor from (one's) citizenships in the world community."[14]

Stateless refugees are also exposed to environmentally specific challenges, whether they are based in rural or urban settings. In his encyclical, *Laudato Si' (LS)* Pope Francis brings to our attention the plight of persons displaced by a changing climate that has led to environmental degradation. He states: "There has been a tragic rise in the number of migrants seeking to flee from the growing poverty caused by environmental degradation. They are not recognized by international conventions as refugees; they bear the loss of the lives they have left behind, without enjoying any legal protection whatsoever."[15] The pope regrets that the world has remained indifferent to the plight of such refugees. He therefore calls on all persons of goodwill and all governments to respond to the needs of this special category of refugees. Given that such refugees are not recognized in the host countries and do not fall under the broader definition of refugees, they are likely to be both stateless and homeless.

Conclusion

Recognition of the urgent need to protect the human rights of stateless refugees, and the correlative duties of those rights, is fundamental to the development of national and international legal frameworks that respond to the precarious situation of stateless and subsequently homeless refugees. It is imperative that measures to support and integrate stateless refugees should not disproportionately fall on the poor who are already struggling to make ends meet. In fact, any form of humanitarian, legal, and political assistance should not pit refugees against already vulnerable citizens. A multidimensional approach to helping stateless-cum-homeless persons is vital to the well-being of the affected persons as well as for the host communities.

Notes

1. UNHCR, *Statistical Yearbooks: Figures at a Glance*, 2017, http://www.unhcr.org/figures-at-a-glance.html.

2. Aileen Thomson, "Report on Gathering at Georgetown Law Center: Addressing the Challenges of Statelessness," *Human Rights Brief*, December 23, 2009, http://hrbrief.org/2009/12/addressing-the-challenges-of-statelessness/.

3. "Understanding Statelessness: Issues, Challenges and Opportunities," *NTS Alert*, February 10, 2010, http://www.rsis.edu.sg/nts/HTML-Newsletter/alert/NTS-alert-feb-1001.html.

4. David Weissbrodt and Clay Collins, "The Human Rights of Stateless Persons," *Human Rights Quarterly* 28, no. 1 (2006): 245–76.

5. K. Linda Kerber, "Toward a History of Statelessness in America," *American Quarterly* 57, no. 3 (2005): 727–49.

6. M. Vicente Pérez, "Human Rights and the Rightless: The Case of Gaza Refugees in Jordan," *International Journal of Human Rights* 15, no. 7 (2011): 1031–54.

7. Zahra Albarazi, "Syrian Refugee or Stateless Refugee: The Challenges of Statelessness in Exile," *London School of Economics: Middle East Centre Blog*, June 2016, https://blogs.lse.ac.uk/mec/2016/09/26/syrian-refugee-or-stateless-refugee-the-challenges-of-statelessness-in-exile.

8. UNHCR, "Lacking a Nationality, Some Refugees from Syria Face Acute Risks, *UNHCR* (December 20, 2013), https://www.unhcr.org/news/latest/2013/12/52b45bbf6/lacking-nationality-refugees-syria-face-acute-risks.html.

9. Albarazi, "Syrian Refugee or Stateless Refugee."

10. A. Riley, A. Varner, P. Ventevogel, and M. Hasan, "Daily Stressors, Trauma Exposure, and Mental Health among Stateless Rohingya Refugees in Bangladesh," *Transcultural Psychiatry* 54, no. 3 (2017): 304–31.

11. Avyanthi Azis, "Urban Refugees in a Graduated Sovereignty: The Experiences of the Stateless Rohingya in the Klang Valley," *Citizenship Studies* 18, no. 8 (2014): 839–54.

12. Azis, "Urban Refugees," 850.

13. William O'Neil, "What We Owe to Refugees and IDPs: An Inquiry into the Rights of the Forcibly Displaced," in *Refugee Rights Ethics, Advocacy, and Africa*, ed. David Hollenbach (Washington, DC: Georgetown University Press, 2008), 27–52.

14. John XXIII, *Pacem in Terris* (April 11, 1963), http://w2.vatican.va/content/john-xxiii/en/encyclicals/documents/hf_j-xxiii_enc_11041963_pacem.html.

15. Pope Francis, *Laudato Si'* (May 24, 2015), 25, http://w2.vatican.va/content/francesco/en/encyclicals/documents/papa-francesco_20150524_enciclica-laudato-si.html.

Violence, Violations, and Homeless Women

Julie George, SSpS

In this essay, I focus mostly on the situation of homeless women in India, since my experiences are based on women's issues in India. To begin with, women are the primary users of a home; thus their housing requirements must be the priority. For women, a home is not just a space that provides shelter; it is also a place of relationship, employment, security, safety, stability, and social interaction. And it means access to basic amenities that come along with a home such as water, electricity, roads, markets, school, hospital, transport, and place of employment, which are the supporting social surroundings that women normally require for an appropriate living. But homelessness restricts women from enjoying these minimum basic rights and requirements.

Women constitute one of the groups most harshly affected by homelessness anywhere in the world. Women who are denied housing and are living on the streets suffer the severest kinds of abuse and violence.

> Homeless women and young girls, with or without families, are vulnerable to physical abuse and harassment and denied a very basic right to lead a dignified life. Incidents of sexual harassment are very common as these women and children are out on the streets all through the day and night. Women very often find themselves in the middle of fights on the streets, protecting themselves and their children from anti-social elements. With frequent cases of children being kidnapped, women are forced to tie their infants to their bodies, ensuring they don't lose them.[1]

Women in all groups are especially vulnerable given the extent of statutory and other forms of discrimination which often apply in relation to property rights (including home ownership) or rights of access to property or accommodation; they are also particularly vulnerable to acts of violence and sexual abuse when they are rendered homeless.[2]

The homeless live in public spaces, ranging from bus terminals to commercial junctions, pavements, street corners, railway platforms, spaces underneath bridges and flyovers, shelter homes, and places of worship. Living in such places also means no access to basic necessities. In some of the cities, the homeless will have to avail themselves of the pay-and-use toilets. Being short of money, they use facilities at railway stations, but if they are caught, hefty fines will be levied on them as well as humiliation by the police. "More than 57,000 people in the city of Mumbai live without shelter, not because they choose to, or because they deserve to, but only because they are forced to do so."[3] People who live on the streets struggle for dignity and face daily battles for things so many of us take for granted, such as toilets, water, food, safety, and a good night's sleep.

Domestic Violence and Homeless Women:
A Tragic Reality

Domestic violence is one of the main causes of homelessness for women, and it is closely tied to a woman's financial independence. Normally, women are more likely to give up their jobs in order to take on caring roles. In the job market, women are often paid less than their male counterparts for the same work, which makes their savings less or zero. When a woman victim decides to leave a violent marriage, it means leaving the matrimonial home; her options are often limited. The abusive husband may have control over her finances, and her capacity to perform well at work may have been diminished by the abuse she suffers, which may also gradually result in her losing her job. Normally the children become the responsibility of the mother, and she needs to find a safe place for both herself and the children to stay safe.

> The cult of true womanhood proclaims that the vocation of women is homemaker. The fulfillment of her true nature and happiness consists in creating the home as a peaceful island in the sea of alienated society, as Eden-Paradise to which men can retreat from the exploitations and temptations of the work-world. Women must provide in the home a climate of peace and happiness, of self-sacrificing love and self-effacing gentility on order to save the family.[4]

Society puts the responsibility of saving the family and marriage solely on the woman.

Today more and more homes are becoming battlegrounds where intimate partner violence forces women and children out of the house. Though women's identity is entwined with a home, the ownership of a house as a capital investment and the largest expenditure in the household budget lies with the male head of the household. Even if women own property, their place is considered to be within the house—and this cult of domesticity perpetuates the low status of women. The market economy devalues domestic work and the policy makers consider it to be "non-work."

Being homeless often means decreased personal safety for women. They are rendered homeless for a multitude of reasons. These include domestic violence, sexual violence, desertion, migration, displacement, and forced eviction. As a women's rights lawyer, I have come across many incidents in which domestic violence plays a greater role in increasing women's vulnerability to homelessness and to further violence, especially when there is a lack of protection by the legal system itself. Abandonment by a husband or the marital family and lack of support from the natal family results in women being thrown out of their homes and onto the streets.

Consider Sindhutai, who was married off at a very young age and abandoned by her husband when she was pregnant. She lived on the street and gave birth to her daughter in a cowshed, cutting the umbilical cord with a sharp stone. Feeling lost and betrayed, Sindhutai started singing and begging in trains and on the streets to make ends meet. She continued to fight for herself and her daughter's existence, and, fearing for their safety, she made cemeteries their home. Miraculously, she managed to rise from these ashes, and today she is taking care of hundreds of children who are sheltered in the homes she runs. She is just one of the fortunate few who have overcome such odds, but the majority of women are not so fortunate.

Our cities are extremely unsafe for women—rape, theft, murder, kidnapping, sexual exploitation, and gender-based violence are common. Some women have no option but to start begging. The homeless women who are single, without any family, are among the most vulnerable. Though there are legal provisions to secure women's rights to remain in their matrimonial homes, the improper implementation of such laws continues to result in victims of domestic violence being thrown out of their homes. Most of the shelters keep women and children only for a short while. Women, especially mothers who are out of the workforce and dependent on their abusive husbands financially, are at risk of homelessness after leaving an abusive marriage.

"Many women report that they have felt unsafe even in shelters, or are survivors of gendered trauma stemming from stays in shelters. Malnourishment and hunger among homeless women is common. In Delhi, residents stated that local police only allow residents to cook at night, which has significantly limited their food intake. If the women try to prepare a meal during the day, police throw away their utensils and food items."[5] Many of these women have left abusive marriages, suffered sexual violence, or have been abandoned by families for mental illness or after the death of a husband. Though the Protection of Domestic Violence Act has ensured women's right to stay in their matrimonial and parental homes, women are harassed in many ways by their husbands until they finally leave the house. "Voices against laws which protect women against domestic violence are getting louder or at least more widely reported because these laws challenge the very core of so-called tradition and culture, the patriarchal family, and impermissible masculine behaviour."[6]

Witch-hunting: Another Sin against Women

"Witch-hunting" is a form of violence against women in different parts of the world in the contemporary era. A patriarchal society that habitually blames women for everything that happens will be more likely to blame women who are vulnerable. "Witch-hunting" can be seen as one of the worst forms of cultural violence against women. Witchcraft in India is still part of the deep-rooted traditional rural culture. Targeting female-headed households for witch-hunting has become a major issue confronting women's movements in all states of North and Western India. Widowed/single/divorced and deserted/Dalit/tribal women are labeled witches by people with vested interests, who then grab their land and homes.

Witchcraft has been seen as a mere superstition for a long time; however, studies and observations by sociologists and anthropologists show that Dalit woman who are rebellious in nature, a threat to the patriarchal system, or widows who possess some property, are the ones who are most often tormented and called a witch. This is a conspiracy to throw them out of the community, to acquire their property, or to suppress their voice. Witch-hunting is also understood to be a manifestation of the low social status of women, whereby the male attitude of dominance and violence against women is concretely legitimized by calling a woman a witch.[7]

Witch-hunts are most common among poor rural communities with little access to education and health services, but with lasting, age-old belief in witchcraft. When an individual gets sick or some dangerous situation arises in the community, the blame falls not upon a virus or disease, but upon an alleged witch. Many studies show that women who are poor and low-caste are easy targets for being branded as witches. Women who are widowed, who are childless, who possess certain features, or who are old and lonely, poor, or socially ostracized are easy targets. Women accused of witchcraft have been treated in an inhuman way: physically abused, stoned, ostracized, and driven from their homes and away from the village and their familiar surroundings and left to die. "In recent years, we have seen the rise of anti-witch-hunt campaigns in both Africa and India, with women and men educating people about the causes of illness and the interests motivating male traditional healers, local leaders, and other frequent accusers. In each case, women's decision to fight back, break their isolation and join with other women has been vital for the success of these efforts."[8]

Deprivation to Destitution: Burdens of Politics, Patriarchy, and History

The deprived sections of society such as the poor, small farmers, daily wage laborers, and women domestic workers, often experience the ramifications of industrialization, globalization, forced eviction, creation of smart cities, and communal riots. The impact of the recent demonetization in the country has affected various facets of the lives, labor, and livelihoods of the marginalized, especially women, leading these deprived sections of the society into destitution.

The unabated modernization of Indian cities has turned them into exclusive zones for the rich and the neo-rich. The preferred new homes of the wealthy sit within secure and digitally controlled gated communities, or within self-contained townships, with many services outsourced to various agencies. The urban working class—waste collectors, domestic workers and service providers like plumbers, electricians, butchers and fishmongers—are not welcome in these smart habitations. If economic relationships in the past were marked by the exploitation of the poor, today a vast number of people find themselves largely irrelevant in the grander scheme of things.[9]

In December 2018, around 35,000 Adivasis (Indigenous people) marched barefoot from Nasik to Mumbai, the financial capital of India, demanding title to their lands, which they had cultivated for generations. Many women were part of the march, and Mathurabai was among them. When she reached Mumbai with tired, bleeding heels, some people from Mumbai distributed footwear. "The farmers from Telangana explained how their wives' suicides due to indebtedness were never counted as farmer suicides. Women farm laborers from Bihar said they were always paid wages in grain and not in cash. Villagers from Mathura, Uttar Pradesh wanted back the 100 acres a politician had seized."[10]

Women do not constitute a homogeneous group. But irrespective of class, race, and age, they are universally discriminated against and experience inequality in all spheres, especially when it comes to their rights, such as to adequate housing. Lack of access to and control over land and house contributes significantly to women's increasing poverty. Ownership, access, and control of land and housing lay the foundation for women's empowerment.

There are many social, economic, and political situations that render people insecure, homeless, and without a sustainable source of livelihood. Women are particularly vulnerable given the low socioeconomic status accorded to them. Women workers from the Scheduled Caste groups constitute the largest section of the unorganized workforce in India. They also form the largest section of landless agricultural workers in the agricultural sector.

In many male-dominated societies, women have always been discriminated against. Gender biases are deeply rooted and are reflected in women's lack of access to and control over land, housing, and property in particular. Women are thrown out of their secure homes due to changes in marital status, such as when they become widows or divorced.

Old age is often an insecure and troublesome time for women, who have to depend solely on their children for their survival. In fact, even customs and traditions cast women out from the social system. There are customs and traditions that do not recognize women's contributions as productive. There is a lack of laws, policies, and programs that are sensitive toward women and the aged, as well as an absence of institutional support in times of distress and homelessness.

In urban settings, women living in the slums survive in deplorable conditions, without proper shelter, adequate water, health, sanitation, or hygiene. The position

of women who are pavement dwellers is worse. These women continuously face the
threat of forced eviction in the name of urbanization and development.

Today, in many parts of the country, forests and land are becoming battlegrounds in the name of development, where the state fights its citizens and throws
them out of their own land and houses. Industrial corridors and other businesses
have created forced migration within the country, triggering massive injustice
against certain communities.

"Women, who are estimated to make up about 10 percent of India's homeless
population, suffer the brunt of a growing crisis brought on by rapid urbanisa-
tion, soaring property prices, and a critical lack of shelters and affordable housing.
Compounding the difficulty is a lack of reliable data on homeless people, and
homeless women in particular."[11] Women and children with no money and no one
to turn to, settle on the pavement, marking their space among other families who
live there. When it rains, they cover themselves with plastic sheets. They have little
protection from the winter cold or the summer heat. The police harass them, and
the local people are annoyed at their presence and curse them. But they cannot
afford to pay rent, and the shelter homes that are provided by the state are also not
good, so the homeless often have no option but to live on the pavement.

There is no quick solution to this problem; many countries are encountering
similar difficulties. So ending urban homelessness in less developed countries such
as India is unlikely, with thousands cramming into already crowded cities. Evictions there are rising: hundreds of homes are pulled down and people are forcibly
removed to make way for metro stations and highways.

Land is important for women because they depend on it for their livelihood.
It provides them with food, nutrition, and income security. "Hunger is chronic
among women and children in many women-headed households. The reason: they
lack access and control over land including village common lands and forests. It is
critical for women, who live in rural areas and depend on agriculture and related
activities for survival, to gain access to, and control over land and to usufruct rights
on village common lands and forests."[12]

In many areas of North India, the Tribals/Adivasis inhabited the land by
fighting against the dangers of wild animals, sickness, and extreme climate. They
prepared the forest and jungles for habitation and for cultivation. "Unfortunately
in the name of development all the laws with provisions to protect the rights of
Adivasis, Farmers, Dalits and labour classes are being amended and the economy of
the nation is being moulded to suit the economy of the capitalistic market."[13] "The
government acquired the land of the small and marginal farmers, mostly Adivasis,
for the so-called development projects under the tags of 'national interest' and
development. Thus, millions of people became landless across the country."[14] Hence
the corporate democracy has made thousands of farmers homeless.

There are undoubtedly strong ties between corporations and the government,
as seen in the following example: "In the state of Jharkhand, 2.1 million acres
of common land was enlisted in the 'Land Bank' and the forest department has

also proposed three wildlife corridors and three sub-corridor projects, where 870 villages will be relocated from the forests."[15] There are also proposals to build industrial corridors, which will further exploit the poor.

> Land acquisition laws were enacted to enable the government to acquire lands provided they were needed for a "public purpose." The infinite malleability of the "public purpose" restriction empowered the government to work these laws excessively. Acquisition laws for instance are used towards land-pooling, a technique by which many parcels of land are pooled together and acquired from several small land owners—amounting to land-grabbing from the poor.[16]

Finally, sexual violence against women has been a regular feature of communal riots, ethnic conflicts, and war anywhere in the world, and female stereotypes continue to influence the violence inflicted during the riots. "Moreover these stereotypes acquire greater significance since they draw on patriarchal conceptions of women as symbols of honour, as sanctified property, and as the biological reproducers of family, community and nation."[17]

Home and Beyond

In many parts of the world, women's rights to adequate housing and land continue to be systematically denied, and the denial of housing and land results in multiple human rights violations. Women's rights to land and housing have been a major concern of the women's movement in India for over two decades. Globally, women's rights to housing and land are becoming an area of growing urgency. In almost all societies, women have historically managed the unpaid care work and fulfilled the responsibilities of looking after the family and children by cooking, cleaning, caring, collecting fuel, fodder, water, taking care of poultry and cattle, and providing food and nutritional protection. Women's contributions to the family and society remain unrecognized, and mostly unpaid; thus, the need for women to be able to secure land and housing has become critical. It is a difficult task to get an accommodation for women victims of violence, desertion, or rejection from the natal or marital family. The effect of family violence continues to be a major driver of homelessness.

Though housing and property rights are guaranteed to women through international documents as well as through constitutions and laws in many countries, often the implementation of these rights is overshadowed by existing patriarchal practices and discriminatory patterns. In India, religion-based family laws and customary laws play important roles in determining women's rights to housing, and they are different for different communities and religious groups.

The gendered construct of social and economic relations within and outside the household and deeply entrenched patriarchal attitudes in the civil society discriminate against women in virtually every aspect, be it policy development, entitlement in government projects, control over household resources, right of inheritance and ownership, and even the construction of housing. Women's human rights include their right to house and property, which is a critical factor in determining their social status, economic well-being and empowerment. Many cases show that women's ownership of property and housing is crucial for reducing gender-based violence; an increase in women's income or ownership of property will increase household resources, which will result in improving women's status and increasing their bargaining power in the household, thereby lowering the risk of gender-based violence.

In an ironic move, "At the end of 2015, the local government of Mumbai cleared a proposal for cow shelters, intended to house homeless cows in the city."[18] Whereas in 2012, the Homeless Collective, a coalition of various nongovernmental organizations working with the homeless in Mumbai, had filed a public interest litigation asking the local government to provide shelters for the homeless as per the standards set out by the Supreme Court, but it was not until January 2016, after three years of litigation, that the local government finally agreed to build thirteen shelters to add to the seven existing ones in Mumbai.

The local governments claim that the lack of space in the city is the biggest stumbling block for developing shelters for the homeless. But this is not so; rather, the issue of homelessness is not treated with the seriousness it deserves. The state's response to homeless women is repulsively insufficient, and the majority of homeless women are left to fend for themselves. For the homeless, life on the streets means frequent eviction and confiscation of bare essentials and identity documents. These evictions are human-made calamities that push these communities back into the vicious circle of deprivation.

Collective action by NGOs has created a powerful movement for the homeless to be included in the census and to be provided with more desperately needed shelters. As long as we are unable to uproot deeply embedded inequality and discrimination, alleviate poverty, create employment opportunities, and bring about gender parity, the situation will not change. Women need to be given ownership rights in the joint family properties. Until such measures are taken and the government's policy making becomes more concerned with people, the fight for dignity and human rights will continue. Nowhere is this more needed than for the women on the street. "Incidents of violence against women and the homeless prompted the Supreme Court order in 2012 that for every 100,000 city population, one homeless shelter must be built across all cities."[19]

Conclusion

Our response to this contemporary call, especially in our urban and rural missions, should be to assist in the transition of women from being victims to being true citizens of the country and to stand in solidarity with them to demand their legal and human rights; to support women-specific shelters providing a safe space for women; and to work toward abolishing the gender pay gap and sexism in all workplaces, especially in our own institutions. Gender inequality in the workplace affects all women, but the way it affects homeless women is rarely talked about; thus, that is a conversation we need to initiate.

As Varghese Theckanath wrote:

> The most important step forward for the Church in urban India is to trace its roots back to the poor. If it placed its best personnel and resources at the service of the elite in the last century, the same has to be done for the poor today. The Church has to physically, psychologically, and voluntarily move to the periphery of society to protect human rights, create gender parity, and help reduce the impact of climate change.[20]

Women's human rights include women's ownership in housing in order to lessen the threat of discrimination and different forms of violence, and to reduce wife-beating, alcoholism, and sale of land. Despite remarkable achievements in the field of women's development and a fairly strong women's movement, violence against women is still a burning issue. Above all, we need to understand that people living on the streets are not thieves, beggars, drug addicts, and miscreants. We need to treat them with respect and dignity. Women, especially those who are homeless, are ten times more vulnerable (to assault, rape, etc.) than men; hence, they require specialized support services to cater for their particular vulnerabilities.

Notes

1. Pooja Yadav and Deeksha Chaudhary, "For Mumbai's Homeless People, Each Day Is a Struggle for Dignity," *Scroll.in,* May 13, 2016, https://scroll.in/article/802788/photo-feature-for-mumbais-homeless-people-each-day-is-a-struggle-for-dignity.

2. UN Committee on Economic, Social, and Cultural Rights, Sixteenth Session, 1997.

3. Yadav and Chaudhary, "For Mumbai's Homeless People."

4. Elisabeth Schüssler Fiorenza, *In Memory of Her: A Feminist Theological Reconstruction of Christian Origins* (New York: Crossroad,1983), 348.

5. Shivani Chaudhry, Amita Joseph, and Induprakashsingh, "Homeless Women and Violence," http://www.hic-sarp.org/documents/Homeless_Women_and_Violence_Shivani_Amita_Indu.pdf. An edited version of this article has been published in *The Fear that Stalks: Gender-based Violence in Public Spaces*, ed. Sara Pilot and Laura Prabhu (New Delhi: Zubaan, 2011).

6. Brinda Karat, "Rights in Reverse," *Communalism Combat*, no. 143 (Mumbai: Sabrang Communications, 2009), 23.

7. National Commission for Women, "Research Study on Violence against Dalit Women in Different States of India by Studying the Sources of Materials That Are Available and Conducting Interview of the Perpetrators, Victims and Witnesses, A Report Submitted by Centre for Alternative Dalit Media (CADAM)," New Delhi (2013): 34, http://ncw.nic.

in/content/research-study-violence-against-dalit-women-different-states-india-studying-sources.

8. https://www.newframe.com/witches-witch-hunting-and-women.

9. Varghese Theckanath, "Is the Church Getting Lost in India's Smart Cities?" *La Croix*, New Delhi, December 10, 2018, https://www.ucanews.com/news/is-the-church-getting-lost-in-indias-smart-cities/84015.

10. Rohini Mohan, "Mumbai to Delhi, Why Farmers like Mathurabai Keep Marching," *Times of India*, December 2, 2018, 19. https://timesofindia.indiatimes.com/home/sunday-times/all-that-matters/mumbai-to-delhi-why-farmers-like-mathurabai-keep-marching/articleshow/66898970.cms.

11. Rina Chandra, "'Too Afraid to Sleep': India's Homeless Women Suffer as Cities Expand," https://mobile.reuters.com/article/amp/idUSKBN1KZ00S (August 13, 2018).

12. http://hlrn.org.in/womens-rights.

13. Dayamani Barla, "Democracy and Increasing Gap between the Rich and the Poor," *Forum for Justice and Peace News Letter*, no. 33 (January–April 2018): 17.

14. Gladson Dungdung, "Democracy and Land Rights," *Forum for Justice and Peace News Letter*, no. 33 (January–April 2018): 15.

15. Ibid., 16.

16. Malavika Prasad, Report on Conversation on Contemporary Struggles towards the Realization of Socio-economic Rights, Center for Legal Philosophy and Justice Education, NALSAR University of Law, Hyderabad (2017): 13.

17. Megha Kumar, *Communalism and Sexual Violence* (New Delhi: Tulika Books, 2017), 11.

18. Yadav and Chaudhary, "For Mumbai's Homeless People."

19. Amarjeet Singh, "Night Life in Delhi," DNA 8/12/2018, https://www.dnaindia.com/delhi/report-night-life-in-delhi-2693439.

20. Varghese Theckanath, "Is the Church Getting Lost in India's Smart Cities?"

The African Elders

Wilhelmina Uhai Tunu, LSOSF

Because our world is faced with emerging issues such as tribalism, escalating poverty, political instability, endless conflict, refugees, fraud, and corruption, we have a responsibility to deepen our collaboration in responding to these issues. Homelessness is another global issue that reminds us that our vocation is not just to pay attention to the effects of things. In Africa, we ought to be committed to developing a system of universal charity and solidarity with the needy, especially the African elders. Guided by Catholic Social Teaching and following the call of our master Jesus Christ who inspires us to follow in his footsteps, to build bridges of unity (Jn 17:21) rather than walls of separation, we need to develop great interest and initiative to work for the vulnerable in Africa, especially the elderly. Now more than ever, the elderly find themselves homeless, isolated, and deserted by their closest relatives. This disheartening and very un-African phenomenon of abandoning elders requires a serious ethical analysis and practical measures to mitigate its effects. Considering the growing need for the protection of the elderly, we are compelled to offer them love and the services necessary to uphold their dignity and health.

This essay presents the African elderly and their roles in traditional African societies as figures of wisdom and upholders of values that ensure the society's integrity. This essay also deals with their roles in contemporary African societies. Here, not only do I look at significant changes that have taken place in the face of globalization but also the contemporary social challenges related to the care of the elderly. I will show that the family networks that used to sustain the vulnerable elderly in traditional African settings are disintegrating, leading to the ethical problem of the abandonment of the elderly. They have the right to proper care, and this right imposes a duty on all people—young and old, men and women. Before venturing into the discussion on the elderly in traditional and contemporary African societies, it is vital to provide a working definition of the elderly from the African perspective.

Definition of "Elderly"

According to the World Health Organization (WHO), there are universally used definitions of old age, but there is no agreement on the age at which a person becomes old.[1] The cause of ageing is a biological truth beyond human control. Old age is also determined by how each society perceives it. Societies in the developed world focus on chronological time to determine the age of a person as young or old.[2] Old age for them therefore begins at "the age of 60 or 65 years, equivalent to retirement age."[3] For Africans, unlike Western people, old age is an experience of concrete change, growth, generation, and passing away of specific things.

African cultures have different connotations of what it means to be "elderly." The term "Mzee" in the Swahili culture refers to an elderly person. "Mzee" is applied within three connotations. First, any parent is an elder to her/his children. Respecting parents is thus mandatory for any child. Second, anybody beyond fifty years of age is an elder, since such persons are a treasury of wisdom and a gift of love for both the church and the world.[4] Third, higher status in the community, particularly when it comes to managerial roles and material wealth, makes one an elder even if she or he is young. Elders are revered not so much for what they do (although that is important) but for who they are. They are known to have different experiences, skills, and knowledge, and these qualities qualify them to be the wisdom reservoir and consequently to be respected by any junior members in the society.

Those who are young in age must prove that they are capable of being revered as elders. For example, among the Masaai people, an ethnic group in Northern Tanzania, a man has to kill a lion as a symbol of true manhood, bravery, power, and leadership.[5] In this situation, even a boy in his teen years can be considered an elder after fulfilling such requirements. Emmanuel Katongole calls this mentality "a culture that exalts warrior virtues and fears the show of affection, for affection is a sign of weakness."[6] African cultures view elders as role models and ancestors. They inculcate values connected to acceptable ways of behavior and conduct, to which members of the society are obliged to conform. In precolonial Africa, values such as respect, responsibility, hospitality, relationality, care, fidelity, solidarity, and social justice were held sacred, and, short of that, painful and shameful penalties were imposed on offenders.

The Elderly and Their Roles
in the Traditional African Society

In the traditional African society, when we speak of care for elders, we focus on the African sense of community where elders are in solidarity with the community and where every member of the community participates in caring for each other. Mutual solidarity here implies that members find support from each other for their individual commitment to the common good.[7] This solidarity depicts the image of the family established in communion. In this regard, elders play key roles in promoting the spirit of responsibility to the young generation for economic livelihood, primarily as farmers in agriculture and animal-rearing, including some significant supplementary activities such as hunting, blacksmithing, and the making of crafts for sale.

With regard to sociopolitical dimensions, elders are leaders and the bedrock for the community. They are the custodians of traditions, customs, and moral integrity. For instance, in regard to marriage, African marriages come into being as a result not of a single ceremony but of many ceremonies with an interfamily association in which elders from both families initiate the whole process, from proper betrothal of a couple, to the engagement, and finally to the marriage ritual itself. During engagement rituals, special elderly women from both families have the role of examining the bride's virginity. The chief patron of the marriage, who is always a man, acts as a go-between for the two families and passes on any needed information. The uncle to the groom acts as a patron and is escorted by a few men and women who give special blessings to the new couple.

Elders are portrayed as wise people who are upholders of justice as well as morality. In traditional African societies, there were no formal institutions of a public power such as courts and legislations. When disputes arose, they were private in nature and concerned relatives or people of the same kinsman. They were solved by an age-old mechanism, utilizing lineage counselors who convened a conclave. Some disputes were taken to relevant authorities such as the council of elders or village committee. Elders did not force them to appear. In earlier African societies, customary adjudication, mediation, conciliation, or coping with wrongdoing was done by shaming and invocation of supernatural forces against the deviant individual. It could also be by means of ordeals, contest, or retaliation, which resulted whenever disputes arose within a family, clan, or a group in a particular society.

In case of any tension and conflict in marriage among couples, elders acted as mediators and reconcilers in order to maintain the perpetuity and sanctity of marriage. The court of family elders, often from both families, ensured the presence of forgiveness, reconciliation, justice, and peace in the marriage. Furthermore, land disputes between two relatives claiming title over land through inheritance were settled by arbitrators in the district courts. They were of the view that since those in the land dispute were relatives, the dispute could be brought to an amicable arbitration by dividing the land equally between the parties. The rationale of these customary dispute settlement methods was to maintain unity, solidarity, and mutual relations within the family, the clan, or the entire society.[8]

Elders as Symbols of Wisdom

The Yoruba people of Nigeria have a wise saying: If you stay away from the elders because of bad breath, you will not learn wisdom. These wise words point to the irrefutable reality that the elders in African societies are rightly considered as wise, experienced, dignified, powerful symbols and upholders of values that ensure the society's integrity and peaceful coexistence. This is because wisdom is envisioned to come and increase progressively with age. It is said that as one advances in age, he or she encounters different practical experiences that will help guide young ones. Following this claim, we can underline that elders impart wisdom through folktales to younger generations. These stories have great significance in handing on knowledge, traditions, wisdom, and moral values, and are good for personal development because they influence the person's perception, attitude, and behavior, as well as the society.[9] Elders are thus custodians of time, and are a repository of traditional wisdom and values. Because of their tested experience they are a link between the old and the modern/contemporary time. They are the bridge between these times. As such, they are reference points. Without sharing their past experiences, we cannot have an identity nor can the future generation have a point of departure.[10] The elderly are like a springboard for the younger generation to grow in leadership, virtues, and uprightness.

In the religious dimension, African Traditional Religions are part of a heritage for the African people. African elders are not only sociopolitical leaders but also religious leaders. They play important roles in offering sacrifices to the Supreme Being, blessing the young, and invoking the assistance of ancestors, who are considered the living dead, whenever the need arises. For example, religious leaders are sought out in cases of poor health and misfortune in the village. Religious leaders uphold a shared belief and confidence in the Supreme Being/God, along with a firm commitment to increase good in the world, preserve it, and pass it to the next generation.[11] Emmy Gichinga points out that in the African life-enhancing cosmos, "elders belong to the group of people who are depositories of God's blessings and wisdom. They conduct rituals and cleansing ceremonies, and in so doing, play a significant religious role."[12] In this wisdom, African Traditional Religion still promotes the art of holiness. Family elders bless work implements for good fortune, and their role is to pray on behalf of family members. Most of these prayers are addressed to God, but others are addressed to the living-dead who act as mediators. John Mbiti confirms this as he rightly says: "The prayers are addressed to the spiritual realities of which African people are very much aware. These realities include God, who is the Supreme Being over all, various types of spirits, personification of natural phenomena and objects, some of which are regarded as manifestations of God."[13]

Blessing of the community is sought from elders whenever a serious undertaking involves risks. The community aspect is emphasized because the religious beliefs and morals of the people are practiced within the community of the living, and the departed members of the community (ancestors).[14] In this spirit of community, elders invoke blessings from ancestors, the living dead, other spirits, and finally from the Supreme Being (God) for a good weather, for rain, good luck during hunting, and other undertakings.[15]

In short, the African elder is thought of as a moving encyclopedia or point of reference. And since tradition is an agreed-upon way of doing ethics in the African worldview, the elders are supposed to keep the tradition, and they also have the moral mandate to hand it over to the next generation.

The Elderly in Contemporary African Society

Significant changes have taken place in the face of globalization, although to a great extent Africans are still immersed in the spirit of their religions as they move on with the world. There has been a great social transformation owing to various factors such as urbanization, advancement in communication technology, and globalization. As a result, people are no longer doing things as they did fifty years ago. However, Africans still maintain some values that give them their identity. For instance, the sense of community, which is visible in team spirit during work, prayers, and other rites and rituals; respect for life of the unborn, the living, and the dead; hospitality; "Ubuntu" brotherhood/sisterhood; and religion are some of the values that Africans still cherish. As role models, the elderly impart these elements to the younger generation.

Population

Globally, the number of elderly people is rapidly increasing. "Ageing is one of the most significant social transformations of the twenty-first century with implications for nearly all sectors of society."[16] According to the United Nations, "The number of older persons aged 60 years and above is expected to double by 2050 and triple by 2100, that is, rising from 962 million globally in 2017 to 2.1 billion in 2050 and 3.1 billion in 2100."[17] Following the United Nations predictions (2017), older persons aged sixty years or over in Africa are expected to account for 9 percent of the African population by 2050.[18]

The elderly in Africa contribute greatly and positively, especially in providing care for their grandchildren and promoting family survival and togetherness in this era of HIV/AIDS. Loving and caring grandparenting is an essential emotional and caregiving support. The elderly are mentors for experience and role models of faith and positive living. Pope Francis's words confirm old age as "a time of grace in which the Lord invites the elderly to persevere and communicate the faith."[19]

Contemporary Social Challenges Faced by the Elderly

In contemporary African societies, the elderly's presence is unnoticed in various institutions, programs, policies, and strategies, which do not include them in the decisions that directly affect them—in some instances, they are excluded completely. Consequently, those who had humble backgrounds lack pensions and universal health coverage just when they are beginning to experience the weakening physical condition of old age. They suffer from poor health due to hunger and malnutrition, lack of clean water, and an increased burden of care. Problems encountered by the elderly in Africa are thus manifold.

Today the traditions and values that used to safeguard the protection of this cumulative population in Africa are under pressure because of the vast social and economic changes. Social marginalization is one of the challenges that is gradually becoming a great threat to the well-being of the elderly. Many young people are not committed to serving older persons with courtesy and compassion. The value of respect for elders is swiftly dwindling in many African societies. The elderly are thus victims of crimes, as some of them are subjected to various forms of abuse, including psycho-physical violence, neglect, rape, and denial of access to basic necessities such as proper health care services, information, good shelter, food, water, and general support by the family and the community. Pope Francis condemns such abuses as he states, "It is inhuman to abuse elders just as it is inhuman to abuse children."[20]

Challenges from the Perspective of Old-Age Care Associations

With regard to family care relations in Africa, families are responsible for providing care and support to the elderly.[21] With the rapid social, cultural, and economic changes, long-term care for the elderly is in question because many young people opt for alternative paths after completing their education and acquiring formal employment. Employment opportunities open the way to multiple responsibilities. Providing care within the family as well as fulfilling career obligations becomes a great social challenge because numerous responsibilities lead to various burdens. Subsequently, conflicts arise between spouses who need to cooperate in caring for the elderly parents and children in the family. Generally, finding a balance between domestic tasks and professional work becomes a question to be analyzed, since people opt not to do the unpaid work that makes them dependent.[22] Family networks that sustained the vulnerable elderly in the traditional African settings are disintegrating. Many frail elderly are in desperation as they are abandoned in villages without proper care and financial support.[23]

Today, employment opportunities are important for the sustainability and development of the family and society. However, both men and women ought to remember that their participation and involvement in the social development of the community should not lead them to neglect care for the elderly. It is dreadful that once elderly people have retired and are no longer productive in socioeconomic development, many of them lack adequate care and are in isolation, as they have nobody to listen to and to share their feelings with. They have no way to participate in economic and social matters that affect them or to air their views in community gatherings.

Although they have contributed greatly to the social and economic welfare of the society, some of these elderly people remain economically poor. They experience socioeconomical and emotional neglect. For instance, with the impact of the HIV/AIDS pandemic, they carry the burden of caring for and supporting their orphaned grandchildren. Nevertheless, some poverty alleviation programs do not recognize their role as participants in social care. Like other human beings, the elderly deserve to be treated with respect. The famous German philosopher Immanuel Kant reminds us that each human person has a priceless dignity that must be respected. He insists that this dignity makes it ethically wrong for some people to abuse others. For Kant, human dignity is a categorical moral principle that says that human persons ought to be treated as ends and not merely as means in implementing one's deliberations. The dignity and contribution of the elderly, therefore, ought to be respected.[24]

Economic and social independence should not lead any individual to abandon their primary duty of caring for others. Everyone needs to bear in mind that caring for the elderly in African families is very crucial, thus cooperation among the family and community members is essential. As African people and thus as a global family, we need to respond to the ethical, social, political, and cultural challenges in today's world by posing questions such as: How can we balance our gender roles in Africa today? Does our cultural African heritage have something to offer to our care relations to elders? How should we blend our values in our modern societies? Indeed, something must be done to revive the traditional African cultures.

Christa Schnabl rightly observes that many modern societies suffer from lack of caregivers as a consequence of the gender equality movement. Caregiving work should not be viewed as belonging to the least well-off members of the society, nor to women, because it is an important part of a shared common social responsibility. We cannot presume that caregiving benefits only the receiver and the giver. Caregiving is a right that has an impact on all people—young and old, men and women. Laurenti Magesa agrees with Schnabl's sentiments on the rights of the people by stating, "Human rights are principally God-given privileges which are believed to be enjoyed by all human beings, and to be enjoyed by them equally, solely by virtue of their being without distinction of birth, race, class, faith, or any other physical or spiritual trait."[25] As a right, receiving and giving care is essential for shaping and framing the communal and economic sustainability of a people.

The Elderly and Homelessness

Homelessness, a state of people without a permanent dwelling, is a violation of basic human rights and a global crisis. It was never experienced in the traditional African communities, but it is becoming an issue in Africa in both rural and urban areas. However, those who are responsible for responding to it lack a comprehensive theoretical framework (due to a lack of research on ageing), and hence have not handled this issue properly. The elderly, in particular, experience homelessness in several African societies. Causes for homelessness differ in societies with regard to circumstances. Poverty, for instance, leads to homelessness as it disintegrates family relations.

In the midst of poverty, social relations are threatened, and caring for the elderly becomes an uphill struggle. Humans ought to have interpersonal relationships in order to enhance social well-being and good care among all, but poverty disrupts such interpersonal and family relationships. In this situation, family members tend to abandon the overly dependent elderly when they are unable to provide basic needs to sustain them. Consequently, the elderly are left alone, helpless and hungry, begging, unable to access sufficient shelter, food, and health care.

The popular traditional African belief was that all that a person did was guaranteed to affect the whole community, for better or for worse. John S. Mbiti confirms this when talking about the African wisdom of social relations, stating: "I am because we are and since we are, therefore I am."[26] Poverty is certainly a serious threat to interpersonal relationships, and it leads to isolation and homelessness.

African traditional heritage was very rich in promoting an environment conducive for human dwelling. The elderly maintained the identity of each particular clan by establishing a permanent home. Jomo Kenyatta, for instance, wrote about *Facing Mount Kenya* as a sign of identity for the Gikuyus of Kenya.[27] The elderly living within the Mount Kenya region, like those in other African communities, do not feel at home if their heritage or historical identity is disturbed. Taking them away from their original environment is violating their cultural and traditional rights. They may be fixed somewhere physically, such as in a developed urban center, but culturally they remain homeless. Homelessness is therefore a result of changes in social structures, like the setup of the family, and changes in its economic status; for example, when their profession becomes too demanding, some people today opt to stop caring for the elderly at home so that they can keep up with their workplace responsibilities.

In defining the physical sense of the Swahili term "Mzee" (elderly), I captured three aspects that qualify a person as elderly: if they are a parent; if they are beyond fifty years of age; and if they hold a special position or status in the community. In the African philosophy, people in these categories were respected. They were traditionally cared for by their children until the end of their lives. Even when children established their homes after marriage, they used to send their children to spend time with their grandparents. Today, Africans have been influenced by Western culture, especially in urban areas. Instead of caring for the elderly, they take them to nursing homes, where they feel homeless because of isolation. And some elderly opt to be taken to nursing homes. But both those who are left at home and those who go to nursing homes feel homeless, and it is almost like killing them psychologically because they develop low self-esteem knowing that their family and community no longer value them. Because of isolation, some of them develop health problems associated with dementia, which is not well understood in Africa, and they are thus mistakenly believed to be suffering from psychosis. Technological solutions to such problems are not available in many health facilities, and where they are available, some families are not economically positioned to handle the resulting medical expenses and other related demands; hence, the family may further neglect their elderly.

To mitigate homelessness, comprehensive awareness and understanding of ageing is essential. Every member in the society needs to know that old age, as a noncontributory phase of life, is not a weakness. And all people ought to be prepared for graceful ageing; policy formulators should include social security for all elderly persons and ensure that families take care of their elderly.

Deliberation on Care for the Elderly

In care relations, people give care and others receive it and vice versa. But, it is not a must that one has to give back the same help as received because people differ in their levels of ability to give or receive. This reciprocity entails that the elderly in Africa get a kind of family support including companionship and satis-faction of basic needs and safety needs.[28] Schnabl says that any help given is a care activity rather than family activity, and she defines care as interpersonal activity, acknowledging the complex vulnerability and dependency of human beings.[29] The care given has to be aimed at supporting the dependent elderly and ensuring her or his well-being.

In conclusion, the human and ethical aspects of care have various dimen-sions, including human bonding, responsibility, and support for others, such as the older members of the society. Care also deals with emotions such as compassion, sympathy, empathy, and approachability.[30] Although care is needed not only for the dependent elderly but for all members in the family, the entire community needs to be sensitive to the care needed by the elderly. It is also crucial to form solidarity groups among the elderly for self-sustainability, through various projects such as the ones offered by the governments, faith-based organizations, community-based orga-nizations, and nongovernmental organizations. These organizations support and encourage the elderly to have activities that not only promote care for their envi-ronment but also act as income-generating projects such as making energy-saving (*jikos*) cookers and tree nurseries. Therefore, it is imperative to appreciate the pres-ence and contribution of elderly persons who even in their seventies and eighties continue to act as figures of wisdom and champions of values that ensure the soci-ety's integrity and the development of both the church and society. Although there are significant cultural and socioeconomic changes and challenges in the face of globalization that affect all of us as a community, we acknowledge that the future of the contemporary generation lies in the present wisdom of its contemporary elderly members.

Notes

1. WHO, "Proposed Working Definition of an Older Person in Africa for the MDS Project." http://www.who.int/healthinfo/survey/ageingdefnolder/en.
2. M. Gorman, "Development and the Rights of Older People," in *The Ageing and Development Report: Poverty, Independence and the World's Older People*, ed. J. Randel et al. (London: Earthscan, 1999), 3–21.
3. WHO, http://www.who.int/healthinfo/survey/ageingdefnolder/en.
4. Keith A. Fournier, "Old Age Is a Time of Grace: Pope Francis Calls the World to Honour the Elderly," *Catholic Online*, October 3, 2014, https://www.catholic.org.
5. Joseph Healey and Donald Sybertz, *Toward an African Narrative Theology*, 4th reprint (Nairobi: Paulines Publications Africa, 2005), 77.
6. Emmanuel Katongole, *The Sacrifice of Africa: A Political Theology for Africa* (Grand Rapids, MI: William B. Eerdmans, 2011), 127.
7. John Tenamwenye, *Solidarity and Its Evangelical Challenge for the Local Churches in Africa Today: A Theological Reflection from the Tanzanian Perspective* (Nairobi: Don Bosco, 2009), 22.
8. G. S. Berman, "Facilitated Negotiation: An Effective ADR Technique," *Dispute Resolution Journal* 30 (April 1995): 18–22.

9. Pauline Das and Mohan L. Raj, "Irula Folk Tales," *The Criterion: An International Journal in English* 5, no. 5 (October 2014), http://www.the-criterion.com/V5/n5/Das.pdf.

10. Laurenti Magesa, *What Is Not Sacred: African Spirituality* (Maryknoll, NY: Orbis Books, 2014).

11. Tanganyika African National Union, *The Arusha Declaration and TANU's Policy on Socialism and Self-Reliance* (Dodoma, 1967), 1.

12. Emmy M. Gichinga, *Counseling in the African Context: A Counseling Guide* (Nairobi: GEM Counseling Services, 2007), 28.

13. John S. Mbiti, *The Prayers of African Religion* (Maryknoll, NY: Orbis Books, 1978), 4.

14. Bénézet Bujo, *The Ethical Dimension of Community, The African Model and the Dialogue between North and South* (Nairobi: Paulines Publications Africa, 1998), 29.

15. Ibid.

16. United Nations, "Ageing," www.un.org/en/sections/issues-depth/ageing/.

17. Ibid. Data from "World Population Prospects: The 2017 Revision."

18. United Nations, "World Population Prospects: The 2017 Revision," www.on.org/en/development/desa/population/publications/pdf/ageing/WPA2017.

19. Little Sisters of the Poor, "Pope Francis Celebrates with the Elderly," September 28, 2018, http://www.littlesistersofthepoor.org.au.

20. Fournier, "Old Age Is a Time of Grace: Pope Francis."

21. http://www.nia.nih.gov/sites/default/files/2017-06/AginginSub-SaharanAfrica.pdf, 9.

22. Christa Schnabl, "Vulnerability, Reciprocity, and Familial-Care Relations: A Socioethical Contribution," in *Catholic Theological Ethics Past, Present, and Future: The Trento Conference*, ed. James F. Keenan (Maryknoll, NY: Orbis Books, 2011), 225.

23. Lilian Muendo, "As Young Kenyans Leave Villages, Sisters Care for Neglected Elderly Left Behind," *Global Sisters Report*, May 31, 2018, http://globalsistersreport.org/news/ministry/young-kenyans-leave-villages-sisters-care-neglected-elderly-left-behind-54076.

24. Michael J. Sandel, *Justice: What's the Right Thing to Do?* (New York: Farrar, Straus and Giroux, 2010), 105.

25. Laurenti Magesa, *Christian Ethics in Africa* (Nairobi: Acton, 2002), 67.

26. John S. Mbiti, *Concepts of God in Africa* (London: SCK, 1970), 108.

27. Jomo Kenyatta, *Facing Mount Kenya: The Tribal Life of the Gikuyu* (London: Secker and Warburg, 1956).

28. Maria G. Cattell, "Caring for the Elderly in Sub-Saharan Africa," *Ageing International* 20, no. 2 (June 1993): 13–19, https://link.springer.com/article/10.1007%2FBF03032491.

29. Schnabl, "Vulnerability, Reciprocity, and Familial-Care Relations," 227.

30. Ibid.

HOMELESSNESS AMONG MILITARY VETERANS

The United States as a Recent Case Study in Political Will and Evidence-based Policymaking

Dennis P. Culhane and Ann Elizabeth Montgomery

Homelessness has been a steady feature of human history. People unsettled or rendered stateless by migrations, famines, and disasters have had to endure survival on the margins of lands they have had to traverse. Yet even accepted members in a society, including those who have had some status, can find themselves displaced or rootless due to a variety of historical circumstances. Chief among these is war, which can render both civilians and soldiers destitute, and often in flight for their survival. In peacetime, as war or military campaigns subside, former soldiers may be without work, family, and community ties. Throughout history, former fighters left stateless, or without a meaningful social role in peacetime, have had to wander and beg for their survival, sometimes stressing local capacity for acceptance. In ancient times, Roman soldiers were a frequent street presence between conflicts, and a source of social tensions (which is no less true in our own time).[1] Former service members, physically but often also emotionally scarred by their military experience, may face particularly daunting challenges on returning to their communities. Some may bear those scars many years after their service has ended. Today, "veteran homelessness" is a problem of global importance.

In this chapter, we consider the problem of veteran homelessness and the need for societal responses, with a particular focus on the United States. Although veteran homelessness afflicts populations worldwide, the problem in the United States has garnered the attention of policymakers, offering a contemporary example of how political will—and the resources that follow—can have a significant mitigating effect on the problem. Access to considerable public resources has enabled the US government to initiate a set of interventions on a scale never before attempted around the issue of homelessness in the United States and, perhaps, in the world. Examining the case of the United States provides an opportunity to reflect on how public sympathies combined with research-informed approaches can promote compassion, respect, and social inclusion for the poorest among us.

Some Social and Historical Context

Homelessness among current and former soldiers has had a long and well-documented history.[2] Ancient historical references discuss the problem of unemployed, destitute soldiers following military campaigns, and their impact on city life and public spaces.[3] Medieval literature includes numerous references to "vagabond" veterans. Their precarious circumstances stood as symbols for insecurities about local social problems and poverty, as well as sources of inspiration for charitable efforts that could instill national pride.[4] That some soldiers remained armed and had some skill with weaponry could cast a menacing shadow on their predicament as well. These historical references share a common attempt to frame the existence of homelessness among soldiers as a public problem demanding some special attention, even if those framings varied in characterizing the issue as a public threat, nuisance, or call to action.

Contemporary accounts of homeless soldiers and veterans likewise carry a variety of meanings, reflecting both a real heterogeneity in conditions and circumstances, as well as the uses to which the problem can be put in varying sociopolitical contexts. The range of conditions facing homeless soldiers is remarkably broad. Boy soldiers in central Africa, left destitute after subsiding conflicts, have become an international cause because their recruitment into these conflicts as children is so troubling, and because the horrors they witness or inflict leave them with lifelong scars. Adult soldiers throughout the world similarly bear the wounds, visible and invisible, of war-related trauma, made worse by their lack of access to work or income on return to society, and their challenges in reintegrating with families and communities.

Continuing conflicts in the Middle East that have included native fighters from the region, as well as international forces from Europe, Australia, and North America, have created a new generation of military veterans with the wounds of war, and their aftermath: disability and joblessness. The global scale of veteran homelessness is daunting, as virtually every corner of the world has produced survivors of war whose traumatic experiences and dislocation from home and community have rendered so many excluded from society.

Veteran Homelessness in the United States

In many poor and developing nations, former soldiers are but one portion of a large population of needy families and individuals; thus, special assistance for reintegration of soldiers after war can be absent. In more developed nations, the cause of veteran homelessness can be used as a political mobilizing force, joining former war supporters and detractors in a common call for national service and reconciliation. The cause of veteran homelessness has been raised by political leaders in the United Kingdom, Canada, and most especially in the United States. In 2009, newly elected United States President Barack Obama set the goal of ending veteran homelessness as a national priority.

The problem of veteran homelessness in the United States is long-standing, dating back to the Revolutionary War.[5] Virtually every war and conflict has left wounded, disabled, and poor veterans in its wake. In the early history of the United States, the armed services often provided a social safety net for disabled soldiers who could not care for themselves, including dormitories and other lodging on military bases. The first formal federal commitment in the United States emerged from the Civil War in 1865.[6] Along with the establishment of veterans' pensions, Soldiers' Homes were established to provide communal living in dormitories on campuses designed as welcoming "asylums," but for Union soldiers only. In 1930, after World War I and given the large number of former soldiers in need of support and rehabilitation, the modern-day United States Department of Veterans Affairs (VA) was established, with its mission of serving the health, income, and social needs of veterans. The agency absorbed the functions of the Soldiers' Homes, which were effectively the backstop against homelessness at the time. Since then, the VA's responses to homelessness among veterans have continued to evolve along with the scientific evidence for treatment and rehabilitation services. With its own scientific research programs, VA is often considered a leader in health care, especially for vulnerable populations. As homelessness emerged anew in the United States in the 1980s, with many veterans among their ranks, both the VA and a variety of private "Veteran Services Organizations" arose to meet the challenge of addressing their needs.

When homelessness initially reemerged as a social problem in the 1980s, Vietnam-era veterans were thought to constitute the greatest proportion. However, as research would later bear out, contemporary homelessness among veterans paralleled the growth of homelessness among their nonveteran peers, and was drawn primarily from the generation immediately after the Vietnam era. However, when the Gulf War in the early 1990s and the later conflicts in Iraq and Afghanistan unfolded after 9/11, a new generation of former combatants began to join the ranks of the adult homeless population. Risk for homelessness among veterans is particularly high for women, those who identify as a racial minority, as well as those with behavioral health challenges, including posttraumatic stress disorder and substance use disorders.[7] People who were relatively low-paid enlistees into the military and who did not progress in the military pay-grade system, as well as people who were discharged for misconduct, are also at significantly greater risk. Additional risk factors for *unsheltered* homelessness among veterans include being male, older age, and lack of receipt of compensation through the VA.

When President Obama declared the goal of ending veteran homelessness, more than 73,000 veterans were estimated to be homeless, with about 40 percent living on the streets, in unsheltered situations, or in other places not intended for human habitation. Since then, there has been a 50 percent decrease in the number of veterans experiencing homelessness, due largely to the comprehensive response carried out by the VA.[8]

Contemporary Response to
Homelessness among US Veterans

Before the Obama Administration's commitment to end veteran homelessness, federal spending by the VA stood at about $300 million annually, most of which supported special programs in health services and transitional housing. By the time the Obama Administration left office, the annual investment had grown to $1.6 billion, funding a broad array of programs and services, from homelessness prevention to permanent housing, for more than 200,000 veterans annually. A powerful combination of forces made this possible, including the political will from the president and cabinet, the bipartisan commitment of the US Congress to fund the initiatives, and public support for the moral imperative that no veteran should be left behind. Eventually, the implementation effort that followed included multiple federal agencies, tens of thousands of federally funded employees, a national effort to engage local communities in identifying and serving veterans, and a research-based framework to support the design of a comprehensive range of evidence-based programs.

The VA's strategy to end veteran homelessness encompasses a continuum of responses: outreach and drop-in services, emergency and transitional housing, homelessness prevention and rapid rehousing, and permanent supportive housing for veterans with the greatest needs. The VA provides income support as well as services to assist veterans in obtaining employment or reentering the workforce. Veterans who have been involved in the criminal justice system are also the subject of programs to avert homelessness, including in-reach to jails and prisons to assist in the transition to the community and a separate "veterans court" program. In addition to these homelessness-specific services, the VA also offers health care services—including those to address behavioral health concerns—and benefits to assist veterans with long-term goals such as increasing their education or purchasing a home.

Since 2009, three key initiatives have been instrumental in addressing housing instability among veterans and reducing the number of veterans experiencing literal homelessness (i.e., living in emergency or transitional housing or on the streets). The first is the VA's universal screen for housing instability: all veterans who present at a VA hospital for health care services are asked whether they have concerns about their housing situation. By asking veterans two simple questions about their housing situation, the VA is able to assess the housing needs of all veterans receiving health care services and link them with housing resources, if needed. In addition, data collected as part of this initiative has allowed the VA to learn more about veterans who use the health care system, their needs related to housing, and the best way to link them with needed resources. Data from the screen for housing instability among veterans has also found that more than 10 percent of veterans who report concerns about their housing situations during health care visits at the VA are living on the streets or other places not meant for human habitation, and they are almost three times as likely to continue to experience homelessness compared with those living in sheltered situations. Veterans living in unsheltered places are particularly vulnerable given their older age, lack of income, and frequent use of acute care.[9]

The second key initiative is the Supportive Services for Veteran Families (SSVF) program, which provides temporary financial assistance and supportive services to prevent homelessness among precariously housed veterans or to assist veterans who have recently become homeless to rapidly return to permanent housing. This program is unique in that the services are funded by the VA but provided by community-based organizations throughout the country, making these services more accessible to veterans in the communities where they live and responsive to their individual needs. SSVF provides flexible services that may effectively respond to the needs of veterans who may be reintegrating in their community following military service, fleeing intimate partner violence, or caring for dependent children or other family members. Since it began serving veterans in 2014, SSVF has assisted an increasing proportion of veterans to transition from unsheltered living situations to permanent housing; during 2016, almost one-half of veterans receiving rapid rehousing assistance by SSVF reported living on the streets or other unsheltered situations when they entered the program.[10] In addition, SSVF can provide assistance to veterans who may have needs not directly related to their housing but that have an impact on their housing stability, such as funds to purchase a work uniform to ensure the veteran is employed.

The third key initiative, permanent supportive housing, is intended to end homelessness among veterans who have experienced long-term or frequent episodes of homelessness and have some disabling condition that makes it difficult for them to maintain housing stability. The US Department of Housing and Urban Development (HUD) and the VA have joined forces to operate the HUD-VA Supportive Housing (HUD-VASH) program, which provides veterans with a rental subsidy to ensure that housing is affordable and supportive services to ensure that it is permanent. In addition, HUD-VASH services are strategically allocated to areas of the country where veteran homelessness is most concentrated, responding to the needs of particular communities. The vast majority of unstably housed veterans who use HUD-VASH remain stably housed for at least one year and may leave the program to move into their own independent housing. The HUD-VASH program is also taking steps to address the low vacancy rates and lack of affordable housing in the United States' most expensive cities by funding entire buildings to house veterans.

Although the VA's comprehensive strategy to address housing instability among veterans has resulted in a significant reduction in the prevalence of homelessness among veterans, particular challenges remain. For example, US veterans are more likely than nonveterans to be living in rural areas, which means they may have less access to the services to address homelessness and other needs, which are often concentrated in urban areas. The population of women veterans is rapidly growing as more women join military service; their exposure to trauma in the context of military service as well as prior to and following service may increase their risk of housing instability. In addition, women veterans tend to be homeless with children and are more likely to be doubling up with friends and family than accessing traditional homeless services, making it difficult to identify them as homeless and to develop holistic responses for their varied needs (e.g., to address housing, trauma, childcare, etc.). In addition, the veteran population generally—as well as veterans experiencing housing instability—is aging, which calls for specific responses to address this particularly vulnerable population (e.g., aging in place, assisted living).

Conclusion

Although veteran homelessness has been present in society for centuries, the example of the United States' response to veteran homelessness indicates that there are solutions to this problem. With focused political will and a variety of deeply funded responses to the needs of the population, veteran homelessness can be addressed, even among those with the greatest needs or those living in the most undesirable conditions. The United States Veterans Administration has developed responses to identify veterans who may be at risk of homelessness, prevent homelessness, or rapidly rehouse veterans who become homeless, and to support veterans in obtaining and maintaining permanent housing. The success of this strategy is apparent in the significant decline in veteran homelessness in the United States over the past decade. However, as more individuals enter military service and ultimately become veterans, the challenge to address their needs and prevent and end experiences of homelessness continues.

Other countries and nongovernmental organizations could learn from the United States' approach, including the research that has helped develop an evidence base of effective programs. However, given the unique circumstances across countries with respect to housing, health, and social policies—and particularly with regard to the differing capacity for social welfare provision—the translation of the United States experience will necessarily be limited. Likewise, garnering the political will for such an effort cannot be expected to translate in every country's social context, especially where rival forces and defeated soldiers may complicate public sympathies for political action. National efforts at reconciliation among previous enemy forces and rival political camps could be accompanied by an outreach effort to support former combatants in their struggles to reintegrate with their communities, and to avoid homelessness and destitution. Nongovernmental organizations, advocacy groups, and social scientists could join forces to support and enable such efforts through program planning, capacity building, and the testing and evaluation of interventions. Hopefully, the United States experience can provide some guidance.

Notes

1. Lukas de Blois, "Army and General in the Late Roman Republic," in *A Companion to the Roman Army*, ed. P. Erdkamp (Oxford: John Wiley and Sons, 2013), 164–79.

2. Linda Woodbridge, "The Neglected Soldier as Vagrant, Revenger, Tyrant Slayer in Early Modern England," in *Cast Out: Vagrancy and Homelessness in Global and Historical Perspective*, ed. A. L. Beier and P. Ocobock (Athens: Ohio University Press, 2008), 64–87.

3. De Blois, "Army and General."

4. Woodbridge, "Neglected Soldier."

5. Kenneth Kusmer, *Down and Out, on the Road: The Homeless in American History* (Oxford: Oxford University Press, 2002).

6. J. R. Ploppert and P. Smits, *The History and Origins of VA's Domiciliary Care Program from the National Home for Disabled Volunteer Soldiers to Mental Health Residential Rehabilitation and Treatment Programs, 1865–2013* (Washington, DC: US Department of Veterans Affairs, 2014).

7. S. Metraux, L. X. Clegg, J. D. Daigh, D. P. Culhane, and V. Kaine, "Risk Factors for Becoming Homeless among a Cohort of Veterans Who Served in the Era of the Iraq and Afghanistan Conflicts," *American Journal of Public Health* 103 (2013): S255–S261.

8. US Department of Housing and Urban Development, "The 2018 Annual Homeless Assessment Report to Congress (AHAR): Point-in-Time Estimates of Homelessness" (Washington, DC: HUD, 2018), https://www.hudexchange.info/resources/documents/2018-AHAR.pdf.

9. T. H. Byrne, A. E. Montgomery, and J. D. Fargo, "Unsheltered Homelessness among Veterans: Correlates and Profiles," *Community Mental Health Journal* 52 (2015): 148–57; A. E. Montgomery, T. H. Byrne, D. Treglia, and D. P. Culhane, "Characteristics and Likelihood of Ongoing Homelessness among Unsheltered Veterans," *Journal of Health Care for the Poor and Underserved* 27 (2016): 911–22.

10. US Department of Veterans Affairs, "Supportive Services for Veteran Families (SSVF) FY 2016 Annual Report" (Washington, DC: Veteran Affairs, 2017), https://www.va.gov/HOMELESS/ssvf/docs/SSVF_FY2016_Annual_Report_508c.pdf.

THE POOR WORKERS IN AN AFFLUENT CITY

Homelessness in Hong Kong

Mary Mee-Yin Yuen

Hong Kong is famous for its skyscrapers, its multicolored, nighttime harbor view scenery, and its free economy. People know it as a developed city, financial center, and shopping paradise. The GDP per capita was US$46,000 in 2017.[1] Foreign Exchange Reserves in Hong Kong reached an all-time high of US$44.34 billion in February 2018.[2] However, this glamorous aspect reflects only one side of the picture. There are 1.4 million poor people in this wealthy city, with a poverty rate of 20.1 percent. Hong Kong indeed has ranked number one for having the biggest wealth gap among all the advanced economies in the world for many years. Its Gini coefficient has shown the enormous gap between the rich and the poor.[3] This is contrary to the Catholic Social Teaching that informs us that "excessive economic and social differences between the members of the one human family or population groups cause scandal, and militate against social justice, equity, the dignity of the human person, as well as social and international peace."[4]

These statistics are not just numbers—they depict the ridiculous inequality in an apparently affluent city. The phenomenon of increasing numbers of low-income workers who are forced to live in indecent conditions or even become homeless reflects the urgency of the city's housing problem. One example is the story of Keung Gor, fifty years old, who lives in a certain corner of the city.

Keung Gor is a cleaning worker with unstable working days, earning only about HK$3,000 (US$400) per month. He used to rent a bed in the Sham Shui Po District, an old district of Hong Kong. The 1,000-square-foot (93 square meters) flat is divided into thirty bed-units. Most of the units have no windows, and bad ventilation. Even worse, bed bugs appeared on Keung Gor's bed every night, biting his hands, feet, nose, and mouth. Disturbed by this, he could sleep for only two hours every night, which seriously affected his work. He asked the owner of the flat to fix the problem but was ignored. In the face of such a bad situation, Keung Gor prefers to sleep on the street. "At least I would not be bitten and woken up. If there is a proper place to live, who wants to sleep on the street?"[5]

Keung Gor's case is not unique in Hong Kong or even in other developed wealthy cities. Some social workers who follow the cases of homeless persons in Hong Kong point out that many homeless people have similar experiences— renting a subdivided unit with high rent, only to find that the unit is extremely small and has hygiene problems. They end up having no choice but to sleep on the streets.

Keung Gor's situation reminds me of the story of Lazarus in the gospel (Lk 16:19–31). Lazarus appeared as an individual with his own story but was invisible to the rich man. Pope Francis has often said that underprivileged people should be described not only by statistics but through very human stories. In the Lenten Message for 2017, he said, "Lazarus teaches us that the other persons are a gift. A right relationship with people consists in gratefully recognizing their value. Even the poor person at the door of the rich is not a nuisance, but a summons to conversion and to change."[6] Keung Gor and other homeless people indeed are human beings whom God loves and cares for, despite their concrete condition as outcasts.

In this essay, I discuss the situation of the homeless who are low-income workers or unemployed in the affluent city of Hong Kong, using both real-life stories and statistics. I examine the reasons for this phenomenon and discuss what we can do in response to this situation.

General Situation of the Homeless

The number of street sleepers in Hong Kong has continued to rise. Official figures from the Social Welfare Department show that the number has increased from 555 in 2013 to 1,127 in May 2018.[7] However, social workers and critics claim that the government's estimation does not reflect a full picture of the problem, as some homeless individuals are invisible because they are reluctant to register as homeless. In a study called the *Homeless Outreach Population Estimation Hong Kong* (HOPE), conducted by a number of local universities and nongovernmental organizations (NGOs) in Hong Kong in 2015, it was found that there were 1,614 homeless people—almost double the government's estimate for that year.[8]

Of these 1,614 homeless, 92.5 percent were male and 7.5 percent were female. The average age was 55, ranging from 20 to 80, with almost 60 percent of interviewees belonging to the age group of 45–64. As for the duration of their homelessness, more than half are long-term street sleepers, that is, five years and above; short-term street sleepers (less than six months) make up only 13.5 percent. Middle-term street sleepers (six months to five years) account for almost 30 percent.[9] According to this study, 780 or nearly half (48.3 percent) are street sleepers living in public spaces such as streets, parks, or bridges. Another 256 people, about one-sixth (15.9 percent) of the homeless take rest or sleep in twenty-four-hour fast-food restaurants. And 578 homeless people, about one-third (35.8 percent), live in temporary shelters or singleton hostels for street sleepers.

Although the government said that it would do its utmost to assist the homeless, many street sleepers felt otherwise. They said that the government sent workers to drive them away from footbridges, and to sprinkle water and disinfectant powder in the parks and playgrounds frequented by homeless people. Sharp stones are spread underneath bridges, or these spaces are surrounded by fences. Some street sleepers think that the government is taking away the last space left for them to stay at night.

In Hong Kong, there are sixteen shelters and hostels, managed by NGOs, which currently provide about 640 beds. Three shelters that are free of charge are wholly funded by Street Sleepers' Shelter Society Trustees Incorporated. Thirteen hostels receive subsidies from the government, and they charge fees less than HK$2,000 (US$250). Street sleepers need a referral letter from a social worker to qualify for a bed in a shelter or hostel, and it can take between two days and six months to get a bed. Usually, people can stay no more than six months at a time. The beds are pest-free, and hot water is available but no air conditioning. Depending on the curfew set by the shelter, people may be locked out after 11 p.m. With this restriction and the limited length of stay, many people are forced to sleep outdoors or in fast-food restaurants.[10]

For example, Ka-hei, a casual worker, had previously stayed in a government-subsidized hostel but was forced to leave after six months. Some social workers observe that some self-funded hostels allow street sleepers to stay for only one to three months at a time due to a lack of space. If the same homeless person wants to return for another stay, it takes at least another year, and he or she must present a referral from social workers.

Phenomenon of McRefugees or McSleepers

Since 2000, the fast-food chain restaurant McDonald's has started to operate twenty-four hours a day in various regions of the world. This policy has attracted homeless people to stay in McDonald's in Japan, China, and Hong Kong. The twenty-four-hour McDonald's has become "the home of the homeless." Sleepers in McDonald's are called by the mass media "McRefugees" or "McSleepers." In contrast to the street, McRefugees said that fast-food restaurants are safer, cleaner, and have no harassment. In McDonald's, they do not need to be afraid of law enforcement officers who forcibly clear the property of or even take away the identity documents of the street sleepers in a harsh and rude manner.

In just five years, there has been a sixfold increase in Hong Kong's so-called McRefugees. According to a study conducted by the nonprofit young adults group Junior Chamber International (JCI) Tai Ping Shan chapter in June and July 2018, 334 people said they had slept in various McDonald's restaurants in the past three months. Of the 110 branches in Hong Kong that operate twenty-four hours, 84 had seen overnight sleepers. This is a significant increase since a similar study in 2013, which found only 57 sleepers. A branch in Tsuen Wan district hosted more than 30 sleepers, the highest among all the branches. Most of them lie on the chairs or the tables to rest or to sleep.[11]

One main reason for people to choose McDonald's is that many sleepers face socioeconomic challenges such as high rents or electricity bills. They cannot afford air conditioning during summer, and there are no windows for airflow in their subdivided units. Thus, they choose to enjoy the air-conditioned McDonald's on hot and humid summer nights. The free wi-fi, cheaper food, and bathroom facilities are other attractive reasons.

Researchers of the above study found that not all of the overnight sleepers were really homeless. More than 70 percent of respondents said they had other places to sleep, such as public housing flats or subdivided units, and the majority had either full-time or part-time jobs during the day. However, they prefer to sleep at McDonald's to avoid conflict with families, to build social relationships with others, to be closer to work, or to seek temporary shelter while waiting for a cheap public rental flat.[12]

The phenomenon of the McSleepers is probably made possible by the tolerant attitude of the chain restaurant. The workers of the chain store seem to be considerate and have not driven the sleepers away. In a statement to CNN, McDonald's Hong Kong said that the company is accommodating to those who stay at the restaurant for extended periods regardless of their reasons for doing so, while still committed to providing a pleasant dining environment.[13] It claims that it welcomes people of all walks of life to visit the restaurants and would not disturb them, but provides attentive service.[14]

Homeless Women

Among the McSleepers is a forty-eight-year-old woman named Monita. She left a shelter operated by a charity group after her three-month stay expired. She said that "there were bullies, thefts, and sexual harassment among the twenty female members"; thus, she did not want to stay there anymore. She tried to complain, but the male staff ignored her. As a welfare recipient, she can only afford to rent a subdivided flat for HK$1,500 (about US$190) a month. She uses the space only to store personal belongings as "there are too many cockroaches and bed bugs."[15]

The issue of street sleepers and homelessness has been closely linked to the issue of economic employment. Because of the structural transformation of the Hong Kong economy, it is more difficult for women to find jobs, especially middle-aged women. Changes in economic and family structure have increased the number of single women, many of whom need to work. Besides economic factors, other reasons for female homelessness are related to family relationships and domestic violence. However, there are few beds or temporary shelters for female street sleepers; support for women is inadequate. Very often, homeless women have to face more dangerous situations as they are more vulnerable to sexual assault and violence.

Challenges of Street Sleepers

The Catholic Church teaches that a proper shelter, in addition to clothing, food, education, employment, and so on, is one of the conditions for leading a truly human life.[16] Without a home, whether they are living on the street or in a shelter or fast-food restaurant, people are deprived of the proper and safe living conditions that would protect their physical health and safety, and they lack social and economic relationships. These threats become more serious with longer durations of homelessness. Homeless people are deprived of their human rights, including autonomy of life and property, the protection of personal privacy, freedom from discrimination and intimidation, and the right to social and political participation. They are marginalized by their society.

According to the International Covenant on Economic, Social, and Cultural Rights (ICESCR), article 11, "Everyone has the right to an adequate standard of living for himself and his family, including adequate food, clothing and housing, and to the continuous improvement of living conditions."[17] ICESCR is applicable to Hong Kong and is stated in article 39 of the Basic Law, the mini-constitution of Hong Kong. Thus, the government of Hong Kong has the responsibility to take appropriate steps to ensure the realization of this right.

At present, the government subsidizes three social service teams that provide services to the homeless. These services include counseling, outreach, personal care, employment counseling, housing referral, and so on, but are far from adequate. Thus, homeless people are often forced to stay on the street. According to the report of HOPE mentioned above, when asked about the reasons for failing to leave homeless life, the main reasons given by the homeless are that private housing rents are expensive (50 percent); work is unstable or they are unemployed (30 percent); income is too low (15 percent); public housing waiting time is too long (20 percent); the conditions of private housing and dormitory environments are poor (10 percent); and so on.[18]

Root Causes of Homelessness

From the various studies shown above, we can see that economic reasons make more people become street sleepers. Professor Wong Hung, a scholar who has studied the poverty problem of Hong Kong for many years, said Hong Kong faces a homelessness epidemic produced by its surging property prices and huge wealth gap. Rising rent and low income are thus among the root causes of homelessness.[19]

Hong Kong is consistently ranked the world's least affordable property market. According to Demographia, an urban planning policy consultancy, since the end of the real estate recession in 2014, prices of houses have risen by nearly 400 percent.[20] The rich have used real estate to gain profits while the poor suffered from ever-increasing rents. Governmental measures to freeze rents have failed to ease Hong Kong's housing crisis. Hong Kong's home prices have been driven higher by rules restricting land use and by land and rent policies. These policies lead to a continuous rise in housing prices and rents, without control or intervention from the government. A few large companies have accumulated huge land reserves and investment property portfolios that enable them to extend their financial power over a wide spectrum of business, ranging from transport, public utilities, supermarkets, and, most importantly, land development. The developer cartel-hegemony increases social and economic unfairness.[21]

Moreover, under the existing political system, the Hong Kong government and real estate development and construction companies are mutually beneficial. The Hong Kong government, which technically owns land, gives long-term lease rights to developers; in turn, Hong Kong's political leaders are elected by 1,200 elites, including property developers and business tycoons. This vicious circle is at the root of the enormous gap between the rich and the poor. Political scientist Barry Sautman argues persuasively that most prominent tycoons strongly oppose expanding democracy and want to maintain the business-centered, small-circle election for Legislative Council functional constituencies and Chief Executive of the government in order to protect their interests.[22]

Furthermore, there is a lack of affordable public housing for the low-income classes. The 2017 Long Term Housing Strategy Progress Report notes that 280,000 public housing units will be built in the next decade. However, the estimated completions in the next five years are much lower than expected. The planning and creation of Hong Kong's New Towns, which were intended to be self-sufficient communities, also create problems for low-income workers. Many residents who have to commute downtown for work find the cost and travel time too high. Thus, some may prefer to sleep in fast-food restaurants to save on transportation costs.

With inadequate public housing and the lack of regulation of private housing, the phenomenon of expensive rent for extremely small living units arises. The market mechanism has failed. People cannot enjoy decent and appropriate residences. In order to protect the right to housing, it is necessary for the government to intervene in the private market, trying to keep a balance between the right to accumulate assets and the right to housing. Rent control and increases in the public housing supply are important means for solving the housing problem.

Apart from rising rents, low income is another root cause of the housing problem. Since 2012, the unemployment rate in Hong Kong has been at a low level of 3.3 percent. However, the high employment rate does not mean that the level of wages for grassroots workers has increased. Low income among workers creates a large number of poor working families. According to the government-published 2017 poverty report, among the 7.8 million population, there are 1.38 million people living below the poverty line. Even after the government's intervention through cash assistance, there are still 1.01 million people living in poverty. It is particularly worth noting that one out of every four children is from a poor family.[23] Poor workers earning little can afford only subdivided units, entailing fire risks, poor ventilation, and poor hygiene. They are not proper homes.

That people live in poverty does not mean that they are lazy or refuse to work. On the contrary, they often have to work very long hours. Wong Hung argues that the culprit of the problem of working poverty is the government's outsourcing system, leaving many workers unable to earn a living wage. The government took the lead in outsourcing work to replace the work of civil servants, in the name of improving efficiency, but this resulted in increased poverty among the workers. The government's major departments have employed more than 37,000 nontechnical staff. Among them, about 30 percent receive an hourly salary of only HK$34.5 (about US$4), which is only the legal minimum wage. Another 47 percent of employees receive only a little bit more than the minimum wage.[24] Such low wages make life very difficult. As pointed out by Hong Kong scholar Nelson Chow, if the government continues to refuse to raise the minimum wage level and examine the relationship between the outsourcing services system and working poverty, the increasingly serious problem of working poverty will never be solved.[25]

Pastoral Responses

The preferential option for the poor is a special priority in the exercise of Christian charity, to which the whole tradition of the church bears witness. Pope John Paul II insisted that it is impossible not to take account of the existence of the realities of the poor, the homeless, and the needy. He highlighted that our daily lives, as well as our decisions in the political and economic fields, must respond to these realities.[26]

Some Christian and non-Christian groups distribute food and daily necessities to the homeless from time to time in order to soothe their immediate difficulties. Apart from the existing shelters, the Sant'Egidio Community in Hong Kong opened the Home of Mercy on November 18, the World Day of the Poor, in 2018. Fr. John Wotherspoon and his team also visit the homeless and have meals with them regularly. They set up a halfway house, the Mercy Centre, in Cheung Chau Island in 2017 for men who face difficulties in reestablishing themselves in society after being released from prison. Some subdivided flats in the downtown area were also rented to help women and families with housing problems.

To lead a life of dignity, many homeless or street sleepers want to earn a reasonable income by their own efforts so that they can rent a proper and decent place to live. Thus, as some NGOs suggested, on the one hand, the government should set up transitional housing with basic medical and rehabilitation services, allowing them to stay at least three years. This would help improve a dire situation. On the other hand, a living wage, more public housing, control of rent and property prices, and improving community infrastructure in the New Towns should be prioritized.

The needs of the poor and the homeless are often not recognized because many people, especially those in power, fail to empathize with the poor and homeless. The culture of mercy that Pope Francis has tried hard to promote is very much needed in Hong Kong, particularly in the business sector. Business ethics and corporate social responsibilities should be strongly advocated. If the owners of flats and land developers do not charge as much as they can but rather keep rent or housing at a more reasonable and affordable level, the housing problem can certainly be eased. If the government ceases to exploit workers by outsourcing their jobs, workers can have higher income to rent a more decent flat. Conversion is needed. As Pope

Francis points out, in the face of poverty, we need a new perspective and lifestyle; we must not be indifferent. This requires us to listen to the cry of the poor, to really meet the poor, to make sharing a way of life, and to try to improve the situation in which the poor are excluded.[27]

Notes

1. Statistics from the Census and Statistics Department, Government of Hong Kong, https://www.censtatd.gov.hk/home.

2. Statistics from the Hong Kong Monetary Authority, https://tradingeconomics.com/hong-kong/foreign-exchange-reserves.

3. The Gini coefficient is an index from 0 to 1 that measures the wealth gap for households. Hong Kong rose to a record high of 0.539 in 2016. That was the highest figure since the city began keeping records on income equality 46 years ago. See United Nations Human Development Reports, "Hong Kong, China (SAR)," http://hdr.undp.org/en/countries/profiles/HKG. Also see Hong Kong Government, "The Gini Coefficients of Hong Kong in 2016: Trends and Interpretations," https://www.hkeconomy.gov.hk/en/pdf/box-17q2-5-2.pdf.

4. Second Vatican Council, Pastoral Constitution on the Church in the Modern World (*Gaudium et Spes*), 1965, no. 29. http://www.vatican.va/archive/hist_councils/ii_vatican_council/documents/vat-ii_const_19651207_gaudium-et-spes_en.html.

5. Keung Gor's story is taken from: I-care Programme of the Chinese University of Hong Kong & City-Youth Empowerment Project, Department of Applied Social Sciences of Hong Kong City University, *Homeless Outreach Population Estimation Hong Kong 2016*, 44. The full report can be found at http://www.cityu.edu.hk/youeprj/hopehk2015_chi.pdf.

6. Pope Francis, "The World Is a Gift, Other Persons Are a Gift," *Message of His Holiness Pope Francis for Lent 2017*, no. 1, http://w2.vatican.va/content/francesco/en/messages/lent/documents/papa-francesco_20161018_messaggio-quaresima2017.html.

7. Statistics from Social Welfare Department, the Government of Hong Kong, 2013–18.

8. I-care Programme of the Chinese University of Hong Kong & City-Youth Empowerment Project, 10.

9. Ibid., 10, 16, 21.

10. Su Xinqi, "Priced Out and Living above a Rubbish Dump: Where Do Hong Kong's Rough Sleepers Go?" *South China Morning Post*, August 12, 2018.

11. Junior Chamber International (JCI) Tai Ping Shan Chapter, *Survey Report on Sleepers of Fast Food Restaurants*, 2018. See https://www.inkstonenews.com/society/study-finds-more-people-sleeping-mcdonalds-hong-kong/article/2158640.

12. Ibid.

13. Jessie Yeung, "Why So Many People Sleep in McDonald's in Hong Kong," *CNN*, May 7, 2018, https://edition.cnn.com/2018/08/06/asia/hong-kong-mcdonalds-sleepers-intl/index.html.

14. Su Xinqi, "Priced Out and Living above a Rubbish Dump."

15. Shirley Zhao, "Number of People Sleeping in Hong Kong McDonald's Branches Skyrockets," *South China Morning Post*, August 5, 2018.

16. *Gaudium et Spes*, no. 26.

17. https://www.ohchr.org/en/professionalinterest/pages/cescr.aspx.

18. I-care Programme, 25, 31.

19. Wong Hung, "Hong Kong New Homeless Epidemic," *CUHK Updates*, February 2015.

20. "Hong Kong Takes Title for Least Affordable Housing for 8th Year," *Bloomberg News*, January 22, 2018.

21. Alice Poon, *Dichan Baquan [Land and the Ruling Class in Hong Kong]*, trans. Shimin Yan (Hong Kong: Enrich Publishing, 2010), 36–39.

22. Barry Sautman, "Hong Kong as a Semi-Ethnocracy: Race, Migration and Citizenship in a Globalized Region," in *Remaking Citizenship in Hong Kong: Community, Nation and the Global City* (London: RoutledgeCurzon, 2004), 127.

23. Government of HKSAR, *Hong Kong Poverty Situation Report 2017* (HK: Census and Statistics Department), 2018.

24. Wong Hung, "Why Does Poverty Continue to Exist?" *HK01*, November 22, 2018, https://www.hk01.com.

25. Nelson Chow, "The Sorrow behind the Bustling City—The True Face of Hong Kong's Poverty," *Ming Pao Daily News*, November 30, 2018.

26. John Paul II, *Sollicitudo Rei Socialis*, 1987, no. 42, http://w2.vatican.va/content/john-paul-ii/en/encyclicals/documents/hf_jp-ii_enc_30121987_sollicitudo-rei-socialis.html.

27. Pope Francis, "Let Us Love, Not with Words but with Deeds," Message of the First World Day of the Poor, November 19, 2017, http://w2.vatican.va/content/francesco/en/messages/poveri/documents/papa-francesco_20170613_messaggio-i-giornatamondiale-poveri-2017.html.

Youth and LGBT

Homeless, Overlooked, and Underserved

Alejandro Crosthwaite, OP

In countless cities in America, hundreds of homeless youth may be seen loitering in strip malls, wandering the streets unsupervised, or sleeping in abandoned buildings, under bridges, or on the couches of relatives, friends, or strangers.[1] In 2017, in one single night, 40,799 unaccompanied youth were counted as homeless. Eighty-eight percent of these homeless youth were eighteen to twenty-one years old; the rest (12 percent) were minors under the age of eighteen. Five hundred fifty thousand unaccompanied youth, in the course of a year, suffered some type of homelessness longer than a week. Half of these youth were under the age of eighteen.[2]

Despite their numbers and visibility, many homeless youths are overlooked and underserved. One reason for this is that, due to the highly transient nature of youth homelessness, it is very difficult to gather and record exact figures that reflect the true nature of the crisis. In turn, this hampers efforts to offer swift and adequate services in response to real need.[3] This is especially true of homeless youth who "couch-surf" among relatives, friends, or strangers. Since these homeless youths are not checking into shelters or sleeping under bridges, they go mostly undetected by groups serving homeless people or by census-gathering tools.[4]

Homeless youth tend to suffer more long-term effects from the stress and trauma of a single episode of homelessness than an adult who has been homeless for an extended period of time.[5] They are also more vulnerable and susceptible to physical, mental, and sexual abuse. They are more vulnerable to engaging in high-risk sexual behaviors, including prostitution; thus they are at greater risk of STD/HIV transmission. They often have unhealthy nutrition practices and poor health. Many have mental health issues, including severe anxiety, depression, and low self-esteem. Homeless youth may fall into substance abuse. They become victims of untimely death.[6] Each year, 5,000 homeless youth die owing to physical and/or sexual assault, illness, or suicide.[7]

It is thus imperative to implement a better methodology to identify homeless youth so that they do not continue to be overlooked and underserved. This will help ensure that timely and direct service systems can be put in place to protect homeless youth from the risks associated with homelessness and that public policy and direct service systems will be developed and realized to address and prevent the causes that put youth at risk of homelessness.

Addressing the Most Prominent Causes
of Youth Homelessness

Youth become homeless for a variety of reasons, but the most prominent causes are poverty; physical, mental, and sexual abuse; involvement in the child welfare and juvenile justice systems; racial discrimination; and, to a surprisingly high degree, homophobia.[8]

Poverty

According to a review of past research conducted by the American Medical Association in 2016, 39 percent of homeless youth worldwide reported poverty as the main reason for their situation.[9] This was especially the case in developing countries (41 percent) but also in North America (34 percent)[10] (and other developed nations [30 percent]).[11] In the United States African American youth have an 83 percent and Hispanics (nonwhite youth) have a 33 percent higher risk of reporting homelessness.[12] The fact that a youth lived in a poor family does not necessarily imply that they were neglected or uncared for. However, due to their situation of poverty, they were more likely to drop out of school, making it more likely that they would face extremely dire economic and social prospects.[13] Youth with less than a high school diploma or GED had a 346 percent higher risk of not finding a job or earning a living wage; they were also more likely to be poor, to suffer from a variety of adverse health outcomes, and to eventually become homeless.[14] In many situations, as the youth got older, their families were unable to continue to support them financially, and thus they were forced to leave their homes—not because they were being kicked out, but because their family's poverty meant they could no longer continue living with them. Youth reporting annual household income of less than $24,000 had a 162 percent higher risk of reporting homelessness.[15]

Physical, Mental, and Sexual Abuse

According to the 2002 *National Incidence Studies of Missing, Abducted, Runaway, and Thrownaway Children*, the latest report on this subject (as of this writing), based on 1999 findings, the primary cause of youth homelessness in the United States is family dysfunction in the form of parental neglect, physical or sexual abuse, family substance abuse, and family violence.[16] This was also the main cause reported by homeless youth in the rest of the developed world as opposed to poverty that tended to be reported among homeless youth in developing countries.[17] Thirty-two percent of homeless youth reported severe family chaos and conflict as the main factor for their homelessness,[18] and 29 percent reported physical, mental, and sexual abuse as a cause.[19]

The 2002 *Sexual Abuse among Homeless Adolescents: Prevalence, Correlates, and Sequelae* report prepared for the US Department of Health and Human

Services states that 21 to 42 percent of homeless youth were sexually abused, and 4 to 38 percent reported this as the leading cause for running away from home.[20] Sixty-eight to 88 percent of homeless youth reported being sexually abused by a family member or someone else that they knew.[21] In 2011, the National Runaway Safeline (NRS) conducted a longitudinal study from data collected since 2003 by the National Longitudinal Study of Adolescent Health, and reported that 10 percent of runaway youth identified emotional/verbal abuse as the reason for running away from their homes whereas 7 percent identified physical abuse or assault as the main reason.[22]

Involvement in the Child Welfare and Juvenile Justice Systems

Homelessness may lead to involvement with the juvenile justice system and vice versa. A survey conducted by the US Administration for Children, Youth, and Families in 2016 discovered that 44 percent of homeless youth had stayed in a jail, prison, or juvenile detention center; 78 percent had at least one interaction with the police, and 62 percent had been arrested.[23] In some cases this encounter with the juvenile justice system was due to a lack of shelter at the time (e.g., arrest for truancy after missing school due to the lack of stable housing, or stealing food or money due to hunger). In other cases, youth may become homeless after their involvement with the juvenile justice system because their families are unwilling to let them return because of family conflict or restrictions imposed by landlords or public housing authorities.[24] This affects, in a disproportionate way, African American and Hispanic (nonwhite) youth, as well as LGBT youth.[25] Encounters with the juvenile justice system tend to be negative and possibly traumatic experiences that have a long-term impact on young persons' lives regarding educational achievement, good health, and economic stability in the future.

Research conducted in 2004 by the University of Pennsylvania discovered that out of 8,251 homeless youth in New York City, 18 percent reported they had been involved in the child welfare system, with 6 percent of these having a history of reporting to shelters during or after their association with family services.[26] Poverty, housing instability, and psychological anxiety because of homelessness force many parents to place their children with relatives, friends, or child welfare services.[27] Children who were placed in the care of child welfare services were 40 percent versus 24 percent more likely than those without child welfare involvement to experience repeated homelessness and shelter admittance.[28] This was especially true of older children and youth who experienced difficulties fitting into shelter life because of typical shelter environments (i.e., little privacy, and alienation from schools and neighbors). These youth tended to have or develop strained relationships with parents, putting them at higher risks of homelessness after leaving shelters.[29] This led the researchers to conclude that "the high rate of crossover between homelessness and the child welfare system suggests the need for service coordination for children in foster home families."[30]

Racial Discrimination

Homeless youth of color are affected by many of the same causes that drive the high rates of homelessness among the general population of color: separate and unequal educational opportunities, racial discrimination in housing and jobs, and higher rates of involvement in the child welfare and juvenile justice systems.[31] African Americans constitute a staggering 40 percent of the population in homeless shelters.[32] African Americans were at a 12.8 percent higher risk than the general population, and a 28.4 percent higher risk than the poor population, of reporting homelessness as well as longer spells of homelessness (an average of 3 versus 2.4 years among the white population).[33] The saddest statistic is that African American children (under the age of five) become homeless at double the rate of their white counterparts.[34] The National Law Center on Homelessness and Poverty argues that "homelessness and the lack of affordable housing in the US have a disparate racial impact, in violation of the US's obligations under the *International Convention on the Elimination of All Forms of Racial Discrimination*."[35] Similarly, racism and discrimination continue to keep unemployment rates high among African Americans, consequently increasing their risk for homelessness.[36] Mass incarceration of people of color, particularly African American men and boys, further increases their likelihood of becoming homeless.[37]

Homophobia

A 2012 study by the Williams Institute at UCLA School of Law estimated that out of the 1.6 million homeless youth in the United States, 40 percent identified as LGBT.[38] This is a shocking percentage considering that LGBT youth compose only 7 percent of the overall population.[39] Accordingly, there is an overrepresentation of LGBT youth among the overall homeless youth population, especially among LGBT youth of color (31 percent African American/Black, 14 percent Latino/Hispanic, 1 percent Native American, and 1 percent Asian/Pacific Islander).[40] Aside from being at greater risk for homelessness, LGBT youth are also more likely to become homeless at younger ages.[41]

There are several reasons why LGBT youth end up homeless: 46 percent reported that they ran away from their homes because of family rejection of their sexual orientation or identification; 43 percent were forced out by their parents, and 32 percent faced physical, mental, and/or sexual abuse at home.[42] A study by Gary Mallon concluded that 56 percent of LGBT youth involved in the child welfare system experienced homelessness because they felt safer on the streets than in their foster or group home.[43] Another study conducted in 2017 by the University of Chicago anticipated that LGBT youth had a 120 percent higher risk of reporting homelessness.[44] LGBT youth also tend to experience longer periods of homelessness and to struggle with more mental and physical health issues than other homeless youth.[45] Finally, other common reasons for why LGBT youth may become home-less include: mental health issues (depression, anxiety, etc.), 65 percent; family abuse (sexual, mental, physical), 54 percent; alcohol and substance abuse, 53 percent; prostitution, 42 percent; sexual assault, 39 percent; involvement in the child welfare (33 percent) and juvenile justice systems (31 percent); and domestic/partner abuse (31 percent).[46]

These are some of the top causes of youth homelessness in the United States. From these causes it becomes quite clear that the vast majority of homeless youth do not "choose" a "street lifestyle." One has to also keep in mind that each case is unique and cannot be reduced to just one or two causes; it might be a complex series of reasons that lead a youth to end up homeless.[47]

LGBT Homeless Youth and Religious Rejection

Research done by San Francisco State University's Family Acceptance Project estimates that up to 40 percent of LGBT homeless youth leave home or are kicked out because of their parents' religious beliefs regarding sexual orientation and identification.[48]

In general, religious affiliation and religiosity are correlated with positive mental health outcomes for young adults and adolescents (i.e., lower levels of depression, fewer suicidal tendencies).[49] However, a strong association also exists between levels of religious affiliation and religiosity and negative attitudes toward homosexuality. Because of these factors, LGBT youth affiliated with a religious community and living in a religious family context report experiencing increased discrimination and internalized homophobia (i.e., negative attitudes, beliefs, feelings, and stereotypes about LGBT people that are directed inward by LGBT youth), as well as sexual identity conflict, depression, and suicidal tendencies.[50] Furthermore, family rejection at young ages can have lasting negative effects.[51]

Although 40 percent of LGBT youth with a religious upbringing reported not experiencing any religious and sexual orientation identity conflict, 43 percent reported experiencing some kind of conflict between their religious beliefs and their sexuality. Thirty-one percent of this latter group reported eventually resolving this conflict, whereas 12 percent reported still experiencing conflict. In general, those in the 31 percent tended to be older than those in the 12 percent group.[52] Additionally, 42 percent of those reporting conflict left their religious affiliation due to the conflict, especially among Christians (34 percent of Protestants and 13 percent of Catholics).[53] Those LGBT youth who left because of sexual orientation identity conflict and internalized homophobia were at greater risk of suicidal thought.[54]

In 2014, as the 2015 Synod of Bishops on the Family was being prepared, Carl Siciliano, the director of the largest shelter in the United States for homeless LGBT youth, wrote an open letter published as a full-page ad in the *New York Times* asking Pope Francis for his support for LGBT homeless youth:

I ask you to take urgent action to protect them from the devastating consequences of religious rejection, which is the most common reason LGBT youths are driven from their homes. . . . What these youths endure is horrific. They endure the torment of being unloved and unwanted by their parents, combined with the ordeals of hunger, cold and sexual exploitation while homeless. LGBT youths who are rejected by their families are 8 times more likely to attempt suicide than LGBT youths whose parents accept them. . . . A teaching's wisdom and efficacy must be judged in part by its outcome. The teaching that homosexual conduct is a sin has a poisonous outcome, bearing fruit in many Christian parents who abandon their LGBT children to homelessness and destitution. How could a good seed yield such a bitter harvest?[55]

Unfortunately, neither the 2015 Synod on the Family nor Pope Francis's Post-Synodal Apostolic Exhortation *Amoris Laetitia* had much to say in response.[56] More recently, the 2018 *Final Document of the Synod of Bishops on Youth, Faith and Vocational Discernment*, after heavy criticism from some sectors of the church,[57] returned to the term "homosexual persons" instead of the controversial "LGBT youth" that appeared in the synod's *Instrumentum Laboris,* a change that was seen as a positive move forward by some sectors of the church.[58] Nevertheless, the 2018 *Final Document* acknowledged that these questions needed "a more in-depth anthropological, theological and pastoral elaboration"; it renewed "its commitment against any discrimination and violence on a sexual basis"; and encouraged "accompaniment in the faith of homosexual persons," so that they can live "their own baptismal vocation, to recognize the desire to belong and contribute to the life of the community; to discern the best way of realizing it."[59] We hope that Pope Francis's post-synodal exhortation will provide the religious, spiritual, moral, and pastoral foundations needed to offer LGBT homeless youth an unconditional spiritual embrace.

A Way Forward in Preventing Youth Homelessness

Society usually classifies homeless youth as juvenile delinquents, which results in their exclusion, criminalization, and oppression.[60] Although juvenile delinquency is often seen as the main cause of youth homelessness, only 10 percent of homeless youth report it as a cause for their homelessness, and this figure might be exaggerated since youth preferred to report delinquency instead of abuse as a cause for their situation.[61]

Providing timely and direct interventions to homeless youth who fall into the cracks because of poverty, abuse, welfare and justice victimization, discrimination, and homophobia is crucial for protecting them from the risks of living on the streets and for supporting positive youth development. Policies and solutions developed and put in place for adult homelessness do not work for this particular population; policies and services need to be specially tailored for children and youth. Even more critical is addressing family/parental needs in order to prevent youth and/or their families from becoming homeless, and addressing behavioral health needs through comprehensive methods that involve both youth and their families. Prevention efforts to minimize family conflict and violence may include family-focused prevention programs such as support groups for parents, parenting skills classes, and conflict resolution skills.

Considering that religious rejection too often causes LGBT youth to experience homelessness, faith communities need to rethink their teaching, preaching, pastoral outreach, and sense of being church so that they may provide parents of LGBT youth with the religious, spiritual, moral, and pastoral foundations for offering their LGBT children unconditional spiritual embrace. Religious communities also need to be more active in protecting LGBT youth from harassment, in enabling them to have access to culturally appropriate support, and to guarantee equal treatment and supportive services. It is important for faith-based and non-faith-based shelters, transitional housing, and permanent housing to promote positive LGBT youth development, provide safe spaces for them, offer family reconciliation services, and connect LGBT youth to faith-based and other community resources and services.

Faith communities, civil society organizations, the private sector, and governments must all do more to meet our common responsibilities for preventing the causes of, and assisting the victims of, youth homelessness. We must recognize homeless youth and youth at risk of homelessness as an extremely vulnerable part of the human family. As Christians, we are reminded by the Gospel that the first human problem the child Jesus faced on earth was a lack of shelter: "[His mother] wrapped him in swaddling clothes, and laid him in a manger, because there was no room for them in the inn."[62] Today, we especially see in the faces of homeless youth the face of the homeless infant Christ. We know that in reaching out to them, standing with them in defending their rights, in working with them and their families for decent housing, we serve the Lord.

Notes

1. The US Department of Housing and Urban Development/Office of Community Planning and Development defines "Unaccompanied Homeless Youth (under 18)" as "people in households with only children who are not part of a family with children or accompanied by their parent or guardian during their episode of homelessness, and who are under the age of 18." It defines "Unaccompanied Homeless Youth (18–24)" as "people in households without children who are not part of a family with children or accompanied by their parent or guardian during their episode of homelessness, and who are between the ages of 18 and 24." See Henry Megan, Rian Watt, Lily Rosenthal, and Azim Shivji, *The 2017 Annual Homeless Assessment Report (AHAR) to Congress* (Washington, DC: US. Department of Housing and Urban Development (HUD)/Office of Community Planning and Development, 2017), 3.

2. HUD, *AHAR*, 1.

3. Nikita Stewart, "Homeless Young People of New York, Overlooked and Under-served," *New York Times,* February 6, 2016, A1.

4. Eric Kurhi, "Couch Surfing Kids: Hidden and Nearly Homeless," *Mercury News,* September 27, 2017, https://www.mercurynews.com/2017/09/26/couch-surfing-kids-hidden-and-nearly-homeless.

5. Ellen Hart-Shegos, *Homelessness and Its Effects on Children* (Minneapolis: Family Housing Fund, 1999), 3.

6. National Council of State Legislatures, "Homeless and Runaway Youth," Denver: NCSL, April 14, 2016, http://www.ncsl.org/research/human-services/homeless-and-runaway-youth.aspx.

7. Ibid.

8. Youth.gov, "Homelessness and Runaway," *Youth.gov*, https://youth.gov/youth-topics/runaway-and-homeless-youth.

9. Lonnie Embleton, Hana Lee, Jayleen Gunn, David Ayuku, and Paula Braitstein, "Causes of Child and Youth Homelessness in Developed and Developing Countries: A Systematic Review and Meta-analysis," *JAMA Pediatrics* 170, no. 5 (May 2016): 438.

10. Ibid., 441.

11. Ibid., 440.

12. Matthew H. Morton, Amy Dworsky, and Gina M. Samuels, *Missed Opportunities: Youth Homelessness in America: National Estimates* (Chicago: Chapin Hall at the University of Chicago, 2017), 12.

13. Russell W. Rumberger, "Poverty and High School Dropouts. The Impact of Family and Community Poverty on High School Dropouts," *SES Indicator*, May 2013, https://www.apa.org/pi/ses/resources/indicator/2013/05/poverty-dropouts.aspx.

14. Morton, *Missed Opportunities,* 12; Rumberger, "Poverty," n.p.

15. Morton, *Missed Opportunities,* 12.

16. US Department of Justice, Office of Justice Programs, Office of Juvenile Justice and Delinquency Prevention, *National Incidence Studies of Missing, Abducted, Runaway, and Thrownaway Children* (Washington, DC: US Department of Justice, 2002), 2.

17. Embleton, "Causes," 439.

18. Ibid.

19. Ibid.

20. US Department of Health, Administration on Children, Youth and Families, *Sexual Abuse among Homeless Adolescents: Prevalence, Correlates, and Sequelae* (Washington, DC: US Department of Health. Administration on Children, Youth and Families, 2002), ES-1–2.

21. Ibid., ES-2.

22. National Runaway Safeline, *Child Abuse and Why Youth Run Away: Hot to Recognize Child Abuse* (Washington, DC: NRS), 2.

23. Coalition for Juvenile Justice, "Youth Homelessness and Juvenile Justice: Opportunities for Collaboration and Impact," *Coalition for Juvenile Justice* 1, no. 1 (June 2016): 1.

24. Ibid.

25. Ibid.

26. Jung M. Park, Stephen Metraux, Gabriel Broadbar, and Dennis P. Culjane, *Child Welfare Involvement among Children in Homeless Families* (Philadelphia: University of Pennsylvania, 2004), 423.

27. Ibid., 424.

28. Ibid., 429.

29. Ibid., 433.

30. Ibid., 423.

31. Jeff Olivet and Marc Dones, "T³ Threads: Changing the Conversation: Racism and Youth Homelessness." *Center for Social Innovation,* June 6, 2016, http://us.thinkt3.com/blog/author/marc-dones.

32. Frederick H. Lowe, "Report: Blacks Comprise More than 40 Percent of the Homeless Population," *BlackmansStreetToday,* February 20, 2018, http://www.north-starnewstoday.com/news/report-blacks-comprise-40-percent-homeless-population.

33. George R. Carter III, "From Exclusion to Destitution: Race, Affordable Housing, and Homelessness," *Cityscape: Journal of Policy Development and Research* 13, no. 1 (2011): 35, 60.

34. Dennis Culhane and Stephen Metraux, "One-Year Rates of Public Shelter Utilization by Race/Ethnicity, Age, Sex and Poverty Status of New York City (1990 and 1995) and Philadelphia (1995)," *Population Research and Policy Review* 18, no. 3 (June 1999): Abstract.

35. National Law Center on Homelessness and Poverty and Los Angeles Community Action Network, *Racial Discrimination in Housing and Homelessness in the United States. A Report to the U.N. Committee on the Elimination of Racial Discrimination* (Washington, DC: National Law Center on Homelessness and Poverty), 1.

36. Devah Pager and Hana Shepherd, "The Sociology of Discrimination: Racial Discrimination in Employment, Housing, Credit, and Consumer Markets," *Annual Review of Sociology* 34 (January 1, 2010): 181.

37. Thomas P. Bonczar, "Prevalence of Imprisonment in the US Population, 1974–2001," *Bureau of Justice Statistics Special Report* (August 2003): 1.

38. Simon Costello, Naomi Goldberg, Richard Hooks Wyman, Jeff Krehely, and David Vincent, *Serving Our Youth: Findings from a National Survey of Service Providers Working with Lesbian, Gay, Bisexual, and Transgender Youth Who Are Homeless or At Risk of Becoming Homeless* (Los Angeles: Williams Institute with True Colors Fund and The Palette Fund, 2012), 3.

39. Ibid.

40. Harbor House, "LGBTQ," n.p.; also see Michelle Page, "Forgotten Youth: Homeless LGBT Youth of Color and the Runaway and Homeless Youth Act," *Northwestern Journal of Law and Social Policy* 12, no. 2 (2017): 18.

41. Eliza Brown, "Homelessness among LGBT Youth: A National Concern," *Child Trends,* November 18, 2013, https://www.childtrends.org/homelessness-among-lgbt-youth-a-national-concern.

42. Ibid.

43. Gerald P. Mallon, *We Don't Exactly Get the Welcome Wagon: The Experiences of Gay and Lesbian Adolescents in Child Welfare Systems* (New York: Columbia University Press, 1998), x.

44. Morton, *Missed Opportunities,* 12.

45. Harbor House, "LGBTQ Youth Overrepresented among Homeless Youth." *Harbor House News,* October 17, 2018, http://www.oceansharborhouse.org/news/lgbtq-youth-overrepresented-among-homeless-youth.

46. Costello, *Serving Our Youth,* 7.

47. Andrew M. Seaman, "Poverty to Blame for Most Youth Homelessness Worldwide," *Reuters,* April 4, 2016, https://www.reuters.com/article/us-health-homeless-youths-idUSKCN0X12BQ.

48. Alex Morris, "The Forsaken: A Rising Number of Homeless Gay Teens Are Being Cast Out by Religious Families," *RollingStone,* September 3, 2014, https://www.rollingstone.com/culture/culture-news/the-forsaken-a-rising-number-of-homeless-gay-teens-are-being-cast-out-by-religious-families-46746.

49. Jeremy J. Gibbs, "Religious Conflict, Sexual Identity, and Suicidal Behaviors among LGBT Young Adults," *Archives of Suicide Research* 19, no. 4 (October–December 2015): 472.

50. Ibid.

51. Lesley University, "The Cost of Coming Out: LGBT Youth Homelessness" *Lesley University*, October 17, 2018, https://lesley.edu/article/the-cost-of-coming-out-lgbt-youth-homelessness.

52. Gibbs, "Religious Conflict," 472.

53. Ibid., 474.

54. Ibid.

55. Alexandra Bolles, "Letter in New York Times Calls for Pope Francis to End Harm to LGBT Youth," *Glaad*, April 13, 2014, https://www.glaad.org/blog/letter-new-york-times-calls-pope-francis-end-harm-lgbt-youth.

56. See Francis, *Post-Synodal Apostolic Exhortation Amoris Laetitia* (Vatican City: Vatican Publishing House, 2015), nos. 130–32; 251.

57. See Diane Montagna, "'LGBT' Should Not Be in Vatican Documents: Archbishop Chaput Tells Youth Synod," *Life Site*, October 4, 2018, https://www.lifesitenews.com/news/archbishop-chaput-lgbt-should-not-be-used-in-vatican-youth-synod-document.

58. Synod of Bishops, *Instrumentum Laboris of the XV Ordinary General Assembly of Synod of Bishops on Young People, The Faith and Vocational Discernment* (Vatican City: Vatican Publishing House, 2018), no. 53. In number 197 it also addresses "young people who decide to create homosexual instead of heterosexual couples and, above all, would like to be close to the Church."

59. Synod of Bishops, *Final Document of the Synod of Bishops on Youth, Faith and Vocation Discernment* (Vatican City: Vatican Publishing House, 2018), no. 150.

60 Embleton, "Causes," 439; Seaman, "Poverty," n.p.

61. Embleton, "Causes," 439.

62. Lk 2:7.

ADDICTION

Drink and Drugs

Tobias Winright

During an interview published the day before the beginning of Lent in the magazine *Scarp de' Tenis* (Tennis Shoes), which, with support from Caritas, serves homeless people in Milan, Pope Francis said, "There are many excuses" people give to justify why they don't give to a person begging on the street, such as "I give money and then he spends it on drinking a glass of wine."[1] Over the years, I have heard friends say similar things, and I, too, have had such thoughts when approached by persons, presumably homeless, begging for some money, whether in Saint Louis or Louisville, Rome or Trent, Maynooth or Sarajevo. Will the street person use the money for alcohol, drugs, or other unhealthy addictions instead of for food, shelter, or other necessities? In an article about Pope Francis's interview, Catholic theological ethicist Beth Haile notes, "When I lived in Boston, it was not uncommon to see a beggar on the street smoking cigarettes or drinking malt liquor. It is easy to say, 'See, that guy doesn't even know how to use money responsibly. Why should I give him more?'"[2] In these attempts to justify their disregard for the beggar's supplication, we see how homelessness and addiction to drink and drugs are commonly—and negatively—assumed to be associated.

This essay investigates the presumed links between homelessness and addiction to drink and drugs. By "drink" I mean alcoholic beverages such as whiskey, beer, and wine, rather than coffee which contains caffeine and can also be addictive. By "drugs" I refer to illegal, rather than legally obtained pharmaceutical, drugs, and to recreational drugs such as opioids (e.g., heroin), stimulants (e.g., cocaine, methamphetamine), and hallucinogens (e.g., LSD). Of course, what's considered to be illegal varies from one state jurisdiction to another, as is the case currently in the United States with the cannabinoid marijuana. Moreover, "addiction" itself will be probed further in what follows. Because very few theological ethicists have treated this topic, especially in connection with homelessness, I begin with an anecdote and a story. As Catholic theological ethicist Joseph A. Selling suggests, "Narrative should be an integral part of any ethical discourse."[3]

Although I have been a theological ethicist for over two decades, I have also worked in the criminal justice system, including as a correctional officer at a large, maximum security county jail in Florida, and as a city reserve police officer. During the 1980s I remember firsthand how the deinstitutionalization of the mentally ill forced many onto the streets. As Paul S. Appelbaum described it at the time, "Pioneer Square in Seattle, Lafayette Park in Washington, the old downtown in Atlanta have all become places of refuge for these pitiable figures, so hard to tell apart: clothes tattered, skins stained by the streets, backs bent in a perpetual search for something edible, smokable, or tradable that may have found its way to the pavement below."[4] Many of these homeless persons, including those who had apparent addictions to alcohol or drugs, were actually reinstitutionalized, even if only temporarily, in city and county jails rather than in mental health facilities. In many US cities, both large and small, this criminalization of homelessness has only increased. For example, according to a recent investigative report appearing in the *Oregonian*, 52 percent of all arrests made in 2017 in Portland were of homeless persons, who make up only 3 percent of that city's general population.[5]

Of course, looking back, I now see the importance of the question raised around that time by Denise Lardner Carmody and John Tully Carmody: Should addiction to alcohol or drugs "be considered primarily a medical problem, a social problem, a moral problem, or a religious problem?"[6] What happened, during the 1980s while I was working in law enforcement, was that homeless persons, addicted to alcohol or drugs, who may have been previously regarded as a mental health problem, were becoming considered a moral, even criminal, problem by much of society. At the time, my gaze on homeless persons who seemed to be addicted to alcohol or drugs included each of these facets, though I probably leaned toward blaming them and viewing their addictive problems as self-inflicted. Yet I gradually came to get to know some of them, especially since a good number were repeat "offenders." I began to see that these persons had stories, histories, life experiences— indeed, that they were not completely autonomous, totally free individuals separate from others, including family members who may have abused or abandoned them, and including the wider civil and social systems and structures, especially economic and political, that in their own ways may also have abused or abandoned them.

Although my personal experiences as a law enforcement officer encountering homeless persons with these addictions made an impression on me, they occurred long ago. Plus, in my subsequent years in lay ecclesial ministry (youth and campus ministry) and as a theological ethicist, I have encountered homeless persons, many with addictions, at soup kitchens, homeless shelters, and parish halls. I could share my own stories, but because I do not have permission from any of these persons, I will draw some from a stirring book by Gary Smith, SJ, *Radical Compassion: Finding Christ in the Heart of the Poor*, in which he writes "about the people with whom I have lived and worked over the past several years as part of my mission on the streets as a priest of the Society of Jesus, the Jesuits."[7] To provide a good sense of the context, Smith observes:

> On my way to work every day, I walk down Third Street in Portland, in a section of the city called Old Town, through a scene played out in the poor areas of every large city in the United States: the unemployed

looking for work; drug dealers furtively hawking their heroin, cocaine, and methamphetamines; residents from the many SROs [single-room occupancy hotels] moving in and out of their buildings; burned-out alcoholics coming off or beginning another day of panhandling and drinking and misery; addicts engaging in the endless hunt for another fix; lines of people waiting to get food or clothes or shelter; the occasional nervous and fatigued prostitute wandering by; individuals talking incoherently to themselves; staff persons from a variety of agencies going about their work; alert police slowly surveying the streets on foot, on bikes, in cars.[8]

I remember such scenes from my own past experiences, and this description of the streets by Smith was on my mind during some runs I made through this area of Portland a few years ago while at an academic conference. Of his book's chapters, though, chapter 5, titled "Crashing and Burning: The Insanity of Drugs and Alcohol," offers vignettes that are most relevant for my assigned task in this present volume. As the chapter's title suggests, most of the stories he shares from his experiences with homeless, poor women and men who are addicted to drugs and alcohol are tragic.

For instance, Smith refers to Lucia, who "has fallen off the wagon," slowly slipping "back into the hell of anger, self-deprecation, and street alcoholism."[9] When she's sober, she "is a shining light of grace and humanity," gifted at building community and caring for the other poor.[10] When intoxicated, however, she is vicious and manipulative. At the same time, she's very vulnerable, especially to predatorial men. There is also Marshall, who is "probably forty-five, but an old-looking forty-five," and who is "an alcoholic, worn down by the sights and emotions of his life's journey."[11] A Vietnam war veteran, alone and in pain, he expresses his concern for the street people who are in despair. In tears, Marshall laments, "I wish I could help them, but I am so [expletive] weak, so trapped in my own body."[12] Another Vietnam vet, Roe, aged forty-three, dies, "probably a result of his chronic alcoholism—he had a seizure that led him to choke to death on his own vomit."[13] And his "self-destructive behavior" was a consequence of "the poison" of his scarred memories of war. Smith will miss Roe, especially his "good-humored, sarcastic zingers" flung at his jogging and his jogging clothes.[14] Then there's Larry, a heroin addict, who was off it but had relapsed, using it even more than before. "This nightmare called drug addiction is like radiation: it slashes through everything—body, soul, relationships, all that is sane and healthy and meaningful."[15] Smith happened to bump into Larry as he was on his way to a bridge from which he intended to jump and commit suicide. Smith writes, "So we talked. We wept. The guy was just beaten by it all: the helplessness, the devastation, the failure, the shame, the constant hustle for dope, the knowledge of what he had become, the sleeping under bridges, the loss of friends, the loss of the woman who once cherished him."[16] After Smith and Larry walked to a church, they separated. Several months later, Larry showed up again, grateful and clean from heroin after detox and time in a rehab center. One more:

Tanya, who with a bipolar condition "was an old thirty-three," dying after "having never come out of her heroin-induced coma."[17] She once attempted to cut Smith with a broken bottle, but they became close nevertheless. He even visited her in jail. Smith recounts:

> Off in the corner of one of the jail modules, Tanya talked to me, some-times sobbing, trying to reconcile her longing for wholeness and the compulsions of destructive behavior. The guilt was thick and paralyzing, like a river of mud. It was disheartening, because there didn't seem to be a way out, short of a long-term regimen of treatment and counseling. I had seen her leave jails before and immediately plunge back into the river of ripping and running. Her judgment was impaired.[18]

These real life (and death) narratives that Smith shares reveal how there is much more to "the" story of homeless persons who are addicted to alcohol or drugs. Actually, there's a matrix that encompasses more than individual freedom and responsibility—that is, more than simply the personal agency that lends itself only to the lenses of moral and criminal culpability. As Stanley Hauerwas has observed,

> The loss of narrative as a central category for social ethics has resulted in a failure to see that the ways the issues of social ethics are identified—that is, the relation of personal and social ethics, the meaning and status of the individual in relation to the community, freedom versus equality, the inter-relation of love and justice—are more a reflection of a political philosophy than they are crucial categories for the analysis of a community's social ethics. The form and substance of a community is narrative-dependent, and therefore what counts as "social ethics" is a correlative of the content of that narrative.[19]

In the United States, the dominant political and economic philosophy reduces social ethics to seeing issues and ills as corresponding to the individual and to freedom. Roger G. Betsworth argues that "the thought and practice of social ethics is rooted in both the plurality and the unity of the American experience." He notes that the reduction of scope in social ethics is because four primary cultural narra-tives, sometimes mutually reinforcing and at other times in tension with each other, "have shaped the sense of self and world for the majority of Americans": the biblical and Puritan story of covenant; the Enlightenment and "gospel of success" story of the individualistic, self-made man; the therapeutic and consumerist story of well-being; and the story of the "mission of America" as destined leader.[20] Betsworth adds, moreover, that these four cultural narratives "belong to the dominant groups," casting others such as Blacks and women—and I would add, homeless addicts to alcohol and drugs—as "outsiders."[21]

Particularly relevant is Betsworth's chapter titled "The Gospel of Success in America."[22] One element of this cultural narrative is a moralism that presupposes "the free and responsible individual" who possesses "the power to shape their own lives."[23] This "story of success" emphasizes industriousness and "the ability of each individual to make personal progress" so that, almost mechanistically (with a logic of cause and effect), "the moral man became an economic success."[24] Benjamin Franklin and his *Autobiography*, calling for such things as frugality and avoiding the tavern, are considered by Betsworth as historically influential in this narrative's gaining deep traction in US culture. Also, McGuffey's *Eclectic Readers* further schooled generations of children in this story. And Andrew Carnegie's article "Wealth," which appeared in 1889 in the *North American Review*, added the element of competition and social Darwinism (i.e., the survival of the fittest) to the mix.[25] Hence, the moralism in which the "story of failure is the flip side": if one is poor, this is due to the person having a "poor character, who will not train himself or herself in the virtues of industry and efficiency."[26] However, Betsworth observes that downplayed or ignored in this narrative of success (or failure) are how one's actions transpire within "an existing web of relationships, in the presence of other persons whose action affects the outcome of the story."[27] An additional shortcoming of the narrative of success is its failure to recognize the "mystery of human life," including its giftedness, contingency, and limits.[28] Indeed, the narrative of success "divides us rather than binds us together," preventing us from "seeing the poor, the stranger, the wayfarer, the widow, and the orphan as brothers and sisters," but instead "as persons who have failed" and "gotten what they deserve."[29] For Betsworth, who is a United Methodist ethicist, this narrative of success is a myopic deception.

In his book's conclusion, Betsworth, like Hauerwas, argues that "narrative is the form of rationality especially appropriate for ethics, and . . . [that] we not only can, but must make judgments that one story is more adequate than another."[30] The narrative of success fails, in my view, to do justice to the homeless persons with addictions to alcohol and drugs described above by Gary Smith, SJ. Just as Betsworth proposes, for a corrective, that "we need to renew our willingness to listen seriously to the outsiders, whose lives and words reveal the many ways we bend our vision of the good to our own self-interest," I have been trying to suggest that we need to include and listen to the stories of the persons Smith encounters on the streets of Portland before addressing the ethics of homelessness and addiction. In other words, we need to avoid the problematic and partial perspective of the narrative of success and its moralizing—evident in the excuses people made at the outset of this essay for not giving money to street beggars and in my own attitude toward homeless persons during my initial years in law enforcement—when attempting to offer a moral analysis of homelessness and addiction to drugs and alcohol.

We can now see that the treatment, though brief, of addiction by Carmody and Carmody is significant. Their coauthored book, *Christian Ethics: An Introduction through History and Current Issues*, was unique, compared to other similar books at the time (1993) and even now, in treating drugs and alcohol as a subsection within the chapter on medical ethics, along with AIDS, abortion, euthanasia, and allocation of health care resources. They begin by noting that some ethicists distinguish between "addiction," based on physical needs, and "habituation," having to do with social practices. Either way, though, Carmody and Carmody raise the question about such "substance abuse": "Should either addiction or habituation be considered primarily a medical problem, a social problem, a moral problem, or a religious problem?"[31] Each of these facets is considered as relevant in their short account.

Carmody and Carmody note the tremendous negative effects of drug and alcohol addiction on family and work, and they add that Christian ethicists should not "overlook the suffering of addicts and alcoholics themselves," whose "self-hatred," as we have seen in Smith's narratives above, "runs deep" and poses "a huge stumbling block to belief in a good God."[32] Carmody and Carmody do not, however, mention homelessness connected with these addictions. After considering policy possibilities, such as legalizing some drugs and providing clean needles for users, and the importance of medical therapy versus criminal punishment, the Carmodys turn more directly to the Christian moral perspective.

Here they note that substance abuse has been regarded as "a species of the sin of gluttony or the vice of intemperance."[33] The focus has been on the abuse of a substance, and that abuse is one of excess, leading to detrimental effects on the users (e.g., their health) and on other people (e.g., endangering them when one is driving or operating machinery). Because we are morally obligated "in conscience to use well what God has given," substance abuse is problematic from a moral and religious perspective. In glancing at pre–Vatican II moral manuals, this is the only Christian moral perspective I find to be evident. For example, in the 1955 English edition of the moral manual, *Moral Theology*, by Heribert Jone and Urban Adelman, the subject of alcohol is treated in the section on the vice of gluttony, which is "the inordinate longing for food or drink," with intemperance in drink, and "its immediate effect the loss of the use of reason," regarded as "a graver sin" (venial if it results only in a partial loss of reason; mortal if it results in complete loss of reason). It is within this section that drugs such as morphine, opium, and chloroform are also mentioned in passing, with "that which was said of intoxicating drinks hold[ing] also for narcotics."[34] For Jone and Adelman, the problem of addiction is a moral one having to do with personal vice. Of course, this shouldn't be surprising, perhaps, since the audience of moral manuals such as theirs was the cleric hearing an individual's confession of sins during the sacrament of penance. Homelessness did not appear as a topic or an issue in their moral manual.

The more ecumenical *Westminster Dictionary to Christian Ethics*, which was a go-to reference work during the 1970s through the 1990s, has entries on addiction, alcoholism, and drug addiction, but none on homelessness or street persons. Nor do the authors of these entries refer to homelessness in connection with them. Unlike the Carmodys, in his extremely short entry the Anglican theologian John Macquarrie conflates addiction with habituation when he defines the former as the "state of being given over to the habitual use of alcohol or other drugs."[35] The other two entries on alcoholism and drug addiction were written by bioethicist H. Tristram Engelhardt, a philosopher also holding a medical degree. On alcoholism he observes that it was for centuries viewed through the lenses of religion, morality, and the law, regarded as "a sin, a vice, and a crime."[36] In the late eighteenth century, alcoholism began to be regarded through a medical lens as a kind of disease. In the end, Engelhardt acknowledges these various perspectives and concludes that "an account of the difficulties will not be fully forthcoming within any one theoretical framework."[37] As for drug addiction, unlike Macquarrie, Engelhardt highlights possible distinctions between addiction, habituation, and dependence. He also considers not only the physical but also the psychological aspects. Again, Engelhardt notes that how drug addiction is characterized depends on the framework being used, whether legal, medical, or religious, which in turn determines whether drug addiction is seen as criminal behavior, disease, or sin.[38]

Like Engelhardt, some Catholic bioethicists have given attention to drug and alcohol addiction. In the fifth edition of their widely used *Health Care Ethics: A Catholic Theological Analysis*, Benedict M. Ashley, OP, Jean deBlois, CSJ, and Kevin D. O'Rourke, OP, include a section titled "Addictions" within the chapter titled "Mental Health: Ethical Perspectives." They see "addiction or dependency" as basically "habituation to some practice harmful to the subject."[39] Their focus is on habituation to drugs, although they note that "one can also be addicted to other detrimental substances or activities, such as alcohol, tobacco, coffee, and excessive food, as well as too much sleep, too much work, and pursuit of sexual pleasure."[40] While mentioning that "traditional ethics" dealt with this problem via the cardinal virtue of temperance, these Catholic bioethicists take into account how drug abuse causes physiological changes that limit human freedom. Their description of how persons with addictions can have a "profound sense of depression that is often worsened by feelings of guilt and shame" echoes the narratives shared by Smith on the streets of Portland. After emphasizing how the virtue of temperance is the "ultimate and only fully satisfactory remedy for addiction,"[41] they express a nuanced approval of programs such as Alcoholics Anonymous (AA), which by its making popular the notion of alcoholism as a "disease" and thereby diminishing the social stigma attached to it, has perhaps also reduced too much "the moral aspect of addiction."[42] Like Engelhardt, these coauthors reckon that there is an interplay between the moral and the physiological when it comes to drug and alcohol addiction. Unlike any of the previously considered authors (except Smith), Ashley, deBlois, and O'Rourke bring up the connection between homelessness and addiction: "It should be recognized, moreover, that drug abuse is promoted by poverty and homelessness and in turn augments these evils. Public policy, encouraged by the medical profession, must aim at breaking this vicious cycle."[43]

Between the moral manuals and the more recent efforts of some theological bioethicists, we see some development, therefore, from a narrower "moralism," which the Carmodys criticize as attempting to address "complicated problems by the simple application of ethical analysis or exhortation."[44] They ask, "How much do genetic endowment, family circumstances, or peer pressure contribute to a given substance abuse? How much is freedom curtailed?"[45] They note that both medical science and social science are attempting to help answer these questions, but also that there remains a great amount of uncertainty, so that "Christian moralists have to proffer their judgments with many qualifications."[46] The Carmodys urge that as much as possible be done to alleviate the social and psychological factors that give rise to addiction, as well as to encourage persons with these addictions to take what responsibility they can and to do their part. Ultimately, they conclude: "Believing that God wants people . . . to thrive even more than such people themselves do, Christian moralists have to assert that nothing—no abuse or sin—separates people from the love of God manifested in Christ."[47] Although the Carmodys do not mention homelessness, I believe that their brief analysis of addiction to alcohol and drugs coheres well with the narratives shared by Smith from the streets of Portland.

When Pope Francis, in response to the question about giving money to the street beggar who might use it only for some wine, went on to emphasize that the way one reaches out to the person asking for help is important, so that it must be done "by looking them in the eyes and touching their hands," I immediately thought of Smith's ministry of presence and accompaniment in Portland. The pope also noted that we should consider our circumstances compared to the street person's, suggesting perhaps the complex variables involved. During my writing of this essay, with its attention to how theological ethics has considered addictions, I have noticed that my own gaze toward the homeless, as I have encountered them on the street, in my neighborhood, and even at a coffee shop, has changed. As we have seen, to address problems such as homelessness and addiction, Catholic theological ethics today must integrate the insights of Catholic social thought, Catholic bioethics, and fundamental Catholic moral theology.[48] Only in doing so will Catholic theological ethics be able to contribute, as Vatican II's *Gaudium et Spes* urged, to the flourishing of the human person "integrally and adequately considered,"[49] and to the common good, which is "the sum total of social conditions which allow people, either as groups or as individuals, to reach their fulfillment more fully and more easily."[50]

Notes

1. Carol Glatz, "Don't Worry How It's Spent, Always Give Homeless a Handout, Pope Says," *Catholic News Service,* February 28, 2017, http://www.catholicnews.com/services/englishnews/2017/dont-worry-how-its-spent-always-give-homeless-a-handout-pope-says.cfm. The editors of the *New York Times* were favorable, https://www.nytimes.com/2017/03/03/opinion/the-pope-on-panhandling-give-without-worry.html.

2. Beth Haile, "Is It Wise to Give Your Spare Change?" *US Catholic* 82, no. 12 (December 2017): 18–22, https://www.uscatholic.org/articles/201708/direct-giving-31134.

3. Joseph A. Selling, *Reframing Catholic Theological Ethics* (Oxford: Oxford University Press, 2016), 46.

4. Paul S. Appelbaum, "Crazy in the Streets," in *On Moral Medicine: Theological Perspectives in Medical Ethics*, ed. M. Therese Lysaught and Joseph J. Kotva Jr., 3rd ed. (Grand Rapids, MI: William B. Eerdmans, 2012), 510.

5. Rebecca Woolington and Melissa Lewis, "Portland Homeless Accounted for Majority of Police Arrests in 2017, Analysis Finds," *Oregonian*, June 27, 2018, https://www.oregonlive.com/portland/index.ssf/2018/06/portland_homeless_accounted_fo.html. According to the authors: "Most often, police arrested homeless people on property, drug or low-level crimes. The vast majority of the arrests, 86 percent, were for non-violent crimes, the analysis found. And more than 1,200 arrests were solely for offenses that are typically procedural—missing court or violating probation or parole." See also Tristia Bauman and Ted Brackman, "Cruel and All Too Usual," *Sojourners* 48, no. 1 (January 2019): 32–35.

6. Denise Lardner Carmody and John Tully Carmody, *Christian Ethics: An Introduction through History and Current Issues* (Englewood Cliffs, NJ: Prentice Hall, 1993), 194.

7. Gary Smith, SJ, *Radical Compassion: Finding Christ in the Heart of the Poor* (Chicago: Loyola Press, 2002), 4.

8. Ibid., 2.

9. Ibid., 65.

10. Ibid.

11. Ibid., 70.

12. Ibid.

13. Ibid., 72.

14. Ibid., 73.

15. Ibid.

16. Ibid., 74.

17. Ibid.

18. Ibid., 75–76.

19. Stanley Hauerwas, *A Community of Character: Toward a Constructive Christian Social Ethic* (Notre Dame, IN: University of Notre Dame Press, 1981), 9–10. See also Stanley Hauerwas and L. Gregory Jones, eds., *Why Narrative? Readings in Narrative Theology* (Grand Rapids, MI: William B. Eerdmans, 1989).

20. Roger G. Betsworth, *Social Ethics: An Examination of American Moral Traditions* (Louisville, KY: Westminster/John Knox Press, 1990), 11, 16.

21. Ibid., 20.

22. For a very recent treatment of the "gospel of success" and health care ministry, see Ramon Luzarraga, "Accompaniment with the Sick: An Authentic Christian Vocation That Rejects the Fallacy of Prosperity Theology," *Journal of Moral Theology* 8, no. 1 (January 2019): 76–88.

23. Betsworth, *Social Ethics*, 53, 57.

24. Ibid., 58.

25. Ibid., 68–69.

26. Ibid., 77.

27. Ibid., 76.

28. Ibid., 78.

29. Ibid., 79.

30. Ibid., 178–79, 181. Betsworth here draws from Stanley Hauerwas et al., *Truthfulness and Tragedy* (Notre Dame, IN: University of Notre Dame Press, 1977), 15–39, 74–76, 82–84.

31. Carmody and Carmody, *Christian Ethics*, 194.

32. Ibid., 195.

33. Ibid.

34. Heribert Jone, OFM Cap, and Urban Adelman, OFM Cap, *Moral Theology* (Westminster, MD: Newman Press, 1955), 56–57. This is the English edition revised in accordance with the sixteenth German edition and containing additions that appear in the seventeenth. A more recent, and much more thorough, treatment of addiction and drinking alcohol is offered by William C. Mattison III, *Introducing Moral Theology: True Happiness and the Virtues* (Grand Rapids, MI: Brazos Press, 2008), wherein he considers the role of family, media, peers, and so on, that influence the why, how, when, and where we drink, but he tends to focus on the transitive effects (e.g., dangerous driving, sexual assault, etc.) and intransitive effects (i.e., bad habits, or vices) that result. To address drinking, Mattison employs the cardinal virtues of temperance, prudence, justice, and fortitude. Although he does not deny the importance of other perspectives—he mentions the sociological (130)—he believes that the virtue approach has been "too often neglected" (130) on this topic. His main audience is students at colleges and universities. See chapter 6, "Alcohol and American College Life," 113–33.

35. John Macquarrie, "Addiction," in *The Westminster Dictionary of Christian Ethics*, rev. ed., ed. James F. Childress and John Macquarrie (Philadelphia: Westminster Press, 1986), 9.

36. H. Tristram Engelhardt, "Alcoholism," in *The Westminster Dictionary of Christian Ethics*, rev. ed., ed. James F. Childress and John Macquarrie (Philadelphia: Westminster Press, 1986), 17.

37. Ibid., 18.

38. H. Tristram Engelhardt, "Drug Addiction," in *The Westminster Dictionary of Christian Ethics*, rev. ed., ed. James F. Childress and John Macquarrie (Philadelphia: Westminster Press, 1986), 163–64.

39. Benedict M. Ashley, OP, Jean deBlois, CSJ, and Kevin D. O'Rourke, OP, *Health Care Ethics: A Catholic Theological Analysis*, 5th ed. (Washington, DC: Georgetown University Press, 2006), 155.

40. Ibid.

41. Ibid., 156.

42. Ibid., 157.

43. Ibid. Currently, data confirm the correlation between homelessness, poverty, and addiction to drug and alcohol; however, causality remains unclear: the relationship appears to be bidirectional. See M. B. Kushel et al., "Revolving Doors: Imprisonment among the Homeless and Marginally Housed Population," *American Journal of Public Health* 95, no. 10 (October 1, 2005): 1747–52. Also, in *Homelessness: Prevalence, Impact of Social Factors and Mental Health Challenges* (New York: Nova Science Publishers, 2014), Colleen Clark writes, "The Substance Abuse and Mental Health Services Administration has estimated that approximately 38 percent of the homeless population is dependent upon alcohol and 26 percent actively abuse other drugs" (126).

44. Carmody and Carmody, *Christian Ethics*, 197.

45. Ibid., 196.

46. Ibid.

47. Ibid.

48. I have in mind here the kind of work offered in *Catholic Bioethics and Social Justice: The Praxis of US Health Care in a Globalized World*, ed. M. Therese Lysaught and Michael McCarthy (Collegeville, MN: Liturgical Press, 2018).

49. Second Vatican Council, *Gaudium et Spes* [Pastoral Constitution on the Church in the Modern World] (1965), no. 51; the phrase is from *Schema constitutionis pastoralis de ecclesia in mundo huius temporis: Expensio modorum partis secundae* (Vatican Press, 1965), 37–38. Louis Janssens's thinking was a major influence here. See Dolores L. Christie, *Moral Choice: A Christian View of Ethics* (Minneapolis: Fortress Press, 2013), and Joseph A. Selling, *Reframing Catholic Theological Ethics* (New York: Oxford University Press, 2016, 2018).

50. *Gaudium et Spes*, no. 26.

Part II

Working to End Homelessness

Global and Ecclesial Strategies

HOMELESSNESS AND SDG 1

Kat Johnson

Despite its impact on individuals and cities across every continent, street homelessness has been left behind in global debate. The word "homelessness" appears nowhere in the United Nations' Sustainable Development Goals (SDGs), which address global concerns from marine conservation to economic growth. Though it is central to issues like inequality, urban life, health, and a number of other SDG target areas, homelessness does not factor into any of the 230 SDG indicators intended to measure the world's progress on our most pressing issues.

Though some populations are more affected than others, street homelessness occurs irrespective of gender, age, family status, or disability. It occurs in nearly all nations and has severe negative impacts both on individuals and on cities. Housing is the foundation for dignified, decent, and rewarding lives: evidence around the world demonstrates that street homelessness dramatically affects health and makes it more difficult to access employment or to exit extreme poverty.

Because most countries do not accurately measure street homelessness, and those that do use different methods, there is not an accurate estimate of the global extent of homelessness. However, the limited data available suggest that this is a challenge on a global scale. For example, in 2005 the Special Rapporteur on Adequate Housing as a Component of the Right to an Adequate Standard of Living reported that "United Nations estimates indicate that approximately 100 million people worldwide are without a place to live. Over 1 billion people are inadequately housed."[1]

This is a problem we must solve: the Universal Declaration of Human Rights recognizes housing as a human right. According to the UN Committee on Economic, Social, and Cultural Rights, the human right to adequate housing consists of seven elements: (1) security of tenure; (2) availability of services, materials, and infrastructure; (3) affordability; (4) accessibility; (5) habitability; (6) location; and (7) cultural adequacy.[2] People experiencing street homelessness do not have access to housing or shelter that meets these criteria, and sometimes are in situations in which not even one of these criteria is met. Street homelessness is the clearest evidence that states are failing to meet their obligation to provide housing as a basic human right.

Although there is a strong case to include homelessness in measuring progress toward a number of SDGs, one of the clearest connections is between homelessness and SDG 1, "End Poverty in All Its Forms Everywhere." Poverty is a causal factor for all forms of homelessness, and it is nearly impossible to exit extreme poverty while experiencing homelessness. There are some references to housing in SDG 1, but the connection between poverty and homelessness could be strengthened by incorporating street homelessness into measures of poverty in wealthy countries, by explicitly including housing as a component of social protection floors, and by including housing as a necessary aspect of improving the resilience of populations vulnerable to climate-related extreme events. A realistic reckoning of the connections between homelessness and poverty in this way would help ensure that country leaders, by meeting separate SDG 1 targets, meet the overall goal of ending poverty.

Poverty within the Sustainable Development Goals

Coordinated by the United Nations, the Sustainable Development Goals (SDGs) are a set of seventeen goals and 230 indicators agreed to in 2016 by representatives of 193 countries. Building on eight Millennium Goals, which expired in 2015, the SDGs are meant to be the world's most pressing challenges to address through the year 2030. They are part of the broader 2030 Sustainable Development Agenda.

Though the indicators are not technically enforceable, these goals matter. There is evidence that the priorities agreed to in the SDGs act as a focal point for philanthropy, businesses, and governments. For example, a 2017 survey of 2,400 business professionals across regions found that 60 percent integrate the SDGs directly into business strategy.[3] The SDG Funders initiative, funded by major foundations such as the Conrad N. Hilton Foundation and the Ford Foundation, tracks foundations' giving alignment with the priorities laid out in the SDGs.[4]

The SDGs' predecessor, the 2000–2015 Millennium Development Goals (MDGs), brought transparency to problems that were previously more abstract. Progress on each of the eight areas targeted by the MDGs was carefully measured, funded across regions, and publicly monitored. They fostered accountability and, less tangibly, peer pressure. The MDGs offered a platform for public and private monitoring, as political leaders received regular questions about progress and strategies for reaching the agreed goals.

It is worth noting that the SDGs and the United Nations' Habitat II and Habitat III agendas each include some version of a goal either to provide adequate shelter for all, to provide adequate housing for all, or to improve the lives of people who are homeless. However, these goals and declarations either do not mention unsheltered homelessness as indicators of progress toward adequate housing (as in the case of the SDGs), or do not have timelines, measurement, or clear goals to prompt action or allow for accountability (as is the case for the Habitat declarations).

The first and most prominent Sustainable Development Goal, "SDG 1," is to "End Poverty in All Its Forms Everywhere." Its success will be measured based on seven targets, which will each be measured by a number of indicators. The full list is available through the Department of Economic and Social Affairs' Statistical Division[5]; three targets are especially relevant to discussion of street homelessness. First, the headline target, 1.1: "By 2030, eradicate extreme poverty for all people everywhere, currently measured as people living on less than $1.25 a day." Second, target 1.3: "Implement nationally appropriate social protection systems and measures for all, including floors, and by 2030 achieve substantial coverage of the poor and the vulnerable." Finally, target 1.5: "By 2030, build the resilience of the poor and those in vulnerable situations and reduce their exposure and vulnerability to climate-related extreme events and other economic, social, and environmental shocks and disasters."

These targets stand out in relation to homelessness in ways that will be further explored in the following sections.

Homelessness and Poverty

Homelessness is connected to poverty, especially extreme poverty, in two general ways. First, poverty is a causal factor of homelessness: being poor makes an experience of homelessness much more likely. Second, being homeless makes escaping poverty nearly impossible.

Causes of homelessness vary as much by person or family as by country or region. The Canadian Homeless Hub provides a helpful classification of three categories of causes of homelessness, which are as relevant around the world as they are in Canada: structural factors, systemic failures, and personal and individual circumstances.[6] At the most general level, however, people become homeless because they cannot access the housing and supports they need in order to be stably housed. A core reason people cannot access housing and support is that they cannot afford them. This can be due to a lack of affordable housing at the structural level; to prohibitively expensive health care, transportation, or other costs; to insufficient income; to a personal network also struggling with poverty; or a combination of these. Someone living in poverty is much more vulnerable to becoming homeless than someone who is financially comfortable.

This is an intuitive idea, and it is also supported empirically by research from a number of economic contexts. In the United States and Europe, rates of homelessness are higher in countries with less generous social programs.[7] Studies from the late 1990s onward in the United States also confirm that subsidies help determine whether families experience homelessness or are successful in exiting homelessness. These include a nine-city study in the United States that found strong housing retention rates for families with histories of homelessness who were offered subsidies. In cities with follow-up data, after eighteen months 88 percent were either still in Section 8 housing (86 percent) or had moved to permanent housing (2 percent). This level of stability held no matter what type of services were offered, or which approaches were used to recruit families—in other words, the housing subsidy was the important factor.[8]

In many countries, the gap between housing and rental costs and hourly wages is significant. The National Low Income Housing Coalition each year reports on

"Housing Wages," the hourly wage a full-time worker must earn to afford a modest rental home without spending more than 30 percent of his or her income on rent and utility costs. In 2016, the housing wage in the United States was $16.35 for a one-bedroom. By contrast, the federal minimum wage was $7.25 per hour.[9] In this environment, it is not difficult to imagine why someone living in poverty or making minimum wage might be more vulnerable to homelessness. In fact, in 2016, in no United States state could a person working full-time at the federal minimum wage afford a one-bedroom apartment at the Fair Market Rent (the fortieth percentile of gross rents for standard units).

In some regions of Asia and Africa, rural-urban migration patterns driven by rural poverty contribute to high rates of homelessness in cities. Voluntary resettlement occurs in response to the pull of economic opportunity, heightened by the absence of such opportunity in rural areas. A 2015 study in Bangladesh showed that rural-urban migrants face "intensified impoverishment risks of landlessness, homelessness, and increased morbidity,"[10] as migrants are far from important family networks and are unaccustomed to urban life. Lack of adequate education or training can prevent access to the social, educational, and economic opportunities that attracted migrants to cities, resulting in low-paying and unstable employment that is not sufficient to cover housing and shelter costs. In this way, rural poverty drives migration to cities, which can lead to continued poverty and, in the absence of family networks, homelessness.

In India, there are several ways in which rural-urban migration is driven by economic considerations and leads to homelessness. For example, rural poverty drives seasonal migrants into the city to pursue work in fields like brickmaking or construction. These migrants stay in urban centers for a portion of the year, sending remittances back to their rural homes, where family members may be struggling to make ends meet. Because they send a portion of their small incomes home, they often cannot afford rent in urban slums or apartments, and instead live at "their workplaces, shop pavements, and open areas in the city," until they return home at the end of their employment.[11]

Experiencing homelessness in turn makes it difficult to get out of extreme poverty. Though data vary across regions, it is generally more difficult while homeless in any country to access employment, recover from health or mental health challenges, and even maintain basic hygiene while living on the street or in a shelter. A qualitative survey of formerly homeless adults in the United States who struggled with mental illness while they were homeless revealed that, among other factors, rules enforced by shelters and difficulty accessing mental health treatment made it challenging to access employment.[12] In addition to these physical and practical concerns, the psychological demands of housing insecurity and homelessness can complicate exits from poverty. People who sleep outside may suffer from chronic sleep deprivation and stress, which can make functioning in a workplace difficult.

Though homelessness makes it more difficult to access employment, many people who are homeless do work. In developing countries, people living on the street or in shelters often turn to the informal sector. Though difficult to measure, this undeclared work can constitute up to 20 percent of the national GDP of some southern and eastern European countries and 48 percent of nonagricultural employment in North Africa, 51 percent in Latin America, 65 percent in Asia, and 72 percent in sub-Saharan Africa.[13] For those who are homeless and can work, there is often an interest and desire to do so. In Spain in 2007, 75.7 percent of people experiencing homelessness in 2005 were unemployed, and 49.6 percent of these were consistently searching for work while seeking stable housing.[14]

Connecting Homelessness and Poverty within the Context of SDG 1

Despite the relationship between homelessness and poverty, especially extreme forms of poverty, neither SDG 1 nor any of its targets or indicators mention homelessness. There are many ways of integrating housing broadly, or homelessness specifically, into SDG 1 targets that could strengthen and make them more meaningful. This would increase the likelihood that meeting SDG 1's targets would indeed help bring an end to poverty. Three options stand out: (1) integrating housing explicitly into discussion of social protection systems; (2) integrating street homelessness as a proxy for extreme poverty in wealthy countries; and (3) including housing as a necessary aspect of improving the resilience of populations vulnerable to climate-related extreme events. There are certainly others, but any of these would provide a starting point.

Including a "Roof" as Part of Social Protection Floors

Implement nationally appropriate social protection systems and measures for all, including floors, and by 2030 achieve substantial coverage of the poor and the vulnerable.

—Sustainable Development Goal 1, Target 1.3

SDG 1 calls for the implementation of social protection systems, including a minimum standard, or a floor, that provides a basic standard of living to individuals in a country. In addition to protecting individuals, social protection floors aim to protect countries from broader shocks and stresses. Public discussion on social protection floors generally focuses on providing a basic income and access to health care. This discussion, and guidance behind Target 1.3, might explicitly include housing as a key component of ensuring that individuals have a basic standard of living. According to "Social Protection: A Coherent Strategy for Shared Prosperity," the CSocD56 Civil Society Declaration, "It is patently clear that people cannot make meaningful contributions to societal development if they are . . . fighting simply for basic survival." People experiencing street homelessness face negative outcomes related to mortality, health, ability to earn a basic income, and other basic elements of survival.

This would not be a dramatic stretch: housing is already part of the debate on social protection. For example, housing is a measure of the social protection expenditure according to the IMF, Eurostat, OECD, and the UN ECLAC.[15] The ILO's *World Social Protection Report 2017–2019* includes housing as a social service on which income security depends. As the most visible manifestation that a state has failed to provide a basic level of social protection around housing, street homelessness should be part of this discussion. Put another way: ensuring social protection requires a roof, not just a floor.

Street Homelessness as a Proxy for Extreme Poverty in Wealthy Countries

> By 2030, eradicate extreme poverty for all people everywhere, currently measured as people living on less than $1.25 a day.
>
> —Sustainable Development Goal 1, Target 1.1

Among the critiques of the first target of SDG 1 is that $1.25 per day is too low a bar to appropriately cover extreme poverty in higher-income countries, where someone living on $5 or even $10 a day would be considered extremely poor. As a result, this target does not do enough to motivate higher-income countries to action. The second target somewhat accounts for differences in economic and development contexts by linking progress to national poverty lines rather than a global standard: "By 2030, reduce at least by half the proportion of men, women, and children of all ages living in poverty in all its dimensions according to national definitions." Still, this target addresses poverty but not the most extreme forms of poverty. There is a need for a clean, global yardstick with a clear set of indicators to assess the most severe forms of poverty worldwide in order to eliminate them. This yardstick should define extreme poverty in a way that would be ambitious for wealthy as well as lower- and middle-income countries to eliminate.

Instead of setting only the global figure of $1.25 per day, this target might instead include metrics for extreme poverty across countries with specific economic profiles. In a model like this, the wealthiest countries might simply use street homelessness as a proxy for, or as part of the definition of, extreme poverty.

Homelessness and Climate-Related Events

> By 2030, build the resilience of the poor and those in vulnerable situations and reduce their exposure and vulnerability to climate-related extreme events and other economic, social, and environmental shocks and disasters.
>
> —Sustainable Development Goal 1, Target 1.5

People without homes are especially susceptible to the impact of climate change. People who live on the street are more exposed to the day-to-day effects of climate change, such as heat and cold, as well as events such as storms and floods. Further, there is evidence that street homeless individuals who have substance use and mental health challenges may make decisions around seeking shelter during an emergency that could lead to harm or mortality during extreme events.[16] Within the indicators measuring progress toward Target 1.5, housing, or at a minimum, shelter, should be discussed as a necessary aspect of improving the resilience of populations vulnerable to climate-related extreme events. People living on the street should also be specifically included and addressed as a subpopulation of "those in vulnerable situations," so that countries are incentivized to account for how they will be protected.

Notes

1. UN Commission on Human Rights, "Report of the Special Rapporteur on Adequate Housing as a Component of the Right to an Adequate Standard of Living," Miloon Kothari: 2005. E/CN.4/2005/48.

2. Office of the United Nations High Commissioner for Human Rights, "The Right to Adequate Housing." Fact Sheet No. 21/Rev.1, https://www.ohchr.org/Documents/Publications/FS21_rev_1_Housing_en.pdf.

3. See *Ethical Corporation*'s Responsible Business Trends Report 2017, http://www.ethicalcorp.com/60-companies-are-integrating-sdgs-business-strategy.

4. The mission and members of the SDG Funders group is available at http://sdgfunders.org/.

5. The formal indicators list is available through the UN Statistical Commission website: https://unstats.un.org/sdgs/indicators/indicators-list/.

6. Canadian Observatory on Homelessness, York University, Toronto. "The Homeless Hub," https://www.homelesshub.ca.

7. Marybeth Shinn, "Homelessness, Poverty and Social Exclusion in the United States and Europe," *European Journal of Homelessness* 4 (2010): 19–44.

8. Debra J. Rog, C. Scott Holupka, and Kimberly L. McCombs-Thornton, "Implementation of the Homeless Families Program: 1 Service Models and Preliminary Outcomes," *American Journal of Orthopsychiatry* 65, no. 4 (1995): 502–13.

9. National Low Income Housing Coalition, "Out of Reach 2016: No Refuge for Low Income Renters," *National Low Income Housing Coalition*, May 25, 2016.

10. Naoko Kaida and Miah M. Tofail, "Rural-urban Perspectives on Impoverishment Risks in Development-Induced Involuntary Resettlement in Bangladesh," *Habitat International* 50 (2015): 73–79.

11. Rameez Abbas and Divya Varma, "Internal Labor Migration in India Raises Integration Challenges for Migrants," *Migration Policy Institute*, March 3, 2014.

12. Daniel Poremski, Rob Whitley, and Eric Latimer, "Barriers to Obtaining Employment for People with Severe Mental Illness Experiencing Homelessness," *Journal of Mental Health* 23, no. 4 (2014): 181–85.

13. Paolo Brusa, "What's Informal about the Informal Economy?" *Homeless in Europe Magazine*, December 28, 2007, 8–11, http://www.multipolis.eu/uploads/documenti/2007_feantsa_brusa_whats_informal_about_informal_economy_EN.pdf.

14. Fundación San Martín de Porres, *Multiple Barriers, Multiple Solutions: Inclusion into and through Employment for People Who Are Homeless in Europe*, Annual Report, European Federation of National Organisations Working with the Homeless, 2007.

15. International Labour Organization, *World Social Protection Report 2017–2019*, p. 203, http://www.social-protection.org,

16. Brodie Ramin and Tomislav Svoboda, "Health of the Homeless and Climate Change," *Journal of Urban Health: Bulletin of the New York Academy of Medicine* 86, no, 4 (2009): 654–64.

Homelessness and SDG 3

Rosanne Haggerty

Not long ago, it didn't seem that much could be done about rates of smoking or deaths from drunk driving. They were in a different category of health issue than providing access to care, finding improved treatments, or preparing for flu season—the problems health care or public health systems typically handled. These were messier. There were legal dimensions, contested policy questions, a need to change individual behaviors and choices, and a general acceptance of these problems as the unfortunate collateral damage of modern life.

Yet this "reality" changed within a generation. Rates of smoking in the United States are now at their lowest since statistics were first collected in the early 1960s; deaths from drunk driving have been cut in half since the early 1980s; and continued, dramatic reductions in smoking and traffic-related deaths and injuries worldwide are key indicators of progress for reaching Sustainable Development Goal (SDG) 3, "Ensure healthy lives and promote well-being for all at all ages." These types of complex health problems *could* be solved, it turned out, but they required a new approach.

Though homelessness is typically discussed in the context of SDG 11 (Target 1: "By 2030, ensure access for all to adequate, safe and affordable housing and basic services and upgrade slums"), this essay reflects on homelessness in the context of SDG 3, and how to increase the probability that SDG 3 can be achieved by making homelessness rare, brief, and nonrecurring for those who experience it.

Homelessness is not referenced in SDG 3, yet there is ample evidence to support our own lived awareness that health and well-being are inseparable from the basic conditions of our lives. The health and well-being of those living on the street or in temporary shelters is profoundly compromised. And for those who would benefit from the specific initiatives of SDG 3—the expectant mothers, newborn infants, those with chronic diseases, or those in need of vaccines or improved health systems or whose lives would be protected by better traffic safety and anti-smoking interventions—investment in these other dimensions of health will be undermined if their beneficiaries are also homeless. It's all connected.

A way to ensure greater success in reaching the SDG 3 goals is to change our approach to homelessness in every community. Recognizing homelessness as a complex health problem, and applying what's been learned about how these types of problems are tamed, is already reducing homelessness in communities that have adopted this approach. The starting point for any community is rejecting the notion that homelessness is inevitable, the unfortunate collateral damage of modern life, and instead making it a problem one's community intends to solve.

Many actors played a role in creating the new reality on smoking and drunk driving: researchers, victims, and family members, schools of public health, and voluntary organizations like the American Cancer Society and Mothers Against Drunk Driving (MADD) that mobilized education and advocacy campaigns and a shared strategy to make smoking and drunk driving socially unacceptable. There were closely coordinated tactics aimed at the range of structures and assumptions that enabled smoking and drunk driving. Smoke-free laws and seatbelt requirements were passed. Lawsuits forced accountability back on cigarette manufacturers, bar owners, and others who profited from the status quo. Treatments, such as nicotine patches, were improved. Funders—insurers, government, philanthropy, employers—created incentives to help smokers quit. Enforcement of driving-under-the-influence laws increased with the help of new technologies, like improved breathalyzers. Penalties for violating relevant laws became more severe. Ultimately, the shift to a solution mind-set has involved all of us in enforcing or living within new norms.

The misdiagnosis of homelessness as a problem of individuals or housing markets alone has impeded the kind of relentless, coordinated, opposite-of-silver-bullet action that shifted the ground on smoking, drunk driving, HIV-AIDS, and other complex health problems. Despite that, dozens of communities in the United States and Canada are now working in this relentless, coordinated, data-driven, whole of community, no-excuses way on homelessness. And they are getting results.

Homelessness and Health

One image captures what for many years was hard to see about homelessness: that it is a health problem.

In the early 2000s, Dr. Jim O'Connell, the founder of Boston's Healthcare for the Homeless[1] and a pioneer in bringing medical care to those living on the street, shared a photo of about a dozen ordinary looking men in their twenties through forties, sitting along a wall in shirt-sleeves on a summer day. The picture had been taken seven years earlier of some of those he and his colleagues cared for on the street. Now, he said, all but one of the youngish-seeming men were dead. The causes of their deaths included liver disease, end-stage renal disease, previous cold or hot weather injuries, HIV-AIDS, and for many, mental health and physical health conditions combined. Dr. O'Connell's research proved that homelessness, when combined with these conditions, had dramatically accelerated what might otherwise have been preventable mortality. The specific causes differed from one individual to the next, as Dr. O'Connell described, but the *principal treatment each man had needed was housing.*

Simply looking at the men in the photograph, it was not evident that a death sentence was upon them. But their story made a powerful case that homelessness was as much a health issue as a housing issue, and that solutions might lie in closing the gap between these two fields.

When modern homelessness became an acknowledged problem in the United States in the late 1970s and early 1980s, the mental health challenges of many of the newly homeless were evident. The de-institutionalization movement had closed asylums without creating the promised system of community-based housing and mental health services. This catastrophic failure was visible in the behavior of those struggling with mental health issues on the street, but the tendency to regard mental health issues as something separate from health issues kept the broader health effects hidden.

My colleagues and I began to see the relationship between housing and health in encountering those moving from homelessness into our permanent supportive housing residences in New York City.[2] Those who had been homeless the longest all seemed to have serious health problems and a history of many encounters with area hospitals. We had prioritized those with serious mental illnesses and those diagnosed with HIV-AIDS when renting out units in our buildings, but found that almost everyone coming from chronic homelessness was in terrible health. Stories of broken health would emerge in conversation or too often, when residents ended up in the hospital. It was far too common to learn of residents with advanced cancer, heart disease, kidney and liver diseases, skin infections and open wounds that wouldn't heal, even tuberculosis. It seemed that despite frequent hospital stays in the past, almost no one had gotten proper follow-up care while homeless, and that returning to the street or a shelter after a hospital stay undid the benefits of whatever treatment they had received.

This was in the mid-to-late 1990s. Within the next decade, our experience that homelessness destroyed individuals' health was confirmed in a series of studies probing the financial and health consequences of homelessness.

Among the influential cost studies, Dennis Culhane's[3] analysis of homelessness in New York City showed that responding to homelessness as a never-ending emergency, with more and more short-term measures, showed up most starkly in health care systems. The costs of providing emergency health care and temporary shelter, plus the cost of jail stays attributable to those experiencing homelessness, nearly matched what it would cost to provide each person with a stable home.

Funds for rent subsidies to help people move into a home were always scarce, however, while, as Culhane pointed out, emergency services were limitless. Shortly after the release of this study, I watched as eight emergency vehicles responded after a disheveled looking man pushing a cart with his belongings fell near a construction crane and was brought by ambulance to a nearby public hospital where he was seen briefly in the emergency room but not admitted. My colleagues and I called various New York City offices to calculate the cost to the public of the incident. $4,800 was the conservative estimate. At the time, this would have paid the gentleman's rent at a small apartment for four months.

A 2006 study by John Billings[4] of high utilizers of New York City's largest public hospital revealed the flip side of the story: that the health care system itself was straining under the burden of treating those experiencing homelessness. Suffering from conditions like cellulitis, schizophrenia, alcohol and substance abuse; and multiple chronic conditions, 58 percent of the patients in their highest utilizer group were found to be without a stable home.

The human costs of homelessness were also becoming clearer.

A 2005 study conducted by New York City's Department of Health and Mental Hygiene (DOHMH)[5] and Department of Homeless Services assessed the health impacts of homelessness on the health of those experiencing homelessness. Death rates of homeless single adults were found to be twice that of nonhomeless adults, rising with the length of time a person remained homeless. Prolonged homelessness was, as a colleague said at the time, a condition with worse mortality rates than many cancers.

The relationship between health and homelessness was increasingly clear, but it was not clear how to integrate the two to drive improvements in health and reductions in homelessness.

A Certain Type of Problem

Problems that are multifaceted, dynamic, and don't clearly live in one space have emerged as a certain type of challenge: *complex problems*. With complex problems, filling in the spaces between pieces of the solution is as important as each component itself. In the case of homelessness, this means that health care providers, organizations assisting the homeless, and operators of housing must learn to function as a single, accountable team.

Complex or "wicked" problems have been defined as those where there is "little or no agreement on the definition of the problem (owing to multiple values, perceptions, and perspectives); clear solutions to the problem, owing to the wide array of possible solutions and trade-offs associated with each; or easily identified causes or authority due to the problem having multiple potential causes, jurisdictions, stakeholders and regulators or implications."[6] Unlike technical problems that can yield to technical solutions (e.g., build more housing), complex problems require distinct mind-sets, approaches, and tools to integrate many moving and changing elements and establish accountability for producing results.

Certain sectors have, of necessity, developed ways to tame complex problems. In advanced manufacturing, aviation, and construction, for example, work is done in teams; real-time, specific data on how all the parts are coming together guide immediate corrective action and testing of improvements. This is also true in global health. Successful campaigns to eradicate diseases, curtail outbreaks, and reduce threats like smoking and drunk driving are among the best examples of complex problem-solving at work. By definition, these are the problems that involve many actors, where lives are at stake, and where it must be the job of everyone involved to assure that the problem is solved, day in and day out, and that nothing, and no one, falls through the cracks.

When complex problems are being solved, they are invisible: your plane lands safely; your Toyota is still going strong after 200,000 miles; no injuries occurred on the local construction site. Complex problems are solvable, but they require a distinct approach.

Not recognizing when a problem is complex generally ends up with lots of money spent and limited progress to show. In places that have defined homelessness as a housing or resource problem alone, homelessness has often continued to increase significantly—in New York City, for example, despite more than 32,000 permanent supportive housing apartments created in recent years and billions more spent on temporary shelter, homelessness is at a near all-time high. Solving a complex problem first requires shared accountability for results.

The idea of a world without traffic fatalities seemed far-fetched until I met with Paul Steely White, who was the executive director of Transportation Alternatives in New York City until late 2018. Paul and his team brought Vision Zero to New York by making it a campaign issue for mayoral candidates in 2013. With Vision Zero came an accountability mind-set: that zero traffic fatalities and serious injuries was the only acceptable goal or measure of a community's performance on a life-and-death issue.

Vision Zero[7] is now an international movement. It began in Sweden in 1997 by turning old assumptions upside down. It stated that road safety was equally a responsibility of communities as of drivers, and that better-designed roads, cars, and policies could make drivers and communities safer. In Vision Zero communities throughout the world, traffic engineers, police, data scientists, and safety advocates—including victims of traffic crashes and their families—regularly review information on where crashes have occurred and develop targeted design and/or enforcement measures to prevent future harms. They continually study patterns to spot emerging problem areas, test interventions, check results, and make improvements. In the five years since Vision Zero was launched in New York, traffic fatalities have decreased by a third.

Our meeting with Paul confirmed what we had seen elsewhere: successful approaches to complex problems transcend their issue-specific concerns. The different areas of focus of Vision Zero with its goal of eliminating traffic casualties, and the Built for Zero movement to end homelessness are less significant than that we think and work similarly with the aim of solving a complex health problem for a whole population.

The similarities begin with a mind-set that the problem is solvable, for everyone, and a commitment to work back from the desired end state. There is the recognition that it must be a team commitment, with all the key actors in a community sharing the goal and accountability for the result.

Real time, specific information is critical (e.g., what were the circumstances of the particular crash? Who specifically is homeless?), and a new culture of testing and improving is needed, with training for teams in problem-solving skills such as quality improvement and data analytics. Tactics must shift as data show how the problem is moving and changing. Investments and policy are flexible and adaptive, driven by what is actually happening on the ground and what is required to make further and future progress.

Within an accountable "system" with these features, the services, housing, advocacy efforts—the activities of organizations engaged in a given complex health issue, if aligned with what is needed and effective—add up to more than the sum of their parts. The anonymity and enormity of problems is stripped away as they become specific, actionable, measurable, and shared.

Measurably Reducing Homelessness to Improve Health and Well-being

If the picture of homeless men in Boston, slowly dying of conditions made lethal by their homelessness, marked a first glimpse into the connection between health and a stable home, a new picture illuminates an unfolding future.

Angie Walker, coordinator of services for the homeless in the city of Rockford, Illinois, is leading the weekly meeting of all the local organizations working to end homelessness in Rockford. Around the table the team is referencing the same prioritized "by-name list" of all those experiencing homelessness in the community. Because they have taken the anonymity out of homelessness and know everyone by name, they know that individuals' circumstances vary widely and that there are multiple paths out of homelessness. Many can resolve their homelessness if they receive the legal, medical, financial, or other help that will resolve the problem that caused them to become homeless. Others will need some financial help for a time to cover the rent while they get back on their feet or find a job. Some will need a whole package of help: an affordable apartment and a support worker to help with health, mental health, or other needs. The group is discussing how to target their resources. They have already ended chronic homelessness and homelessness among military veterans, and they are well on their way to ending youth homelessness. They are steadily moving toward making all homelessness rare, brief, and nonrecurring. Behind Walker on the wall is a chart showing Rockford's month-by-month progress and the changes they've seen as the result of rigorously testing their latest ideas for reaching zero. Long-term homelessness with its lethal health risks is becoming a thing of the past

Rockford, population 360,000, is northwest of Chicago. It resembles many "Rust Belt" cities that flourished during the manufacturing era and have struggled as factories closed and jobs disappeared in the latter part of the twentieth century. It is a typical American community. Rockford's approach to homelessness had been typical as well, largely focused on providing temporary shelter and other emergency assistance to the homeless.

We met the Rockford leaders for the first time when the city joined the 100,000 Homes Campaign,[8] organized by Community Solutions, the not-for-profit I lead. This campaign brought together communities across the United States to identify and house 100,000 chronically homeless and medically vulnerable individuals experiencing homelessness during a four-year period. We aimed to learn together what it would take to go beyond providing services to actually *ending* homelessness.

The insight at the heart of 100,000 Homes was that the way communities organized their response to homelessness was the key ingredient in whether they would end it. We had learned through our early work as developers of permanent supportive housing that it was too often no one's job to end homelessness in a community: Not-for-profits provide services or advocated for more services. Government agencies focused on compliance with rules. Amid rising homelessness, rising spending, and a rising awareness of the health risks of homelessness, we wanted to learn with others how to fill this accountability gap and get people housed. We aimed to restore a sense of urgency to the issue by highlighting the health consequences for those experiencing homelessness.

More than 105,000 people were housed by the 186 communities that participated in 100,000 Homes. But no community had ended homelessness by the time the campaign ended in July 2014. Rockford was one of the 70 communities that stepped forward again when we asked for volunteers prepared to figure how to finish the job and get all the way to a sustainable end to veteran and chronic homelessness in their city or county. The new effort is Built for Zero.[9]

In eleven places, Built for Zero communities have now ended chronic or veteran homelessness, and another 32 are well on their way, showing steady reductions. What has evolved is a methodology for approaching homelessness as a complex problem. It draws on the mind-set, tools, and skills developed in sectors that deal successfully with complex problems and produce reliable systems that protect vulnerable people from harm:

1. A shift of *belief*, from seeing homelessness as inevitable and unchangeable, to solvable
2. A shift of *organization*, from individual programs to a whole community response, anchored by a clear "command center" structure with all key actors represented, with all sharing data, and with a clear structure for decision making
3. A shift in *information*, from generalized or estimated data on homelessness, to by-name, real-time data on how it is being specifically experienced by each individual or family
4. A shift in *culture*, from compliance and rigid planning to problem solving and iterative testing and improvement
5. A shift in *investments*, from historic spending practices to flexible, data-driven, targeted investments to fill gaps in a community's housing/health system.

Making these shifts involves a community team learning new problem-solving skills. These skills are needed to end homelessness but in addition to face every complex problem: how to collaborate across divisional lines; how to establish a fact base for an issue or condition and to use valid information to monitor progress; how to pose ideas for testing and improvement rather than argumentation; how to facilitate meetings and conversations to reach decisions and clear next actions. Ways to teach these practices have been figured out in various sectors, but few organizations working with the homeless had been exposed to data analytics, human-centered design, quality improvement, and other proven methodologies for taming complex problems. Training communities in these skills, coaching them in working through each barrier to zero, and clearing their path in any way possible is the work of our Built for Zero team.

We've also seen the profoundly social nature of change: communities exceed what they imagine they are capable of when they are part of a larger movement and drawing on one another's learning and momentum. Built for Zero is a movement to end homelessness, a methodology, and a learning collaborative. We bring community teams together throughout the year for them to share what is working and what hasn't, and to celebrate each other's progress and support each other's resolve and momentum through the demanding journey.

The belief that homelessness can be ended is spreading. In addition to Built for Zero in the United States, a Canadian Built for Zero movement is also under way, and the Institute of Global Homelessness,[10] an initiative of London-based Depaul International and DePaul University in Chicago, has launched A Place to Call Home. This involves a dozen vanguard cities, spread across six continents, that are testing approaches to reduce or end street homelessness. The goal: have 150 cities achieving measurable reductions in street homelessness by 2030, in line with the Sustainable Development Goals.

Whether homelessness increases or decreases by 2030 will directly affect attainment of SDG 1 (End poverty in all its forms everywhere), SDG 11, and SDG 3, but weaves through every goal as a last-mile indicator. Will the most vulnerable and marginalized be reached by progress on quality education, inequality, food security, decent work, gender equality, accountable institutions, and every environmental or global partnership goal? Progress in ending homelessness is a powerful measure.

Notes

1. Boston's Healthcare for the Homeless, https://www.bhchp.org.

2. The author founded and from 1990 to 2010 led Common Ground Community (now Breaking Ground), a developer and operator of housing for the homeless, https://breakingground.org.

3. Dennis Culhane, Stephen Metraux, and Trevor Hadley, "Public Service Reductions Associated with Placement of Homeless Persons with Severe Mental Illness in Supportive Housing," *Housing Policy Debate* 13 (2002): 107–63.

4. John Billings and Tod Mijanovich, "Improving the Management of Care for High-Cost Medicaid Patients," *Health Affairs* 26 (2007): 1643–55.

5. New York City's Departments of Health and Mental Hygiene and Homeless Services, *The Health of Homeless Adults in New York City* (December 2005), https://www1.nyc.gov/assets/doh/downloads/pdf/epi/epi-homeless-200512.pdf.

6. Horst Rittel and Melvin M. Webber, "Dilemmas in a General Theory of Planning," *Policy Sciences* 4, no. 2 (June 1973): 155.

7. In the United States, the Vision Zero Network supports participating cities, https://visionzeronetwork.org.

8. For case study and independent evaluation of 100,000 Homes Campaign see https://www.world-habitat.org/world-habitat-awards/winners-and-finalists/the-100000-homes-campaign/ and https://www.urban.org/sites/default/files/publication/44391/2000148-Evaluation-of-the-100000-Homes-Campaign.pdf.

9. Launched in January 2015 as *Zero:2016*. https://www.community.solutions/what-we-do/built-for-zero.

10. Institute of Global Homelessness, https://www.ighomelessness.org/a-place-to-call-home-initiative.

Homelessness and SDG 11

A Neoliberal Paradox?

Toussaint Kafarhire, SJ

Some major African cities have been busy face-lifting in the last twenty years. They keep revamping the obsolete infrastructure system inherited from colonial days. As the process of changing the face of the continent continues, urbanization promises a better life not only through expanding one's cultural experiences beyond the confines of rural and traditional realms and providing chances to acquire a better education, but also through exposure to multicultural friendships and cosmopolitan values. Such prospects explain why people choose to migrate from rural to urban settings. Seeing the hopes for social, economic, and political transformations generated by urbanization, rural populations keep migrating to the cities to benefit from these improved living conditions.

The urbanization of Africa is growing rapidly, as shown by the increasing number of urban dwellers in major African cities. Only 5 million people lived in Lagos in 1980, for instance, as compared to its 20 million residents today. Likewise, in 1980, 7,135,507 out of 26,357,462 people in Zaïre (now the Democratic Republic of Congo), or 27.1 percent of the general population, lived in urban areas. In 2018 the population size has reached 84,004,989, and people living in cities are estimated at 33,989,753 or 40.5 percent of the general population.

The trend toward greater urbanization and the gentrification of certain neighborhoods, which forms the basis of the neoliberal paradox in Africa, are undeniable. But the rural to urban exodus has made the housing situation in cities more precarious, forcing the poor living in slums to become homeless altogether. In 2016, a UN-Habitat report noted that "sub-Saharan Africa alone accounts for 56 percent of the total increase in the number of slum dwellers among developing regions between 1990 and 2014. [Yet], the number of slum dwellers in sub-Saharan Africa has grown in tandem with growth in the region's urban population."[1] In light of this, the neoliberal promise that "a rising tide will lift all boats" seems contradictory, and raises questions. Why has increased urbanization in Africa created more homelessness and marginalization than less? And why is there still a lack of good social policies to tackle the problem of homelessness?

This chapter is a reflection on this neoliberal paradox. It is divided into three parts. The first section introduces the reality of homelessness in the changing context of revamping African cities. It uses Nairobi, in Kenya, as a metonym for homelessness on the continent. The second section examines the neoliberal development paradox and argues that neoliberalist welfare ideology puts absolute value on market operations at the expense of economic and social justice policies. And the third section focuses on the United Nations' Sustainable Development Goals (SDGs), more specifically, SDG 11, which invites the cities of the future to become more inclusive, more humane, safer, more resilient, and more sustainable. For "urban areas will [indeed] be increasingly critical for achieving all SDGs and integrating the social, economic and environmental goals set forth in the 2030 Agenda."[2] Indeed, true development, according to Catholic Social Teaching (CST), is always holistic and entails moral commitment to the welfare of all, including the generations to come and the future of our planet. The conclusion draws a parallel between SDG 11 and CST, as the former resonates with Pope Francis's spirituality of stewardship of our common home, which he develops in his 2015 encyclical *Laudato Si'*.

Africa at a Historic Crossroads

Africa stands today at a historic crossroads. Almost six decades after their independence, African nations are gradually moving away from old colonial ties, expanding their global outreach and seeking new business opportunities beyond the traditional postcolonial Western partnerships. They count a younger and vibrant generation of intellectuals who have embraced the ideals of globalization. These African enthusiasts have shed the old grudges against the past and the racial inferiority complex, and now regard the world as their home. While demanding a fair share of the benefits of human progress—including greater freedom, participation, and human dignity—this generation of Africans prefers to live in urban settings. It is thus involved in building the kind of future it wants for itself and for its children.

The African urban landscape is changing fast everywhere. In the last twenty years, impressive transformations have affected the urban infrastructures inherited from colonial times. In Nairobi, Kinshasa, Luanda, Abidjan, Dakar, Accra, and Lagos, to name but a few, the transformation of African major cities is remarkable in the latest development trends. No other city exemplifies the current trends in urbanization better than Nairobi. The Kenyan capital is undergoing infrastructure changes that include construction of new estates, shopping malls, and commercial centers; revamping of an obsolete railway system; construction of new roads; and gentrification of whole neighborhoods. The Jomo Kenyatta International Airport (JKIA) has been upgraded to the standards of comfort for all modern airports. Nairobi has become the hub for most international gatherings taking place in Africa. Yet while the city is bubbling with so much economic and cultural activity, a whole segment of the population is still left out. These invisible homeless people blend in with the urban population in the streets of Nairobi, roaming day and night in search of something to eat. This contradiction between the rapid rate of urban development and the worsening of conditions for the poor requires a more in-depth analysis for better social policies.

Urbanization, as Joan Clos notes, is an "untapped tool for development and economic growth."[3] But this "untapped tool for development and economic growth" seems to ignore the plight of homeless people. The focus is on improving physical infrastructures rather than on investing in human beings and enabling them to shape the kind of future they want. A neoliberal opportunism has rendered sightless decision makers who pursue monies and labor loans from new donors such as the Chinese government and its companies. This too is the reality of Nairobi's urbanization trend, where the experience of homeless people remains unchanged despite the economic boom the city is experiencing.

I recently met a twenty-six-year-old Nairobi street-dweller who spends most of his time around the Globe cinema roundabout. He had come to Nairobi two years before to look for a job, and all he wanted was a new opportunity in life. Unfortunately, he still has not found employment. Although homeless, he says he avoids hanging out with other street homeless youth because whenever a crowd of street people is spotted by the police, they are suspected of plotting some mischief. He sleeps in shops' verandas on rainy days and has developed new habits—a euphemism for new addictions—like chewing *khat* (or Miraa).[4] His dream is to be able to return to school one day.

Another man, probably in his mid-sixties, living in Ngara (an area in northeastern Nairobi), shares a heartbreaking story about his current state of separation from his family. He was once married and had three children from that marriage. But he neither gets to see them today nor does he have the courage or the intention to look for them. "Why would I?" he asks rhetorically. "I have no money to help them, anyway." The level of despondency he has reached shows how cruel and dehumanizing poverty can be. As he grows tired of his homeless situation, his dream is to find a job, perhaps as a watchman, or anything that can allow him to earn some money to pay rent. He recalls that the last time he paid rent, it cost him about Ksh 2000 per month (about US$20).

These two stories show that behind every face of a homeless man or woman, there is a painful experience and shattered dreams, but also hope. The marginalization of the worst-off increases along with the number of homeless people. According to some UN-Habitat statistics, about 199 million Africans lived in slums in 2005, representing 20 percent of the world's total slum dwellers. In 2010, the same UN agency stated that 72 percent of all African urban dwellers lived in slums and informal settlements.[5] Despite the proliferation of construction sites, more than 60,000 children are destitute and live as homeless in Nairobi alone.[6] The poor are affected even more negatively by the destruction of their neighborhoods, without compensation, through urbanization trends.

In the wake of its new constitution in 2010, the Kenyan government developed a policy framework, the National Child Protection, in 2011, showing the specific roles of government—at the county and the national levels—in protecting the rights of children. The policy hoped to "deliver a more integrated approach to child protection and drive improvements across all systems and all jurisdictions. It also provided a mechanism for engaging non-state partners, including non-state actors, children, and the broader community at the national level."[7] Yet eight years later, the government's response to street homelessness has been either sluggish or inappropriate. The Kenyan national welfare policy was delegated to county governments, defining its role as that of coordinating and aligning children's activities with county governments' plans and programs, but critics have argued that there are no clear guidelines on whose responsibility it is to cater for the welfare of street children, or for the youth and families living on the streets. Additionally, as county governments were tasked with mobilizing resources on behalf of children, facilitating training for children's officers and area advisory councils, and implementing the National Data Information System in every subcounty, the national and the county governments continue to argue about whose responsibility it is to house and rehabilitate street children.

In May 2017, efforts by the Kenyan police to remove children from the Nairobi city streets and return them to their respective homes or enroll them in the Nairobi County government care centers (including rehabilitation centers in Shauri Moyo, Joseph Kang'ethe, Kayole, and Bahati)[8] were a fiasco. Program managers still deny that children were admitted into any of these centers, and street families that were involved feel they were not treated with dignity by these state agents. A young man who witnessed this police action explained that the Nairobi County government officials arrested members of street families and forced them to work without pay. "While we are in need of the basic human necessities like food, shelter and clothing, the *askaris* [police] told us that we should go back to our homes almost as if it was a choice to be on the street." Another individual claimed that the *askaris* from the Nairobi County government harassed them all the time. Having neither a place to sleep nor bedding to cover himself at night, he confided that both his parents are still alive, though he hasn't seen either of them since leaving home three years ago. Remembering how his parents mistreated him, he explained that, "All we want is an alternative to this kind of life, a place to sleep and even go back to school."

Why have developments in urban infrastructure not improved the lives of slum-dwellers and homeless people? What is the meaning of all the housing and infrastructure growth if slums and homeless people keep increasing? The neoliberal development agenda raises the question about priorities between human dignity and the transformation of urban infrastructure.

Paradoxes of the
Neoliberal Development Model

Regardless of their location, age, or experience—whether in Lagos, Kinshasa, Luanda, Nairobi, or elsewhere—most homeless people do not choose street life because it is more appealing to them. As the few personal stories above illustrate, most of them are actively hoping and looking for a job to escape the harshness of street life. They did not end up in the streets because they were too lazy to work, and homelessness does not stem from individual failure alone—it also epitomizes the disruption of the African traditional family system and cultures.

Take for instance the trickle-down theory that says that a rising tide will lift all boats, which was used to sell globalization ideals in the early 1980s and 1990s. This belief paved the way for the gradual privatization that reduced the role of the state to the protection of property rights, enforcement of contracts between stakeholders, and regulation of the money supply for sound exchange.[9] As a theory of welfare, neoliberalism advances the argument that the states' only role is to promote strong private property rights, free markets, and free trade. Thus, homeless people are to blame for their failure in life and deserve their current conditions. While the neoliberal ideology is used to obfuscate, exonerate, and justify the historical and institutional processes that produced the complex realities of the kind of societies we live in, homelessness is blamed on individual failures. But to ignore the history of institutions and ideas that produced the societies we live in would be misleading. As French historian François Dosse notes, the past is indeed the most cumbersome presence and, possibly, the richest.[10] For there can be no existence of the present without the presence of the past, nor can there be lucidity and understanding of the present without consciousness of the past.

Providing an interpretative framework within which individualism, faulty historical processes, and the resulting institutions are extolled at the expense of the common good and the human dignity of the poor, the neoliberal ideology equated the optimization of economic performance through market efficiency and technical progress with development. As Jesuit priest Peter Henriot suggests, every form of social organization, including government policies, the function of society, and even the role of the state, were all subjected to this unrestricted free market.[11] Hence, while overlooking the forms of systemic distortions and historical processes in the neoliberal development model, most social policies and distributional justice imperatives were relegated to the back seat in the neoliberal world order.

As a result, African postcolonial states lost their power to control and orient their social policies, on the one hand, and, on the other hand, multinational corporations become kings because they can contribute more monies in taxes upon which most postcolonial states increasingly depend. The corporations can decide under which conditions social policies are adopted and implemented, or whether to provide social relief through humanitarian organization, reducing citizens from subjects of rights to objects of charity. In such an environment, citizens no longer constitute the right source of the state's legitimacy where the delocalized needs, wishes, and interests of consumers are central to the benchmarks of good governance and economic development. As a result, many states feel no obligation to work toward social justice, seeking instead to promote the market interests of the few super-wealthy.

SDG 11 and Catholic Social Teaching

It becomes critically important to address the question of whether urbanization in Africa is affecting only physical space or if these current development projects perpetuate the trend of marginalizing whole segments of the population. The question becomes that of learning whether the transformations affecting most African capital cities are merely cosmetic or if they ever reach those who need and deserve them the most. Can and should African cities uncritically follow this neoliberal model of growth that concentrates wealth in the hands of few at the expense of the many? If the current physical transformations of African cities follow the dictate of the neoliberal development while ignoring the imperative to update social infrastructures, then the problem is a serious one. As well, the trickle-down promise of globalization benefits is but a remote dream.

The transformation of most African cities today is made possible thanks to Chinese development loans. China has become the most important driving force behind current trends in African urbanization. In 2017, for instance, China launched a ten-year project conducted by the Chinese multinational company Haite to build an industrial city in the city of Tangier, in Morocco. With an estimated project cost of US$10 billion, the city is expected to host up to 200 different Chinese companies.[12] Another Chinese multinational enterprise, the China Republic's Consortium Citic (CRCC), has invested US$6.2 billion in Algiers to build a portion of the East-West highway. The work is conducted by China Railways Construction Corporation, the same company that is rehabilitating 633km of railway between Dakar and Kidira at a cost of 1.15 billion Euros. The Harbour Engineering Company (CHEC), another Chinese company, is modernizing the seaports both in Cote d'Ivoire's capital, Abidjan, at US$1.2 billion and Cameroon's town of Kribi at US$1.422 billion. Sinohydro is constructing electric dams in Benin at a cost of 405 million Euros, and a similar project is being implanted in Gabon at a cost of US$398 million. Huawei, the Chinese electronic giant, is installing 2,000km of optic fiber in Burkina Faso at 175.3 million Euros. In 2007, China signed a contract worth $6 billion with the government of the Democratic Republic of Congo in a barter of minerals exploitation for infrastructural development (roads, hospitals, stadiums). In short, the degree of China's involvement in development projects in Africa is simply astounding.

Fearing Beijing's hunger for resources, which would not only erode the influence of Western countries since the colonization period, but also saddle the vast central African nation (DRC) with unmanageable debt, the question becomes an ethical concern. Is this neoliberal development approach viable when it shows little care for the environment, the human cost, and the future of our planet?[13]

The UN's SDGs are an expression of the global consciousness reached about our common future. Our human consciousness is the faculty that we have to inform our perception and interpretation of the reality in which we live. In the words of Irish Jesuit scholar and philosopher of science Patrick Heelan, "Human consciousness has sensory experience, it produces new insights, it tests for relevant truth in the world, and makes free value-laden decisions . . . , it adds meanings to the physical and neurological codes and signals, technically called information, to which it is responding."[14]

The SDGs suggesting inclusiveness and sustainability need to be factored in our definition and practices of development today. This is what the Catholic tradition views as social justice, where, more than redistribution of goods, the concern of development should be primarily focused on the fundamental dignity of all. Justice concerns the way in which major social arrangements distribute fundamental rights and duties. The state, as the central institution, is tasked with the redistribution of primary social goods, the regulation of political relations, and the balancing of individual subjective preferences with the common good.[15]

Conclusion

It is important to understand the level of *subtle* penetration of the neoliberal ideology into Africa during the last three decades through politics, economics, and culture. This ideology has led us to take for granted a model of development that ignores and leaves out the dimension of the poor in its calculation. That is where we need to understand and operationalize new changes in planning development, which first has to happen at the level of human consciousness before it trickles down into our practices and institutions. The human condition, social action, and historical institutions are all a result of the dominant cultural self-understandings and the construction of meaning. To that effect, SDG 11 proposes that the global community should confront the new emerging trends and the challenges posed by a neoliberal model of urbanization. That is, SDG 11 calls for the world to "halt uncontrolled urban sprawl, reverse the growth of urban slum populations, institute smart, safe and efficient urban transport systems, improve urban environments through creating safe spaces, manage air pollution and municipal solid waste, as well as promote sustainable buildings, ecosystem corridors and consumption and production patterns."[16]

Pope Francis's encyclical *Laudato Si'* can also inspire a conversation on urbanization that seeks to achieve inclusiveness and sustainability. His call is to include everyone in the "new dialogue" about our common future—regardless of their faith traditions, historical trajectories, social conditions, political identities, or any artificial boundaries that have been created to provide a wrong and false sense of security to some groups of people at the expense of others. This new and inclusive dialogue is needed because "the environmental challenge we are undergoing, and its human roots, concern and affect us all."[17] This entails the nonhuman world, that is, nature and the universe as the extension of the human mind. Given the environmental externalities created by a neoliberal model of development, Pope Francis warns that "our world has a grave social debt towards the poor who lack access to drinking water, because they are denied the right to a life consistent with their inalienable dignity."[18] To quote the pope at length:

> Generally speaking, there is little in the way of clear awareness of problems which especially affect the excluded. Yet they are the majority of the planet's population, billions of people. These days, they are mentioned in international political and economic discussions, but one often has the impression that their problems are brought up as an afterthought, a question, which gets added almost out of duty or in a tangential way, if not treated merely as collateral damage. . . . This is due partly to the fact that many professionals, opinion makers, communications media and centers of power, being located in affluent urban areas, are far removed from the poor, with little direct contact with their problems. *They live and reason from the comfortable position of a high level of development and a quality of life well beyond the reach of the majority of the world's population.* This lack of physical contact and encounter, encouraged at times by the disintegration of our cities, can lead to a numbing of conscience and to tendentious analyses which neglect parts of reality. . . . Today, we have to realize that a true ecological approach always becomes a social approach; it must integrate questions of justice in debates on the environment, so as to hear *both the cry of the earth and the cry of the poor.*[19]

Our response to urbanization and homelessness should therefore consider the "reality" of all human beings—including the not-yet-born—in order to shape policies that ensure the common good. Our common future depends on the care we show to our planet and the concern we have about the multiple crises we face today, including the social, political, and ecological crises. All might be exposed to suffer the consequences of human activities but some bear a greater responsibility in creating these conditions while others are more vulnerable to their externalities. In these times of climate change awareness, those with greater responsibility have an "ecological debt" vis-à-vis the poor who are ill prepared— both economically and technologically—to confront these problems, especially our homeless brothers and sisters.[20]

Notes

1. UN Habitat, *World Cities Report 2016: Urbanization and Development. Emerging Futures* (Nairobi: United Nations Human Settlements Programme, 2016), 58.

2. UN Habitat, *Tracking Progress toward Inclusive, Safe, Resilient, and Sustainable Cities and Human Settlements. SDG11 Synthesis Report-High Level Political Forum 2018* (Nairobi: United Nations Human Settlements Programme, 2018), 7, http://uis.unesco.org/ sites/default/files/documents/sdg11-synthesis-report-2018-en.pdf.

3. UN Department of Public Information, Africa Renewal (April 2016), 4, https:// www.un.org/africarenewal/magazine/april-en-2014.

4. *Khat* (Catha Edulis) is an Arabian shrub considered to be a stimulant that grows at high altitudes in regions such as the Arabian Peninsula or East Africa. See Lamina, Sikiru, "Khat (Catha edulis): The Herb with Officio-Legal, Socio-Cultural and Economic Uncertainty," *South Africa Journal of Science* 106 (March/April 2010): 1.

5. http://mirror.unhabitat.org/content.asp?cid=5454&catid=578&typeid=8#.

6. As a matter of fact, the number of children living and working in the streets is estimated to be between 300,000 and 400,000 across Kenya. For statistics, see http://www.smilefoundationkenya.com/background/statistics-of-street-children.html.

7. The National Council for Children Services, *The Framework for the National Child Protection System for Kenya*. 2011, 6, https://resourcecentre.savethechildren.net/sites/default/files/documents/5429.pdf.

8. Lillian Mutavi and Stella Cherono, "Controversy Rocks Crackdown on Street Children in Nairobi," http://nairobinews.nation.co.ke/news/crackdown-street-children-nairobi/.

9. Noreena Hertz, *The Silent Takeover: Global Capitalism and the Death of Democracy* (New York: HarperCollins, 2001), 15–25.

10. François Dosse, "Michel de Certeau et l'Écriture de l'Histoire," *Vingtième Siècle: Revue d'Histoire* 2 (April–June 2003): 145.

11. Peter J. Henriot, SJ, "Globalization: Implications for Africa," *Sedos*, January 12, 1998, https://sedosmission.org/old/eng/global.html.

12. AFP, "Morocco's Tangier to Host Chinese Industrial City," https://www.dailymail.co.uk/wires/afp/article-4332940/Moroccos-Tangiers-host-Chinese-industrial-city.html.

13. See Christiana Peppard and Andrea Vicini, eds., *Just Sustainability: Technology, Ecology, and Resource Extraction* (Maryknoll, NY: Orbis Books, 2015).

14. Patrick Aidan Heelan, "Consciousness, Quantum Physics, and Hermeneutical Phenomenology," in *The Multidimensionality of Hermeneutic Phenomenology*, ed. Babette Babich and Dimitri Ginev (Basel: Springer International, 2014), 94.

15. See John Rawls, *A Theory of Justice*, rev. ed. (Cambridge, MA: Harvard University Press, 1999), 3–10.

16. UN Habitat, *Tracking Progress Towards Inclusive, Safe, Resilient, and Sustainable Cities and Human Settlements,* 109.

17. *Laudato Si',* no. 14. (Hereinafter *LS.*)

18. *LS*, no. 30.

19. *LS*, no. 49. Emphasis mine.

20. *LS*, no. 51–52.

STRATEGIES FROM ABOVE

Government

Dame Louise Casey, CBE, CB

Governments of all political persuasions, across all continents of the globe, in countless cities and countries, take, or say they are taking, action on homelessness. Their motivations and the steps they take may differ, but most often some form of action is put in place.

Politicians and politics are central to this work. Homelessness can be solved—people do not have to live and sometimes die on the streets. It is a choice we make as a community, and as a society, and it is a choice politicians and governments make on our behalf—whether to allow it, to prevent it, or to attempt to end it.

Government, as defined by the *Oxford English Dictionary*, is "the group of people with the authority to govern a country or state" and "the system by which a state or community is governed." More important, governing is "having authority to conduct the policy, actions, and affairs of a state, organization, or people."

When a government decides it will use its power, its money, its authority, and its policy-making prowess to tackle homelessness is when we have most often seen, and continue to see, the most effective work done to help tackle the now-global problem of homelessness.

Street homelessness in the United Kingdom was reduced numerically from thousands of people sleeping out on the streets to hundreds, in a concerted effort in a short period of time by the Labour Government elected into power in 1997. Following that, for over a decade the numbers sleeping out on the streets remained low and only began rising after a change of government in 2010. Today the numbers of people have risen back into the thousands.

The 1997 Labour Government chose to use its power to solve this problem, and since 2010, governments have chosen not to use that power. The United Kingdom is an example of success and failure in a country that is affluent and relatively economically stable, and indeed where politicians across the political divides would say they were committed to "ending homelessness" and would condemn each other for any failures to do so.

When governments do take action, they tend to do so because street homelessness is a potent symbol of whether the society over which they govern is caring or uncaring. People, sometimes including children, sleeping on pavements, in doorways, in subways, at stations, in the back streets is not easy to ignore (nor should it be).

Tackling homelessness is the responsibility of us all as decent human beings. And of course, it is not only the duty of government to take action—there are other agencies that are uniquely placed to act. However, it is government that should develop and execute "strategies from above"; their people are best placed to make sure that, as a community, we can strive to solve the problem in an effective and coordinated way.

Government also uniquely has the power to prevent homelessness, to ensure the right solutions are in place for those who are currently homeless, and to make sure once people are helped off the streets that their life is one built to keep them permanently away from homelessness.

It is an easier choice to alleviate only the symptoms and not the causes of homelessness, but this is a short-sighted decision. To hand out food on the street or provide a warehouse full of cot beds may be better than leaving people hungry or without any shelter in the short term. But governments—and all of us—should not withdraw after this stopgap help is put in place. Government should be concerned about solving the problem long-term, about preventing homelessness altogether— ensuring that, for example, there is a job and shelter for someone leaving prison so they do not go back to a life of crime; that there are homes available for those who cannot afford their own housing; that children in foster or state care receive the emotional and physical comfort they need; and that people are offered the right education or help with employment to prevent them from being condemned to a life on the streets.

Government and Politics

Governments, be they central, local, federal, state, or municipal, often take action on the visible forms of homelessness. Sometimes this is because there is a pressing political situation that means it is expedient for them that action is taken and is seen to be taken. For example, the death of a homeless person in a subway near the UK Houses of Parliament caused a national outcry and a new call for action to tackle homelessness.[1]

Much was made of the links between street panhandling and crime in the Mayor Rudy Giuliani period in 1990s-era New York City. Public concern about street crime and drugs became associated with the Giuliani's decisions to reduce shelter beds available to the homeless and to step up police arrests on those living on the street.

It is also true that generally positive developments such as hosting the Olympic Games can catapult homelessness and housing up the political agenda—sometimes in positive ways, but sometimes less so. In Atlanta in 1996, Seoul in 1998, Beijing in 2008, and Brazil in 2016, thousands of people were forced to move out of their homes to make way for redevelopment connected to the games, and nearby areas were cleared of encampments.

Governments react to public opinion, journalistic discourse, and political, economic, and financial pressures.

The public often has conflicting responses to street homelessness. Sometimes they react with compassion and sometimes with anger. Public anger means homeless people are attacked or abused on the streets. Public compassion means homeless people are offered food and money. This dynamic, then, is replicated in politics. In some countries, it is a criminal offense to sleep on the street, whereas in others significant public resources are directed by governments to provide help.

In British political history, tackling homelessness has been motivated by different beliefs, but often the resulting action has been similar. Put simply, those on the left of politics (the social democrats or the socialists) would argue that they prioritize addressing homelessness because it is an issue of equality. And those on the right of politics (the conservatives) would argue that they prioritize it because they believe that they have a duty to provide for those less fortunate than themselves. This is similar in many Global North countries, where the left seeks to create legal rights for homeless people, and the right would be more likely to reduce rights but provide relief in the form of services.

Advocates, campaigners, activists, or service providers can work with both these manifestations of political ideologies as they often end up delivering broadly similar outcomes—additional money for services to help homeless people, new laws or rights to empower homeless people, or new methods to quantify or evaluate what is happening.

In 1997, the Labour Government was elected into power with a commitment to solve street homelessness (which at the time was called "rough sleeping"). It was one of the first priorities of the newly created Social Exclusion Unit set up and staffed by the government, which wrote a report about how the problem should be addressed. The report marked a new way of policy making. The analysis was thorough; the strategy was developed collaboratively with campaigners and service providers; and it set a national, defined, and enumerated target to reduce street homelessness.

In the foreword to that report, the Prime Minister at the time, Tony Blair, wrote:

> There are good reasons for aiming to end rough sleeping. It is bad for those who do it, as they are intensely vulnerable to crime, drugs and alcohol, and at risk of serious illness, and premature death. And rough sleeping is bad for the rest of society. The presence of rough sleeping on the streets will attract others—often young and vulnerable—to join them. Many people feel intimidated by rough sleeping, beggars, and street drinkers and rough sleeping can blight areas and damage business and tourism.[2]

This is interesting because it balances the compassionate response to the homeless person with a tougher view of what the public would want and expect according to the political philosophy of the day. "Tough and tender" in equal measure was a hallmark of that Labour Government across a range of policies, and as such represents the approach of many countries across Europe and the Global North in terms of their attitudes toward solving homelessness.

Key to government strategies are the crucial tests of whether that government simply wants to be seen to be doing something about the problem, whether they want to take action to alleviate the symptoms, or whether they actually want to solve the problem completely. To solve it we need to be able to define it.

Definitions and Enumeration

There is no universally accepted definition of homelessness, and it is a contested issue in research and policy circles. In many countries, homelessness is defined (if it is at all) narrowly to include only those found using or sleeping on the streets and those in emergency accommodation (often referred to as shelters). This applies worldwide—not only in countries with huge economic problems but countries across Europe and the rest of the Global North.

As homelessness is measured using different definitions and different methodologies, this makes it easier for governments not to contrast their nation with others to assess how their performance compares. In 2015, the Institute of Global Homelessness worked with researchers, service providers, and policy makers to develop a framework for definition measurement that captures the full extent of homelessness categories.[3]

The framework covers all types of homelessness, from those unsheltered on the street to those in unsuitable forms of housing or encampments. It addresses a range from the street homeless of Bangalore, to those trapped in transitional housing in Chicago, or to those living in shacks or slum dwellings in Santiago. The broad definitions and categories acknowledge and validate the size and scale of the homelessness problem, while providing a structure within which countries or agencies can prioritize their issues.

Advocates, campaigners, service providers, and politicians not in power often want the widest definition possible in order to be able to advocate for either the biggest problem or specific interest groups within that number. Governments, however, often want to limit the definition of what they consider to be the problem and therefore often only count or enumerate what they want to focus on.

There is some sense in both sides of this argument, as advocates and service providers must do their utmost to help the largest number of people they believe need help and advocate how this should be done. Politicians, however, are publicly accountable for any successful or failing endeavors a government achieves and have to choose priorities on which to focus their money and power.

Sometimes there is common ground across political differences and across the agencies involved—and where there is common ground on definition, enumeration of scale, and collaborative action, there can be success.

The United Kingdom in 1997 was one example of where government recognized homelessness using a broad definition (it is the only country where a family can be accepted, counted, and helped as homeless while living in a property that is no longer suitable for their personal conditions), and where, at the same time, they prioritized certain subgroups. The two high-priority subgroups were those sleeping on the streets and families with children being put into hotels or motels. The motivation of the government was the welfare of the homeless people and also the financial cost of using hotels and motels for homeless families.

The UK administration is not alone in focusing on high-profile subgroups of homeless people. Both the George W. Bush Administration in 2002 and the Obama Administration in 2009 in the United States focused on the "chronically homeless" category, with Obama then going on to set targets for ending homelessness among veterans. Both of these initiatives were welcomed by campaigners, service providers, and the public.

These are examples of where government and the wider community agreed on a priority, a definition, and a measurement, and took successful action on homelessness. Action from above by government often operates within a framework of legislation, rights, targets, and goals.

Legal Frameworks, Rights, Targets, and Goals

Politicians often see the way they can exert their power for governing and sometimes for change via two distinct lenses: legal—the ability to pass laws that can then be shaped in a court of law—or fiscal—the ability to raise money and spend money that changes the economic life of the public they serve and the country they govern. There are very few countries that have any legal rights to housing to end homelessness, and even where they are enshrined in legislation, they are rarely legally enforceable.

Governments of all political persuasions are reluctant to institute a legal right to housing even for roofless or street homeless people. The UK is an exception to this, but even in the UK, there is no right to shelter for a street homeless person. Governments, their lawyers, and officials will often be wary of a rights-based framework as it is potentially unlimited in its scope. They can also be concerned that it encourages an adversarial and legalistic framework rather than solving problems as they see them.

There is evidence around the world of the existing legislation within countries being deployed to great effect. The size and scale of the street homeless population in India is huge (known to be greater than the entire population of the UK), and it was a very significant court case that has created huge changes. "The Order of the Supreme Court of India in the matter of E. R. Kumar & Others vs. Union of India & Others, dated 11/11/2016, Writ Petitions" concerns the right to shelter of homeless persons in urban areas. It says: "The Supreme Court directs a Committee to be constituted which will be responsible for the physical verification of the available shelters for urban homeless in each State/UT (Union Territory) and also verify whether the shelters are in compliance of the operational guidelines for the Scheme of Shelters for Urban Homeless under the National Urban Livelihoods Mission (NULM)."[4]

Around 240 shelters opened in Delhi because of this judgment, with the court directing that there should be one shelter per 100,000 of the population. The shelters may be of mixed quality and safety, but nevertheless if an area can prove the numbers of people that are homeless on the streets, this can force the hand of the state to react.

Governments also make decisions based on cost, such as whether something could be done with less money or whether the problem is costing a disproportionate amount of money that could be directed elsewhere. The challenge here is that the quality of evidence needed to make the case for different fiscal decisions is hard to achieve. Many lobbying groups make claims that they then cannot substantiate.

There are some notable exceptions—a US homelessness researcher has carried out pioneering work in this area. One study showed that long-term and repeatedly homeless people were found to cost the US taxpayer a great deal as compared with the general population. One example became famous, with one homeless person shown to be "costing" the state almost $1 million in additional public spending over the course of his life; he was known as the "Million Pound Man."[5]

Governments around the globe make pledges for change—job creation, protection of the environment, cracking down on drugs or crime, and many others, including tackling homelessness. For targets and goals to be effective, governments need to lead them effectively. Often the more successful are led by prime ministers, presidents, or other significant leaders so that the whole of the government and the community are challenged to play their part.

Definition and measurement must be clear, but so too must the policy intention or there is a risk that numerical targets will miss the point. For example, to reduce the number of people sleeping on the streets, more action needs to be taken than just opening a shelter at the time of the enumeration. That is not solving homelessness by governing—that is manipulating the public and letting down homeless people.

A strategy from above by government is one that prevents homelessness, tackles whatever problems homeless people face once homeless, and makes sure their life is built positively away from the street.

Personal vs. Structural

Politicians often decide that homelessness is either "structural" (meaning systemic, such as lack of housing or infrastructure) or "individual" (meaning personal, therefore being about drug, alcohol, or mental health issues). This is often a manifestation of their political philosophy, or an expedient reading of the situation they find themselves in—for example, it is easier to blame someone for being a drug addict rather than recognize the need for money to build more housing.

Two of the most significant researchers in poverty and homelessness have made sense of these issues. Nicholas Pleace weaves the structural and individual factors together. Structural issues such as shortages of housing or high levels of unemployment create the conditions within which homelessness can occur, but people with personal problems are significantly more likely to suffer from these adverse conditions and therefore end up homeless. His colleague, Suzanne Fitzpatrick, correctly broadens what structural factors would include. For example, if a child was born into a family that could not cope and ended up in foster care, then that is a systemic issue, rather than a personal failure of the child.[6]

The solution to many social problems lies in addressing multiple and complex problems. Unable to single out a "silver bullet" that will solve the interdependent and intractable web of problems, governments often pick those that are easier to address, and are often persuaded to do so by single-issue campaign groups, service providers, or activists.

Put simply, a campaigner might advocate for a new law or new structural solutions (a right to housing or a number of new homes). The service provider might advocate that funding more services like theirs will solve the problem—be that more hostels or shelters, more rehabilitation treatment, and so on. Alone they will not make the impact needed.

Solving homelessness is almost always going to be a combination of structural and personal factors. That is where good government is needed. Analysis of what the problem is, agreement on what the most needed resource or most pressing concern is, strong collaboration on a goal that does profit one person, party, or organization.

Building more homes without tackling the drug addiction that is trapping someone on the street will not solve the problem. Blaming someone for alcoholism and not giving them an option to get treatment and a home will not solve the problem.

Prevention and Resettlement vs.
Treating the Symptoms: The UK Experience

In the United Kingdom, there was a huge change in policy thinking in the 1980s and 1990s that moved away from only providing temporary shelter for homeless people to resettling them away from the streets and the lifestyle completely. There was a recognition that stopping people from recycling back into the same system would not only save money but also be more effective on a human level. This policy change began during a period in the 1980s where vast numbers of people were becoming poorer and where there were significantly increasing levels of homelessness.

What is important about this development is that it paved the way for money to be spent and action to be taken to prevent people from becoming homeless in the first place, to provide more than a roof for homeless people, and to provide real help to sustain a life away from the streets. Money to assist vulnerable people with their rent or a financial deposit for a flat became available. Support to help people deal with their alcoholism, together with a hostel bed, was provided. Access for those who moved out of the "homeless system" to jobs and education became more accepted.

"Prevention as well as cure" became the hallmark of the new Labour Government from 1997—supported by the pioneering work of its Social Exclusion Unit, which analyzed how problems could be solved as opposed to merely mitigated. This emphasis on prevention has continued under successive UK Governments, as illustrated by the Homelessness Reduction Act of 2017, which was passed by Parliament under the Conservative Government.

A successful preventative strategy on homelessness has to be able to understand what is going on in people's lives *before* they are homeless in order to be able to prevent those problems from then creating homelessness.

It has to be able to get to the bottom of what it would take to help the stock of people currently out on the streets to come inside successfully, by understanding fully their needs, vulnerabilities, and the choices they are prepared to make.

It needs also to know the frequency with which people return to the streets, so that routes off the streets for them can be made more effective. If people are frequently returning to the streets, then the strategy is not working long-term.

In order to fully understand how to best deploy resources to end homelessness, information and data has to be forensically gathered and analyzed. Often researchers refer to three areas where data is required—stock (those currently on the street), flow (where people were before and what is happening to them across the system), and prevalence (how frequently are people returning to the street).

On prevention, sometimes action can be simple if the understanding and will is there. For example, it became clear that when prisoners were released on a Friday afternoon in London they were significantly more likely to end up homeless, as all the services required to support them were closed over the weekend. If they were released on a Monday morning when more services were open, then the likelihood of ending up homeless was reduced. Other simple steps would include hospitals checking that a patient has a home or hostel to be discharged to or giving landlords a chance to complain about a tenant before evicting them to see if anything can be done can help prevent homelessness.

All these are actions that can be put in place if there is the right type of data and information on what is happening in people's lives prior to their homelessness—and so too can bolder measures to prevent homelessness and social exclusion. For example, the 1997 Labour Government gave greater rights and help for children growing up in foster care. It gave veterans a new deal so that when they left the armed forces, they received a resettlement package that helped them adjust to civilian life. This showed how governments could take the lead to help solve homelessness in partnership with others.

The strategy in the UK that both prevented and resettled homeless people had a third, central element. It focused on the homeless people who were the most vulnerable, those that had some of the greatest physical and mental health problems and had often been out on the streets for the longest. This entailed the development of new approaches including new types of outreach on the streets, where workers were able to help the homeless person through the system from the street to a home and beyond. It provided permanent housing for those homeless people who could not or would not move into a shelter or hostel but would take up their own home with support (an early "Housing First"–style model). And it provided treatment and support to the most vulnerable, including providing options for shelters and housing where homeless people did not have to be sober to move off the street.

This strategy (that combined prevention, new ways of working with vulnerable people out on the streets, and effective resettlement of people away from the streets) led to a successful reduction in the numbers of people on the streets in the UK and it remained successful until 2010.

Strategies from Above: Government

There are many compelling reasons why governments should take action on homelessness and lead the community efforts needed to solve the problem. Whether they are local, state, or municipal, they hold many of the powers and levers for improving the systems responsible, such as the foster care system, the roads or subways that homeless people use to sleep in, and the fiscal and legal tools to create change.

These are powers that they can choose to use for good—to solve homelessness. And like all of us in this global community, they have a moral imperative to do so.

Notes

1. Sarah Marsh, "Death in Westminster: A 'Wake-Up Call' on Homelessness," *Guardian*, December 20, 2018, https://www.theguardian.com/society/2018/dec/20/death-in-westminster-a-wake-up-call-on-homelessness.

2. UK Cabinet Office, "Annual Report on Rough Sleeping" (1998), https://webarchive.nationalarchives.gov.uk/20120919185722/http://www.communities.gov.uk/documents/housing/pdf/156723.pdf.

3. Volker Busch-Geertsema, Dennis P. Culhane, and Suzanne Fitzpatrick, "Developing a Global Framework for Conceptualising and Measuring Homelessness" (July 2016), https://www.sciencedirect.com/science/article/pii/S0197397515300023.

4. The Order of the Supreme Court of India in the matter of E. R. Kumar & Others vs. Union of India & Others, dated 11/11/2016, Writ Petitions, http://www.indiaenvironmentportal.org.in/content/437577/order-of-the-supreme-court-of-india-regarding-right-to-shelter-of-homeless-persons-in-urban-areas-11112016.

See the Writ itself: http://www.indiaenvironmentportal.org.in/files/shelter%20for%20homeless%20Supreme%20Court%20Order.pdf.

5. Dennis P. Culhane, "The Cost of Homelessness: A Perspective from the United States," *European Journal of Homelessness* 2, no. 1 (2008): 97–114.

6. Suzanne Fitzpatrick, Deborah Quilgars, and Nicholas Pleace, eds., *Homelessness in the UK: Problems and Solutions* (Coventry: Chartered Institute of Housing, 2009).

STRATEGIES FROM ABOVE

Caritas and Beyond: Getting Our Ecclesial Act Together

Pat Jones

> And one came to your back door
> all bones and in rags, asking the kiss
> that would have transformed both you
> and him; and you would not,
> slamming it in his face,
> only to find him waiting at your bed's side.

—R. S. *Thomas*, "Biography," in *Collected Poems, 1945–1990*

Having a home is a basic condition for human flourishing. It is also a form of social belonging, which both calls on and contributes to social solidarity. When people have the foundational structure of a home, they can recover their dignity and freedom and participate in society. When the streets contain people sleeping in doorways and under bridges, the social body is wounded. In contemporary Western liberal democracies, even after the fractured politics of recent decades, there is still a social contract in which we assume a social safety net is in place. The rising indicators of every kind of homelessness in England tell a different story. We are now a wealthy society in which some of the most vulnerable among us find the doors of society slammed in their faces.

The most visible sign of crisis is the disturbing increase in people sleeping rough, up 169 percent since 2010. This is the face of homelessness that everyone encounters if they choose to notice it. Less visible are those living in hostels or inadequate temporary accommodation, where families typically share a single room in dangerous, badly converted office blocks. They may have shelter but not an adequate basis for their lives. Local authorities already struggling with deep budget cuts forced upon them by austerity policies look wherever they can for places to house the homeless families they are legally compelled to assist, but the vast reduction in social housing stock limits what they can do. Young people are disproportionately likely to experience homelessness, resulting from family breakdown, insecure income, and other vulnerabilities.[1] Meanwhile, at the regional and national level, politicians promise strategies and make commitments to end rough sleeping.[2]

The analysis provided by academics and other experts demonstrates how the impacts of welfare reform have deepened the crisis and lays bare the political decisions that have led to this situation.[3] Welfare policy has turned in the direction of capped benefits, gatekeeping access to scarce resources, and imposing punitive sanctions in response to minor failures to comply with regulations. The restructured benefit system now being implemented, the much-maligned Universal Credit, seems on current evidence to push groups further into the precarity that often leads to homelessness.[4] Political attention has been forced toward the dysfunctional housing market that is also implicated in homelessness, but the structural issues at stake are deeply embedded in neoliberal economics and are complex to unpack. Housing has become a commodity in a marketplace rather than a social good to be secured in stable ways.

This brief sketch describes one political context, that of England, at a particular time. The dynamics that combine to cause or increase homelessness have a different history and configuration in each place, and the details matter. The ways in which welfare systems have evolved and the stability or otherwise of housing policy, as well as the economic and political context, vary from country to country. There is some common ground and potential for countries to learn from each other about alternative policies and effective strategies. There is also a lesson we have learned painfully in the UK. While housing policy and economic structures move relatively slowly, homelessness can increase rapidly as a cumulative effect of multiple factors, both personally and externally enforced. Progress in reducing street homelessness in the 1990s has now been reversed. Changes to benefit policies and rising costs in the private rented sector have pushed those barely surviving into crisis. Personal trauma can upend what seem to be secure life structures. People turn to the threadbare social safety net and find it lacking.

This matters most of all for those described in social policy as experiencing multi-exclusion homelessness. They have complex and overlapping needs, indicating that the solution to homelessness does not end with the provision of accommodation. Those who have spent years living on the street often acquire other vulnerabilities such as substance abuse or untreated mental health conditions, and live on the peripheries of society. In material terms, achieving change in their situation involves access not only to housing but also to health care and other services associated with social inclusion. Just as important is relational support and recognition of personhood, which is the strength of voluntary agencies.

This is the context in which the ecclesial response to homelessness is embedded and in which ecclesial actors have to find a position and strategy. The tradition and narrative of Catholic charity pushes primarily toward a response of *caritas*, loving concern and material aid as an outflow of faith. For Benedict XVI, this outflow is how the church "acts as a subject with direct responsibility, doing what corresponds to her nature."[5] Francis is more direct, proposing that "each individual Christian and every community is called to be an instrument of God for the liberation and promotion of the poor, and for enabling them to be fully a part of society."[6] His recognition of homelessness as social exclusion and his personal actions of solidarity with homeless people invite a renewed ecclesial engagement. Meeting with homeless people in Washington, DC, in 2015, he asked: "Why are we homeless, without a place to live? And those of us who do have a home, a roof over our heads, would also do well to ask: Why do these, our brothers and sisters, have no place to live? Why are these brothers and sisters of ours homeless?"[7] It is less evident that the ecclesial response takes these questions seriously by addressing the structural and political as well as the material dimensions of homelessness.

In this chapter, I examine ecclesial responses to homelessness, using the Catholic community in England and Wales as a case study and drawing out some tensions and questions that need further work. I argue that while the practical response to people who are homeless is strong, ecclesial action and voice addressing the structures and policies implicated in homelessness is uncertain and limited, and the contribution that Catholic social ethics could make is indistinct at best. The ecclesial response reflects an overdependence on the principle of *caritas,* and points to the need to expand and communicate the Catholic narrative on homelessness using other core principles of Catholic Social Teaching (CST). I propose that the concept of the common good in particular is essential in order to construct an ecclesial response that aims not simply to alleviate but also to end street homelessness.

Outflow, Vocation, Strategy, and Voice

At least four streams can be identified in ecclesial response to homelessness. The first is *outflow*, the least strategic and most widespread, the ordinary reality of how church members give both funds and a share of their goods and time to support people who are homeless. Some belong to organizations such as the Society of St. Vincent de Paul; others volunteer with the charities and projects working in this field, including voluntary interfaith night shelters and Nightstop schemes providing overnight accommodation to homeless young people in crisis.[8] Organized Catholic charities both within and beyond Caritas structures depend on this bedrock of solidarity, which extends to other areas of vulnerability as well as homelessness. The impulse for this activity happens in many ways, prompted by the instincts of faith in response to the Gospel, or communal ecclesial commitments to projects or charities, or from personal exposure or political disquiet at what is visible around us.

The second is found in the *vocational* commitment of lay Catholics who work in sectors of public and political life where they hold influence and power in relation to policies, structures, and social perceptions that have a bearing on homelessness. Some consciously acknowledge the influence of a Catholic worldview and its underlying theological convictions in their ethical principles and commitments; others may not. There are allies here for organized Catholic response and depths of strategic insight and expertise often barely used.

The third stream is the development of *strategy* by Catholic charitable organizations working in public spaces to respond to homelessness. Many belong to Caritas structures at diocesan or national level; some do not. A significant number grew from the work of religious congregations and still hold to the inspiration of their founding charisms. They work with different populations ranging from young people and street sleepers to women whose lives are affected by prostitution. Some accept substantial government funds and work as delivery partners for statutory services; others avoid what they see as potential controls or constraints and prefer the freedom and risks of reliance on voluntary funding. The services they provide include night shelters and other forms of emergency accommodation; day centers providing meals, hygiene facilities, and companionship; temporary and supported accommodation; advice, advocacy, access to education, and support in finding employment. Where possible, they seek a public voice, either individually or working through the Caritas network in a coordinated way. Some point to and use the inspiration of Catholic Social Teaching; others draw on the Gospel or their founding visions, mediating these in organizational values and culture. Their Catholicity is expressed in how they enact their particular ethical narratives in the conditions of secularity, and their links to institutional Catholic structures help keep their roots and inspiration alive and generative in their work.

The final stream is the public *voice* of the institutional church, offering moral perspectives for society and calling both politicians and civil society to account. This is the least active mode of response, despite the aspirations in papal encyclicals.[9] Although there is strong episcopal support for practical response to homelessness, there is an absence of theological and ethical analysis of the wider context and almost no official public Catholic voice.[10] A recent report from the Bishops' Conference agency, Caritas Social Action Network, has however broken a silence of decades. The report, titled "Abide in Me," sets out "a national framework for new and renewed Catholic social action," although it is focused on housing rather than homelessness.[11]

This pattern reflects both the messiness and the expansive Catholicity of social mission, reaching far beyond institutional structures and membership. In responding to homelessness, Catholics work with other Christians, other faith communities, and secular organizations. In charities belonging to Caritas networks, the majority of staff may not be church members or indeed profess any faith, but they work with passion and commitment within the moral horizons to which the charities hold tenaciously. The charities work on and across the boundaries of the visible church, exercising necessary freedom, discernment, and autonomy as they negotiate the risks and the gains of being entangled in politics.

The concept of ecclesial strategy is revealed to be problematic. The ecclesiological structure of each of the four streams of activity above is different, and the possibilities of alignment and collaboration in pursuit of a social good such as ending homelessness are impeded by the resulting tensions. It may be desirable for each Catholic parish to participate in a street homeless count in their area; but they may not see this as a priority. It may be arguable that the Bishops' Conference should take a prophetic stand on homelessness policy, pressing the government hard for change; but the bishops rarely make specific judgments on social matters in a unified voice. Catholic charities meanwhile must make judgments, accept risks, and live with compromises while somehow remaining tethered to instincts and principles rooted in a Catholic worldview and social ethic.

Underlying Ethical Frameworks

The disparate streams of Catholic responses work against a deeper ethical grasp of what is at stake. The characteristic emphasis of activists and practitioners on provision of services tends to crowd out deeper reflection. Yet what is happening on the ground would benefit from critical reflection and could provide insights to refresh Catholic social thought. There is a question here for Catholic social ethics, about whether there are principles, insights, and perspectives that will genuinely serve the activists and practitioners and enable conversation that crosses ecclesial borders and engages all those working within the broad scope of Catholic social mission. Catholic social thought has the potential to underpin and extend the moral perspectives held in the charities' narratives, strengthening their resistance to what John Coleman terms the isomorphic tendencies of other cultures and ideologies.[12] In the urgency of their daily work, it is difficult for charities to work out how to do this or where to find the access points. Such conversation is needed equally within ecclesial communities, to expand horizons of concern and action and to resource episcopal public voice.

What could such a conversation offer? It could start from how we understand and construct homelessness. In the Institute of Global Homelessness (IGH) definition of homelessness as "lacking access to minimally adequate housing," the authors point to the conceptual base supplied by the "enforced lack" criterion used in thinking about poverty.[13] To speak of an enforced lack points in a very different direction from that taken when discussing homelessness in terms of "need." It means we have to ask how the enforcing happens and which structures and actors are involved. The definition also avoids constructing the homeless person as a collection of needs and directs us toward the issues of access to housing and judgment of what is adequate. The IGH definition approaches homelessness from a social policy perspective, but works on common ground with the only substantial document on this theme issued from the Holy See, *What Have You Done to Your Homeless Brother?*[14] The Pontifical Council text locates homelessness as a structural and social concern, "the result of a whole series of economic, social, cultural, physical, emotional and moral factors that specifically bear down on those who have never been integrated into the current social system."[15] Like the IGH, the document recognizes that homelessness is an injustice, a "lack of something which is due," a failure of both the state and society and a matter of human rights.[16] It articulates a simple but profound principle: that property is at the service of the human person.[17] This principle alone interrogates the commodification of housing and the financialization of housing markets in the UK that intersect with globalized capitalism but also reflect local political decisions.

There is a gap between the narrative of *caritas,* the classical instinct of Christian faith to help those in need that dominates the culture of Catholic concern about homelessness, and the reality of what causes and constitutes homelessness, and what is involved in ending it. The risk is that interpreting what we see on our streets only in terms of need obscures the equally crucial dimension of recognizing what homelessness means: that we have constructed—or allowed—a society and politics in which we are willing to tolerate the enforced homelessness of many. The danger of Catholic generosity is that we think it is sufficient to give material aid. This limits our engagement in several significant ways.

The first requires recognition of how we are implicated in other people's homelessness. Kelly Johnson, in her study of begging as a practice within Christian tradition, starts from how uncomfortable people feel when encountering beggars, because they bring forth our own uncertainty and fears. The reason, she suggests, is that "the beggar sees an alarming truth about humanity, about me, that had things been done differently, that beggar could have been any one of us."[18] She describes this as an "untidy corner of ethics," containing questions we would prefer not to address, about areas such as property rights, altruism, justice among strangers, and the usefulness and meaning of giving. When the focus is enlarged from begging to street homelessness, other obscured questions tug at our consciences, about whether the social safety net exists and how our own economic and political choices are implicated. Danny Dorling, working from the discipline of human geography, comments that in England and Wales, "We now have more housing than we have ever had before, per person and per family. We just share it out more unfairly than we have ever done before."[19]

The ethical reflection that could illuminate a deeper ecclesial response to homelessness has to square up to a more complicated understanding that involves those of us who have homes as well as those who do not. As a Catholic community we hold a social ethic rooted in a theological worldview that encompasses more than generosity and loving concern for those most in need. We are equally called to seek the welfare of the city, the social arrangements that most clearly conform to the vision of the Kingdom. Although we know that all politics are provisional, we also know that our salvation has a social aspect, as we seek the implications of the Gospel for the social order. This becomes concrete in how we understand and respond to homelessness, as neighbors and as citizens, and how we convince others that homelessness matters to those who are not homeless. This takes ecclesial response into uncomfortable places of political debate and personal discernment. It asks us to move beyond giving aid alone and to answer Francis's questions in our own context. Catholic social ethics can provide frameworks to help us avoid the ideological traps of polarized politics and root reflection in properly theological horizons.

So, we cannot abstain from the hard work of ethical discernment in relation to welfare and housing policy. The moral complexity of what seem to be social goods but in practice act both to sustain some lives and damage or constrain others is troubling and does not submit to clear judgments or strategies. The professional Catholic charities already know this. It is their daily reality, negotiating with the inadequacies and dysfunctional habits of statutory provision, finding occasional allies and empathy, and practicing a counternarrative of person-centered holistic response. They recognize the absence of the conditions people need in order to flourish, and work with those who come to their services to co-construct the basic goods and securities people need. Their experience discloses a combination of power and powerlessness. They know that the agency of the people with whom they work is crucial; they cannot choose for people the steps that rebuild social belonging. Front-line workers accompany the human process of change and carry some of its weight while wrestling with the systems that are meant to provide the safety net but so often do not. Their colleagues use whatever access and opportunities are within their reach to advocate for better policies and legislation, but their organizational capacity for analysis and ethical reflection is modest as such work is hard to fund. The absence of a larger Catholic conversation drawing on social teaching and ethics and oriented toward the particular dynamics of homelessness and social welfare in the context of this nation leaves the charities to their limited resources.

There are insights in the charities' work that offer fresh perspectives to other streams of ecclesial response. Charities frequently present their work as a response to need and social exclusion and tell the stories of clients now flourishing. There is another dimension of their experience that is less often articulated. There is reciprocity in their work, in which the staff and volunteers are also enabled to flourish by their participation in a common task. Jon Sobrino comments that when richer churches help churches who work with the poor and oppressed, they find that they not only give, but also receive, and "what they receive is of a different and higher order."[20] The perspectives on our own lives, our faith, and our politics that come from encountering the experience of homelessness are potentially transformative for each of us. The material inequalities built into any social assistance only make sense when we acknowledge this incomplete and asymmetric reciprocity.

A Bigger Canvas: Ecclesial Response to Homelessness in the Horizon of the Common Good

The insights held in the experience of professional Catholic charities embody a larger ethical framework than *caritas*. Safe and adequate housing is above all a condition needed for people to be able to seek their own fulfillment, and it cannot be achieved *for all* without a social contract and political economy committed to such a purpose. The common good is too often left as a distant horizon or an abstract idea in Catholic ethical discourse. Yet although we do not know precisely what it looks like, we can pursue it as a process, using what Patrick Riordan terms "elements that guide investigation."[21] For Riordan, discovery or construction of the common good must be inclusive of everyone and of all the dimensions of human well-being. The Catholic social instinct has always reached for this inclusion. It has also always wrestled with the kind of political order that will best serve human community and social justice. A focus on the common good does not dispense with the need for *caritas*. In Thomas Bushlack's account, *caritas* is the distinctive element that Christians bring to the common ethical task of seeking social goods in shared practical reasoning. Bushlack also argues that the efficacy test of the common good is found in the extent to which it allows all, especially the vulnerable, what they need to flourish and participate.[22] The common good concept directs our attention to the shared, reciprocal, interdependent nature of our citizenship, our humanity, and our salvation. When we examine homelessness through the lens of the common good, we can see more of what needs to be done.

The common good framework has another significant advantage. It provides ethical common ground that reaches across the streams of ecclesial response to homelessness and across the porous borders of social mission. Its theological context and horizon are generative and engaging, and offer horizons of meaning to those who join the work of Catholic charities while bringing other ethics and commitments. The task of working out in each context how we can organize what the welfare state first sought, a floor below which no one should fall, is almost a proxy for the question of what the common good means. It puts before all of us the questions asked at our door and by the people sleeping on our streets.

Conclusion

Ecclesial response to homelessness is messy and diverse. It is not likely to respond to attempts at greater strategic alignment, but it is possible to propose a sense of direction that encompasses a larger purpose than material help, however loving. The common good offers a framework to move beyond *caritas* and draw disparate actors into a dynamic framework. The work that Catholic social ethics can do matters here, constructing a narrative that connects theological insights, ethical principles, and social realities in particular places, inviting those working in the different streams of ecclesial response to discover and work from a full Catholic vision.

Notes

1. www.homeless.org.uk.

2. In August 2018, the government announced a strategy to end rough sleeping by 2027, allocating £100 million. Ministry of Housing, Communities and Local Government. "Rough Sleeping Strategy" *GOV.UK* (August 2018), https://assets.publishing.service.gov.uk/government/uploads/system/uploads/attachment_data/file/733421/Rough-Sleeping-Strategy_WEB.pdf.

3. See, for example, the Homelessness Monitor published by https://www.crisis. org.uk/ending-homelessness/homelessness-knowledge-hub/homelessness-monitor/. The National Audit Office has reported on the impact of welfare reform: see www.nao.org.uk.

4. www.northern-consortium.org.uk.

5. Pope Benedict XVI, *Deus Caritas Est* (December 25, 2005), 29, http://w2.vatican. va/content/benedict-xvi/en/encyclicals/documents/hf_ben-xvi_enc_20051225_deus-caritas-est.html.

6. Pope Francis, *Evangelii Gaudium* (November 24, 2013), 186, http://w2.vatican. va/content/francesco/en/apost_exhortations/documents/papa-francesco_esortazione-ap_20131124_evangelii-gaudium.html.

7. Pope Francis, "Visit to the Charitable Center of St. Patrick Parish and Meeting with the Homeless" (September 24, 2015), https://w2.vatican.va/content/francesco/en/ speeches/2015/september/documents/papa-francesco_20150924_usa-centro-caritativo. html.

8. Night Shelter schemes bring together a rota of churches and other religious sites to provide overnight shelter in an area, using a common referral system. Nightstop is a federation of voluntary hosting schemes coordinated by Depaul UK, www.depaulcharity.org.

9. Pope Benedict XVI, *Caritas in Veritate* (June 29, 2009), 9, http://w2.vatican.va/ content/benedict-xvi/en/encyclicals/documents/hf_ben-xvi_enc_20090629_caritas-in-veritate.html; Pope Francis, *Evangelii Gaudium,* 182–83.

10. Although the bishops of England and Wales have not expressed a Catholic public voice on homelessness since 1990, the Irish and Australian Bishops' Conferences have both issued documents in 2018. See *A Room at the Inn?* https://www.catholicbishops.ie/ wp-content/uploads/2018/10/2018-Oct-01-Bishops-pastoral-letter-on-Housing-and-Homelessness-A-Room-at-the-Inn.pdf, and *A Place to Call Home*, www.catholic.org.au.

11. Caritas, "Abide in Me," *CSAN*, November 2018, www.csan.org.uk/wp-content/ uploads/2018/11/Abide-in-Me-CSAN.pdf.

12. Institutional isomorphism describes the process by which institutions within a sector gradually come to resemble each other in their norms and behavior. John Coleman, SJ, "Institutions," in *The Blackwell Companion to Catholicism*, ed. James Joseph Buckley, Frederick Christian Bauerschmidt, and Trent Pomplun (Oxford: Blackwell, 2007), 403–18.

13. Volker Busch-Geertsema, Dennis Culhane, and Suzanne Fitzpatrick, "A Global Framework for Understanding and Measuring Homelessness," *Institute for Global Homelessness*, 2015. Joanna Mack and Stewart Lansley define poverty as "an enforced lack of socially perceived necessities" in *Poor Britain* (London: Allen and Unwin, 1985), 39.

14. Pontifical Council for Justice and Peace, "What Have You Done to Your Homeless Brother?" (December 27, 1987), http://theolibrary.shc.edu/resources/homeless.htm.

15. Ibid., II.2.

16. Ibid., III.2.

17. Ibid.

18. Kelly S. Johnson, *The Fear of Beggars: Stewardship and Poverty in Christian Ethics* (Grand Rapids, MI: Eerdmans, 2007), 14.

19. Danny Dorling, "Has Brexit Burst the British Housing Bubble?" *New Statesman* (October 16, 2016), https://www.newstatesman.com/politics/uk/2016/10/has-brexit-burst-british-housing-bubble.

20. Jon Sobrino, *The Principle of Mercy: Taking the Crucified People from the Cross* (Maryknoll, NY: Orbis Books, 1994), 146.

21. Patrick Riordan, *A Grammar of the Common Good* (London: Continuum, 2008), 28.

22. Thomas Bushlack, *Politics for a Pilgrim Church: A Thomistic Theory of Civic Virtue* (Grand Rapids, MI: Eerdmans, 2015), 214.

STRATEGIES FROM BELOW

Subsidiarity and Homelessness

William T. Cavanaugh

When people say, "We ought to be doing more to help the homeless," the "we" is often understood as the state, that is, national and local government agencies. There are some good reasons to think that if the state has any responsibility for the welfare of its citizens, then it ought at least to ensure that those citizens are not sleeping on park benches in subzero temperatures. There are those who are opposed in principle to any government provision of goods that the market should provide, but such voices do not get much credence from those who advocate for the homeless, nor should they. The idea that the market will provide if left alone is one of the most pernicious forms of magical thinking that afflicts the contemporary world, and one that is refuted by the thousands sleeping rough on the streets. Letting the market provide housing in San Francisco, for example, is why homelessness has reached epidemic proportions there, with two-thirds of the homeless having been forced from their previous homes by skyrocketing prices. When we think the alternatives are either state or market, people who advocate for the homeless gravitate toward the state. We tend to think of the state as our friend, to which we can appeal to solve the problem of homelessness.

But the reality is more complicated. The state is a meeting place of different stories about the way things are that are often at cross-purposes with each other. One story that is told about the state is that it is the provider of the common good; others view the state more minimally as a safety net that at least prevents the worst from befalling individuals. People disagree on this role of the state, but virtually all agree that one of the state's key roles is to protect private property rights. In this role, the state becomes one of the primary promoters of homelessness. In this brief chapter, therefore, I suggest that we should approach the state with a certain measure of ambivalence. On the one hand, appealing to the state for aid can be an important part of our strategy for addressing homelessness. On the other hand, to get to the root cause of homelessness, Christians will need to tell a more profound story about the way things are, one in which goods are essentially common and God responds personally to the needs of all.

I begin by discussing the state and subsidiarity in Catholic social thought, and then I discuss three different practices of subsidiarity with regard to homelessness.

148

The State and the Common Good

The *Catechism of the Catholic Church* regards the state, like the family, as natural to human being.[1] The state has authority in order "to ensure as far as possible the common good,"[2] but the idea that the state will in fact ensure the common good is not taken for granted. The *Catechism* adds that authority "is exercised legitimately only when it seeks the common good,"[3] thus recognizing the possibility that the state and other authorities will not live up to the ideal in practice, and thereby lose legitimacy. At the same time, even in theory, the *Catechism* recognizes that the ideal is not for the state to have sole responsibility for the common good. The *Catechism* encourages widespread participation in voluntary associations and institutions at all levels,[4] and instructs that "in accordance with the principle of subsidiarity, neither the state nor any larger society should substitute itself for the initiative and responsibility of individuals and intermediary bodies."[5]

There are different ways of reading the principle of subsidiarity in Catholic thought. One approach is to see it as a purely procedural principle, within a fundamentally positive view of the modern expansion of state power, to determine at what level problems are most efficiently addressed.[6] A more critically aware approach, in my judgment, is one that sees the expansion of state power at the expense of intermediate associations as inherently problematic. The growth of state intervention in the twentieth and twenty-first centuries has been accompanied by the withering of robust intermediate associations like neighborhoods, families, churches, unions, fraternal organizations, and other bodies that stand between the state and the individual. The withering of such social networks—and the reduction of social life to the oscillation between state and individual—has contributed to the explosion of street homelessness.

More than a procedural principle, subsidiarity is critical of the modern state because it is based in a Christian anthropology of people as being born for living in personal communion with one another. As Robert Vischer has written, when the state in actual practice seeks "either to marginalize intermediate associations or remake them in the state's own image," subsidiarity's support for the integrity and autonomy of such associations can serve as a "subversive wrench in the collective enthronement of individualism."[7] Vischer does not want to do away with the state. "Subsidiarity does, however, reframe our image of the modern state, envisioning it as a resource for localized empowerment and coordination, rather than as the arbiter and provider of the social good."[8]

There are a number of ways in which the modern state tells a story that is in tension with the common good. In the first place, what is "common" stops at the borders policed by the nation-state. Instead of a truly common human good, the nation-state establishes divisions among peoples, some of which directly affect homelessness. As we have seen in recent years, the resettling of refugees has been disrupted by a strident insistence on securing "our" borders against "them." Within our borders, the same dynamic of dividing us from them exacerbates homelessness by distinguishing those who are deserving of attention from the state from those who are not. Undocumented homeless have a much harder time getting government help for housing.

In the second place, states reinforce the privatization of common goods through the absolutization of private property rights. We often suppose that states unite all within their borders, and stand above divisions of class. However, one of the fundamental roles of the state is to protect property rights, and that means protecting the rights of those who already have property; this is not an accidental but a fundamental and essential role of the state. By prioritizing the protection of private ownership of property over the social use of property, the state contributes to homelessness in many different ways:

- zoning laws that discourage affordable housing, homeless shelters, and services for the homeless in certain areas, in order to protect the market value of properties;
- enforcement of laws that protect the absolute right of ownership regardless of its social purpose or lack thereof, e.g., evicting squatters from vacant houses or unused land;
- laws and policies that protect and encourage private development, even if it means gentrification and displacement of lower-income people;
- laws and policies that protect and encourage property speculation, so that speculators reap massive benefits when property prices peak—thus rendering housing unaffordable for many—but are protected when the bubbles produced by speculation burst, as in 2008;
- the criminalization of homelessness via laws that "protect" even public spaces from being used by homeless people, e.g., anti-vagrancy laws that prevent people from sleeping, cooking, bathing, etc. in public parks;
- ordinances that encourage evicting homeless people from semi-public businesses, such as shopping malls or fast-food places;
- policies that connect education funding to property taxes, ensuring that the wealthy have good schools and the poor do not.

Most of the above are not immutable, but all flow naturally from the state's mandate to protect private property and to allow the market to set the price of access to such property. In more general terms, the state is a marketplace in which those with money have much more access to power and benefits than those without money. Access to money becomes the measure of the value of human persons. Those with money therefore have a wildly disproportionate effect on elections and policies, so the state often exacerbates rather than alleviates the underlying conditions of poverty that cause homelessness—lack of access to health care, good education, unionized jobs, treatment for drug addiction, and so on.

None of this means that we should stop trying to get governments to take care of homeless people. But we need to be realistic and recognize that caring for the homeless is in tension with the state's mandate to protect absolute property rights, and therefore protect the propertied classes. Rather than see the state simply as the keeper of the common good, we would do better, as Vischer says, to see it as a *potential* resource for localized organization and empowerment.

Practices of Subsidiarity

Here I would like to explore briefly three types of practice from below with regard to homelessness. All three are examples of subsidiarity, and they have strengths and limitations.

The first type of practice involves creating local institutions and networks to deal with homelessness. My parish church participates in a local initiative called Housing Forward in which churches and synagogues provide spaces to shelter people overnight, volunteers to staff shelters and drop-in centers, and funding to pay for permanent staff to work with homeless people to find permanent housing. Housing Forward works with, and receives funding from, a large variety of community partners, businesses, and local governments. It participates as well in the federal Housing and Urban Development (HUD) department's recently implemented Coordinated Entry program, a process to make sure that people facing homelessness are quickly identified, assessed, and connected to a range of services based on their abilities and needs. Housing Forward is the lead agency for Coordinated Entry for suburban Cook County, Illinois. This is a good example of what Vischer calls envisioning the state "as a resource for localized empowerment and coordination." Here, local congregations take the lead in inviting chaos into their physical spaces and bringing together the lives of some of their members with people who are experiencing homelessness and many other related problems. The federal government and local governments participate in a limited coordinating role.

Housing Forward is effective, locally organized, and flexible, but is nevertheless an organization that requires a certain level of bureaucracy. What if the money raised were simply given to the homeless? This is a second, more radical, approach to subsidiarity. When enacted at a society-wide level, it tells a subversive story about the privatization of common goods, an issue that the first approach does not directly address.

In 2009, the aid organization Broadway gave thirteen chronically homeless men in London £3000 each, with no strings attached. Some had been on the streets for decades, many with substance abuse problems. They were free to spend the money as they wished, on the assumption that they knew their own needs best. The expectations of the social workers monitoring the experiment were not high, but they were surprised by the result. The men were frugal, spending an average of just £800 the first year, on things like a hearing aid, a cellphone, a dictionary, gardening classes. Within two years, nine of the thirteen had housing. All were making progress. And the cost of the experiment was a fraction of the annual sums previously spent on policing, court appearances, and social services for the thirteen men.[9]

This experiment is touted by advocates of a Universal Basic Income, or UBI, an old idea that has been getting renewed attention lately.[10] The fundamental proposal is a guaranteed payment from the government to every citizen, regardless of their work status, wealth, or merit, with no strings attached. Proponents see it as a way to provide a floor under people—or a roof over their heads—to allow them to escape poverty. There is increasing evidence, based on limited experiments in a variety of countries, that social programs and development schemes do not work as well as simply giving people money and allowing them to decide how best to use it. Proponents argue that it is both economically and politically feasible, and point to the surprising fact that Richard Nixon and Milton Friedman both supported a UBI.[11] I will skip over the question of feasibility, and address the question of desirability, from the point of view of Catholic Social Thought.

UBI at first glance seems like the opposite of subsidiarity, a massive increase in the top-down paternalism of the welfare state. But it's not. The UBI is premised on the idea that people at the ground level know their own needs better than the state. The main thing poor people lack is money; they might spend it on job training, or housing, or more nutritious food, but they, not government functionaries, decide. One of the functions of government that the UBI would greatly diminish is the sorting of the deserving from the undeserving poor, usually based on the willingness to work. Governments employ armies of civil servants to ensure that recipients of aid—if not entirely disabled—are either applying for or working at sufficiently low-paying and demeaning jobs. People recoil from the idea of free money with no requirement to work, on the false assumption that cash disincentivizes work.[12] Even illness does not release people from the demand to work; Kentucky has recently required work in order to receive Medicaid. Work makes a person "deserving" of help.

It is important to see that this sorting of deserving from undeserving poor is not an accidental but an essential function of the modern state. As guarantor of private property, the state enforces a certain theodicy about how property came to be in the hands of those who have it. Those who have property, we are told, deserve to have property. This explains why people are horrified by the specter of the idle poor, but not by the reality of the idle rich. For owners of capital, it is possible to receive a large income while doing no work of any kind. Heirs of fortunes made by someone else's work need not lift a finger, and yet the 2017 tax bill doubled the tax exemption for such unearned inheritances to $22 million for couples. Work is a requirement for the poor but not for the rich because the state, as guarantor of private property, tells a story about the genesis of wealth. Karl Marx characterizes the story this way:

> In times long gone by there were two sorts of people; one, the diligent, intelligent, and, above all, frugal élite; the other, lazy rascals, spending their substance, and more, in riotous living. . . . Thus it came to pass that the former sort accumulated wealth, and the latter sort had at last nothing

to sell except their own skins. And from this original sin dates the poverty of the great majority that, despite all its labor, has up to now nothing to sell but itself, and the wealth of the few that increases constantly although they have long ceased to work. Such insipid childishness is every day preached to us in the defense of property.[13]

UBI tells a different story, one in which creation is the common property of all humanity. A UBI would ensure that everyone have at least some share in the common patrimony that no one of us living today did anything to deserve: the abundance of natural resources, the fruits of centuries of progress in technology and social organization, and so on. As Philippe van Parijs and Yannick Vanderborght point out, the correct term for the taxes that would be required to fund a UBI is not "redistribution" but "distribution"; they "are not levies on what was created out of nothing by today's producers, but rather fees to be paid by these producers for the privilege of using for their personal benefit what we have collectively received."[14] The language of *ex nihilo* here invites theological interpretation; God, not the capitalist, is the creator. According to Aquinas, all things are God's, and therefore, with regard to their use, "man ought to possess external things, not as his own, but as common, so that, to wit, he is ready to communicate them to others in their need."[15] The "social mortgage" on wealth, to use John Paul II's term,[16] refers not only to the common destiny but also to the social origin of wealth, and ultimately its origin in God. We are all beggars before God, all equally undeserving of God's grace, but all nevertheless invited to the eschatological banquet.

It is precisely here, however, that I feel it necessary to note some reservations about cash transfers from the state as a means to end homelessness. The corporal works of mercy in the Christian tradition are based on Jesus' eschatological vision in Matthew 25. Those invited to the heavenly feast are those who fed the hungry, gave drink to the thirsty, clothed the naked, visited those in prison, and so on. And when they did so, they encountered Christ himself in the form of the poor. What becomes of this encounter with Christ if a UBI is enacted? In the Catholic tradition, solidarity with those who suffer is meant to be free, personal, and communal; the UBI is designed to be obligatory, impersonal, and individual. Indeed, the depersonalization of care for the poor is sometimes touted as a boon of cash transfers; recipients of aid are spared the humiliation of encounter with a giver. But I worry that the well-to-do will also be spared the humiliation of the encounter with Jesus in the poor. James Keenan defines mercy as entering into the chaos of others,[17] and it is this encounter with the frailty of others that opens up one's own frailty, and that often transforms people into agents building real communal structures of solidarity in the world. I worry that relying on cash transfers could promote a "culture of indifference," to use Pope Francis's words, on the assumption that everybody is fine as long as they are getting a monthly check. I worry that money could substitute for grace.

Depersonalized solutions to homelessness will not strike at the root cause of homelessness, which is the privatization of common goods and the individualization of society. To enact a more profound story about the common origin and destiny of material goods, we need to enact a more profound story about the common origin and destiny of people. More than a distribution of money, we need a distribution of people in community, finding ways of living that bring vulnerable and less vulnerable people together. The church cannot simply leave the care of the homeless to the state, but needs to create spaces that pull people with property out of their comfort zones and put them into contact with the chaos of others.

A third approach to homelessness, then, happens at a more personal level that is neither institutionalized nor monetized. It happens as it does in the parable of the Good Samaritan, with the Samaritan simply responding in an immediate way to the needs of the wounded Jew. As the Greek text of Luke's gospel says, the Samaritan was "moved in his bowels" by the sight of the wounded man, flesh calling out to flesh. As Ivan Illich comments,

> This is an act which prolongs the Incarnation. Just as God became flesh and in the flesh relates to each one of us, so you are capable of relating in the flesh, as one who says ego, and when he says ego, points to an experience which is entirely sensual, incarnate, and this-worldly, to that other man who has been beaten up.[18]

Illich sees the early church practice of having a "Christ room" in one's own home for those experiencing homelessness as an extension of this incarnational approach to the needy. Unfortunately, Illich argues, this approach gets marginalized as care for the poor is increasingly institutionalized and bureaucratized from the late middle ages onward. Illich does not want to do away with all institutions, but he wants to do more to resist their depersonalizing and disincarnating effects.

Dorothy Day and the Catholic Worker represent one example of this third approach in the contemporary era. Catholic Worker houses of hospitality are not institutions but homes into which people invite strangers. Matthew 25 was the center of Dorothy Day's personalism: the homeless person should be treated as Christ. "The mystery of the poor is this: That they are Jesus, and what you do for them you do for Him. . . . The mystery of poverty is that by sharing in it, making ourselves poor in giving to others, we increase our knowledge of and belief in love."[19] The confusion of the poor and the not poor in the sharing of poverty; the location of both poor and non-poor in the same body, the Body of Christ; the relativization of private property in the sharing of a home; the consequent breaching of the boundaries between what is mine and what is yours—all of this tells a different story about the common origin and destiny of both material goods and of human persons. Dorothy Day did not simply want to house the homeless without questioning the injustices of the system that produces homelessness at its root. The root is the privatization of the common goods that God has created and given to all to enjoy together. The answer is to share life together and confuse the boundaries between what is mine and what is yours. Dorothy Day's criticisms of "Holy Mother the State"[20] were not simply a procedural critique of the level at which social problems were addressed. They were part of a broader enacted vision of all people as members or potential members of Christ's body.

Conclusion

Solutions to homelessness are likely to come in all three of the above forms, and more. Multifaceted problems need multifaceted solutions. In addressing the problem, however, we should not forget to think simultaneously big and small. We need to think big in analyzing not simply the symptoms but the root causes of homelessness in the overarching stories we tell about the origin and destiny of material goods. We need to think small in remembering that each person experiencing homelessness is a person with a different story, and our solutions need to be personalist as well.

Notes

1. *Catechism of the Catholic Church*, 2nd ed. (Vatican City: Libreria Editrice Vaticana, 1997), §1882. (Hereinafter *CCC*.)
2. Ibid., §1898. "By common good is to be understood 'the sum total of social conditions which allow people, either as groups or as individuals, to reach their fulfillment more fully and more easily'"; ibid., §1906. The internal quote is from *Gaudium et Spes*, 26.
3. *CCC*, §1903.
4. Ibid., §1882, 1893.
5. Ibid., §1894; cf. §1883.
6. An example of this approach is J. Bryan Hehir, "Religious Ideas and Social Policy: Subsidiarity and Catholic Style of Ministry," in *Who Will Provide? The Changing Role of Religion in American Social Welfare*, ed. Mary Jo Bane, Brent Coffin, and Ronald Thiemann (Boulder, CO: Westview Press, 2000), 97–120.
7. Robert K. Vischer, "Subsidiarity as Subversion: Local Power, Legal Norms, and the Liberal State," *Journal of Catholic Social Thought* 2, no. 2 (Summer 2005): 288.
8. Ibid. I discuss these two approaches to subsidiarity in more detail in my book *Field Hospital: The Church's Engagement with a Wounded World* (Grand Rapids, MI: Eerdmans, 2016), chap. 6.
9. Rutger Bregman, *Utopia for Realists: How We Can Build the Ideal World* (New York: Little Brown, 2017), 25–27.
10. See, for example, Philippe Van Parijs and Yannick Vanderborght, *Basic Income: A Radical Proposal for a Free Society and a Sane Economy* (Cambridge, MA: Harvard University Press, 2017), and Guy Standing, *Basic Income: A Guide for the Open Minded* (New Haven: Yale University Press, 2017).
11. Bregman, *Utopia for Realists*, 77–100.
12. Studies by the University of Manchester, the World Bank, the medical journal *Lancet*, and others have shown that poor people tend to work harder when they receive no-strings cash; see ibid., 27–33.

13. Karl Marx, *Capital: A Critique of Political Economy*, trans. Samuel Moore and Edward Aveling (New York: International Publishers, 1967), I.713–14.

14. Van Parijs and Vanderborght, *Basic Income*, 107.

15. Thomas Aquinas, *Summa Theologiae,* (II-II.66.1-2).

16. Pope John Paul II, *Sollicitudo Rei Socialis*, §42, http://w2.vatican.va/content/john-paul-ii/en/encyclicals/documents/hf_jp-ii_enc_30121987_sollicitudo-rei-socialis.html#-27.

17. James Keenan, SJ, *The Works of Mercy: The Heart of Catholicism*, 3rd ed. (Lanham, MD: Rowman and Littlefield, 2017), 5.

18. Ivan Illich, *The Rivers North of the Future: The Testament of Ivan Illich*, ed. David Cayley (Toronto: Anansi, 2005), 207.

19. Dorothy Day, "The Mystery of the Poor," *Catholic Worker*, April 1964, 2.

20. See, for example, Dorothy Day, "On Pilgrimage," *Catholic Worker*, April 1956, 3, 6.

STRATEGIES FROM BELOW

The Catholic Worker: Building the
New within the Shell of the Old

Kelly S. Johnson

Steve Hergenhan, a skilled carpenter, was homeless. Dorothy Day guessed that he might have refused to pay his taxes because he hated cars and did not want to pay for roads. "At any rate, he lost his little house on the side of the hill and ended up in New York, on a park bench during the day, telling his grievances to all who would listen, and eating and sleeping in the Municipal Lodging House, which then maintained the largest dormitory in the world, seven hundred double-decker beds."[1] In the early days of the Catholic Worker, during the Depression, Day and her collaborator Peter Maurin invited Hergenhan to stay with them. He wrote for their newspaper, built a house on the movement's first farm, and gardened to feed visitors. He criticized the Worker for not differentiating between the deserving and undeserving poor; he had no patience with anyone who did not earn her or his own way. When young people in the movement dismissed his ideas and were ungrateful for his work, he grew resentful and stormed off. He came back, though, when he got sick. At St. Rose's Cancer Hospital, Day visited him regularly, reading him her retreat notes. He asked, in these late days, for baptism. Day wrote that the priest who came to the hospital "finished the job, he performed the outward signs, he recited the Latin prayers in a garbled monotone in the back of his throat, and despite the lack of grace in the human sense, Grace was there, souls were strengthened, hearts were lifted."[2] Hergenhan died alone one morning, still frustrated because his life could have been so much more. The Catholic Worker remembered this bitter, argumentative, talented man, without illusion and with reverence for the sacred mystery that is the human person.

The Catholic Worker is not a shelter, a social service organization, or a campaign to end homelessness. It is a movement that confronts the violence of the world with the peacemaking of the cross, offering a comprehensive criticism of modern society and a program of direct action, in the words of the founders, "to build a society in which it is easier to be good." Because the Catholic Worker is an "organism" rather than an "organization," as co-founder Peter Maurin (1877–1949) put it, its houses vary widely in both size and style. Some are urban and some are rural. Some communities are quite small; the homes of families are often shared housing with another family or a few individuals at a time. Some offer food and

157

clothing for hundreds, while housing a relatively small circle of people for a longer period. Others offer temporary shelter to transient guests, including migrants and refugees. In many cases, Catholic Worker houses welcome those who have nowhere else to go and who, in fact, never do go anywhere else, becoming family, collaborators, and hosts themselves. Some two hundred communities that call themselves Catholic Worker and others that draw on the tradition of the Catholic Worker without using that name make time and space for people to eat and sleep, to wash and to talk, to grieve and invent, as a way of "building a new society within the shell of the old."[3]

Making the Encyclicals Click

Peter Maurin, a French peasant and self-taught philosopher, rode the rails as an itinerant worker, was arrested as a vagrant, and slept in the flophouses of New York. One time a priest who had sent Maurin money to travel for a speaking engagement demanded the money back after they met, saying Maurin was just "a Bowery bum."[4] When Dorothy Day (1897–1980), a journalist for radical left newspapers and a recent convert to Catholicism, met Maurin in 1932, he had developed a synthesis based on wide reading in history, philosophy, theology, and economics. Maurin convinced Dorothy Day to start a newspaper to popularize the ideas of Catholic Social Teaching as a more profound and lasting solution to social problems than either communism or capitalism. Day called the paper *The Catholic Worker* (as a contrast to the Communists' *Daily Worker*) and filled it with stories of workers' struggles for justice, as seen in the light of Catholic tradition. The paper also featured Maurin's "Easy Essays," sing-song teachings designed to be memorable. He wrote

> The political problem
> Is not a political problem;
> It is an economic problem.
>
> The economic problem
> Is not an economic problem;
> It is an ethical problem.
>
> The ethical problem
> Is not an ethical problem;
> It is a religious problem.[5]

Maurin said that he wanted "to make the encyclicals click."[6] He advocated the example of St. Francis's voluntary poverty, as in Leo XIII's *Auspicato Concessum* (1882); widespread small-scale ownership of property, in accord with *Rerum Novarum* (1891); the call of all people to holiness in Pius XI's encyclical on St.

Francis de Sales, *Rerum Omnium Perturbationem* (1923); and the laity's role in Catholic Action as described in *Quadragesimo Anno* (1931).

Maurin's plan of action began with "roundtable discussions for the clarification of thought." Good conversation about important issues would produce better insights and build relationships, moving people from "I" to "we." "He made you feel that you and all men had great and generous hearts with which to love God," wrote Dorothy Day.[7] Maurin attributed his approach to the personalism of Emmanuel Mounier.[8] For the Worker, "personalism" means that every person, as a creature made for a supernatural end with God, finds fulfillment in openness to others. A good social order arises from and is built around that personhood. This is the sense in which Catholic Workers speak of the movement as anarchist: personal responsibility in relationships, rather than the violence of the bureaucratic state, organizes the good society and so is the central principle of Catholic Worker life.

Maurin found the economic corollary in distributism, which calls for widespread ownership of property for the sake of responsible and creative contribution to the common good.[9] Each person uses property to work creatively and responsibly, to make what is both beautiful and useful. Maurin argued that both usury and industrial labor undermine an economy of good work. Craft guilds, cooperative forms of business, and credit unions were needed to support this society of small-scale ownership and work.

> Christianity has nothing to do
> With either modern capitalism
> Or modern Communism,
> For Christianity has
> a capitalism of its own
> and a communism of its own.
> Modern capitalism
> Is based on property without responsibility,
> While Christian capitalism
> Is based on property with responsibility.
> Modern communism
> Is based on poverty through force
> While Christian communism
> Is based on poverty through choice.[10]

Drawing on Peter Kropotkin's thought about the need to connect scholarship and labor,[11] Maurin also proposed "agronomic universities," where unemployed workers and scholars would live together on the land, each helping the other create a better social order. Life together on the land could counter homelessness, unemployment, dehumanizing work, intellectual disconnection from reality, the habit of mistaking money for wealth, and pressures against welcoming children into a family. Integrating worship into that life of community and work on the land would foster a culture in which love of God and of neighbor could be reconnected to work, so that labor could be personal and beautiful as well as useful.[12]

The Catholic Worker is best known, however, for the middle component of Maurin's program, its houses of hospitality, where those who need shelter would be welcomed, as Maurin often repeated, "at a personal sacrifice." Maurin called for bishops to take the lead in providing hospitality, but also for every parish and indeed every Catholic home to welcome those in need. "There are guest homes today/ in the homes of the rich/ but they are not for those who need them."[13]

> We have parish houses for the priests,
> Parish Houses for educational purposes,
> Parish Houses for recreational purposes,
> but no Parish Houses of Hospitality . . .
> We need Parish Homes
> as well as Parish Domes.[14]

Though Peter Maurin is often criticized for holding a romantic view of premodern life, he was no armchair philosopher. Even before he and Day began the Catholic Worker, Maurin had given his life over to a bold experiment in truth: practicing work as a gift and accepting voluntary poverty as part of, not a failure of, a Christian economy.[15] By "voluntary poverty," Maurin meant neither a grinding, degrading lack of necessities nor the uncluttered "simplicity" that is really another form of luxury. He meant, rather, the costly and practical openness to God and to one's fellow humans that would make a personalist society possible. This kind of voluntary poverty is not a danger sniffing around the edges of prosperity, looking for a way in; it is the home fire, the source of freedom to love one's brothers and sisters in deed and not just in word.

Maurin also saw his companions on the street as authoritative agents of change. "Although you may be called/ Bums and panhandlers/ You are in fact Ambassadors of God."[16] By refusing the rule that says each economic player must strive for independence, these "ambassadors" stir up an economy that recognizes mutuality. Those who beg are not a social problem to be solved; in their struggle, the Spirit of God is calling all humanity to a new life. A church filled with that Spirit and resplendent in the traditional works of mercy would attract collaboration from "the unpopular front": "Humanists, who try to be human to man; Theists, who believe that God wants us to be our brother's keeper; Christians, who believe in the Sermon on the Mount as well as the Ten Commandments; Catholics, who believe in the Thomistic Doctrine of the Common Good."[17]

Direct Action "At a Personal Sacrifice"

But Day and Maurin did not wait for bishops or parishes or other lay people to act. People came to them in need, and Day began finding room. First, she rented such apartments as she could for them, skipping payment of some of her own bills to pay for the miserable cheap rooms. Eventually the growing community opened houses of hospitality in New York's Bowery, and quickly other houses began opening across the United States and beyond.[18]

These houses are not shelters. They are, rather, homes where people make room for other people to become part of the household. Many Catholic Worker communities, in fact, refuse to register as tax-exempt organizations. In a 1989 roundtable discussion on the practice of hospitality, Gayle Catinella of St. Francis House in Chicago remembered Miss Minnie, who "lived out of two bags, slept sitting up in a chair every night with two coats on" when she arrived. She stayed for years, gradually settling in to sleep in a bed, bathe regularly, and wear clean clothes. Since space was limited, she and Gayle became roommates. When Miss Minnie had to move out to a nursing home where, it turned out, she did not receive her medication and adequate care, Gayle felt the pain and guilt of any family member who sees a loved one suffering.[19] Miss Minnie was not a client or a case. She was a friend. As Debbie McQuade explained in the same meeting,

> Anyway, that's the kind of attitude to have with the guests, so that you really like them as persons. Sometimes later you do things to help them, but what you need to do first is just like them and accept them. If they don't change or get their life together or allow you to be helpful, that's all right. You'll still like them. If they change, that's great, but if they don't, that's okay, too.[20]

Personalism in hospitality means the goal is not to make people productive members of society or well-adjusted citizens (and certainly not to fix them to make one's own life easier) but to encounter them, allowing them to be and to become themselves as fully as possible. For many who have been caught between bureaucratic systems of aid and the invisibility of being on the streets, the personal welcome creates space for healing to happen.

Catholic Worker farms offer particular opportunities for healing. Slim's mother dropped him off with some Catholic Workers in 1937 and never came back. Always quiet, he became silent and withdrawn in the confusion of the city. When the community moved him to the first Catholic Worker farm on Staten Island, he was so delighted that he rolled in the grass exuberantly. He remained a gentle, beloved member of Catholic Worker farm communities until his death in 2005. "Here, Slim had children and dogs around him. He had jobs. In the spring and fall he raked leaves, he hauled water, he took out the garbage. In the winter he shoveled snow, cutting paths between the houses and then as his imagination led, pathways to utopia, you might say."[21]

This sort of personal hospitality leaves no room for romantic illusions. A visitor to a Catholic Worker community once asked, "Does Jesus live in this house?" The resident answered, "Yes, he does. And he doesn't flush." Catholic Workers know about intimidation and theft, drug and alcohol abuse. Responses are pragmatic, each community setting its own standards. Some communities will call on police to report crimes and for help with violent behavior. But because of their commitments to pacifism and personalism, Catholic Worker communities tend to manage conflict themselves, planning ahead to ensure that those who are "on the house" are not alone in case of a problem and developing personal skills and tactics of teamwork to de-escalate conflict. For Catholic Workers, the violence of the street is a reality to handle, one more part of the social disorder we all suffer, alongside consumerism, militarism, and an economy that serves the fantasy of endless growth. It is not a reason to stop being hospitable. "Love in practice is a harsh and dreadful thing, compared to love in dreams," as Fr. Zosima says in one of Day's favorite books, *The Brothers Karamazov.*

"The Cross, That Mighty Failure"[22]

Catholic Workers are accustomed to complaints that this long-range, local, and personal program does not do enough to change systems or even meet immediate needs. Do the works of mercy, in fact, end up supporting the status quo, rather than changing it? Catholic Workers themselves do not pretend that their hospitality is unambiguous. Day wrote with characteristic frankness, "Many left the work because they could see no use in this gesture of feeding the poor, and because of their own shame. But enduring this shame is part of our penance."[23] Facing the reality of misery that cannot easily be fixed is a necessary part of knowing the truth about the world and about ourselves. After forty years in the movement, Frank Cordero wrote, "I've discovered being a Catholic Worker is not the answer to our national social ills and sins of denial. Being a CWer is more like taking an antidote, something you need to do to keep honest, with eyes wide open to the matrix of lies that drives our modern US way of life."[24]

Day recognized that the Worker was not the single solution. She referred to many different ways of practicing the works of mercy, because so much good work is needed: "Building, increasing food production, running credit unions, working in factories which produce for true human needs, working in the smallest of industries, the handcrafts—all these things can come under the heading of the works of mercy, which are the opposite of the works of war."[25] Nevertheless, she chose to give her energy to chopping vegetables and serving soup, accompanying people to medical appointments, defusing arguments that threaten to turn into fights.[26] Others continue to choose the same.

The Worker accepts its limitations as part of its calling to be with the poor. As Murphy Davis of The Open Door (a house of hospitality in Atlanta founded by a Presbyterian community) wrote,

> We still wonder how we'll get the work done next week and where the money will come from to pay the bills. It often seems that we spend more

time burying the dead, saying goodbye, and dealing with tragedy than celebrating victories. How strange it seems to affirm that this is precisely how God has gifted us. If we had somehow become a successful ministry, we sure would not have moved into such close familial ties with the poor.[27]

That poverty is not resignation. The works of mercy, after all, include "instructing the ignorant" and "admonishing the sinner," and under those headings, Catholic Workers turn from "comforting the afflicted" to "afflicting the comfortable." In Lent of 2018, Kaleb Havens of the LA Catholic Worker chained himself to a fence on Skid Row and went on a hunger strike, outside a building that had once housed a hundred and fifty homeless people. The building now warehouses property, while human beings outside of it are left to find their own way in a city that offers glittering prospects to those who can pay and squalor to those who can't. Havens collaborates with longtime Skid Row activists, including General Dogon, in a campaign demanding that new market-rate developments include social services and low-income housing. "The keys had been handed over to big money, and landowners get to write all of the laws," says Havens. The ongoing campaign aims to "give power back to the people." Even in protest, the spirit of penance and prayer lingers. For Havens, thirty days camped on Skid Row, living on broth and tea and coconut water was a part of "balancing the scales," a way of "taking my white privilege and doing prophetic witness."[28]

Havens's action was just one link in a long chain of work by other activists, among them Jeff Dietrich and Catherine Morris, longtime leaders of the LA Catholic Worker. Dietrich is known around Skid Row for putting his body on the line, literally, when city dump trucks arrived to trash the possessions of the homeless, but also by blocking the mayor's bathroom to provide an object lesson in the importance of getting porta-potties in place for the homeless and by occupying a bulldozer set to prepare a site for the new cathedral, whose expense Dietrich saw as a betrayal of the church's duty to love the "least of these."[29] Dietrich, when accused of "enabling" homeless people, answered, "Yes, we believe in enabling people living on the streets, people who've been discarded by society, so they can live with as much dignity as possible. I guess that's right, homeless enablers are what we are."[30]

Whether by protest or hospitality, the Worker sees changing this social order as a spiritual struggle, as well as a material and political one. Day advocated "the little way," a teaching of a nineteenth-century French contemplative nun St. Therese of Lisieux. Lacking occasion for heroic virtue as a martyr or missionary, Therese offered to God her small acts of devotion, such as remaining silent when a co-worker in the laundry splashed her with dirty water. Therese held that any act of love, offered to God, had results far out of proportion to its size. Therese saw this as realism: because human action is always imperfect, always small, anything people do becomes great only because it is given entirely to God, who does all things.

Day found in "the little way" the essential spirituality for the twentieth century. "With governments becoming stronger and more centralized, the common man feels his ineffectiveness. When the whole world seems given over to war and the show of force, the message of Therese is quite a different one." Therese's teaching clears a path through both despair and grandiose aspirations. As the atom is small and explosive, so the small, hidden act of complete self-surrender to God "has all the power of the spirit of Christianity behind it. It is an explosive force that can transform our lives and the life of the world, once put into effect."[31]

"The little way" frees Catholic Workers to act boldly in accord with conscience, even if they cannot see how the action can be effective in addressing the enormity of the problem. Each action of faith, no matter how great the powers arrayed against it, is an opportunity to build the new within the shell of the old. The cross is, as Day wrote, a "mighty failure," and it gives believers the courage to take risk faith themselves.

Conclusion

Since Dorothy Day's death in 1980, the Catholic Worker has continued to tell stories and argue about ideas. Should Catholic Workers be more devoted to or more critical of traditional Catholic practice and the leadership of the bishops? How should relations to the state and police be navigated? What forms of protest are truly nonviolent? How deeply is the Worker shaped by white privilege and how should it change to address that? In his remembrance of Casa Juan Diego founder Mark Zwick, Michael Baxter wrote, "The tradition of the Catholic Worker is what makes it possible to debate its aims and means, and only by debating its aims and means can the movement develop and deepen over time."[32]

The Catholic Worker is unfinished. Its life offers no conclusions, no victory, no clean fixes, and that is consistent with Maurin's synthesis, which at its heart is about persons sharing in the life of a crucified God. Pope Francis could have been describing the Catholic Worker when he wrote, "I prefer a Church which is bruised, hurting and dirty because it has been out on the streets, rather than a Church which is unhealthy from being confined and from clinging to its own security."[33]

Notes

1. Dorothy Day, *The Long Loneliness* (New York: Harper & Row, 1952), 193.
2. Ibid., 199.
3. Catholicworker.org offers a directory of communities, which at present lists 174 in the United States and 29 elsewhere, including houses in the Philippines, Uganda, and South Korea.
4. Day, *Long Loneliness*, 280.
5. From "Christopher Dawson, 'Culture Rooted in Religion,' arranged by Peter Maurin." Maurin Papers, Series 10, Box 1, Folder 9. Marquette University Archives, The Dorothy Day–Catholic Worker Collection. Thanks to Marc Ellis for pointing out this essay and to Phil Runkel for locating it in the archives.
6. Day, *Long Loneliness*, 194.
7. Ibid., 171.

8. For an introduction to Mounier (and a number of Maurin's other influences), see Mark and Louise Zwick, *The Catholic Worker Movement: Intellectual and Spiritual Origins* (Mahwah, NJ: Paulist Press, 2013).

9. A seminal statement of distributism is G. K. Chesterton, *The Outline of Sanity* (New York: Dodd, Mead, 1927). For an example of a recent revival, see Gene Callahan, "Distributism Is the Future," *American Conservative* (March 1, 2016): 26–29.

10. Peter Maurin, *Easy Essays* (Chicago: Franciscan Herald Press, 1984), 37–38.

11. *Fields, Factories, and Workshops*, ed. George Woodcock (Montreal: Black Rose Books), 165–81.

12. The emphasis on crafts continues to the present day. See Brian Terrell, "CW Struggle for the Land," *Catholic Worker*, August–September, 2017, 3.

13. Maurin, *Easy Essays*, 8.

14. Ibid., 10–11.

15. Day, *Long Loneliness*, 178–79.

16. Maurin, *Easy Essays*, 8.

17. Ibid., 146.

18. For an insider view of this early hospitality, see Kate Hennessy, *The World Will Be Saved by Beauty: An Intimate Portrait of My Grandmother* (New York: Scribner, 2017).

19. Rosalie Riegle Troester, ed. and comp., *Voices from the Catholic Worker* (Philadelphia: Temple University Press, 1993), 170–71.

20. Debbie McQuade, interview, *Voices*, 173.

21. Tom Cornell's obituary for Theodore Roosevelt Ridlon, known as Slim, appeared in *The Catholic Worker*, March–April 2007, and is part of a collection of such obituaries: *Ambassadors of God: Selected Obituaries from* The Catholic Worker, ed. Amanda W. Daloisio, Dan Mauk, and Terry Rogers (San Jose, CA: Resource Publications, 2018).

22. Dorothy Day, "On Pilgrimage," February 1969, in *On Pilgrimage: The Sixties* (New York: Curtis Books, 1972), 360.

23. Day, *Long Loneliness*, 215–16.

24. Frank Cordero, "In Gratitude for Eighty-Five Years of the Catholic Worker Movement," *Catholic Worker*, May 2018, 4.

25. Day, "On Pilgrimage," February 1969, 361.

26. Robert Coles, *Dorothy Day: A Radical Devotion* (Reading, MA: Addison-Wesley, 1987), 102.

27. Peter Gathje, ed., *A Work of Hospitality: The Open Door Reader, 1982–2002* (Atlanta: Open Door Community), 12.

28. Interview with the author, December 18, 2018.

29. "Times Are Changing under Pope Francis," *National Catholic Reporter*, December 6, 2013, https://www.ncronline.org/news/justice/times-are-changing-under-pope-francis.

30. Interview with Kurt Streeter, "A Couple's Commitment to Skid Row Doesn't Waver," *Los Angeles Times,* April 9, 2014, https://www.latimes.com/local/la-me-c1-catholic-workers-20140409-dto-htmlstory.html.

31. Robert Ellsberg, ed., *Dorothy Day: Selected Writings* (Maryknoll, NY: Orbis Books, 1992), 202.

32. "Mark Zwick 1927–2016," *Catholic Worker*, January–February 2017, 3.

33. Apostolic Exhortation *Evangelii Gaudium* (November 24, 2013), 4, http://w2.vatican.va/content/francesco/en/apost_exhortations/documents/papa-francesco_esor-tazione-ap_20131124_evangelii-gaudium.html.

Theological-Ethical Foundations

THE MINISTRY OF ACCOMPANIMENT AMONG THE UNHOUSED

Reconceiving the Spiritual Works of Mercy

María Teresa (MT) Dávila

Attending to the dignity of unhoused persons demands care for physical as well as spiritual needs. "Housing first" initiatives, for example, provide ample evidence of the importance and success of attending to their material well-being as part of comprehensive efforts to improve the quality of life of the unhoused.[1] But wholeness and human dignity in integral human development requires accompanying the pursuit of material development with attention to spiritual well-being.[2] Integral human development asks that we seek the material, as well as the cultural, political, and spiritual integrity and flourishing of all members of a community. Aptly, the Christian tradition offers both corporal and spiritual works of mercy to help the faithful orient themselves toward marginalized and impoverished persons and communities for the task of building wholeness, reconciliation, integrity, and dignity for all.[3]

Homeless ministries of accompaniment focus on the spiritual works of mercy and seek to meet and walk with the unhoused where they are, physically and spiritually. Through ritual, prayer, conversation, and sharing in simple meals, the ministry of accompaniment attends to the spiritual integrity of the unhoused. Social and personal stigma, shame, and the psychological toll of the physical challenges of homelessness greatly challenge the human spirit. They lead to feelings of self-hate, brokenness, and alienation. This is exacerbated by the very real alienation and hate many of our communities feel toward the unhoused, who are often not permitted inside our churches, public spaces, or businesses. Ministries of accompaniment offer a form of spiritual welcome and reconciliation without judgment, regardless of the stage in a person's journey toward becoming housed. It is in the course of practicing these ministries that the spiritual works of mercy prove to be a mutual task of building wholeness for all participants, housed and unhoused.[4] Rather than being charitable acts of largesse by those who possess an abundance of a particular resource toward those who lack in that resource—as the corporal works of mercy are sometimes understood—ministries of accompaniment engage the spiritual works of mercy from the common understanding of all being God's children in profound need of God's mercy and reconciliation.

Chaplains on the Way is one such ministry of accompaniment.[5] Through walking the streets of Waltham, Massachusetts, offering different forms of ecumenical worship and prayer, accompaniment and conversation in simple meals, and visiting members of the community who are hospitalized or jailed, it offers key ministries from which many in the community would typically be excluded in traditional religious settings. I have come to understand the spiritual works of mercy as the practice of broken people, sharing their spiritual gifts in mutuality, in the trust that Christ, as one who walked the way of the cross as a completely broken man, restores and reconciles all. Participation in the life of Chaplains on the Way and the witness of its ministers and community members inform this understanding. This chapter reconceives the spiritual works of mercy interpreted through the lens of homeless ministries of accompaniment. First, I present the spiritual works of mercy with unhoused communities as a matter of love and justice because they seek to restore an integral part of the dignity of every person through attending to their spiritual well-being. This is followed by a closer look at the ministry of accompaniment through the work of Chaplains on the Way. These experiences highlight how an understanding of the spiritual works of mercy as practices of mutuality among a broken people is a significant shift from the common misunderstanding of the works of mercy as spiritual gifts bestowed by the spiritually pure and gifted unto the sinning and wayward soul. The final section looks more closely at one particular practice of Chaplains on the Way: the Way of the Cross during Holy Week. This ritual is experienced as one of the most broken spaces in the Christian tradition as the community accompanies a broken Jesus to his crucifixion. As such, this opens space for acknowledging our own need for God's mercy and for inclusion in a spiritual community that helps communicate that mercy. During the Way of the Cross, members of the Chaplains on the Way community are challenged to envision what reconciliation and wholeness in Christ could look like from the particular experience of being unhoused.

The Spiritual Works of Mercy and Human Dignity

Attending to the spiritual life of the unhoused combines the requirements of justice and mercy. By exploring how spiritual well-being and development is part of a person's dignity and integrity, we acknowledge the centrality of the spiritual works of mercy in protecting their dignity. The concept of integral human development in Catholic Social Teaching provides a view of the material well-being of persons and communities that is intimately related to their political, spiritual, educational, cultural, mental/intellectual, and social well-being. This view is grounded on the Catholic vision of human dignity centered on the person in community as created by and in God, with rights and dignities that no event or condition—imprisonment, homelessness, war, sickness, disability, employment, or socioeconomics—can alter. Integral human development extends beyond a mere floor of basic material and political rights for human survival. It promotes the integrity of the person and his right to flourish economically, culturally, politically, socially, and spiritually. In articulating a vision for development that takes into consideration the fullness of the human person, the church proposed that human development must be measured in dimensions that went beyond material and economic progress.[6]

Pope Paul VI redefined development as a process that "cannot be limited to mere economic growth."[7] In 1987, John Paul II added that "collaboration in the development of the *whole person and of every human being* is in fact a duty of all towards all, and must be shared by the four parts of the world."[8] For Benedict XVI, integral human development "requires a transcendent vision of the person, it needs God: without him development is either denied, or entrusted exclusively to man who falls into the trap of thinking he can bring about his own salvation, and ends up promoting a dehumanized form of development."[9]

Integral human development acknowledges the transcendental nature of the person: their relationship with and directionality toward God. At a practical level this transcendental component must be balanced with a diversity of religious traditions and experiences often present in the different communities that take shape around homeless ministries.

Including the transcendental or spiritual life of a person as part of an effective approach to the development of the whole person is an attempt to be authentic to the truth of the fullness of the person as created by God. Attention to the spiritual and religious life of persons and communities recognizes how religious life can support the economic development and social integration of the poor and provide a sense of belonging, stability, forgiveness, resilience, and other positive markers that greatly affect the life prospects of persons and communities.[10] Integral development points to the goal of attending to the whole person, seeing sustained relationships with God and others as key elements of personal and communal wholeness.

Finally, inclusion and participation in communities of support and with which people deeply identify further helps us understand the spiritual works of mercy, and the ministries of accompaniment that embody them, as a matter of justice for unhoused communities. Martha Nussbaum's Capabilities Approach as a model for development includes dimensions such as human participation, a sense of belonging, the exercise of imagination, and the engagement of emotions, play, and other nonmaterial dimensions as crucial for the development of persons, communities, and nations.[11] Often the unhoused have experienced tragic rejection not just by their families and other loved ones, but by the very faith communities that anchored their day-to-day lives before becoming unhoused. In addition, the shame of homelessness and internalized guilt that many unhoused feel about their life circumstances often keeps them from approaching faith communities in which they might find welcome and support.

As a matter of justice, the unhoused are owed the same welcome and sense of religious belonging as their housed counterparts. Most development models agree that spiritual wellness contributes significantly to the life prospects of poor communities, and Catholic Social Teaching insists that human development fails when it does not consider the whole person, which includes the spiritual/transcendental dimensions. Care for the spiritual life of the unhoused is a matter of justice, of attending to their whole being, and aiming for their best life prospects.

Ministry of Accompaniment
as a Spiritual Work of Mercy

James Keenan describes mercy as "the willingness to enter into the chaos of another. Because God is merciful God enters into our chaos."[12] It is, first and foremost, a form of recognition of the other and his or her worth as a human being, as well as the conditions that affect or threaten that worth. That in itself proves transformative as so much of the suffering of the poor is made invisible in society. Second, entering the chaos of another is done in recognition and imitation of God's mercy for us. In the case of the spiritual works of mercy, we enter the chaos of another not from the stance of an abundance of resources on our part, since we are first required to acknowledge our own deep need for mercy.[13] Rather, from that place of shared spiritual vulnerability and poverty, we become "spiritual caretakers of others."[14]

To this effect, the ministry of accompaniment with the unhoused brings a character of mutuality to the spiritual works of mercy. At Seattle Mennonite Church, engaging in any ministry *toward* the unhoused meant asking hard questions about who parishioners were for that population and who they wanted to be as a faith community.[15] Their efforts to ensure that their ministry to the unhoused not become "transactional" led them to a ministry of presence that was centered mainly on listening:

> It all begins with one-on-one, human-to-human connections. It doesn't come about when the person of relative privilege seeks to save or change the person who is suffering. Instead, there must be a deep listening for the words, the dreams, the hopes that are already within the individual.[16]

In transactional forms of ministry, those offering ministry are often seen as having more resources, being morally superior, having more knowledge than those receiving, suggesting a mere redistribution of resources.[17] A transactional model of redistribution is often applied and seen in the practice of the spiritual works of mercy and ministries of accompaniment when those engaging in these ministries lord their spiritual largess over others, or pretend to be spiritually superior. This imbalance leads to resentment because it tends to highlight largess, while disregarding the recipient's spiritual richness, resilience, and resources.[18]

Ministries of accompaniment are indeed a form of becoming incarnate in the suffering of the unhoused, meeting them and walking with them *precisely where they are*. Jude Tiersma Watson speaks of incarnational urban ministries this way: "When we choose to cross barriers into another class and culture, we choose to undergo the physical and emotional experiences of our neighbors, identifying with them in their struggles and joy."[19] As we engage in the spiritual works of mercy, we are called to acknowledge our own suffering and weakness.[20] It demands awareness and reflection on our own brokenness as humans on a shared journey toward wholeness.

The ministry of accompaniment at Chaplains on the Way in Waltham, Massachusetts, seeks to meet the spiritual needs of individuals where they are. The "on the Way" happens along a walking route that maps out the city of Waltham's warming, free meal, and day centers, as well as some of the churches that offer hospitality to the different kinds of rituals, prayers, and groups going on at various times during the day. The walk takes place early in the morning and again in the afternoon. The walk in the morning ends at a local fast food restaurant where chaplains offer community members they have met along the way conversation and a simple meal. Some mornings members of the community already know to meet the chaplains there and are waiting for them by the time they finish their walk. Conversations at that time focus on listening to health and housing woes, family concerns, personal struggles, and updates on others who might not have come around in a while. Listening is the first act of mercy: providing comfort to the afflicted in the form of acknowledging their humanity, and their concerns as real and valid. Chaplains also make a point of announcing any special gatherings that day and later in the week. These range from prayer circles, meditation, walking a labyrinth, meals to be shared in community, and worship services. The conversation often ends by asking people if they have any needs for which they wish to pray. We don't always see everyone at the next event that day. Especially if this is in a traditional worship space, sometimes there are wounds and memories that make people hesitate to enter a church or space for organized prayer or worship. Those who do join find a community where their whole selves are received, where they are never judged. Because Chaplains on the Way is not a fixed shelter, it does not have any rules regarding sobriety of participants for any of the activities. As long as participants are not a threat to others or to themselves, they are welcome.

If we understand the spiritual works of mercy as owed in justice to the unhoused, we can consider five concrete ways in which ministries of accompaniment promote their human dignity in the way described above:

1. Acknowledging participants' whole stories, including their narrative of how they became unhoused. The ministry of accompaniment does not place limits on what community members get to share in prayer and conversation. The spaces created for participants welcome their narratives about family, loss, sexual and intimate partner violence, drug dependency, job prospects, relationships, love, and hope.
2. Building communities of spiritual belonging and care. These spaces welcome both community members ecstatic to be welcomed in a worship space, as well as some who are incredibly suspicious and even resentful of the church. In these spaces, the priority is to offer comfort to the afflicted, to help them see the chaplains and other community members as respecting their worth, and co-travelers in the journey toward healing whatever brokenness we bring to these spaces.[21]

3. Instructing their understanding away from a God who judges and condemns toward a God who embraces in mercy and compassion. Often community members have been on the receiving end of much religious violence. The Bible and a particularly stern image of God have been used to shame the unhoused, or judge their circumstances as morally reprehensible. The result is often a vision of God as loving only those whose circumstances God approves of, making the unhoused feel that they are outside of God's mercy, care, and forgiveness.

4. Forgiveness of past wrongs. The spiritual burdens carried by the unhoused are often heavy and long-term. Some represent very serious events in which the person has significantly wronged a loved one, or themselves. Some might seem trivial or even silly to the listener, but they nevertheless constitute a heavy burden for that person. Because the unhoused frequently feel excluded from traditional communities of faith they see themselves outside the boundaries of God's forgiveness. And even when we hold services of healing and reconciliation, community members might express that even when God forgives them, they are not ready to forgive themselves. In such cases, it makes a difference simply to open space where we can carry these burdens together, where forgiveness is offered, and the path to forgiving the self is open.

5. Praying for their needs. One of the ways in which ministry with the unhoused attends to the worth and human dignity of all gathered is incorporating their prayer requests, their life experiences, and challenges. Participants come believing that their concerns are not worthy to be brought up in communal prayer. They either feel they have no right to do so by virtue of some past wrong or not having attended a religious service in some time, or that their particular concerns are altogether inappropriate for communal prayer. By incorporating prayers for the chaplains or prayer leaders, we communicate our shared need for God's mercy and care, that the prayer space has no exclusions, and that there is no spiritual or moral superiority separating the ministers from the unhoused.

Finally, praying for deceased members of the community and attending to their collective mourning is a central element of ministries of accompaniment. For the unhoused, untimely death and tragedy is part of their daily experience. Many have medical conditions that go untreated for months or even years; drug addiction and overdoses threaten them constantly; and sheer human cruelty toward their population makes them vulnerable to attacks. Praying for the deceased members of the community is a final act of acknowledging their full worth before the community and before God. It is impactful to see the concern we have for each other when a member is in the hospital, lost or not seen for some time, or has passed away. Collective mourning and prayer also become a witness to the dignity and worth of the remaining community members who understand that in that space and in that community, they are acknowledged as full heirs of God's promises of redemption.

The Way of the Cross:
Broken Space for Restoring Wholeness

The Way of the Cross is the most broken space in the Christian story. It is that journey that signals the defeat of the Jesus project to his followers, close friends, and family. While the cross and Jesus' death on it are later interpreted as the first moment in Christ's victory over death, the journey to the cross has all the indications of personal and corporate failure and defeat. It is a space that the unhoused easily recognize as their own, even if they put some moral or existential distance between them and the figure of Jesus. The broken space of the Way of the Cross welcomes our brokenness and loss because for the first time in our own broken story, we are walking with Jesus as co-equals: like Jesus, many who are gathered have served time, been spat on by others walking by, have lost the love, welcome, and respect of friends and kin, and have nothing but the burden on our back to call our own. And as we gather and pray through this broken journey, we too are aware that our own death may likely be as untimely, unjust, and tragic as Jesus' death.

Praying the Way of the Cross at Chaplains on the Way has become a place where confession and mercy meet for both housed and unhoused. Stopping at each station opens up space for contemplation, personal prayer, and communal prayer. As Jesus' body becomes more broken with each insult, the weight of the cross, the violence of the moment, participants find space to bring their own brokenness in a safe moment of shared vulnerability. These experiences correspond to the spiritual work of comforting the afflicted: "Comforting is always an act of acknowledging, not so much the loss, but the self-understanding of the afflicted one. . . . By participating in the life of mercy we may discover the dignity of the human person that sparkles oftentimes when they are most vulnerable."[22]

A thirst for reconciliation is often the most vocalized need: reconciliation with a child, a spouse, a parent, a sibling, those loving relationships most affected by the conditions that brought the person to become unhoused. Although the Way of the Cross is sometimes a reminder of these broken bonds in their life, it also draws people closer in faith to a God who suffers with them, and who reconciles all, even after immense violence and hurt. It is a vision of healing and wholeness that we can all hold, shape, and share together, even if for a brief afternoon.

On one occasion, as each station prompted prayers particular to the situation on the image, I was overwhelmed by the image of Mary contemplating her dying son. A number in the group prayed for children: children of incarcerated women, children in war-torn countries, and, of course, their own. I added the prayer that had welled up inside me, for my own children, specifically one who struggles with mental health needs. Tears flowed copiously down my face as I placed my concerns for my child at the image of Mary at the feet of a crucified Jesus. At that point I felt I had failed the community, imposing my own concerns on those already suffering because of their housing situation and the conditions that caused this. I was embarrassed and felt like a fraud. But the community gathered that day understood mental health needs, the deep loss that can come with it, the chaos, the unpredictability. They heard my prayer, they nodded, they understood, and they too raised it up to Mary's gaze. My failure was not in uttering the prayer, but in not seeing them as a community of mutuality. I feared that my vulnerability would bring them further hurt. I had forgotten that what we bring to others in the ministry of accompaniment and the spiritual works of mercy is nothing but our broken selves, ready to be vessels of unmerited and unending mercy.

Conclusion

The centrality of tending to the spiritual well-being of the unhoused as part of honoring their worth and human dignity points to the role the spiritual works of mercy play in development conversations. The ministry of accompaniment offers a setting and sets of practices that adapt to many of the challenges, spiritual and corporate, experienced by the unhoused: lack of transportation, suspicion and wariness toward religious establishments and churches, overwhelming feelings of rejection, alienation, and lack of worth. Efforts at housing the homeless and providing other benefits for their material flourishing must take into account how spiritual well-being becomes an asset in considering their long-term life prospects.

However, many of the metrics of development do not apply to the spiritual works of mercy. The type of goals set by housing first initiatives, for example, cannot be applied to the ministry of accompaniment. What does success look like after a year of accompaniment in Chaplains on the Way? How do we measure building trusting relationships? Enabling reconciliation? How do we quantify building spaces of shared vulnerability and brokenness for the spiritual development of all? In the practice of the ministry of accompaniment, the goal is ultimately to be vessels of mercy already freely poured out for our healing among communities that don't often get to have mercy shown to them.

Certainly, a both/and approach is needed. It is important to be able to quantify mental and physical health and well-being of populations whom Christians are called to serve. This is a requisite of being good stewards of the resources states, churches, and donors provide for such development work. One way to add a quantifiable measure for the spiritual works of mercy with the unhoused could be to evaluate the spiritual resources truly available to these communities, the level of welcome offered to the unhoused, and whether there are missions of accompaniment continually operating in the area. This would be distinct from measuring "outreach" programs such as soup kitchens, food pantries, and clothing closets often provided by local churches. While these offer a certain kind of spiritual welcome, they do not represent spaces where all in attendance share from their own broken selves, from the common acknowledgment that all are in profound need of God's mercy, and where all are welcome to bring their spiritual vulnerabilities. In addition, these might have restrictions regarding sobriety and past criminal record for participants, constrained by child protection protocols, therefore not truly open to all.

Ultimately, practicing the spiritual works of mercy with the unhoused establishes communities of mutuality and shared vulnerability that might be unsettling to many development models or outreach programs. And yet these are necessary spaces for honoring the full person of those whose life prospects we would like to affect for the better. In turn, they also become essential spaces for the spiritual integrity of those offering accompaniment, redefining the spiritual works as communal experiences for wholeness and healing of all who gather.

Notes

1. See, for example, Deborah Padgett, Victoria Stanhope, et al., "Substance Use Outcomes among Homeless Clients with Serious Mental Illness: Comparing Housing First with Treatment First Programs," *Community Mental Health Journal* 42, no. 2 (April 2011): 227–32; and Susan Collins, Daniel Malone, et al., "Project-Based Housing First for Chronically Homeless Individuals with Alcohol Problems: Within-Subjects Analyses of Two-Year Alcohol Trajectories," *American Journal of Public Health* 102, no. 3 (March 2012): 511–19.

2. Geoff Heinrich, David Leege, and Carrie Miller, *A User's Guide to Integral Human Development (IHD): Practical Guidance for CRS Staff and Partners* (Baltimore: Catholic Relief Services, 2008), 2, 5–6.

3. James Keenan, *The Works of Mercy: The Heart of Catholicism,* 3rd ed. (Lanham, MD: Rowman & Littlefield, 2017). Specifically, Keenan suggests that the spiritual works of mercy help the faithful shift their gaze or attention to the needs of others that often go unseen, as opposed to material needs that are easier to perceive.

4. Ibid., 84.

5. Chaplains on the Way, http://www.chaplainsontheway.us. My engagement with Chaplains on the Way has been varied throughout the past ten years. On a yearly basis, I lead the Way of the Cross during Holy Week, the focus of the last section of this chapter. Throughout the years, I have mentored and directed seminary students doing their field education training with the unhoused. And my homelessness and housing insecurity course has Chaplains on the Way as a partner for the students' journey. I have also participated in the "walks" described in the third section of the chapter as a key element of the ministry of accompaniment.

6. Paul VI, *Populorum Progressio* (On the Development of Peoples) (1967), http://w2.vatican.va/content/paul-vi/en/encyclicals/documents/hf_p-vi_enc_26031967_populorum.html, Section I: Man's Complete Development. Number 13 in particular speaks to this anthropological commitment and duty of the church: "Sharing the noblest aspirations of men [*sic*] and suffering when she [*sic*] sees these aspirations not satisfied, she wishes to help them attain their full realization. She offers man her distinctive contribution: a global perspective on man and human realities."

7. Paul VI, *Populorum Progressio,* 14.

8. John Paul II, *Sollicitudo Rei Socialis* (On the Twentieth Anniversary of *Populorum Progressio*) (1987), #32, http://w2.vatican.va/content/john-paul-ii/en/encyclicals/documents/hf_jp-ii_enc_30121987_sollicitudo-rei-socialis.html. Emphasis mine.

9. Benedict XVI, *Caritas in Veritate* (On Integral Human Development in Charity and Truth) (2009), #11, http://w2.vatican.va/content/benedict-xvi/en/encyclicals/documents/hf_ben-xvi_enc_20090629_caritas-in-veritate.html.

10. Heinrich, Leege, and Miller, *A User's Guide to Integral Human Development (IHD)*, 6. In this document, Catholic Relief Services refers to spiritual well-being as an "asset" in the life of the poor, one that combines positively with other assets to build on development goals and concrete and measurable improvement on life outcomes.

11. See Martha Nussbaum, *Creating Capabilities: The Human Development Approach* (Cambridge, MA: Harvard University Press, 2011).

12. James Keenan, "The Evolution of the Works of Mercy," in *Mercy*, ed. Lisa Cahill, Diego Irarrázaval, and João Vila-Chã (London: SCM Press, 2017), 33.

13. Keenan, *Works of Mercy*, 91.

14. Ibid., 85.

15. Jonathan Neufeld and Melanie Neufeld, "Companionship on Seattle Streets: From Transaction to Mutuality in Ministry," *Vision* (Spring 2014): 16.

16. Ibid., 19.

17. Ibid., 16.

18. Ibid., 17.

19. Jude Tiersma, "What Does It Mean to Be Incarnational When We Are Not the Messiah?" in *God So Loves the City: Seeking a Theology for Urban Mission*, co-edited with Charles Van Engen (Eugene, OR: Wipf and Stock, 2009), 8.

20. It's important to acknowledge my original reluctance to engage the spiritual works of mercy as a topic for personal and scholarly reflection. Alice Camille in "The Dark Side of the Works," *US Catholic* (May 2016), puts it best: "Particularly when we engage the spiritual works of mercy, we could use a generous helping of 'patience, kindness, gentleness, and self-control,' along with our correction of the sinner and advice of the ignorant. Otherwise we risk a bout of zeal that may well be righteous, but will be experienced more like an assault when visited upon those we're determined to assist with our superior wisdom. Works of mercy, after all, have to feel merciful in their execution, and not like being on the receiving end of a firing squad" (48–49). Working in the area of the culture wars has made me wary and suspicious of claims of fraternal correction or instructing the ignorant, when in reality the intervention or discussion feels more like the "firing squad" Camille describes. It was through the ministry of accompaniment with the unhoused, and having children of my own, that opened up the spiritual works of mercy as a practice in the mutual embracing of another's brokenness, enabled because Christ first became broken for us, a journey and sharing that cannot take place if I am not aware of my own brokenness. Keenan's observation affirms this: "While the beneficiary of the corporal works is the recipient, it is the reverse among the spiritual works: often the beneficiary is the one who practices the spiritual works." Keenan, *Works of Mercy*, 84. Much more work ought to be done on the spiritual works of mercy, particularly on whether the language with which they have been traditionally labeled and described really conveys what is taking place among those involved. This would be a valuable and necessary contribution to a church and a people of faith desperate to understand themselves as agents of forgiveness, instruction, comfort, and healing.

21. James Keenan describes how these spaces relate to the spiritual works of mercy: "The reconciling spirit is the one who creates the space that everyone believes they can enter, where they will be forgiven, welcomed, and respected." *Works of Mercy*, 93.

22. Ibid., 99–100.

BLESSED ARE THE POOR IN SPIRIT

A Response to Homelessness by
a Reading of Matthew's Beatitudes

James F. Keenan, SJ

In this essay, I apply the work of the late Yiu Sing Lúcás Chan, SJ, and in particular, his study of the Beatitudes, to homelessness—I use both his exegesis and the
ethical analysis that he developed in *The Ten Commandments and the Beatitudes:
Biblical Studies and Ethics for Real Life.*[1]

Chan writes that the attributes in the Beatitudes were key features of the identity of Jesus. They make sense only if we see them as filling out the image of the one
we wish to follow. They are the eschatological attributes for those who want to enter
the Kingdom of God, for the Kingdom of God is no other than Jesus himself. These
attributes for the disciple are also the very identifying traits of the master.

Chan highlights the broad moral relevance of the Beatitudes in history. Augustine claimed that the Sermon on the Mount was the complete, perfect teaching of
Christian morality. In *Veritatis Splendor,* Pope John Paul II called the Sermon on
the Mount "the *magna carta* of Gospel morality,"[2] and added that the Beatitudes are
"a sort of *self-portrait of Christ.*"[3]

In their eschatological orientation, Matthew's Gospel proposes the Beatitudes as a way of following Jesus Christ, who is preparing us for the Kingdom
of God: he is giving us a blueprint, both personally and communally, of the
attributes we need to enter the Kingdom that Jesus is bringing in. Moreover, the
Beatitudes have a much greater coherence than is normally acknowledged. They
need to be read dynamically, in that the macarisms build one upon another until
finally one realizes that one is climbing a ladder of ascent into the Kingdom. From
the beginning, they look perfectionistic, but once we begin to take the first few
steps, we realize that each step, in a way, empowers the others. Like any notion
of personal or communal growth, until we begin the program, we really are not
able to see where the program is taking us. This "ladder-like" approach was in fact
named as such by early Church Fathers, most notably John Climacus (579–649).[4]
And, it is only by climbing the ladder that we begin to see their internal connect-
edness and logic.

With this in mind, let us begin the ascent.

176

The First Beatitude, Matthew 5:3

Blessed are the poor in spirit, for theirs is the kingdom of heaven.

Significantly, the beatitude tells us that the "poor in spirit" are blessed by God; it echoes Isaiah 61:1 where they are the ones who receive God's good tidings. Chan writes:

> Regarding the notion of "poor," the Greek term πτωχος employed here generally means "beggar." Exegetes inform us that there are several Hebrew equivalents, such as *ani* ("poor"/"afflicted"), *dal* ("weak"), and *ebyon* ("needy"). Thus, the term "poor" refers not only to those who are poor with few possessions but especially those who are socially and economically needy and dependent (such as those being forced to beg). Indeed, the condition of poverty is never regarded as a blessing; and yet the person who is in such a condition can be blessed. Moreover, the term also refers to those who are in special need of God's help (e.g., Psalm 12:5) and have nothing to rely upon except God (e.g., Amos 2:6–7).[5]

These poor, whose economic and spiritual poverty has left them in a state of complete alienation, are, in a word, the homeless. They are the poor in spirit.

Recognizing a virtue for each of the beatitudes, Chan argues that to be "poor in spirit" is the equivalent of having the virtue of humility, a spiritual emptying out: "humility means accepting the complete poverty of our human condition."[6] This is what the poor in spirit experience: only in God do they find their needs met. Discarded by all in society, reduced to begging, they have only God as their hope and to God they come, suppliant. That stance, that humility, is the foundation of any Christian anthropology.

The Second Beatitude, Matthew 5:4

Blessed are they who mourn, for they shall be comforted.

For the second beatitude, Chan wants us to know about who are these blessed mourning? He turns to exegetes who write that the grieving in the second beatitude is directed to the poor in spirit in the first.

Chan is mindful of those ethicists and preachers who think otherwise, who try to claim that the beatitude is a summons to mourn; sounding like grief counselors, they suggest that Christ is counseling us to mourn, for if one denies one's own grief, one will never know the comfort and happiness that follows.

Chan responds: "No one is being told to mourn!"[7] Those in the second beatitude are already mourning. Reminding us of the ladder of ascent, Chan helps us see that we are mourning not for our own losses but for those brothers and sisters who are poor in spirit. Moreover, we are not mourning for those who elect a poverty of spirit, but rather for those whose condition is so bereft of any human good.

Chan writes, "The object of mourning is not so much one's own suffering or sins, but rather the concrete human experience of poverty and suffering encountered by community members. Mourning points to an other-oriented moral value."[8] Then emphatically he adds: "Such is the lot of the disciples of Christ—when our brothers and sisters suffer, we cannot help but mourn." He adds, the beatitude "is about a certain disposition that genuine disciples have with one another, such that if one suffers, the other mourns as well."[9]

When Chan looks for an apt virtue, he finds solidarity naturally as the virtue of the second beatitude.[10] The attitude related to solidarity is not comfort, but rather mourning itself. Chan writes: "In mourning the self tries to identify with the other. Mourning is then the ready subordination of one's own comfort and well-being to the suffering of others." He adds, "In this way, one allows one's private life to be touched by the pain and suffering of the other."[11]

Grieving is an "other-centered attitude," a way that one trains one's own capacity for solidarity with the other by entering into the experience of the other's lot and loss. Not until I fully grasp the loss of the homeless can I resonate with the condition of my sibling who is homeless. Mourning is itself "a truthful expression of the virtue of solidarity."[12]

Listening is a very fine practice for those who mourn in solidarity with another. It allows one to grasp what the other's condition is. The one who suffers needs to be able to find one's voice and speak one's own grief and loss. Listening allows the other to speak, to say the harsh things that no one wants to hear. Listening allows the sufferer to express the disappointment, the abandonment, the hurt, and the misery. When we hear their lament, we inevitably mourn and enter more deeply into another's condition—so many who suffer are looking to be heard.

You may say, yes, but they want a reply! Of course, they do. But you who are mourning are only beginning to learn the ascent of the beatitudes. You have other steps to go before you can begin to do the work of fasting in the fourth beatitude or the work of righteousness in the eighth beatitude. Christ is teaching us to ascend to a capacity to work for these, in the first steps. Now being humble and in solidarity, we must move to the third beatitude.

The Third Beatitude, Matthew 5:5

Blessed are the meek, for they shall inherit the earth.

Climbing the ladder further, Chan takes us to the third beatitude, the meek who will inherit the earth. Here, he surveys the work of biblical theologians and uncovers how inclusive the term is. It appears often in the Septuagint as a word for the *anawim*, the poor, the remnant, those completely left behind. In other words, the meek are again effectively the poor in spirit. But meekness is also an attribute of biblical leadership, both of Jesus and of others in the community (Mt 11:29; Lk 7:36–50; 1 Pet 3:4; Tit 3:2). Moreover, meekness is an ethical attribute of leadership elsewhere. In Jewish literature, meekness marks the sage and the ruler. In Greek literature, it marks the quality of both the true philanthropist and the true philosopher. Meekness is certainly an attribute for a fairly inclusive group of people.[13]

Looking at meekness more as an attitude than a condition, Chan sees it as a transformative virtue, especially as it tempers those whose power can move toward domination. Meekness finds its correlative in gentleness, and in this sense, Chan writes: "The virtue of meekness helps transform our desire to dominate into a vital force to serve."[14] In this way, we can see how we can "emphasize it as a virtue for the poor and the powerful."

Here he turns to Monika Hellwig's astute observation that the powerful "need to unlearn those patterns of behavior that control and dominate others and that 'defend' their possessions and prestige at the cost of others."[15] In a fairly remarkable application to social context, Chan also explores how meekness would look in the corporate world.

When the powerful become champions of justice, they need to develop interiorly a new modesty, an ability to stand as one among others, as one not expecting the head place at the table. Meekness allows the powerful to enter the community as a member instead of as its leader. Meekness allows the powerful to use their power gently, not narcissistically, but compassionately, that is, truly in an other-directed way. Meekness tames the powerful so that their work is truly righteous. Without meekness, they are not able to inherit the earth.

This beatitude seems to be addressed to those who want to serve the homeless but whose own positions of self-importance keep them from being able to enter into true solidarity with the poor. They inevitably "condescend" in their assistance; they want to assist, but they do so from their positions of importance. They try to accompany, but they continue to think of themselves as morally superior.

The third beatitude calls all those who want to assist the homeless to spend some time in learning meekness as a step to better respond to the needs of the poor in spirit. Here then, we begin to see that this ladder of ascent helps us to become trained in the way of the Lord. The ascent becomes empowering, but through an inversion: we grow in power as we surrender it.

Now that we are climbing the ladder, we might do well to study the remaining five beatitudes, but we must remember where we began, with the beggar, the homeless, and realize that all the stages of the beatitudes are built on our capacity to appreciate and respond to their condition. Now that we have learned humility, solidarity, and meekness, we can turn to the fourth and begin our fast for righteousness.

The Fourth Beatitude, Matthew 5:6

Blessed are those who hunger and thirst for righteousness, for they will be filled.

Chan points out:

The original macarism alludes to Psalm 107:5, 8, 9 where God will satisfy
the hungry and the thirsty. However, in the Old Testament, the images of
hunger and thirst have a religious significance as well: It points to an active
seeking (and not just a longing) for God and desiring for God's teaching
and the words of the Law as one desires for food and drink (Psalms 42:2;
143:6; Isaiah 32:6).[16]

The notion of the ladder of ascent leads us to see that the beatitudes are a
training school for Christian discipleship; the exercises of fasting here are not public
fasts in order to protest something, but rather private actions that aim to transform
the one who mourns for the poor in spirit and who struggles to become meek. In
order to pursue these virtues, the disciple is now instructed to practice asceticism so
as to become more capable of these virtues. By fasting, we try to see the righteousness of humility, solidarity, and meekness; this asceticism aims to develop within
the exercitant a deeper hunger for God's righteousness.
    Chan adds: "It is also an ongoing process that does not end until that desire is
fulfilled."[17] This ongoing process he calls a striving, writing that "the object of our
hunger and thirst should be God's righteousness. Therefore, striving for God's righteousness means continually and totally orienting one's heart (including emotions,
thinking, and behaviors) to do what God's righteousness demands."[18]
    Chan identifies this practice of striving for God's righteousness dynamically,
with the virtue of fortitude. This is not simply a fortitude that tenaciously stays put,
but rather one that dynamically and courageously pursues God's righteousness. It
is, therefore, a practice that needs to be accompanied by prayer. "Praying (with the
Lord's Prayer in particular) helps focus on social transformation; as we pray, we
are invited by God to bring God's kingdom on earth and to deliver others from all
forms of indebtedness."[19]

The Fifth Beatitude, Matthew 5:7

Blessed are the merciful, for they will receive mercy.

Chan notes that "starting with 5:7 the remaining four beatitudes are added by
the evangelist from his own sources, for no parallels are found in the Lukan version.
It is suggested that the first three of these four macarisms are taken from a tradition
that reflects the concerns for greater righteousness."[20]

The fifth beatitude is a call to act, to see that the virtue of mercy is the call, as I define it, to enter the chaos of another.[21] Having ascended the ladder, we are at the point where we can encounter the chaos of the poor in spirit.

In the middle of his own work, Chan provides a moving confessional narrative of his own experiences of acting through mercy and therein encountering human misery, a misery that convinces him that he can never walk away from these poor in spirit.

> During my formation as a Jesuit priest, I have been privileged to live in different countries, in both the developed and developing world. One concrete experience common to all is the reality of human misery around us: In Manila, every Sunday, I served the children who live in those "smokey mountains" and spend their entire day picking up "valuables" from the garbage dump. In Belfast, Ireland, I attended funerals of those who died in sectarian conflicts and visited prisoners who are imprisoned because of their fight for an end to colonization. In a remote island in the Pacific Ocean that is simply known as "within the US missile testing range," I too worked with a group of islanders whose community was completely abandoned by the outside world and their environment and natural resources exploited by the Army. In the post Khmer Rouge Cambodia, I lived day and night with a group of landmine victims who struggle to resume a simple life in spite of their physical disability. In my daily reflection, a simple but only too familiar question raised is, "Why these unnecessary miseries?"[22]

Here Chan introduces us to the centrality of mercy in the tradition of the scriptures. He writes:

> In the first place, being merciful and compassionate is a proper attitude towards the human condition noted in the first beatitude—the poor, the outcasts, and even outsiders (9:10–13; 15:21–28). Second, as in the Jewish tradition, to be merciful and compassionate is a fundamental demand (9:13; 12:7). Third, mercy is regularly demonstrated by Jesus' words (18:23–35) and examples (9:27–31). Indeed, the demand for mercy is placed at the center of Jesus' proclamation and challenges the disciples to show mercy to all, including one's enemy (5:43–48).[23]

The centrality of mercy in the scriptures, Chan notes, reflects the fact that mercy is the way we understand the actions of God toward humanity.

> Creation is God's merciful act that brings order into the chaos of the universe; the incarnation is God's entry into the chaos of human existence;

and the redemption is God's mercy that delivers us from the chaos of slavery to sin. . . . Mercy is emphasized by Scripture as the condition for salvation. In short, God who is mercy first shows mercy to us.[24]

Being merciful is therefore a definitive way of imitating God. More than that, mercy is a way of being faithful to God, of participating in God's works, of being most like God in God's ways. Chan writes,

> Matthew cites Hosea 6:6 ("For I desire steadfast love and not sacrifice") twice in his understanding of mercy as a fundamental demand (9:13; 12:7). Here, ἔλεος is used to render the Hebrew term ḥesed ("steadfast, covenantal love of God for the people"). Thus, ἔλεος connotes the idea of loyalty within a relationship, especially loyalty to God. In other words, acts of mercy are concrete expressions of loyalty to God and what God desires of the people.[25]

By entering into affinity with God, by entering into the chaos of the poor in spirit, we enter into the world of God where mercy is exchanged. Thus, being merciful we receive mercy. Mercy is, if you will, its own reward.

The Sixth Beatitude, Matthew 5:8

Blessed are the pure in heart, for they will see God.

The move from the practice of mercy in union with God leads to a new level of capacity in the ever-ascending disciple. Now, the disciple is able to practice mercy well: being meek and in solidarity with the poor in spirit, able to think and act well with them, there is little to compromise the practice of mercy. Being other-directed, a new level of integration has been given to the disciple such that the reconciling work of mercy lives now, in an ongoing way in the disciple.

For this reason, Chan points rather quickly to the comprehensive significance of "purity of heart." Referring to both the Old Testament and New Testament, he notes:

> The Greek term "heart" or καρδία and its Hebrew equivalent *leb* is a comprehensive term. It is at times used interchangeably with the word "soul" (ψυχή)—it can refer to the true self (e.g., Matthew 13:15), the place of emotions (e.g., Acts 14:17), the desire or will (e.g., Proverbs 6:18), the intellect (e.g., Mark 2:6), or the inner space where one encounters the deity (e.g., Psalm 27:8). For Matthew, the heart is clearly the source of outward speech and conduct (15:18–19) as well as the realm of inner life (9:4).[26]

The comprehensiveness of the heart, he writes, connects with the singularity of "the phrase 'pure in heart' (καθαρὸς τῇ καρδίᾳ)," which "is understood within the

Jewish tradition as 'an undivided obedience to God without sin' and is an important virtue."[27] In simple terms, it points to "singleness of intention" and that one should "'will only God's will' with one's whole being."[28]

Chan argues that "pure in heart" "points to neither external purity nor single-heartedness alone but a sense of *integrity* between one's interior life and external actions."[29] He adds, "The pure in heart emphasizes the integrity of one's whole being and understands such an attitude as a fundamental, all-encompassing virtue."[30] For this reason, he notes, the virtue of the sixth beatitude is integrity.

How does one maintain this virtue of integrity? Chan suggests "one growing popular practice," the daily "examen of conscience," as suggested in the *Spiritual Exercises of St. Ignatius*. This is a prayer exercise where "one tries to find the movement of the spirit in one's daily life and through it, to identify the incongruence between one's inner movements and external actions. Examen helps us to be more sensitive to the longings and sources of our own spirit and hence becomes more open to God."[31]

The Seventh Beatitude, Matthew 5:9

Blessed are the peacemakers, for they will be called children of God.

Practicing and receiving mercy leads to a purity of heart, the reconciliation of the warring factors within oneself. This integrity within oneself is a well-won achievement and grace. Now, this seventh beatitude follows the sixth and is about the disciple whose integrity reflects the reconciliation of many of one's own parts; having learned of the hard-won reconciliation in one's self, one becomes a peacemaker among others. Thus one can reconcile others to act together for the poor in spirit.

Referring to the word "peacemaker," Chan notes:

> The term implies a positive action and thus is best applied to someone who seeks to bring peace (i.e., peacemaker) rather than a pacifist *per se*. Some further suggest that it envisions the notion of reconciliation, which in turn implies forgiveness. In both cases, the pursuit of peace is a requirement for following Jesus, for he is the one who brings peace (Luke 2:14) and God is the principal peacemaker (especially by forgiving sins) and a God of peace (Romans 16:20).[32]

Chan notes that it is through peace that one can work for justice, for the peace that Christ speaks of is not simply the absence of conflict or the stability of order, but more importantly the reconciliation of others, so that they together can work for justice. In effect, the peacemaker is the one of integrity who effectively leads others in the work of justice for the poor in spirit. "An exegesis of the Greek and Hebrew terms for peace shows that peace is paralleled with 'justice,'" and is closer to the concept of righteousness than to that of tranquility or order.[33]

Chan provides a helpful summary of how the seventh beatitude expresses the fullness of the achievement of all the previous beatitudes. Arguing that it is mistaken to view peace and justice as incompatible, he writes:

> Genuine peace is built upon justice. Thus, the cultivation of the virtue of peacemaking implies the simultaneous attainment of the virtue of justice at the same time. Moreover, since genuine peace is achieved by means of neither force nor passive acceptance of injustice at any cost, the virtues of meekness and fortitude are called into place respectively: meekness insists on patience and the rejection of violence, while fortitude demands active seeking of peace and endurance. In this way, the third and the seventh beatitudes are closely connected to each other.
>
> Still, the virtues implied in the second beatitude, such as solidarity and the virtuous act of mourning, are also relevant to peacemaking, for they motivate us to assist others in achieving peace. Also, in order to avoid the building up of those stumbling blocks to peace, one needs to cultivate the virtue of humility as well.
>
> Finally, since peacemakers inevitably encounter opponents in the process of making peace, the virtue of mercy (and its particular practice of forgiveness) that leads to transformation of relationships and eventual reconciliation, is crucial to the whole process of peacemaking and restoring the rightful relationships.[34]

The Eighth Beatitude, Matthew 5:10–12

Blessed are those who are persecuted for righteousness' sake,
for theirs is the kingdom of heaven. Blessed are you when people revile
you and persecute you and utter all kinds of evil against you falsely on
my account. Rejoice and be glad, for your reward is great in heaven, for
in the same way they persecuted the prophets who were before you.

Remembering that it is Christ who first aims our attention at the poor in spirit, Chan notes that the phrase ἕνεκεν ἐμοῦ ("on account of me") "states clearly that the proper cause of persecution is Jesus and his teaching."[35] Thus in verse 12, the syllogism "for in the same way they persecuted the prophets who were before you" recalls the Old Testament tradition (and theme) that "suffering from persecution is part of the prophet's vocation (e.g., Nehemiah 9:26)."[36]

Chan notes that the promise of the eighth macarism is the same as that of the first beatitude. He concludes that 5:10–12 "tells us that those who suffer from various kinds of physical and/or verbal persecution for the sake of righteousness as the prophets did and as the disciples do now, on account of Jesus and his teaching, will be rewarded greatly in the eschatological coming of the kingdom of Heaven.

Still, they should rejoice and be glad right now because of the guarantee of this reward."[37]

Noting that by forming an *inclusio* with the first beatitude, this expanded eighth beatitude "sums up the basic thoughts and forms a high point for the ethical teaching of the whole Beatitudes: the attitude of humility identified in the first beatitude reaches its climax in the cultivation of the highest virtue of bearing persecution for righteousness's sake."[38]

In sum, by working for the poor in spirit through solidarity, meekness, fortitude, mercy, integrity, and peacemaking, the disciple becomes finally the poor in spirit. The call to serve the homeless is a call to become truly able to serve them precisely by becoming like them, humble and persecuted.

Notes

1. Yiu Sing Lúcás Chan, SJ, *The Ten Commandments and the Beatitudes: Biblical Studies and Ethics for Real Life* (Lanham, MD: Rowman and Littlefield, 2012). This book was later published in India and then translated into Chinese and published in China. All subsequent citations from the book will simply be noted as "Chan."

2. Chan, xvi, from John Paul II, *Veritatis Splendor*, sec. 15, http://w2.vatican.va/content/john-paul-ii/en/encyclicals/documents/hf_jp-ii_enc_06081993_veritatis-splendor.html.

3. Ibid., sec. 6.

4. Chan, 153, 164.

5. Ibid., 161.

6. Ibid., 164.

7. Ibid., 171.

8. Ibid.

9. Ibid.

10. Meghan J. Clark, *The Vision of Catholic Social Thought: The Virtue of Solidarity and the Praxis of Human Rights* (Minneapolis: Fortress Press, 2014).

11. Chan, 172.

12. Ibid., 173.

13. Ibid., 178–80.

14. Ibid., 180.

15. Ibid., 181. From Monika K. Hellwig, "The Blessedness of the Meek, the Merciful, and the Peacemakers," in *New Perspectives on the Beatitudes*, ed. Francis A. Eigo (Villanova, PA: Villanova University Press, 1995), 193.

16. Chan, 185.

17. Ibid., 188.

18. Ibid.

19. Ibid., 189.

20. Ibid., 193.

21. See James F. Keenan, *The Works of Mercy: The Heart of Catholicism* (Lanham, MD: Rowman and Littlefield, 2017).

22. Chan, 195.

23. Ibid., 194.
24. Ibid., 196.
25. Ibid., 194.
26. Ibid., 201–2.
27. Ibid., 202, citations from respectively, Hans Dieter Betz, *The Sermon on the Mount*, ed. Adela Yarbro Collins (Minneapolis: Fortress, 1995), 134; Ulrich Luz, *Matthew 1–7: A Commentary*, trans. James E. Crouch (Minneapolis: Fortress Press, 2007), 196.
28. Chan, 202, citation from Glen H. Stassen, "The Beatitudes as Eschatological Peacemaking Virtues," in *Character Ethics and the New Testament*, ed. Robert Brawley (Louisville, KY: Westminster John Knox Press, 2007), 252.
29. Chan, 202.
30. bid., 203.
31. Ibid., 205.
32. Ibid., 210.
33. Ibid., 211.
34. Ibid., 213.
35. Ibid., 221.
36. Ibid.
37. Ibid.
38. Ibid., 222.

Homelessness and Hospitality on the Ground

A Methodological Proposal for Catholic Social Teaching

Daniel Franklin E. Pilario, CM

> If only we had a better house, if our house had a stronger door, it would have not been easy for the police to enter and shoot my husband.

> —Widow of a victim of extra-judicial killing in the Philippine War on Drugs

What resources, perspectives, and experiences can we draw from formal Catholic Social Teaching and broader Catholic social thought to help us understand and interpret street homelessness in a global context?[1] In answering these questions, I have at least two options. First, I can survey the official body of Catholic Social Teaching and see where and how it talks about homelessness. Second, I can retrieve and examine some concrete stories in the Christian social tradition and see how they can inspire us to respond to homelessness in our times. The first option is not very promising. The *Compendium of the Social Doctrine of the Church* cites "housing" and/or "homelessness" in only four numbers (166, 365, 482, and 535)—mostly in a passing mention as both a basic human right and a pressing situation. Beyond the sporadic mention of "homelessness" in the encyclicals and speeches of the popes, we find at the international magisterial level the following documents: Pontifical Council for Justice and Peace, *What Have You Done to Your Homeless Brother? The Church and the Housing Problem* (1987); and Pontifical Council for the Pastoral Care of Migrants and Itinerant Peoples, *Guidelines for the Pastoral Care of the Road* (2007).[2] There are also several bishops' conferences that issued some statements on this theme.[3] Since these sources are not substantial, many writers are at a loss for where to find resources on homelessness in official magisterial documents.

Thus, I proceed with the second option in the hope that "movements from below" can lead us toward more fruitful reflection. It is not new knowledge that official social encyclicals were first inspired by ordinary Christians and movements who were trying their best to respond to the social challenges of their own times.[4] I will thus reflect on three narratives located in different times in the history of Christianity: the *Basileias* of Cappadocia initiated by Basil the Great; the Houses of Hospitality started by Dorothy Day; and the housing project *Gawad Kalinga* of the Philippines, originally run by a charismatic group called the Couples for Christ. I intend to draw lessons from their praxis toward some methodological proposals for rethinking Catholic Social Teaching.

The *Basileias* of Cappadocia

These days have brought us naked and homeless people in great number; a host of captives at everyone's door; strangers and refugees are not lacking, and on every side, there is begging and stretched out hands are there to see. Their house is the open-air; their lodgings are the arcades, the streets, the deserted corners of the market; they lurk in holes like owls and birds of the night. Their clothing is tattered rags; their means of subsistence depends on the feeling of human compassion. Their food is anything thrown by the passers-by; their drink is the springs they share with the animals. . . . They live a brutal and vagrant life, not by habit but as a result of their miseries and misfortunes.[5]

This is not a news item from Manila or Calcutta, Rio de Janeiro or Lagos, though their situations sound similar. It comes from the homily of St. Gregory of Nyssa, one of the Cappadocian fathers, written sometime in 378 CE, describing the situation of Cappadocia in Central Anatolia at the heart of present-day Turkey.

Beyond their usual association with the theology of the Trinity or the Arian controversy, the Cappadocian Fathers (Basil of Caesarea, Gregory of Nazianzus, and Gregory of Nyssa) were the foremost champions of the poor in early Christianity.[6] Cappadocia experienced intense famine sometime in 368 CE onward; they were experiencing dry summers and harsh winters. On the one hand, there was an acute lack of food, and the hungry poor were unprotected from the cold; children were left at church doors; and lepers were not taken care of. On the other hand, merchants were hoarding, and the wealthy did not want to share, while the emperor was persecuting the Christian believers. We see two main Christian responses of the Cappadocian fathers to the situation: prophetic preaching and practical advocacy.

Because of limited space, let me focus on St. Basil of Caesarea. He was born to a rich family (ca. 330 CE), studied philosophy in Constantinople and Greece, and came back to Caesarea to become a teacher in rhetoric. He toured Egypt and Palestine and was later associated with a certain ascetic community led by Macrina, his elder sister. He came back to Caesarea to be ordained a priest, and he succeeded Eusebius as bishop in 370 CE.

The first Christian response was Basil's preaching on stewardship of property, the use of wealth, and the temptation of greed: "To the Rich," "I Will Tear Down

My Barns," "In Time of Famine and Drought," and "Against Those Who Lend at Interest."[7] Probably delivered in 368, these homilies were strong words when most of the area suffered from drought, hunger, and famine while the rich were not willing to share. A member of the aristocratic class himself, Basil exhorted the wealthy to share their worldly goods as their way to salvation. He used stories from the Bible—the rich fool who hoarded wheat in his barn, the young man who went away sad because he had a lot of possessions, and other passages—to make his point. He also used everyday metaphors. To bring out sharing as a natural tendency, he described sheep grazing together in one field, yet yielding to each other in order to live. To exhort his hearers against greed, he pointed out that rivers overflow their banks in order to nourish the surrounding fields. But to connect greed for wealth and greed for power, he resorted to the same river metaphor but highlighted a contrary tendency, that is, the power of water to destroy and dominate the lands and plants around it. "Nothing withstands the influence of wealth," Basil preached, "everything submits to its tyranny, everything cowers at its domination. . . . Leading yokes of oxen, the wicked plow, sow, and harvest what is not their own. If you dispute with them, they come to blows with you; if you complain they accuse you of assaulting them."[8] Basil, of course, was preaching to his own kind—the aristocratic class of his time. It was not to incite people to revolution and topple the existing order along the line of Marx's later views. It was an exhortation to generosity toward the community-unity ideal of the early Christian communities. "Let us zealously imitate the early Christian community," he said, "where everything was held in common—life, soul, concord, a common table, indivisible kinship—while unfeigned love constituted many bodies as one and joined many souls into a single harmonious whole."[9]

This brings us to Basil's second response: the construction of a "new city," which Gregory of Nazianzus calls the *Basileia*. This impressive practical initiative is a complex of guest houses and hospices located at the outskirts of Caesarea on the land donated by Emperor Valens himself and by Basil's own family. The settlement complex included a home for the poor and foundlings, some kind of hospital, a workshop in which the poor could hone their skills; and hostels for travelers, etc.[10] With resources coming from the wealthier classes, there was free medicine for patients, homes for the homeless and training workshops for trades and livelihood that would enable the poor to find employment, for example, in farming, carpentry, weaving, metal work, and so on. In his funeral oration for his bishop-patron Basil, St. Gregory of Nazianzus said:

> Go a little outside the city, and gaze on the new city: the storehouse of piety, the common treasury for those with possessions, where the superfluities of wealth as well as necessities lie stored away because of his persuasion—shaking off the moths, giving no joy to thieves, escaping struggles with envy and the onrush of time—where disease is treated by philosophy, where misfortunes are called blessed, where compassion is held in real esteem.[11]

In a new context after the rise of Constantine in the fourth century, the aristocratic leaders—of whom Basil was one—tried to apply their Greek learning into the Christian frame made visible in their concrete response to the social challenges of Cappadocia. Beyond the dominant cenobitic ideal within strict monastic enclosures, Basil's monastic social enterprise—despite its traditional rhetoric—signaled a new prophetic direction toward an engaged monastic spirituality of his time.[12]

Houses of Hospitality: Dorothy Day

Within the month [September 1933] we had started the first women's House of Hospitality. Already we had rented an old apartment in a condemned tenement on Fourth Street to put up three of the men who had joined with the work. Already three more were sleeping in the little store on Fifteenth Street which was also an office, a dining room and a kitchen where meals were being served. Teresa and I slept in an adjoining apartment here. . . . Margaret came back from the hospital with her baby to this apartment and we all participated in the care of the baby when she was ill.[13]

This is the account of Dorothy Day on the first "house of hospitality" in New York in 1939, six years after its first foundation by the Catholic Worker movement. Founded by Dorothy Day and Peter Maurin, the *Catholic Worker* was first a newspaper publication that aimed "to popularize and make known the encyclicals of the Popes in regard to social justice and the program put forth by the Church for the 'reconstruction of the social order.'"[14] With Catholic Social Teaching as inspiration, Dorothy and Peter wanted to educate the workers on the church's teachings on laborers' rights, war and peace, justice, and other issues of the day. Under the editorship of Day, *Catholic Worker* also carried items on crucial issues of the day, such as pacifism and racial discrimination. By 1938, its circulation reached 190,000. However, it also had its critics from all sides—from communists, who thought it was too bourgeois and pacifist; from traditional Catholics, who saw it as too radical and communistic.

The newspaper encouraged the creation of "houses of hospitality" in all dioceses to give shelter to the homeless poor. And to "walk their talk," the members of the Catholic Worker movement rented apartments in New York and opened the first house of hospitality, which served as an editorial office, homeless shelter, community meeting area, feeding center, and gathering space for prayer. Dorothy and the members were the first ones to live there together with the poor that they took care of. Originally, these were conceived of as halfway houses where the homeless and unemployed would get temporary shelter and be transferred to rural farms when they were ready. As it developed, it was also the place of long breadlines serving more than 1,000 persons at a time, a workers' school, and many other purposes. So there were three pillars to the Catholic Worker movement: the newspaper, houses of hospitality, and small sustainable rural farms; the houses and farms took quite a while to materialize, however. In 1939, there were only twenty-three houses and four farms under the Catholic Worker movement. At present, there are 216 communities in the United States and 33 in other parts of the world.[15]

I will note three aspects of these houses of hospitality: First is the emphasis on *littleness* "because we wish each house to be run on a family plan rather than like an institution."[16] Students and scholars live together with the poor and the homeless. Everyone was invited into the house activities during the week, including study sessions, manual work, prayer times. The first houses were located in the poor immigrant districts, among Chinese and Italians who later helped them despite initial prejudices—a case of the poor helping the poor. Littleness, family spirit, and a personal approach to charity were a concrete application of the philosophy of personalism that lies at the foundation of the Catholic Worker movement. Dorothy Day transformed the philosophical personalism of Peter Maurin into the care of the actual human person through the corporal and spiritual works of mercy. Against the agency of the state to which works of "charity" are relegated in both capitalist and communist systems, she argued for the personal care that each Christian must provide. "No, we are not denying the obligations of the State," she wrote, "but we do claim that we must never cease to emphasize personal responsibility. When our brother asks us for bread, we cannot say, 'Go be thou filled'. We cannot send him from agency to agency. We must care for him ourselves as much as possible."[17]

The second aspect I observe is the emphasis on the transcendent dimension of social action. Day believed that the conception of the modern state—both communist and capitalist—has lost the inherent transcendent purpose of the social body. It has fully entrusted the care of human persons to the all-powerful system, losing its divine dimension in the process. Dorothy herself displayed this concern on the personal level. Paul Elie writes: "Her comrades said she would never be a good Communist, because she was too religious—a character out of Dostoevsky, a woman haunted by God."[18] And Dorothy writes: "I can sit in the presence of the Blessed Sacrament and wrestle for that peace in the bitterness of my soul . . . and I can find many things in Scripture to console me, to change my heart from hatred to love of enemy."[19] This belief in the transcendent dimension is the foundation of all her social action, her pacifist stance against all wars, and her protest against two rival social systems of the time—capitalism and socialism. But above all, this also makes Dorothy see the poor as the image of Christ.[20]

The third aspect is the assurance of permanent commitment to the homeless who come. The contemporary word often used to describe this is *sustainability*. "We believe that when we undertake the responsibility of caring for a man [*sic*] who comes to us," Day wrote, "we are accepting it for good."[21] For Day, the work of hospitality is the work of a lifetime:

> We know that men [*sic*] cannot be changed in a day or three days, nor in
> three months. We are trying 'to make men.' And this cannot be done

overnight. Some, indeed, are shiftless and some dishonest; but our aim is to try to see Christ in these men and to change them by our love for them; and the more hopeless a case seems the more we are driven to prayer, which as it should be.[22]

Gawad Kalinga Housing Project:
Couples for Christ in the Philippines

The third story from the ground is that of the *Gawad Kalinga* Housing Project in the Philippines. From the 1980s up to the present, the Philippines has seen the rise of a strong Catholic family movement led by lay couples called the Couples for Christ (CFC)—a trans-parochial community which has now spread to more than a hundred countries worldwide. It presently claims a membership of around a million people spread across 76 different countries.[23] It started out as a renewal program for married couples that branched out to different groups in the family: Kids for Christ, Youth for Christ, Handmaids for Christ (widows), and Servants of the Lord (widowers). It is the only ecclesial movement in the Philippines that is approved with Pontifical Right by the Vatican and considered among the International Association of the Faithful.

In recent years, it launched its social action arm, a housing program for informal settlers and street families called *Gawad Kalinga* (GK), which literally means "to give care." In no time, so-called GK villages sprouted like mushrooms all over the country. It was widely recognized[24] as an effective response to Philippine homelessness, which is one of the worst in the world. GK involves all sectors of society (academia, business corporations, government agencies, etc.) as they are encouraged to put their human and financial resources into building houses for the poor and to organize them into Christian communities, sharing with them the spirituality of Couples for Christ. Called the CFC "outreach program," the GK became very successful since the CFC is present in almost all parishes and dioceses all over the country. Its leader, Tony Meloto, is a member of the Couples of Christ himself and was assigned as *Gawad Kalinga* head by the International Council. He has received national and international awards[25] that cite *Gawad Kalinga* as a program that effectively responds to the housing crisis in the Philippines.

But more recently, the Couples for Christ split, and its housing outreach was disowned by its original group. The whole story is too complicated to tell here,[26] but *Gawad Kalinga* and its leaders were accused by the more conservative members of the movement with veering away from the group's original spiritual mission; the charge was that they had turned the family spiritual renewal movement into social activism.[27] They were also accused of accepting donations from companies that were allegedly manufacturing contraceptives. And when this sensitive "pro-life" chord was struck, some sectors of the hierarchy from the Bishops' Conference level up to the Roman Curia pressured the group to abdicate the direction of the whole project. Stanislaw Cardinal Rylko, then the president of the Pontifical Council for the Laity, was of the same opinion and reprimanded the leaders of *Gawad Kalinga*. Cardinal Lopez Trujillo[28] of the Pontifical Council for the Family also wrote to prevent them from receiving donations from companies producing contraceptives. At the moment, the Couples for Christ movement has split into several groups and *Gawad Kalinga*, now disowned as a Catholic project, has been forced to transform itself into an NGO, still continuing in its mission to house the homeless, but without links to its original faith inspiration.[29]

Homelessness and Hospitality: Approaches to Catholic Social Teaching

What can we learn from these movements of hospitality for homeless peoples? Let me mention two methodological points: a proposal to shift the emphasis of CST from the universal to the particular, that is, to listen to narratives from the ground on how actual communities address the problem of homelessness; and a call to recognize the ambiguity of "institutionalization" in our housing initiatives.

Catholic Social Teaching: Beyond the Universal

Charles Curran[30] has already analyzed the shift in CST methodologies over time, that is, from the deductive approaches to historical consciousness, from deriving universal teachings based on "unchanging principles" of natural law to historically sensitive methods as championed by *Octogesima Adveniens* (40).[31] This crucial text signals a move from what was once a classicist and deductive methodological view of Catholic Social Teaching to more historically sensitive and inductive approaches. Curran also mentions the shift in CST from a more legal ethical model to a more personalist view of the human person, in its emphasis on freedom, respect for one's conscience, equality, and participation.

Posing these narratives of "hospitality from below" does two things in the spirit of the shifts mentioned above. On the one hand, these stories show attempts made by different Christian communities to "analyze with objectivity their situation," "shed on it the Gospel's unalterable words," and to draw from them "norms and principles of reflection and directives for action" (*OA* 4). Beyond looking for principles from "official Catholic thought," these principles are in fact generated on the ground. In these lived experiences, one sees the actual hits and misses, the successes and failures, of discernment and action experienced by these Christian communities. On the other hand, these stories also give us utopias—"forward looking imagination" by evoking the "inventive powers of the human mind and heart" as they provide a critique of present realities (*OA* 37).

In order to develop new theological resources inspired by CST to help us reflect on the issue of homelessness, our proposed methodological option is to start from real stories on the ground. By looking at the *Basileias*, the Houses of Hospitality, and *Gawad Kalinga*, we are led to imagine (not imitate) what a Christian response should be for our times. I imagine that there are millions of these narratives. I do not just mean we should be doing a historical study of the past history of the whole Christian social tradition. I also mean asking present persons and communities to narrate how they engage as Christians the issues and problems of homelessness in their own contexts. We can propose different platforms for people to tell their stories—in film or in print, in the form of personal accounts, community reflections or pastoral strategies. For these lived experiences are theologies in themselves—real acknowledged sources for Catholic Social Teaching.

These stories from the ground can be discerned in two directions—as concrete applications of Christian social tradition but also as critical appropriation of Catholic Social Teaching in context. There is a running thread in all the narratives we have seen above: all these initiatives were applications of Jesus's command: Whatever you do to the least of my sisters and brothers you do it to me. . . . I was homeless and you made me welcome (cf. Mt 25). All these attempts were contextual: Basil, an aristocrat himself, challenged the wealthy by being a prophet who unmasked the hypocrisy of his own kind. Dorothy Day lived the social injunction from below, starting from her own experience of loneliness and alienation, and living with the homeless in spaces that she considered home for the rest of her life. In fact, she died in one of them. *Gawad Kalinga* is a concrete response to an acute situation of homelessness in a Third World country, inspired by the families' encounter with the Gospel in their lives. It is considered an "outreach," to borrow their language, because the Good News could not just be contained within families. It needs to reach out to other families.

However, these concrete narratives from the ground can also critique, challenge, augment, and move forward the conceptualization of housing and homelessness in Catholic Social Teaching and even in the secular discourses about them. One observable development in our contemporary times is the assertion of housing as a "human right," not only in the *Compendium of Catholic Social Doctrine* but also in many United Nations documents.[32] The provisions and conditions therein are hopeful and laudable: security of tenure, availability of services like drinking water, sanitation, energy for cooking, waste disposal, affordability, habitability, accessibility to employment, schools, child care, protection from forced evictions, and so on.[33] But the standards are so ideal that in most cases, especially in Third World contexts, they are unattainable.

In the present context of the Philippines, for instance, a house is not only a basic human right, it is also a precondition to the most basic of all rights—the right to life. In recent years of President Duterte's administration when the police forces have been "cleaning society" of drug addicts, innocent lives have been lost, and many are still in danger. There is an estimated number of more than 27,000 persons killed without trial. Police forces just barge into houses even in the middle of the night and shoot their targets. The words of a widow whose husband was summarily killed inside their house while he was sleeping keeps haunting me: "If only we had a better house, if our house had a stronger door, it would have not been easy for the police to enter and shoot my husband."[34] Housing in this context is not only a human right; it is a door to the most basic of human rights—the right to life. What is needed is not much. It is quite basic: a roof, a wall, and door to protect them from the elements and the human forces of death—a view which highly complicated debates among international housing advocates on "adequate housing" can easily forget.[35]

Hospitality: Beyond the Institutional

One lesson from the narratives above is the need to address homelessness through sustainable social structures that recent Vincentian initiatives call "systemic change."[36] The Cappadocian *Basileias*, the Catholic Worker's houses of hospitality, and *Gawad Kalinga* were their concretizations in history. The *Basileias* were self-sustaining communities; they still existed at least one century after Basil's death.[37] Dorothy Day's breadline and *Gawad Kalinga's* housing project would not have survived without some level of organization and structural commitment. But the move toward institutionalization is also ambiguous. Day insisted on "family spirit" and "littleness" from the start—or, to use some current words, on mutuality and inclusivity. For it has always been recognized that institutions by nature push others to the fringes; instead of being welcoming, they tend to exclude, as Max Weber already warned us in the "routinization of charisma."[38]

It was against the backdrop of the ambiguity of the institution that the Cappadocian fathers exerted their prophetic sermons that struck at the heart of the system—the wealthy, the usurers, and indirectly the church leaders and the empire.[39] Even within the context of the same feudal aristocratic class, Basil claimed the Gospel as the platform of his prophetic denunciation. The expulsion of *Gawad Kalinga* from the Catholic fold is a concrete illustration of Christian hospitality turning itself into exclusion because the church institution favored the purity of its doctrines over and above the dignity and lives of the homeless.

Dorothy Day and the Catholic Worker Movement also turned the critique toward the church institution itself: "The Church is the cross on which Christ was crucified." Thus, even as she decided to be baptized in the Catholic Church, Dorothy also believed that

> one must live in a state of permanent dissatisfaction with the Church. . . . When I see the Church taking the side of the powerful and forgetting the weak, and when I see bishops living in luxury and the poor being ignored or thrown bread crumbs, I know that Jesus is being insulted, as He once was, and sent to his death, as He once was.[40]

If we translate Basil's sermons in the context of homelessness, it is the same message: our big houses and buildings are not ours; we stole them from the homeless. And if the institutional church remedies this situation a little through our faltering housing programs, we are not doing "charity." We are only giving them back what is theirs in justice. And one must do it not in the spirit of condescension but in love. To borrow an expression of Vincent de Paul from the movie *Monsieur Vincent*, "It is only for your love alone that the poor will forgive you the bread you give to them."

I do not intend to give a conclusion to these reflections, as they are meant to be exploratory. This is an invitation to share narratives of hospitality on the ground vis-à-vis the problem of homelessness in the global world. Unlike top-down approaches, there are no clear principles to be applied; only concrete stories with all their frictions, ambiguities, and difficulties, hoping that God's inspiration can reveal itself on the rough grounds where people walk in fidelity to the Gospel. In closing, a quotation from the philosopher Ludwig Wittgenstein may be a helpful guide for our modest proposal: "We have got on to slippery ice where there is no friction and so in a certain sense the conditions are ideal, but also, just because of that, we are unable to walk. We want to walk: so we need friction. Back to the rough ground!"[41]

Notes

1. This essay is a revised version of a paper presented at the conference titled "Homelessness and Catholic Social Teaching" and organized by the Institute of Global Homelessness (DePaul University, Chicago) in Rome, November 29–December 2, 2017.

2. Pontifical Council for Justice and Peace, *What Have You Done to Your Homeless Brother? The Church and the Housing Problem*. Document on the Occasion of the International Year of Shelter for the Homeless (Vatican: Polyglot Press, 1987); Pontifical Council for the Pastoral Care of Migrants and Itinerant Peoples, *Guidelines for the Pastoral Care of the Road* (2007), http://www.vatican.va/roman_curia/pontifical_councils/migrants/pom2007_104-suppl/rc_pc_migrants_pom104-suppl_orientamenti-en.html.

3. See, among others, United States Conference of Catholic Bishops, "A Right to a Decent Home: Pastoral Response to a Crisis in Housing" (February 20, 1975); USCCB, "Homeless and Housing: A Human Tragedy, A Moral Challenge" (March 24, 1988), http://www.usccb.org/issues-and-action/human-life-and-dignity/housing-homelessness/upload/homelessness-and-housing.pdf. Irish Catholic Bishops' Conference, "A Room at the Inn? Pastoral Letter on Housing and Homelessness," https://www.catholicbishops.ie/wp-content/uploads/2018/10/2018-Oct-01-Bishops-pastoral-letter-on-Housing-and-Homelessness-A-Room-at-the-Inn.pdf (11.15.2018). Catholic Bishops' Conference of the Philippines, "I Was Homeless and You Took Me In: Pastoral Statement on the Homeless" (July 1997), http://cbcponline.net/i-was-homeless-and-you-took-me-in.

4. See, among others, Marvin Krier Mich, *Catholic Social Teaching and Movements* (Mystic, CT: Twenty Third Publications, 1998).

5. Gregory of Nyssa, "On the Love of the Poor," in Helen Rhee, *Wealth and Poverty in Early Christianity* (Minneapolis: Fortress Press, 2017), 72.

6. See also Susan Hollman, *The Hungry Are Dying: Beggars and Bishops in Roman Cappadocia* (New York: Oxford University Press, 2001); Bryan Daley, "The Cappadocian Fathers and the Rhetoric of Philanthropy," *Journal of Early Christian Studies* 7, no. 3 (1999): 431–61; idem, "The Cappadocian Fathers and the Option for the Poor," in *The Option for*

the Poor in Christian Theology, ed. Daniel Groody (Notre Dame, IN: University of Notre Dame, 2007), 77–88; Rhee, *Wealth and Poverty in Early Christianity*.

7. For the translation of these homilies, see Basil the Great, *On Social Justice,* trans. with introduction and commentary by C. Paul Schroeder (Crestwood, NY: St. Vladimir's Seminary Press, 2009).

8. Basil the Great, "To the Rich," in *On Social Justice*, 51.

9. Basil the Great, "In Time of Famine and Drought," in *On Social Justice*, 86.

10. Edward Smither, "Basil of Caesarea: An Early Christian Model of Urban Mission," in *Reaching the City: Reflections on Urban Mission for the 20th Century* (Pasadena, CA: William Carey Library, 2012).

11. Cf. Daley, "The Cappadocian Fathers and the Rhetoric of Philanthropy," 432.

12. Anna Silvas, "Interpreting the Motives of Basil's Social Doctrine," *Journal of the Australian Early Medieval Association* 5 (2009): 165–75.

13. Dorothy Day, "House of Hospitality," *Catholic Worker,* May 1939, 1, 3, 4. Cf. http://www.catholicworker.org/dorothyday/articles/342.pdf.

14. Dorothy Day, "To Our Readers," *Catholic Worker*, May 1933, 4; "Aims and Purposes," *Catholic Worker*, February 1940, 7 in http://www.catholicworker.org/cw-aims-and-means.html.

15. "Directory of Catholic Worker Communities," http://www.catholicworker.org/communities/directory.html.

16. Dorothy Day, "House of Hospitality," 3, http://www.catholicworker.org/dorothyday/articles/342.html.

17. Dorothy Day, "House of Hospitality: Conclusion," http://www.catholicworker.org/dorothyday/articles/450-plain.htm.

18. Paul Elie, *The Life You Save May Be Your Own: An American Pilgrimage* (New York: Farrar, Straus and Giroux, 2003), 17.

19. Dorothy Day, "In Peace Is My Bitterness Most Bitter," *Catholic Worker,* January 1967, 1, 2, http://www.catholicworker.org/dorothyday/articles/250.pdf.

20. Dorothy's words: "I watched that ragged horde and thought to myself, 'These are Christ's poor. He was one of them. He was a man like other men, and He chose His friends amongst the ordinary workers. These men feel they have been betrayed by Christianity. Men are not Christian today. If they were, this sight would not be possible. Far dearer in the sight of God perhaps are these hungry ragged ones, than all those smug, well-fed Christians who sit in their homes, cowering in fear of the Communist menace." Cf. http://www.catholicworker.org/dorothyday/articles/435.html.

21. Dorothy Day, "House of Hospitality," http://www.catholicworker.org/dorothyday/articles/342.html.

22. Ibid.

23. The Vatican website reports: "CFC has some 980,600 members, and is present in 76 countries as follows: Africa (16), Asia (18), Europe (24), North America (8), Oceania (6), and South America (4)." Cf. http://www.va/roman_curia/ pontifical_councils/laity/documents/rc_pc_laity_doc_20051114_associazioni_en.html#COUPLES FOR CHRIST.

24. Cf. Gawad Kalinga; cf. http://www.gk1world.com/GlobalCredibity.

25. For the awards received by Gawad Kalinga, cf. http://www.gk1world.com/Global-Credibity.

26. I have written about this controversy in D. F. Pilario, "Catholic Social Movements in the Philippines: Clashes with Institutional Powers," *Journal of Catholic Social Thought* 10, no. 2 (2013): 383–99.

27. The documents of this crisis are found on this site: http://www.cfcffl.org/documents/documents.htm. See also "The CFC-GK Strife and the Rest of the Laity," http://www.cbcpnews.com/?q=node/960/23400.

28. Cf. http://www.cfcffl.org/documents/documents/ltr_of_card_lopez-trujillo_re_pharma_20071126.pdf.

29. Cf. "Gawad Kalinga: Building Communities to End Poverty," http://www.gk1world.com.

30. Charles Curran, *Catholic Social Teaching 1891—Present: A Historical, Theological and Ethical Analysis* (Washington, DC: Georgetown University Press, 2002), 53–100.

31. Pope Paul VI writes: "In the face of such widely varying situations, it is difficult for us to utter a unified message and to put forward a solution which has a universal validity. Such is not our ambition, nor is it our mission. It is up to the Christian communities to analyze with objectivity the situation which is proper to their own country, to shed on it the light of the Gospel's unalterable words and to draw principles of reflection, norms of judgment, and directives for action from the social teaching of the Church" (*Octogesima Adveniens*, 4).

32. Cf. "UN Housing Rights," http://www.housingrightswatch.org/page/un-housing-rights.

33. Office of the United Nations High Commissioner for Human Rights, *The Right to Adequate Housing*, https://www.ohchr.org/Documents/Publications/FS21_rev_1_Housing_en.pdf.

34. For my personal involvement in resistance against this violent program on Duterte's "war on drugs," see Inday Espina-Varona, "Deadly Surveys: Philippines Steps Up Drug War Dragnet." *La Croix International*, September 2, 2017, https://international.la-croix.com/news/deadly-surveys-philippines-steps-up-drug-war-dragnet/5811. Gail DeGeorge, "Spotlight on World Leaders Overshadows Filipino Poor Caught in Country's Drug War," *National Catholic Reporter*, November 16, 2017, https://www.ncronline.org/news/justice/spotlight-world-leaders-overshadows-filipino-poor-caught-countrys-drug-war. Joy Watford, "Finding Hope in the Dark," http://www.positivelyfilipino.com/magazine/finding-hope-in-the-dark. Antje Phöner, "Der Präsident kennt kein Erbarmen," https://missio.com/images/Dateien/missiomagazin/14-21_philip-EJK_2018-03.pdf. Kaela Malig and Andrea Taguines, "The Children Who Cried Papa," http://childrenwhocriedpapa.com.

35. Cf. Mercy Law Resource Center, *The Right to Housing in Comparative Perspective*, https://law.yale.edu/system/files/area/center/schell/mlrc_housing_report-_2018.pdf.

36. Cf. Famvin Vincentian Encyclopedia, "Systemic Change," https://famvin.org/wiki/Systemic_Change.

37. A. Sterk, *Renouncing the World Yet Leading the Church: The Monk-Bishop in Late Antiquity* (Cambridge, MA: Harvard University Press, 2004).

38. Max Weber, *The Theory of Social and Economic Organizations*, trans. A. M. Henderson and Talcott Parsons (New York: Free Press, 1947).

39. Cf. Rhee, *Wealth and Poverty in Early Christianity*, 55–86.

40. Dorothy Day, *The Long Loneliness* (New York: Harper, 1952), 149–50.

41. Ludwig Wittgenstein, *Philosophical Investigations* (Oxford: Blackwell, 1953), §107. For its implications to theology, see D. F. Pilario, *Back to the Rough Grounds of Praxis: Exploring Theological Method with Pierre Bourdieu* (Leuven: Leuven University Press and Peeters, 2005).

HUMAN RIGHTS, HUMAN FLOURISHING, AND THE RIGHT TO HOUSING

Ethna Regan, chf

This essay discusses the role of human rights discourse in ethics, and briefly examines the Universal Declaration of Human Rights (UDHR), which has shaped human rights theory and practice worldwide for seventy years. The gradual acceptance of human rights within Catholic theological ethics will be explored, and the essay will conclude by looking specifically at what is meant by a right to housing.

Human Rights are both self-evident and deeply contested in contemporary ethics. Rights have a broad and complex history, expressed at different times in terms of liberties, natural rights, and human rights. There is a considerable body of scholarship that points to "liberty before liberalism," not just in the natural rights thinking of medieval law and religion, but "the deeper genesis and genius of many modern rights norms in religious texts and traditions that antedate the Enlightenment by centuries, even by millennia."[1] What role, then, do human rights play in contemporary ethics?

I argue that human rights language is a dialectical boundary discourse which holds in tension the universal and the particular, the individual and community, theory and practice, the religious and the secular, the abstract and the concrete. The dialectical tension between these various elements is necessary in order that human rights discourse does not become focused merely on the protection of the rights of individuals insofar as those rights do not infringe the rights of other individuals. Rights are also protective of a larger ethical vision expressed in terms of human flourishing. Defining rights as a boundary discourse in ethics, pointing toward the larger questions of human flourishing and ecological sustainability, challenges the view of rights as a trump in the game of moral reasoning. Although there has been "an erosion of the belief in the universality of human aspirations" in the postcolonial period,[2] there has also been considerable caution about the claims of cultural relativism. The "cultural preference" approach to human rights is often proposed by those who are not obviously under threat, or those who perceive human rights as an obstacle to power and control. Abdullahi A. An-Na'im examines the cross-cultural legitimacy of universal human rights and argues that this universal legitimacy can be enhanced by exploring the possibilities of cultural reinterpretation and reconstruction through "internal cultural discourse and cross-cultural dialogue."[3] Locating rights as a boundary discourse in ethics facilitates this kind of dialogue.

Human rights focuses on what we need to be *protected from* and *provided with* in order to flourish as human beings. Human rights are a contemporary expression of natural rights and facilitate the basic goods of human flourishing. The question of qualification or limitations of rights tends to be addressed mainly in terms of the legality of state restriction of human rights, but, in a world where 100 million people have no home at all, it is a question for global economics as well as a matter of distributive justice. Human rights emphasize human equality, defined by John Finnis as "the truth that every human being is a locus of human flourishing which is to be considered with favor in him as much as in anybody else."[4]

The Universal Declaration of Human Rights: Foundational and Enduringly Relevant

The Charter of the United Nations (1945) and the UDHR (1948), together with the 1966 International Covenants on Civil and Political Rights (ICCPR), and on Economic, Social, and Cultural Rights (ICESCR), are the most significant instruments for the international protection of human rights. The charter laid out the general principles for a morality of human rights and the UDHR outlined the normative content. These documents emerged from the tragedy of war which was foremost in the minds of the delegates from fifty nations who gathered for the 1945 San Francisco Conference that marked the founding of the United Nations. It is worth noting—in the context of this book on street homelessness, which includes significant nongovernmental voices—the "extraordinary and unprecedented influence" of religious and secular NGOs (both present in San Francisco and sending submissions from a distance) in the support and articulation of these documents; these groups are normally considered extrinsic to diplomatic affairs.[5]

Much is made, particularly in contemporary postliberal thought, of a perceived weak philosophical justification in the UDHR. In a desire for a negotiated consensus, a number of justifications were explored in the complex discussions that led to its formulation. It begins with a statement about the human person and what is common to humanity: "Whereas recognition of the inherent dignity and of the equal and inalienable rights of all members of the human family is the foundation of freedom, justice and peace, in the world . . ."[6]

The UDHR is grounded neither in an appeal to God nor to nature, but to human dignity. This appeal seems to presuppose a latent common grasp of its meaning, with no specific definition offered. It is not a univocal term and, as Gabriel Marcel observes, "dignity" often suffers from a "verbal inflation" that aims to compensate verbally for actual widespread deterioration.[7] Dignity may offer a thin normative basis, but such a basis is nonetheless important, constituting potentiality for agreement about human rights across differences of faith and culture. The emphasis on "recognition" of that inherent dignity is a challenge to legal positivism—which holds that the only rights are those conferred by the laws of states—a view that renders the individual vulnerable to legally sanctioned violations of their rights. Most significantly, the UDHR combines civil, political, social, economic, and cultural rights in one declaration under a single preamble. The mandate is that every society should protect civil and political freedoms, and the accompanying mandate is that every society—within its resources—should make provision for food, housing, health, education, and social security for "everyone."

This "everyone" is not an isolated individual, but a located person whose rights find expression in the context of family, marriage, country, community, and in the dynamics of association, public service, trade unions, and educational and cultural life. Article 29 states that community (with its inherent duties) is necessary for the flourishing of the human personality: "Everyone has duties to community in which alone the free and full development of his/her personality is possible." The UDHR does not codify human duties but leaves them to domestic law and governance. Though it has been suggested that our time is marked by a "twilight of duty,"[8] and selfish and trivial appeals to rights are sometimes presented as normative, advocacy using human rights language is often how people express their sense of duty to and solidarity with others.

Legally, the UDHR is regarded as part of international customary law, due to the frequency with which it has been used as a reference in, or incorporated into, other legal instruments. It constitutes a shift in international law from the absolute sovereignty of nation-states to the principle of humanity. Nations are accountable to the international community for the way they treat their own people. Failure to protect the rights of its citizens, including social and economic rights like food and housing, weakens the claims of a state to political legitimacy.

The declaration, the most translated document in the world, influenced the setting of standards and the establishment of norms through declarations and legally binding conventions covering a wide variety of specific aspects of international human rights. There are nations that have ratified only one of the 1966 covenants, but no nation has withdrawn from its recognition of the UDHR. Reliable human rights indicators point to considerable progress in civil and political freedoms worldwide, but improving the process of implementation of social and economic rights—including food and housing—remains one of the key challenges seventy years later.

Human Rights and Catholic Social Teaching: From Hostility to Advocacy

Belief in the inherent dignity of the human person is the foundation of Catholic Social Teaching. At the heart of the development of this teaching is the discovery and articulation of the concrete implications of human dignity in interpersonal, social, structural, and international terms. The ultimate theological justification for engagement with human rights is the doctrine of *imago Dei*. "So God created humankind in his image, in the image of God he created them; male and female he created them" (Gen 1:27 [NRSV]). Although the concept of human rights is not explicitly present in the Torah, Judaism points theology toward the concept of inalienable human dignity, based on this "astonishing assertion" that God created human beings in God's image.[9] The history of theological anthropology is an attempt to come to terms with the meaning of this assertion about the human person. The appeal to human rights is now a constituent dimension of Catholic Social Teaching's advocacy for human dignity across the world. However, the acceptance of the notion of human rights by the church, and the incorporation of that discourse into its social teaching, was a slow and complicated process.

The defensive position of the Catholic Church in the nineteenth century resisted attempts to engage positively with the new intellectual milieu of the period. It was hostile to the conception of liberties associated with the Enlightenment, perceiving therein an idea of freedom lacking any normative framework that would maintain a proper relationship among freedom, justice, and order. The first systematic treatment of human rights in official Catholic Social Teaching, Pope John XXIII's encyclical *Pacem in Terris* (1963), was issued between the first and second sessions of Vatican II.[10] When John—then Angelo Roncalli—was Papal Nuncio in Paris in the 1940s, he participated in discussions about the drafting of the UDHR. This was the time of the establishment of UNESCO, and Roncalli was influential in ensuring that the Catholic Church would make connections with the United Nations and its organizations. *Pacem in Terris* recognizes the role of the United Nations, and makes special reference to the UDHR, seeing therein "a solemn recognition of the personal dignity of every human being."[11] Due to the reference to economic rights in Pope Leo XIII's encyclical *Rerum Novarum* (1891)[12] and other influences—including the work of the American theologian John A. Ryan—the Catholic tradition did not have the same difficulty with socioeconomic rights as it did with civil and political rights.[13] *Pacem in Terris* is a major development because of its endorsement of civil and political rights, contributing to what Donal Dorr describes as a "decisive move away from the right" in Catholic Social Teaching.[14]

Bryan Hehir contends that historically the "neuralgic point of conflict between Catholic teaching and democracy was the idea of religious freedom."[15] The full acceptance of human rights as a legitimate mode of ethical discourse was the major contribution of the Second Vatican Council to Catholic Social Teaching. This full acceptance was shaped by a number of factors, the most significant of which was the formal recognition of the right to religious freedom in *Dignitatis Humanae* (1965). The aim of this Declaration on Religious Freedom was to develop "the teaching of recent popes on the inviolable rights of the human person and on the constitutional order of society."[16] The council stressed that a person may have duties to the truth, but the truth has no rights. The subject of rights is the human person, in truth or error, based on the dignity of that person in their discernment and decision making, founded on the gifts of rationality and freedom. The dynamic of freedom is one of movement from personal freedom to the freedom of the church. John Rawls summarizes the trifold ethical, political, and theological significance of *Dignitatis Humanae*:

It declared the ethical doctrine of religious freedom resting on the dignity of the human person; a political doctrine with respect to the limits of government in religious matters; a theological doctrine of the freedom of the Church in its relations to the political and social world. All persons, whatever their faith, have the right of religious liberty on the same terms.[17]

The impact of the conciliar legitimation of the right to religious freedom is seen in the fecundity of Catholic intellectual and practical engagement with human rights after Vatican II.

Liberation theologians, while pastorally involved with the reality of human rights violations in Latin America, were initially reluctant to engage with the discourse of human rights. They viewed it as founded on an individualistic liberal anthropology and expressed concerns that the focus on civil and political rights, enforceable in a judicial context, overlooked the violations of homelessness, hunger, and poverty. As the church became increasingly involved in the defense of human rights during periods of repression, liberation theology developed a distinctive engagement with rights discourse linking it with the preferential option for the poor. The affirmation of the rights of the poor—especially their social and economic rights—does not negate the universality of human rights, but such affirmation points toward authentic universality in the form of historical and concrete realization. The specific contribution of liberation theology lies in its emphasis on the need for systemic and structural fulfillment of the rights of the poor, whose rights become the test for the paradox of universality. A distinctively theological perspective is found in Jon Sobrino's reflections on the mysticism of human rights. He presents the struggle for the rights of the poor and oppressed as a kind of mystagogy into the life of God.[18] Those who defend the rights of the poor and oppressed bring the mercy and tenderness of God to bear on situations of suffering and are further initiated into the mystery of God through that experience.

Since Vatican II, critical engagement with human rights is found in theology, missiology, and ethics. Human rights has emerged as a major theme in the social documents of episcopal conferences worldwide. Integrating human rights perspectives in development and advocacy work, founded on these theological and ethical principles, has enabled Catholic agencies to collaborate—in a spirit of critical reciprocity—with other secular and religious agencies. At the Second Vatican Council, however, no one could have envisaged the revelations of crimes and scandals that have scarred the reputation of the Catholic Church. These failures, together with issues of human rights *ad intra*, test the credibility of the church's promotion of human rights *ad extra*. Despite these failures, the contemporary challenges of social, global, and ecological justice make the church's continued promotion of human rights, especially the rights of the poorest of the poor, an urgent imperative. Within that imperative, the situation of the homeless poor needs to be treated as a violation of the right to housing, a violation that merits the same attention as that given to torture and executions.

Restoring the Currency of Housing as a Human Right

The UN Special Rapporteur on the right to housing, Leilani Farha, stated that because of the commodification of housing and the connections between the political elite and real estate wealth, "housing has lost its currency as a human right."[19] This reflects a neoliberal economic climate which contracts the public sphere and emphasizes the role of the market in allocating resources. There is also some philosophical ambivalence toward the idea of a right to housing and continuing challenges in the enforcement of social rights, more generally.

Article 25 of the UDHR refers to housing in its codification of the right to an adequate standard of living. Conceptions of "adequacy" can run a continuum from minimal to expansive, but the UDHR links adequacy to "the health and well-being" of person and family. The motivation for the inclusion of this article was that "everyone should be able, without shame and without unreasonable obstacles, to be a full participant in ordinary, everyday interaction with people" and, evidently with street homelessness in mind, should not be forced to meet basic needs "by degrading or depriving themselves of their basic freedoms, such as through begging, prostitution, or bonded labour."[20]

The ICESCR is the most important UN instrument to enshrine the right to housing (article 11.1) and to stipulate the responsibility of states to "take steps" to realize this right.[21] The interpretation of the covenant has moved housing toward consideration as a discrete right derivative of the right to an adequate standard of living. The Committee on Economic, Social, and Cultural Rights (CESCR), the UN expert body that considers the five-year reports submitted by member states on their compliance with the ICESCR, has issued important comments on the right to housing. Although nonbinding, CESCR's comments have helped concretize the general reference to housing (in 11.1) and have influenced international perspectives on the right to housing, especially General Comment No. 4: The Right to Adequate Housing, and General Comment No. 7: Forced Evictions.[22] Comment No. 4 addresses the "disturbingly large gap" between the standards set out by the covenant and the reality of homelessness worldwide, including in some of the richer nations. It stresses that a right to housing should not be interpreted narrowly to refer to minimal shelter, but as "a right to live somewhere in security, peace and dignity."[23] Most important, it fleshes out the concept of adequacy by outlining seven essential elements of adequate housing that must be considered in any context: (a) legal security of tenure; (b) availability of services, materials, facilities, and infrastructure; (c) affordability; (d) habitability; (e) accessibility; (f) location; and (g) cultural adequacy.[24] At the very least, a basic minimum of each of these elements must be in place if housing is to be considered adequate. Measures to address adequate housing could include a mix of public and private sector measures, but the obligation and responsibility to meet the right to housing rests with state parties.

The right to housing finds implicit and explicit expression in other regional human rights instruments. The communitarian approach to rights in the African Charter on Human and People's Rights (1981), which codifies rights in the context of family, community, tribe, society, and state, does not codify an explicit right to housing.[25] However, scholars note that the African Commission, which oversees the implementation of the charter, implies "the right as arising from the requirements of other articles in the African Charter," including the rights to property (14) and the right to protection of the family (18.1).[26] The jurisprudence of the African Commission while dealing largely with issues of forced evictions and land rights, nonetheless "illuminates the connections of the right to housing to other rights, and foregrounds the social and communal aspects of housing that are often ignored in other jurisdictions."[27]

The new constitution of South Africa (1996) contains an explicit right to housing, for provision of housing was seen as key to undoing the exclusion of apartheid, an indicator of how housing is related to the larger issue of social justice and human flourishing.[28] The right to housing, as Justice Albie Sachs commented in the judgment on the important *Joe Slovo* case, "is as much about access to moral citizenship as it is to access to adequate housing" for "those whose lives have been spent in systematised insecurity on the fringes of organised society."[29] It is outside the scope of this chapter to examine the successes and failures of the inclusion of a constitutional right to housing in post-apartheid South Africa, but it is acknowledged that it strengthened the legitimacy of a right to housing internationally.

The Inter-American System composed of two principal bodies, the Inter-American Commission on Human Rights (IACHR) and Inter-American Court of Human Rights (IACtHR), is charged with interpreting and applying a number of regional human rights instruments in the member countries of the Organization of American States (OAS). The American Convention on Human Rights (ACHR, 1969) refers only to home in the context of the right to privacy. None of the region's key human rights instruments contain an explicit right to housing. However, one of the most interesting and controversial contributions comes from the IACtHR's development of a right to a *vida digna*, as an interpretation of article 4 of the ACHR on the right to life. This judgment was made in its landmark "Street Children" case involving the 1990 arbitrary detention, torture, and murder of a group of street children and youth in Guatemala. "The fundamental right to life includes, not only the right of every human being not to be deprived of his life arbitrarily, but also the right that he will not be prevented from having access to the conditions that guarantee a dignified life (*vida digna*). States have the obligation to guarantee the creation of the conditions required."[30] The court's jurisprudence thus expanded the interpretation of the right to life, reminding us that "inherent in the concept of the right to life are considerations regarding quality of life."[31] It also offers an integrative example of the indivisibility of civil and political rights and economic, social, and cultural rights in the context of the right to life. It is true, as Jo M. Pasqualucci argues, that "the difficulty arises in determining the point at which the State is liable for a violation of the right to a dignified life;"[32] nonetheless, the negative duty on states not to interfere with the right to life is thus augmented to include a positive duty not to prevent people having access to housing and other basic necessities for a *vida digna*.

The Revised European Social Charter (RESC, 1996) is the only regional instrument that contains provisions explicitly related to the right to housing: "Everyone has a right to housing" (article 31).[33] The obligations that arise from this right are the obligation (i) to promote access to housing of an acceptable standard; (ii) to prevent and reduce homelessness with a view to its gradual elimination; and (iii) to make the price of housing accessible to those without adequate resources. However, not all states included in the Revised Charter have accepted the provisions of article 31, and those which have are facing challenges meeting the accompanying obligations.

The right to housing is recognized in the most extensive treatment of homelessness in Catholic Social Teaching, *What Have You Done to Your Homeless Brother? The Church and The Housing Problem* (1987). This document, the result of a worldwide consultation of episcopal conferences and oriental churches, challenges states not to adopt a cultural preference approach to the right to housing. In regions where a large part of the population, individuals or families, spends its entire life on the streets, it is "sometimes presented as a pretext that the lack of housing is proper to a certain type of culture. Anything which does not meet the basic needs of a person, alone or in a family, cannot be considered part of any authentic culture."[34] There can be no cultural contraction of the concept of *imago Dei* in the implementation of the right to housing.

Despite the considerable challenges that mark the acceptance and the implementation of the right to housing in human rights instruments, the emerging jurisprudence gives evidence of a gradual explication of the meaning, scope, and content of the right to housing, and of the nature and extent of state obligations. This complex body of case law—dealing with street children, street homelessness, inadequate housing, forced evictions, discrimination, right to property, right to life, privacy, protection of the family—gives evidence of the nexus of rights that the issue of homelessness is part of.

Conclusion

Human rights, broadly conceived in ethics and theology, together with the gradual international codification of a right to housing, are key foundations of the policy and practice of Catholic theological ethics in relation to homelessness. Human rights discourse specifies: (i) fundamental—and universal—human equality founded on human dignity; (ii) the basic goods—including housing—necessary for a *vida digna* and for human flourishing; (iii) the freedoms—including the freedom to be "somewhere in security, peace, and dignity"—essential for the development of human capabilities;[35] and (iv) the significance of these provisions and protections for the development of social and global justice. Each child, man, and woman whose home is the street is a subject of human rights and a locus of human flourishing, "which is to be considered with favor in her or him as much as in anybody else."[36]

Notes

1. Quentin Skinner, *Liberty before Liberalism* (Cambridge: Cambridge University Press, 1998); John Witte Jr., *The Reformation of Rights: Law, Religion, and Human Rights in Early Modern Calvinism* (Cambridge: Cambridge University Press, 2007), 344.

2. Richard Falk, "Human Rights," *Foreign Policy*, no. 141 (March–April, 2004): 18.

3. Abdullahi A. Na'im, "Toward a Cross-Cultural Approach to Defining International Standards of Human Rights: The Meaning of Cruel, Inhuman, or Degrading Treatment or Punishment," in *Human Rights in Cross-Cultural Perspectives: A Quest for Consensus*, ed. Abdullahi A. Na'im (Philadelphia: University of Pennsylvania Press, 1992), 27.

4. John Finnis, *Natural Law and Natural Rights* (Oxford: Clarendon Press, 1980), 221.

5. See Paul Gordon Lauren, *The Evolution of International Human Rights: Visions Seen* (Philadelphia: University of Pennsylvania Press, 1998), and John S. Nurser *For All Peoples and All Nations: The Ecumenical Church and Human Rights* (Washington, DC: Georgetown University Press, 2005).

6. The United Nations General Assembly, "Universal Declaration of Human Rights," 217 (III) A (Paris, 1948), http://www.un.org/en/universal-declaration-human-rights.

7. Gabriel Marcel, "The Existential Background of Human Dignity," *The William James Lectures—Harvard 1961–62* (Cambridge, MA: Harvard University Press, 1963), 158–59.

8. Gilles Lipovetsky, *Le Crepuscule du Devoir* (Paris: Gallimard, 1992).

9. Eugene B. Borowitz, "The Torah, Written and Oral, and Human Rights: Foundations and Deficiencies," in *The Ethics of World Religions and Human Rights*, ed. Hans Küng and Jürgen Moltmann, *Concilium* 2 (1990): 26.

10. John XXIII, *Pacem in Terris*, April 11, 1963, http://w2.vatican.va/content/john-xxiii/en/encyclicals/documents/hf_j-xxiii_enc_11041963_pacem.html.

11. Ibid., nos. 142–45, 144.

12. Leo XIII, *Rerum Novarum*, May 15, 1891, http://w2.vatican.va/content/leo-xiii/en/encyclicals/documents.

13. See John A. Ryan, *A Living Wage: Its Ethical and Economic Aspects* (New York: Macmillan, 1906).

14. Donal Dorr, *Option for the Poor and for the Earth: Catholic Social Teaching* (Maryknoll, NY: Orbis Books, 2012), 118.

15. J. Bryan Hehir, "Catholicism and Democracy: Conflict, Change, and Collaboration," in *Change in Official Catholic Moral Teachings: Readings in Moral Theology No. 13*, ed. Charles E. Curran (New York/Mahwah, NJ: Paulist Press, 2003), 22.

16. Second Vatican Council, *Dignitatis Humanae* (1965), 1, http://www.vatican.va/archive/hist_councils/ii_vatican_council/documents/vat-ii_decl_19651207_dignitatis-humanae_en.html.

17. John Rawls, *The Law of Peoples with "The Idea of Public Reason Revisited"* (Cambridge, MA: Harvard University Press, 2001), 166–67.

18. Jon Sobrino, "Human Rights and Oppressed Peoples: Historical-Theological Reflections," in *Truth and Memory: The Church and Human Rights in El Salvador and Guatemala*, ed. Michael A. Hayes and David Tombs (Herefordshire: Gracewing, 2001), 157.

19. UN Human Rights (March 2, 2017), Statement of the Press Conference by the Special Rapporteur on the right to adequate housing, Leilani Farha, https://www.ohchr.org/EN/NewsEvents/Pages/DisplayNews.aspx.

20. Asbjørn Eide, "Adequate Standard of Living," in *International Human Rights Law*, ed. D. Moeckli, S. Shah, and S. Sivakumaran (New York: Oxford University Press, 2010), 235.

21. The United Nations General Assembly, 1966, "International Covenant on Economic, Social, and Cultural Rights," *Treaty Series* 999 (December): 171.

22. CESCR General Comment No. 4: The Right to Adequate Housing (Art. 11 (1) of the Covenant) Adopted at the Sixth Session of the Committee on Economic, Social and Cultural Rights, on 13 December 1991 (Contained in Document E/1992/23).

23. CESCR General Comment No. 4, 7.

24. CESCR General Comment No. 4, 8.

25. Organization of African Unity, "African Charter on Human and Peoples' Rights," June 27, 1981, http://www.achpr.org/instruments/achpr.

26. Jessie Hohmann, *The Right to Housing: Law, Concepts, Possibilities* (Oxford: Hart, 2014), 76.

27. Ibid., 82.

28. See A. Sachs, "The Creation of South Africa's Constitution," *New York Law School Law Review* 41 (1997): 669–83.

29. *Residents of Joe Slovo Community, Western Cape v Thubelisha Homes and Others* (CCT 22/08), Judgement, June 10, 2009 [2009] ZACC 16 per Sachs J, note 39 and Para. 331. South African Legal Information Institute (SAFLII), http://www.saflii.org/za/cases/ZACC/2009/16.html.

30. "Street Children" (Villagrán-Morales et al.) v. Guatemala, (1999), par. 144, http://www.corteidh.or.cr/docs/casos/articulos/seriec_63_ing.pdf.

31. Jo M. Pasqualucci, "The Right to a Dignified Life (*Vida Digna*): The Integration of Economic and Social Rights with Civil and Political Rights in the Inter-American Human Rights System," *Hastings International and Comparative Law Review* 31, no. 1 (2008): 2.

32. Ibid., 31.

33. Council of Europe, "European Social Charter (Revised)," 1996, https://rm.coe.int/168007cf93.

34. Pontifical Council Justitia et Pax, *What Have You Done to Your Homeless Brother? The Church and the Housing Problem* (Washington, DC: USCC Office of Publishing and Promotion Services, 1987), III.2.

35. Martha Nussbaum identifies the right to housing as part of a set of rights in the area of property and economic advantage which "can be analysed in a number of distinct ways, in terms of resources, or utility, or capabilities." The right to housing can be seen as a right to a resource necessary for a decent level of living, or "as a right to attain a certain level of capability to function." In her list of central human capabilities, Nussbaum identifies adequate shelter within the capability of "bodily health", and "being able to hold property"

as a component of the capability of "control over one's environment." Martha Nussbaum, "Capabilities and Human Rights," *Fordham Law Review* 66, no. 2 (1997): 273–300, 294, 287–88, http://ir.lawnet.fordham.edu/flr/vol66/iss2/2.

36. Finnis, *Natural Law and Natural Rights*, 221.

Modeling a Personal Solidarity in a World of Exclusion

Meghan J. Clark

"Willy was a familiar face to many in the area of the Vatican. He attended daily Mass in Sant'Anna parish in the Vatican and spent his days and nights on the streets around St. Peter's Square."[1] In March 2015, Willy, an eighty-year-old homeless man, was buried in Vatican City, laid to rest near where he last called home. As one engages in moral and theological reflection on homelessness in our communities, a lived and incarnational solidarity is personal and social, marked by a commitment to the full and equal human dignity of each person and of the one human family. We can illuminate a way, through building a culture of encounter and solidarity, of becoming more fully human together.

In this essay, I examine Catholic Social Teaching (CST) on solidarity as an important resource for theological and ethical reflection on homelessness.[2] Within CST, solidarity often appears ambiguous and amorphous, as if a catchall.[3] This is most clear in the *Compendium of the Social Doctrine of the Church*, which offers the following definition: "Solidarity highlights in a particular way the intrinsic social nature of the human person, the equality of all in dignity and rights and the common path of individuals and peoples towards an ever more committed unity."[4] For brevity and clarity, I am focusing on the ways *Gaudium et Spes* invokes solidarity by providing a clear framework for a Christian theological ethic of solidarity. *Gaudium et Spes* uses solidarity (1) to recognize and reflect on the observable reality of an increasingly globalized and interdependent world; (2) to develop a moral response to this economic and political reality; and (3) as a prism for understanding Jesus's relationship to humanity in the incarnation.[5] This essay addresses the first two uses of solidarity together and argues that they culminate in viewing solidarity as a social virtue. Pope Francis develops the connection between solidarity and the incarnation, as identified through attention to Jesus's relationship to humanity in the incarnation and condemnation of the throwaway culture. Ultimately, as Christine Firer Hinze notes, "Solidarity and the option for the poor disclose the very identity of the church."[6]

Solidarity in CST from John XXIII to Benedict XVI: Developing a Social Virtue

Identified as an attitude, a duty, a principle, and a virtue, solidarity is at once complex and multifaceted. Although Pius XII is the first pope to use the word *soli-*

210

darity, it is John XXIII who introduces it into modern CST.[7] Both John XXIII and Paul VI point out a growing "spirit of solidarity" born out of the recognition of increasing interdependence and globalization.[8] This section briefly examines the development of solidarity as a moral concept in CST, culminating in its status as a moral virtue in which persons and communities make "a firm and persevering determination to commit oneself to the common good; that is to say the good of all and of each individual because we are all really responsible for all."[9]

Interdependence, for CST, is both an observable condition and a moral question connected to issues of human dignity. The full and equal human dignity of each individual person provides a base foundation for solidarity; as Paul VI explains, "There can be no progress toward the complete development of man without the development of all humanity in the spirit of solidarity."[10] This is the first context of solidarity identified above—solidarity relates to the fact of interdependence and a growing sense of interconnectedness within the global community.[11] CST identifies this as an awareness, spirit, or attitude of solidarity. This emerging sense recognizes that, as Shaji George Kochuthara notes, "Injustice done anywhere in the globalized world will adversely affect peace, harmony, and development in other parts of the world. Globalization leads to real development only when it is sought in solidarity."[12] When Paul VI links the development of the individual to the development of all humanity, he envisions human flourishing as something expansive and inclusive. Each and every human person living now and in future generations is included.

The equality and universality of human dignity is crucial, according to philosopher Charles Taylor, because otherwise the rhetoric of solidarity becomes easily twisted so that "we feel a sense of moral satisfaction and superiority when we contemplate others."[13] Examining the scandal of poverty, Bryan Massingale explains, "Because what they possess is undesirable and they don't possess much, and can't get more, the poor are literally and figuratively 'worthless'—unwanted, unnecessary, and expendable. In a consumer-driven society, the poor are at best, irrelevant; at worst, they are a burden."[14] Unfortunately, in practice, the dignity of homeless men and women is often easily ignored. Indifference to street homelessness is one of the more glaring examples of exclusion in which "human beings are themselves considered consumer goods to be used and then discarded."[15] The second step in CST's theological ethic of solidarity requires identifying and clarifying our responsibilities for others and "a desire to make the conditions of life more favorable to all."[16] Practically, John Paul II identified "the need for a solidarity which will take up interdependence and transfer it to the moral plane."[17] For this reason, the recognition of interdependence alone is not sufficient for an ethic of solidarity, for "when this interdependence is separated from its ethical requirements, it has disastrous consequences for the weakest."[18]

Most of the Catholic social tradition in the last sixty years has focused on developing the theory and application of these first two aspects: the descriptive awareness of interdependence and the normative obligations for all that flow from it. David

Hollenbach notes, "Solidarity leads members of a community to recognize their well-being is shared. The relationships linking them with other members of the 'we' are themselves key aspects of the common good they share."[19] The synthesis of the first two uses culminates in solidarity as a virtue applying to both individuals and communities. In *Sollicitudo Rei Socialis*, John Paul II defined the virtue of solidarity "as a firm and persevering determination to commit oneself to the common good; that is to say the good of all and of each individual because we are all really responsible for all."[20] He went on to state that it is an "undoubtedly Christian virtue" and that "solidarity must play its part in the realization of this divine plan, both on the level of individuals and on the level of national and international society."[21]

The virtue of solidarity is both personal and communal. As Uzochukwu Jude Njoku notes, "Solidarity requires a balanced understanding of the personal and the social (structural). Both ought to regulate the other. . . . [and] challenge the structural to create such enabling conditions that promote the dignity of each person."[22] As I have argued elsewhere, its end "is participation in the universal common good. To be more specific, it is the participation by all in the universal common good."[23] The practices by which one habituates the virtue of solidarity is by practicing respect for human dignity and human rights.[24] The combination of human agency, human dignity, and human rights are mutually essential to achieving solidarity. As Marie Vianney Bilgrien argues, "Compassion, empathy, and mercy move solidarity into action and help sustain the disposition."[25]

Practically, this requires active participation by all, not just lip service or symbolic presence at the table: "Active participation is required in order for the equality, mutuality, and reciprocity of human dignity to be present."[26] Duties of solidarity cannot be one-directional. As theologian M. Shawn Copeland notes, "Solidarity is a wrenching task: to stand up for justice in the midst of injustice; to take up simplicity in the midst of affluence and comfort; to embrace integrity in the midst of collusion and co-optation; to contest the gravitational pull of domination."[27] Questions of solidarity begin with justice as a requirement, for as Benedict XVI notes in *Caritas in Veritate,* "I cannot 'give' what is mine to the other, without first giving him what pertains to him in justice. If we love others with charity, then first of all we are just towards them."[28]

Within the context of street homelessness, this requires the sustained participation of the homeless in decision making and planning. As Gerald Beyer argues, "Participation in Catholic social thought denotes a substantive contribution to society; it is not just a formal, procedural task to be valued in abstract from the ends served by it."[29] Within the complexities of contemporary society, especially the reality of social media and consumerism, Vincent Miller cautions against a sense of "virtual solidarity" as sufficient for the virtue in which the digital or virtual becomes "a substitute for concrete political solidarity," which must be lived as an embodied reality.[30] As persons and communities, we are called to cultivate the virtue of solidarity through practicing respect for the human rights of persons experiencing street homelessness.

Pope Francis and Solidarity with Christ

Gaudium et Spes connects solidarity with the incarnation by explaining human relationality, as when it states, "This communitarian character is developed and consummated in the work of Jesus Christ. For the very word made flesh willed to share in human fellowship. . . . This solidarity must be constantly increased until the day on which it will be brought to perfection."[31] Since the Second Vatican Council, each pope has reflected on solidarity and signaled connections between solidarity and Jesus, yet it remained an underdeveloped aspect until Pope Francis. "A faith that does not draw us into solidarity is a faith which is dead, it is deceitful. . . . Faith without solidarity is a faith without Christ," Francis stated provocatively during his pastoral visit with the people of Bañado Norte in Paraguay.[32] Francis's unique contribution to CST on solidarity is a focus on learning from Jesus as a model of solidarity, and on lived solidarity as an encounter with Christ.[33] In particular, Francis focuses on solidarity with homeless persons as a privileged place of encounter with Christ.

In *Evangelii Gaudium*, Pope Francis lamented and decried the world of exclusion in which we live. Surveying the global economic and political reality, he stated, "Today everything comes under the laws of competition and the survival of the fittest, where the powerful feed upon the powerless. As a consequence, masses of people find themselves excluded and marginalized: without work, without possibilities, without any means of escape." And he went on to clarify that "exclusion ultimately has to do with what it means to be a part of the society in which we live; those excluded are no longer society's underside or its fringes or its disenfranchised–they are no longer even a part of it. The excluded are not the 'exploited' but the outcast, the 'leftovers.'"[34] Street homelessness is one particular locus of this— pushing the marginalized without homes even further into the shadows, where even their basic humanity is questioned.

In response, Francis invites everyone to reject this world of exclusion by building a culture of encounter and of solidarity. God enters into our reality through our fragility and finitude, "by becoming close to us, by showing true solidarity, especially to the poor and needy."[35] Jesus's identification with the marginalized and excluded is the most important element here. Thus, Francis argues, "our faith in Christ, who became poor, and was always close to the poor and outcast, is the basis for our concern for the integral development of society's most neglected members."[36] We are called to build a culture of encounter and solidarity, remembering that "to love God and neighbor is not something abstract, but profoundly concrete: it means seeing in every person's face the face of the Lord to be served."[37]

On his pastoral visits, his most impactful and challenging speech usually comes when he is among those on the margins—those living in poverty, the homeless, refugees, etc. Sharing lunch at a homeless shelter in Washington, DC, Pope Francis reminded all that "the Son of God came into this world as a homeless person. The Son of God knew what it was to start life without a roof over his head," and we all are invited into relationship with him, as "Jesus keeps knocking on our door in the faces of our brothers and sisters, in the faces of our neighbors, in the faces of those at our side."[38] He chastises the developed world for its throwaway culture and lack of solidarity: "I want to be very clear. There is no social or moral justification, no justification whatsoever, for lack of housing. There are many unjust situations, but we know that God is suffering with us, experiencing them at our side. He does not abandon us."[39]

His emphasis is to resituate the center of Christianity on the peripheries, as well as to refocus attention on the Gospel challenge of Matthew 25 and on the radical identification of Jesus with the poor and marginalized. Incarnational solidarity relocates mercy and the love of God as important components of universal human dignity. In these encounters with homeless persons, this is where one encounters the face of Christ. Here, human dignity is deeply personal, not just universal—it is in the face of the other that one sees the face of Christ. Thus, the deep ties between the option for the poor and solidarity, as a principle and as a virtue, becomes clearer for CST. This is further clarified and deepened by Francis, who urges that solidarity must be "lived as the decision to restore to the poor what belongs to them."[40]

Speaking to the World Meeting of Popular Movements in Bolivia, Francis focused on the 3 L's—land, lodging, and labor—as "sacred rights," and insisted:

> The future of humanity does not lie solely in the hands of great leaders, the great powers and the elites. It is fundamentally in the hands of peoples and in their ability to organize. . . . Each of us, let us repeat from the heart: no family without lodging, no rural worker without land, no laborer without rights, no people without sovereignty, no individual without dignity.[41]

This is an all-encompassing vision of globalized justice as participation situated within CST's holistic valuing of persons and communities aligned with justice and subsidiarity. Social and economic structures are important and must be changed so that the poor become "dignified agents of their own destiny."[42]

In Francis's development of solidarity, the centrality of universal human dignity is intimately tied to Jesus as taking on that humanity in the incarnation. In this connection between Jesus, mercy, and solidarity, "Jesus no longer belongs to the past but lives in the present and is projected toward the future; Jesus is the everlasting 'today' of God."[43] The encounter with the living God necessarily involves encounter with those on the margins, as the flesh of Christ.

Modeling Incarnational Solidarity with the Homeless in a World of Exclusions

Through the efforts of the Office of Papal Charities, led by (now) Cardinal Konrad Krajewski, seeking solidarity with the street homeless population of Rome is a public and consistent theme of the Francis papacy. As a result, "Pope Francis's

Homeless Guests 'Are All Moving' to St. Peter's Square."[44] Not everyone is thrilled that homeless men and women are moving from the shadows of Termini station to the area around St. Peter's Square, with the Vatican providing sleeping bags. Yet when asked by journalists why they have come to St. Peter's, the people answered because at St. Peter's Square they are treated with human dignity. In addition to food and showers, individuals have been invited to tours of the Sistine chapel, music in the Vatican gardens, and dinner inside Vatican City. Programs include summer day trips to the beach.[45] Emphasizing that persons experiencing homelessness are full members of the community for the Jubilee Year of Mercy, Francis added a special *holy door* at a homeless shelter in Rome.[46]

On its own, this outreach is not ending street homelessness in the city of Rome. It does not represent significant structural changes, nor is it the answer to street homelessness around the globe. Neither Pope Francis nor Cardinal Krajewski presents their pastoral plan as a panacea to street homelessness. Instead, it models a radical prioritizing of the full and personal human dignity of each person encountered. It stands with those on the margins and acknowledges that they are full persons—spiritual, social, and even artistic—and not merely needs to be met. It illuminates a path toward solidarity with homeless men and women in our communities. In his 2016 World Day of Peace Message, Francis explains, "As creatures endowed with inalienable dignity, we are related to all our brothers and sisters, for whom we are responsible and with whom we act in solidarity."[47] As a starting point, it is an example of what Nichole Flores calls *aesthetic solidarity,* which can serve as a "foundation for attentive relationships" that "take the reality of the exploited person seriously, thus empowering that person to communicate her experiences in a way that is both personally and socially meaningful" and also "form a basis for relationships characterized by mutuality and equality without diminishing difference."[48]

Solidarity, as both a virtue and a deep connection to Christ, is a lived reality. It must be practiced and cultivated by persons and communities through personal encounters. Thus, as Kelly Johnson notes, "Strangerliness is a habit that has been learned slowly. We will unlearn it with difficulty and we will not do so without making changes in our finances, our locations, our ways of doing business, and our encounters with strangers."[49] Solidarity is an active process. Using the example of accompanying migrants, Mark Potter posits "five movements of the spiritual exercise of solidarity" that help engage both body and spirit in a relationship of equality, mutuality, and reciprocity, which brings forth "a genuine confrontation with the sin" so prevalent in a world of exclusion, and recognizes that solidarity "is not something that can be done alone—it requires the agency and gift of grace extended by another, in this case, the poor."[50]

When questioned about giving money to homeless persons on the street, Pope Francis urged giving to homeless persons without hesitation or judgment about what they may or may not do with the money.[51] Yet, he qualified, arguing that you should not throw money in a cup as you are walking. Instead, stop, look him or her in the eye, touch their hands, speak to them, and give. Why is this important? Because it creates a human encounter. In a truly human encounter, the human dignity of both persons is recognized and therefore embraced. Reflecting on the Parable of the Good Samaritan, according to Gustavo Gutiérrez, it is by leaving our path and entering into the path of another that we "become neighbor" to one another. And "the Samaritan becomes the neighbor for the wounded person. And the wounded becomes the neighbor of the Samaritan."[52]

Solidarity is a social virtue that urges us to be one human family and to work for greater justice in society. At the same time, it is deeply personal. As I drive home in Queens, New York, I strive to embrace Pope Francis's injunction as I encounter homeless men and women lining the side of the road. In a momentary encounter, it is possible to see and affirm the humanity of persons experiencing homelessness. Ultimately, solidarity is both an invitation to become more fully human together and to more deeply ponder the mystery of the incarnation in which the word was made flesh in solidarity with humanity. It is through recognition that those on the margins are the flesh of Christ that it becomes truly possible to see that we are also the flesh of Christ. Thus solidarity, like peace, "is both God's gift and a human achievement. As a gift of God, it is entrusted to all men and women who are called to attain it."[53]

Notes

1. Carol Glatz, "Homeless Man of Deep Faith Given Funeral Burial in Vatican City," *National Catholic Reporter*, February 25, 2015, https://www.ncronline.org/news/people/homeless-man-deep-faith-given-funeral-burial-vatican-city.

2. This essay is an expanded version of a presentation delivered at a Symposium on Street Homelessness and Catholic Social Teaching in Rome, December 1, 2018.

3. For more detail on the development of solidarity in Catholic Social Teaching, see Gerald Beyer, "The Meaning of Solidarity in Catholic Social Teaching," *Political Theology* 15, no. 1 (2014): 7–25; Marie Vianney Bilgrien, *Solidarity: A Principle, an Attitude, a Duty or the Virtue for an Independent World?* (New York: Peter Lang, 1999); and Meghan J. Clark, *The Vision of Catholic Social Thought: The Virtue of Solidarity and the Praxis of Human Rights* (Minneapolis: Fortress Press, 2014).

4. Pontifical Council for Justice and Peace, *Compendium of the Social Doctrine of the Church* (2005), 192, http://www.vatican.va/roman_curia/pontifical_councils/justpeace/documents/rc_pc_justpeace_doc_20060526_compendio-dott-soc_en.html.

5. See *Gaudium et Spes* (December 7, 1965), http://www.vatican.va/archive/hist_councils/ii_vatican_council/documents/vat-ii_const_19651207_gaudium-et-spes_en.html. (Hereafter cited as *GS*.) *GS* references solidarity in 3, 4, 32, 38, 48, 57, 75, 85, and 90.

6. Christine Firer Hinze, "Over, Under, Around, and Through: Ethics, Solidarity, and the Saints," *CTSA Proceedings* 66 (2011): 35.

7. Beyer, "Meaning of Solidarity," 9. Beyer writes of the pope: "In his 1939 encyclical *Summi Pontificatus*, he argues 'the first page of Scripture' (Gen 1:26–27) undergirds the law of 'human solidarity and charity,' revealing our common origin and that all human beings are created in the image of God."

8. It is also worth noting that prior to John XXIII, the word *solidarity* was sometimes viewed with suspicion within European Catholic circles as potentially problematic, given historical connections to the French Revolution and in modern times, to socialism. For more on this history see Steinar Stjernø, *Solidarity in Europe: The History of an Idea* (Cambridge: Cambridge University Press, 2005), 75–85.

9. Pope John Paul II, *Sollicitudo Rei Socialis* (December 30, 1987), 38, http://w2.vatican.va/content/john-paul-ii/en/encyclicals/documents/hf_jp-ii_enc_30121987_sollicitudo-rei-socialis.html. (Hereafter cited as *SRS.*)

10. Pope Paul VI, *Populorum Progressio* (March 26, 1967), 43, http://w2.vatican.va/content/paul-vi/en/encyclicals/documents/hf_p-vi_enc_26031967_populorum.html (Hereafter cited as *PP*).

11. *GS* 4.

12. Shaji George Kochuthara, "Globalization in Solidarity," *Political Theology*, 15, no. 1 (2014): 62.

13. Charles Taylor, *A Secular Age* (Cambridge, Mass: Belknap Press of Harvard University Press, 2007), 696.

14. Bryan Massingale, "The Scandal of Poverty: 'Cultural Indifference' and the Option for the Poor Post-Katrina," *Journal of Religion and Society* Supplement Series 4 (2008): 58.

15. Pope Francis, *Evangelii Gaudium* (November 24, 2013), 7, http://w2.vatican.va/content/francesco/en/apost_exhortations/documents/papa-francesco_esortazione-ap_20131124_evangelii-gaudium.html. (Hereafter cited as *EG*.)

16. *GS* 57.

17. *SRS* 26.

18. *SRS* 17.

19. David Hollenbach, SJ, "The Glory of God and the Global Common Good: Solidarity in a Turbulent World," *CTSA Proceedings* 72 (2017): 56.

20. *SRS* 38.

21. *SRS* 40; "One's neighbor is then not only a human being with his or her own rights and a fundamental equality with everyone else, but becomes the living image of God the Father, redeemed by the blood of Jesus Christ and placed under the permanent action of the Holy Spirit."

22. Uzochukwu Jude Njoku, "Re-thinking Solidarity as a Principle of Catholic Social Teaching: Going beyond *Gaudium et spes* and the Social Encyclicals of John Paul II," *Political Theology* 9, no. 4 (2008): 540.

23. Clark, *Vision of Catholic Social Thought*. 112–13.

24. Ibid.

25. Bilgrien, *Solidarity*, 105–6.

26. Meghan J. Clark, "Anatomy of a Social Virtue," *Political Theology* 15, no. 1 (2014): 30.

27. M. Shawn Copeland, "Toward a Critical Christian Feminist Theology of Solidarity," in *Women and Theology*, ed. Mary Ann Hinsdale and Phyllis H. Kaminski (Maryknoll, NY: Orbis Books, 1995), 18.

28. Pope Benedict XVI, *Caritas in Veritate* (June 29, 2009) 6, http://w2.vatican.va/content/benedict-xvi/en/encyclicals/documents/hf_ben-xvi_enc_20090629_caritas-in-veritate.html.

29. Beyer, "Meaning of Solidarity," 17.

30. Vincent J. Miller, *Consuming Religion: Christian Faith and Practice in a Consumer Religion* (London: Continuum, 2005), 76.

31. *GS* 32.

32. Pope Francis, "Visit to the People of Bañado Norte" (Address, Paraguay, July 12, 2015), http://w2.vatican.va/content/francesco/en/speeches/2015/july/documents/papa-francesco_20150712_paraguay-banado-norte.html.

33. For a more detailed treatment of Pope Francis's Christological approach to solidarity see Meghan J. Clark, "Pope Francis and the Christological Dimensions of Solidarity in Catholic Social Teaching," *Theological Studies* 80, no. 1 (March 2019): 102–22.

34. *EG* 53.

35. Pope Francis, "Meeting with the Academic and Cultural World" (Address, Cagliari, September 22, 2013), https://w2.vatican.va/content/francesco/en/speeches/2013/may/documents/papa-francesco_20130521_dono-di-maria.html.

36. *EG* 186.

37. See note 35 above.

38. Pope Francis, "Visit to the Charitable Center of St. Patrick Parish and Meeting with the Homeless" (Washington, DC, September 24, 2015), https://w2.vatican.va/content/francesco/en/speeches/2015/september/documents/papa-francesco_20150924_usa-centro-caritativo.html.

39. Ibid.

40. *EG* 189.

41. Pope Francis, "Address of the Holy Father at the Second World Meeting of Popular Movements" (July 9, 2015), Santa Cruz de la Sierra, Bolivia, http://w2.vatican.va/content/francesco/en/speeches/2015/july/documents/papa-francesco_20150709_bolivia-movimenti-popolari.html.

42. Pope Francis, "Meeting at the General Assembly of the United Nations Organization" (September 25, 2015), New York, http://w2.vatican.va/content/francesco/en/speeches/2015/september/documents/papa-francesco_20150925_onu-visita.html, http://www.vatican.va.

43. Pope Francis, *The Church of Mercy: A Vision for the Church* (Chicago: Loyola Press, 2014), 10.

44. Barbie Latza Nadeau, "Pope Francis's Homeless Guests are Moving to St. Peter's Square," *Daily Beast*, March 4, 2014.

45. Josephine McKenna, "Pope Francis Treats Homeless to Pizza and a Swim at the Beach" (August 15, 2016), https://www.ncronline.org/news/vatican/pope-francis-treats-homeless-pizza-and-swim-beach.

46. Pope Francis, "Opening of the 'Holy Door of Charity' and Celebration of the Holy Mass" (Homily, Rome, December 18, 2015), https://w2.vatican.va/content/francesco/en/homilies/2015/documents/papa-francesco_20151218_giubileo-omelia-porta-carita.html.

47. Pope Francis, "Overcome Indifference and Win Peace" (World Day of Peace Message, January 1, 2016), 2, http://w2.vatican.va/content/francesco/en/messages/peace/documents/papa-francesco_20151208_messaggio-xlix-giornata-mondiale-pace-2016.html.

48. Nichole Flores, "Beyond Consumptive Solidarity: An Aesthetic Response to Human Trafficking," *Journal of Religious Ethics* 46, no. 2 (June 2018): 372–73.

49. Kelly S. Johnson, *The Fear of Beggars: Stewardship and Poverty in Christian Ethics* (Grand Rapids, MI: Eerdmans, 2007), 220.

50. Mark Potter, "Solidarity as Spiritual Exercise: Accompanying Migrants on the US/Mexico Border," *Political Theology* 12, no. 6 (2011): 830–42.

51. Michael O'Loughlin, "Pope Francis Says Give to the Homeless, Don't Worry How They Spend It, as Lent Begins," *America Magazine,* February 28, 2017.

52. Joshua McElwee, "Gutierrez at Vatican: Church Must Be Samaritan, Reaching Out to Others," *National Catholic Reporter*, February 28, 2014, https://www.ncronline.org/blogs/ncr-today/gutierrez-vatican-church-must-be-samaritan-reaching-out-others.

53. Pope Francis, "Overcome Indifference and Win Peace," 1.

HOSPITALITY

Joseph McCrave

This chapter argues that hospitality may serve as an appropriate, effective, and necessary response to homelessness.[1] It suggests that the kind of hospitality that reaches such potential, however, is one oriented toward outreach rather than the more typical model of reception.

Thus, the discussion here begins with the concept of "Jesuit hospitality" as developed by two contemporary theological ethicists. This concept explains how and why hospitality may be practiced in the mode of outreach. The chapter then offers methodological clarifications and developments for the concept of hospitality as a virtue, and finally applies the analysis of hospitality to responses to homelessness, discussing the overall shape of such responses as well as examples at the interpersonal and structural levels.

Jesuit Hospitality

James F. Keenan argues for the recovery of the virtue of "Jesuit hospitality."[2] Although Keenan's discussion concerns the mission of the Society of Jesus—his own religious order—he rightly suggests that the understanding of this virtue enhances the understanding of hospitality in contemporary theological ethics generally. Keenan distinguishes two modes of hospitable action with roots in the Christian tradition.

On the one hand, there is the hospitality associated with "the receiving church." In this common model, the host welcomes a guest into a certain home or community, sharing not only material resources but fellowship and a way of life.

As Keenan describes, this hospitality finds inspiration throughout Scripture and early Christian practice. In the Hebrew Bible, God "tends to our needs as a host ministers to a guest." This represents a "divine practice," which "becomes normative for God's chosen people."[3] In the Gospels, Jesus is rejected, yet remains the paradigm of hospitality, including at the Last Supper and even on the cross.[4] Hospitality has a "special significance" for the apostle Paul, who is welcomed by early Christian communities. The early church depended on and enacted hospitality in this mode: "whether it was the patron hosting the *ekklesia* or the *ekklesia* hosting either the apostolic preachers or later the neighbor in need. In all instances, the host was in her domicile."[5] Over time, the hospitality of the receiving church was exemplified especially by Benedictine spirituality and practice.[6]

On the other hand, there is the hospitality associated with "the sending church." This is the mode in which Keenan locates "Jesuit hospitality." The notion is surprising as, unlike Benedictines, Jesuits are not famed for their hospitality. Yet Keenan argues that the order practices hospitality in this second mode.

Keenan argues that Jesuits exercise their ministry through "journeying" toward those who are neglected and dwelling with them.[7] Thus, "ministry does not expand from Jesuit community; rather, community occurs where Jesuit ministry is."[8] Jesuit ministry in refugee camps is a paradigm case.[9] This "redefines a classic religious charism that was generally associated with practices within specific domiciles. One does not think ordinarily of hospitality on the road. . . . But our practice of hospitality is on the road because that is where those in need are."[10]

Such hospitality identifies more closely with "the itinerant Paul" than the communities that received him, "for Paul is welcoming his hosts into God's world."[11] It finds an exemplar in "the Good Samaritan."[12] It may also appeal to the incarnation itself, in light of the particular form that it takes in this world. This begins with the birth of an exiled savior come to call us home.[13]

Hospitality, Outreach, and Exclusion

The two modes of hospitality may be considered as specific charisms of particular religious orders, as in the case of the Jesuits and Benedictines. In theological ethics, however, we may consider these modes as different ways that anyone may embody hospitality in response to different situations.

Theological ethicist Kate Ward has demonstrated this point by her insightful application of "Jesuit hospitality" to the problem of economic inequality, in dialogue with Pope Francis's encouragement of the practice of "encounter."[14] Ward also highlights that both proposals resonate with contemporary feminist work on hospitality.[15] This work tends to envisage hospitality as: across difference; risky; marginal; and, mutual.[16] Her explication of the problem of inequality illuminates the need for a certain kind of hospitality (informed by all three sources) in response.

Ward notes that for Francis, "the worst effect of widespread inequality is exclusion."[17] Francis argues that "exclusion ultimately has to do with what it means to be a part of the society in which we live; those excluded are no longer society's underside or its fringes or its disenfranchised—they are no longer even a part of it."[18] As Ward summarizes Francis's vision, inclusion means "not mere subsistence, nor mere access to consumer goods, but full participation in those goods that members of society create through their life together,"[19] such as education, health care, and employment.[20]

For Ward and Francis, inequality is not natural or inevitable, but a product of human choice. It has structural causes, which cannot be transformed by the virtue of hospitality alone. But inequality is also a "virtue problem," that is, "both an indicator of virtue deficits in society, and a factor which contributes to their formation."[21] As rich and poor grow apart, the human flourishing of both is impeded.[22] For the poor this is because of exclusion itself and the consequent challenges in developing virtues (for example, that of self-care). For the wealthy this is because virtues such as "solidarity, compassion, and justice" remain underdeveloped.[23]

In societies where rich and poor are distant, proactive outreach is necessary. Embodied as such, the virtue of hospitality is an appropriate response to exclusion. As a virtue, it also contributes to the flourishing of those who develop it.

Hospitality as a Virtue

Hospitality is a virtue, then, which may be embodied in two basic modes. Recognizing the wider resonances and applications of "Jesuit hospitality," I now describe hospitality in this mode as "hospitality as outreach." I term the mode that resembles the "Benedictine" style, "hospitality as reception."

To name hospitality as a virtue signifies that it is a morally praiseworthy trait; an excellence of character.[24] To become a hospitable person is to become more fully human, as Ward emphasizes.

In the Aristotelian and Thomistic traditions, a virtue is the mean between vices of "deficiency" and "excess."[25] Hospitality, then, is clearly opposed to the vice of inhospitality, a deficiency. Inhospitality can be expressed in direct oppression of those in need but also in passive indifference. We might name the vice of excess, simply, "false hospitality." It is a semblance of virtue, which might impose "hospitable" relations coercively, instrumentalize others for self-gratification, or, assume that they have nothing to offer. Hospitality as the "mean" reminds us that we can go wrong not only by excluding those in need but by the way in which we reach out to them.

The cardinal virtues that Keenan proposes in another discussion offer a way to locate hospitality among other virtues.[26] Keenan suggests that instead of envisaging cardinal virtues as governing "powers of the soul," as did Aquinas, we understand them as governing different spheres of relationships. He names cardinal virtues of self-care, fidelity, and justice. In order, these govern the way in which we relate to ourselves, particular others close to us, and other human beings generally.[27] As with the classical cardinal virtues, prudence is the fourth. Prudence names the ability to order the other virtues, directing them in practice and deciding in cases of conflict.[28]

I suggest that hospitality is the virtue that lies at the intersection of fidelity and justice. When we express hospitality, we receive or approach the other to whom we may have no unique bond. In terms of (prior) relationship, we may owe them only what we owe to any other human being: the essential yet general demands of justice. In hospitality we transform the relationship, choosing to encounter another person—paradigmatically "the stranger"—as one of particular importance to us. The two modes of hospitality have this in common.[29] Still, hospitality as a virtue does not replace justice—still less contradict it—but complements it.

I here consider hospitality an "acquired" virtue, like the cardinal virtues.[30] Its authentic development is not limited to Christians even as it receives distinctive specification within the Christian tradition. Hospitality may be formed within Christian communities[31] and enacted by ecclesial bodies.[32] Yet such formation also directs Christians themselves beyond the church and into the world.[33]

Hospitality as Outreach in Response to Homelessness

The Dynamics of a Hospitable Response

I assume here that, like economic inequality, homelessness is a problem of exclusion.[34] To be homeless among the homed is to lack access to the basic good of shelter, as well as the more complex social good of "home."[35] Yet it is also to be *excluded* from access to *further* goods precisely on account of the condition of homelessness.[36] Such exclusion is sometimes supported by grossly misleading social constructions of homelessness, such as the narrative that it is caused by individual failings.[37]

In order to see how hospitality might respond, we may consider the different dynamics of the two modes.

In hospitality as reception, the host awaits, receives, and incorporates the guest into a particular home or community.

In hospitality as outreach, the "host" journeys to, meets, and accompanies the "guest" into society. These dynamics, which feature in the parable of the Samaritan in Luke 10:25–37,[38] are appropriate to respond to the exclusion of homeless persons. The dynamics of "journeying," "meeting," and "accompanying" respond to exclusion that takes the forms of invisibility, instability, and material barriers to inclusion, respectively.

In "journeying," the hospitable person becomes aware of those on the margins and attends to them. The Samaritan first approaches the other before he "sees," feels "compassion," and "comes even closer."[39] This dynamic responds to the invisibility of homeless persons. They may be "invisible" in that, when we do encounter them, "we act as if they do not even exist."[40] Or they may be "invisible" because they are "the hidden homeless" (unrecorded), yet still suffering exclusion.[41]

In "meeting," the hospitable person addresses another's needs as they are and shares in community outside of her or his own familiar environment.[42] The Samaritan addresses the man's wounds with what he has, on the road (10:34). This dynamic does not emphasize the need to receive the other (into an existing order) as much as to be receptive to the other.[43] Thus, it is appropriate given the complex network of needs created or exacerbated by the instability that homelessness involves. Moments of assessment and understanding may be necessary prior to full "solutions."

In "accompanying," hospitality as outreach assists others "who do not find the world a welcoming place."[44] Its welcome is "not into a particular domicile but into a world where God labors."[45] The Samaritan leads the man to the inn (10:34); a point of rest that will ultimately serve to facilitate the man's resumption of *his* journey.

The telos of hospitality as outreach is therefore inclusion within society itself as the basis for the flourishing of the person to whom it is offered. This reminds would-be respondents to address the material barriers to inclusion that homeless persons face.[46] In the model of outreach, hospitality is not opposed to but rather aligns with the goal of exiting homelessness. To offer "a bed for the night" may remain vital (here there is overlap with hospitality as reception). The notion of welcome into the world, however, frames offers of temporary shelter within this wider goal.[47]

Interpersonal Hospitality: The Case of Soup-runs

A practice that may embody hospitality as outreach is that popularly known (in the UK) as a "soup-run." This is where small-scale voluntary organizations (often churches) facilitate the mobile distribution of food and other provisions around urban centers. They target "rough sleepers," but are prepared to serve anyone. They aim to engage personally with those whom they serve.

In 2005, the charity Shelter produced a balanced assessment of soup-runs.[48] It noted that soup-runs have attracted criticism for failing to serve those whom they target or, where they do, enabling a "street lifestyle." Critics may perceive soup-runs as "naïve and irresponsible philanthropy [that] does not fit with today's strategic responses to street homelessness."[49] Overall, the assessment supports the idea of soup-runs but offers correctives for good practice. Regarding both support and correction, their recommendations align with hospitality as outreach.

Regarding the value of the practice, soup-runs clearly journey to those in need, who may be unable to use mainstream services. Shelter affirms that while this sometimes includes those who are not street homeless (e.g., the recently rehoused), these people usually access the service for "two legitimate reasons," namely, "food poverty" and "social isolation."[50]

Soup-runs also meet those in need, creating community where they are. Shelter affirms that people who benefit from soup-runs "value the opportunity to talk informally to someone who isn't from an 'official agency.'"[51] "Nonjudgmental 'acceptance'" is important for such people.[52]

For Shelter, soup-runs must signpost pathways toward exiting homelessness. Hospitality as outreach supports this view because of its telos of social inclusion. Soup-runs often do not do this, but they can: meeting "immediate needs" is "an effective . . . way of starting a positive supportive relationship, which can be built upon by street outreach teams."[53] With appropriate "provision of information," "soup-runs can and do play an important role in enabling people to begin to exit homelessness."[54]

To name "hospitality" as a "virtue" does not endorse responses to homelessness that are immune from practical, evidence-based considerations. A virtue-based analysis holds that soup-runs (etc.) must be prudential. For instance, while there is little evidence to show that soup-runs, in general, keep people on the streets, in specific areas of "overprovision," they might. One example of prudence here, then, is the co-ordination of soup-runs to avoid "overprovision."[55]

Structural Hospitality

An ethic of virtue is sometimes considered as an alternative to, rather than a resource for, structural reform.[56] Furthermore, hospitality is often contrasted with virtues such as justice and solidarity—even where it is thought to complement them—as offering interpersonal rather than structural solutions.[57] I maintain that the virtue of hospitality may guide attempts to reform structures.[58] Parallel work for justice—which may focus especially on preventing homelessness—is essential; yet social structures can and must become more hospitable to those who are homeless. Here I can only clarify how we might speak of hospitable/inhospitable structures.

One important account of social structures is provided by critical realist sociology, which Daniel K. Finn appropriates for theological ethics.[59] In this school, structures are "systems of human relations among (preexisting) social positions."[60] Some structures "possess a kind of collective agency, as when Microsoft announces it will hire 300 more employees, but that agency occurs only through the persons within the structure." The more important causal impact of structures "is through the various restrictions, enablements and incentives they present to the personal agents within them."[61]

In brief, this suggests that we may speak meaningfully of hospitable/inhospitable social structures in two ways.

First, in terms of "a kind of collective agency." We may think of this as the external causal impact of structures (the impact on those outside of the structure). If a structure is inhospitable in this way, decisions are made by individuals within it that cause states of affairs that, as a matter of fact, exclude certain populations. Even without defending any specific account of collective agency here, the ascription of moral evaluation ("inhospitable") to such an impact is meaningful as a presumptive judgment on the intentions of individual agents who contributed to the decision.

For example, a company may be inhospitable with respect to its policy, formal or informal, not to consider for employment anyone whose address is recognized as a homeless "hostel." Or again with respect to its decision to use "defensive architecture" such as "anti-homeless spikes" on its physical premises.[62]

Second, we may refer to the "restrictions, enablements and incentives" structures to offer to persons operating within them. The opportunities and/or costs of certain choices affect how persons within structures act. Insofar as habitual action forms virtues and vices, this also affects the kind of moral agents these persons become over time. Structures may be hospitable "structures of virtue," then, in that they encourage persons, ultimately, to grow in hospitality.[63]

An example that illustrates the basic point is that of donation points for homeless funds within city centers, which attempt to make people more generous by making it easier to give money to appropriate causes.[64]

I have referred to "soup-runs," above, to draw attention to interpersonal hospitality within them. But the way in which a "soup-run" is structured facilitates this hospitality. Within the structure it is understood that the positions (say, "server") and "served person") relate in a particular way (for example, the former meets the latter with unconditional acceptance) even before individuals enact this.

Such structural encouragement can occur on a wider scale. In the UK, the national-level theater company Cardboard Citizens invites people with experience of homelessness to tell their stories, through the theatrical medium, as actors and writers.[65] Through the creative reevaluation of the meaning of "performer" and "audience member," and of who adopts these positions, this structure enables a radical, mutual hospitality. Those who are not homeless are welcome to listen to those who are or have been.

At the level of the legal system, recurrent proposals to criminalize "rough sleeping" advance the cause of an inhospitable structural device.[66] Such a change would modify the meaning of the position of "rough sleeper" and discourage or prevent hospitality toward people in this position.

Conclusion

In sum, Keenan's analysis of Jesuit hospitality lays the foundation for understanding hospitality as a virtue that operates in two basic modes, historically associated with "the receiving church" and "the sending church." Taking up the latter, Ward shows that hospitality as proactive outreach or encounter is a necessary response to the exclusion created by economic inequality. I suggest that as an acquired virtue, hospitality stands at the intersection of fidelity and justice, calling us to attend to the stranger with special attentiveness. In the mode of outreach, such hospitality is necessary insofar as homelessness is also a problem of exclusion. The specific dynamics of journeying, meeting, and accompanying are appropriate to address this exclusion where it manifests itself as invisibility, instability, and material barriers to inclusion. This understanding of hospitality does not only support and correct interpersonal actions but exhorts us to work for the reform of social structures toward the inclusion of persons who are homeless, and the formation of hospitality in others.

Notes

1. This essay focuses on the moral responsibilities of those who are not homeless (to respond), while affirming that hospitality itself involves encounter in a spirit of mutuality.

2. James F. Keenan, "Jesuit Hospitality?" in *Promise Renewed: Jesuit Higher Education for a New Millennium*, ed. Martin R. Tripole (Chicago: Jesuit Way, 1999), 230–44.

3. Ibid., 231.

4. Ibid., 231; Lk 22:7–38, 23:43.

5. Keenan, "Jesuit Hospitality?" 237.

6. Benedict of Nursia, *The Rule of St. Benedict in English*, ed. Timothy Fry, OSB (Collegeville, MN: Liturgical Press, 1981), no. 53.

7. Keenan, "Jesuit Hospitality?" 237; John W. O'Malley, "To Travel to Any Part of the World: Jeronimo Nadal and the Jesuit Vocation," *Studies in the Spirituality of Jesuits* 16, no. 2 (1984): 1–20.

8. Keenan, "Jesuit Hospitality?" 236.

9. *Jesuit Refugee Service*, https://jrs.net.

10. Keenan, "Jesuit Hospitality?" 241.

11. Ibid., 240.

12. Ibid., 241; Lk 10:25–37.

13. Keenan, "Jesuit Hospitality?" 238.

14. Kate Ward, "Jesuit and Feminist Hospitality: Pope Francis' Virtue Response to Inequality," *Religions* 8, no. 4 (2017): 71.

15. Influential texts include Christine D. Pohl, *Making Room: Recovering Hospitality as a Christian Tradition* (Grand Rapids, MI: W.B. Eerdmans, 1999); Letty M. Russell, *Just Hospitality: God's Welcome in a World of Difference*, ed. J. Shannon Clarkson and Kate M. Ott (Louisville, KY: Westminster John Knox Press, 2009).

16. Ward, "Jesuit and Feminist Hospitality," 5–7.

17. Ibid., 2.

18. Pope Francis, *Evangelii Gaudium* (2013), http://vatican.va, no. 53.

19. Ward, "Jesuit and Feminist Hospitality," 2.

20. Pope Francis, *Evangelii Gaudium*, no. 192.

21. Ward, "Jesuit and Feminist Hospitality," 9.

22. Kate Ward and Kenneth R. Himes, "'Growing Apart': The Rise of Inequality," *Theological Studies* 75, no. 1 (2014): 118–32.

23. Ward, "Jesuit and Feminist Hospitality," 3. This echoes Lisa Tessman's proposal that oppressors may be subjectively happy but not flourish: Lisa Tessman, *Burdened Virtues: Virtue Ethics for Liberatory Struggles* (New York: Oxford University Press, 2005).

24. Stephen Pope, "Virtue in Theology," in *Virtues and Their Vices*, ed. Kevin Timpe and Craig A. Boyd (Oxford: Oxford University Press, 2014), 393–414.

25. Thomas Aquinas, *Summa Theologiae* I-II, q. 64. My account of virtue in this chapter is Thomistic in inspiration.

26. James F. Keenan, "Proposing Cardinal Virtues," *Theological Studies* 56, no. 4 (1995): 709–29.

27. Ibid., 723.

28. Ibid., 724.

29. For instance, Benedict, *Rule*, no. 53.1.

30. Aquinas, *Summa Theologiae* I-II, q. 63, aa. 2-4. I leave open that there may be an additional "infused" form of hospitality.

31. Stanley Hauerwas, *A Community of Character: Toward a Constructive Christian Social Ethic* (Notre Dame, IN: Notre Dame Press, 1981).

32. Luke Bretherton, *Hospitality as Holiness: Christian Witness amid Moral Diversity* (Aldershot: Ashgate, 2006).

33. Lisa Sowle Cahill, "The Natural Law, Global Justice and Equality," in *Searching for a Universal Ethic: Multidisciplinary, Ecumenical, and Interfaith Responses to the Catholic Natural Law Tradition*, ed. John Berkman and William C. Mattison III (Grand Rapids, MI: Eerdmans, 2014).

34. I leave open whether homelessness is caused by, exacerbated by, or merely parallels economic inequality itself.

35. My treatment of street homelessness is based on paradigm cases drawn from the UK context. This includes those living in temporary accommodation and hostels as well as

"rough sleepers." See Shelter, *Green Book: 50 Years on—The Reality of Homelessness for Families Today* (2016), https://england.shelter.org.uk.

36. A philosophical perspective is Keith Burkham, "Homelessness, Virtue Theory and the Creation of Community," in *The Ethics of Homelessness: Philosophical Perspectives*, ed. G. John M. Abbarno (Atlanta: Rodopi, 1999). A practical report is Nicola Robinson and Shelter, *Response—Tackling Social Exclusion* (2004), https://england.shelter.org.uk.

37. Courtney Cronley, "Unravelling the Social Construction of Homelessness," *Journal of Human Behavior in the Social Environment* 20, no. 2 (2010): 319–33.

38. I refer to the translation in Luke Timothy Johnson, *The Gospel of Luke* (Collegeville, MN: Liturgical Press, 1991). Interestingly, Johnson treats the Samaritan and the story of (the hospitality of) Mary and Martha (10:38–42) as one pericope (10:25–42).

39. See the commentary of Johnson, *Gospel of Luke*, 173.

40. Burkham, "Homelessness," 79.

41. Shelter, *Green Book*, 21–22.

42. For a creative account of how churches *as such* might do so for homelessness, see Willis Jenkins, "Neighborhood Ethics: Christianity, Urbanism and Homelessness," *Anglican Theological Review* 91, no. 4 (2009): 539–58.

43. Keenan, "Jesuit Hospitality," 241.

44. Ibid.

45. Ibid., 240.

46. The following documentary reveals examples such as the difficulty of managing paperwork when homeless and of the lack of a private address for applying for employment and education: *Seriously*, "After Cathy," produced by Adele Armstrong, aired November 20, 2016, on BBC Radio 4, https://www.bbc.co.uk/radio4. See also Shelter, *Green Book*, 64–68.

47. See the "A Bed Every Night" initiative in Greater Manchester, UK, which began on November 1, 2018, https://bedeverynight.co.uk.

48. Shelter, *Food for Thought: Soup-Runs and Soup-Kitchens—A Good Practice Briefing* (2005), https://england.shelter.org.uk.

49. Ibid., 5.

50. Ibid., 19.

51. Ibid.

52. Ibid., 3.

53. Ibid., 19.

54. Ibid.

55. Ibid., 17–18.

56. Both early Latin American liberation theologians and their opponents, for example, maintained a sharp distinction here. Gregory Baum, "Class Struggle and the Magisterium: A New Note," *Theological Studies* 45, no. 4 (1984): 691.

57. Christopher P. Vogt, "Fostering a Catholic Commitment to the Common Good: An Approach Rooted in Virtue Ethics," *Theological Studies* 68, no. 2 (2007): 394–417.

58. Kristin E. Heyer, *Kinship across Borders: A Christian Ethic of Immigration* (Washington, DC: Georgetown University Press, 2012), offers a compelling analysis of hospitality in relation to social structures and immigration.

59. Daniel K. Finn, "What Is a Sinful Social Structure?" *Theological Studies* 77, no. 1 (2016): 136–64.

60. Ibid., 162.

61. Ibid., 152.

62. Maryam Omidi, "Anti-Homeless Spikes Are Just the Latest in 'Defensive Urban Architecture,'" *Guardian*, June 12, 2014, https://www.theguardian.com.

63. Although based on a different definition of a social structure, see Daniel J. Daly, "Structures of Virtue and Vice," *New Blackfriars* 92, no. 1039 (2011): 341–57.

64. BBC News, "Contactless Donation Points Unveiled by London Mayor," November 28, 2018, https://www.bbc.co.uk/news/.

65. https://www.cardboardcitizens.org.uk.

66. BBC News, "Oxford City Council 'Criminalising Homelessness.'" April 13, 2015, https://www.bbc.co.uk/news.

Local Responses

FINDING A HOME

The Experience of Street Children at the "Household of Hope" in Yaoundé, Cameroon

Joseph L. Mben, SJ

This essay is a reflection on the experience of the "Household of Hope" (Foyer de l'Espérance in French) with street children in Yaoundé, the capital city of Cameroon. It will try to draw theological insights from that experience. The first section introduces the work of the Household of Hope, focusing on its activities and interactions with street children. The next section provides a brief evaluation of this work, and the third section offers ethical insights flowing from this particular experience. However, before moving further, I would like to offer a conceptual clarification of the notion of street children.

Understanding the Concept of Street Children

A street child or youth is a "young person who spends the majority of his or her time on the streets of large towns/cities and sleeps rough on the street all or part of the time."[1] The term "street" is to be understood in the broadest sense of the word as "all urban public spaces young people make use of and inhabit."[2] Van Blerk indicates that there are identity markers that set street children apart.[3] These are "drug use, criminal activity and begging, sleeping rough, and a disheveled appearance."[4] Street children are one category of homelessness, whose understanding varies according to background and perspectives.[5] The main theory remains the housing theory, which emphasizes homelessness as the absence or lack of adequate housing.[6] "Living in the streets," like street children, epitomizes the housing theory. This approach may include people living rough, in emergency accommodation, in accommodation for the homeless, in institutions, in nonconventional dwellings, and people living temporarily in conventional housing with family and friends.[7]

Another theory looks at prehomeless conditions and includes people in precarious housing arrangements who are at risk of homelessness.[8] The next theory looks at the homeless as people who have become isolated from society and social networks.[9] All this illustrates the difficulty of defining homelessness in a satisfactory way. In this essay, I consider the three-dimensional approach of the UN Human Rights Council on homelessness: (1) homelessness as the absence of home understood broadly and not limited to spatial considerations; (2) homelessness as a form of systemic discrimination and social exclusion; and (3) homelessness as rights holders who are resilient in the fight for survival and dignity.[10]

To this definition, one needs to add gender considerations that tend to be over-looked when looking at homelessness. One reason is that women "tend to conceal their homelessness by staying with friends and family whenever possible;"[11] if they have to sleep rough "they try to remain less visible for fear of abuse."[12] Moreover, for many women homelessness may be tied to a lack of safety or security, to divorce, or to not owning their own place.[13]

The Household of Hope

As mentioned earlier, the Household of Hope (henceforth HoH) is located in Yaoundé, Cameroon, and it is a group of initiatives that aim at the social and/or family reintegration of street children and young prison inmates.[14] It is a Catholic institution headed by a Spanish Jesuit priest named Alfonso Ruiz Marrodàn, SJ, who has been working with street children in Chad and Cameroon for more than two decades. He has been the head of the institution for more than fifteen years. The HoH counts fourteen permanent staff including a nun, nine paid volunteers, and many unpaid volunteers, most of whom are nuns, religious brothers, seminarians, and students.[15] Most of the people working in the HoH are lay people. Although "street children"[16] appears as an umbrella notion, in practice the HoH divides the youth into two categories of age. Those who are between seven and seventeen years old are considered children, and those who are between seventeen and twenty-one years old are young people.[17] The street children involved with HoH come from the whole country and even from neighboring countries such as the Central African Republic and Chad.[18]

Activities

This institution began in 1977 and received a formal approval from the local bishop in 1987 and from the state in 1994.[19] It runs five different projects: the action street for boys, the action street for girls, the Brother Yves Lescanne home, Noah's Ark home, and the social and educational center of Yaoundé's central prison.[20] For the sake of space, I will not consider the last two aspects, because they are primarily directed to actual or former young inmates.

The action street project goes on in the streets to meet with boys and girls, and welcomes them respectively in the Brother Antonio counseling center for boys, and the counseling and orientation center for girls.[21] This particular project involves visiting police stations to look for street children in police custody and working with the department of social affairs. Overall, the action street for both boys and girls involves a four-step strategy: personal and group follow-up, education, contacting families, and a follow-up after the reintegration.[22] Personal and group follow-up involves welcoming, listening, counseling, and group meetings with all the children. Education here means respecting the rules of the center, taking care of domestic chores (for boys and girls), caring about personal and environmental cleanliness, having spontaneous and organized leisure, performing manual work, and having educational discussions. Making contact with families follows a process where information is gathered from the young homeless. Reaching out is done by the educators of the center or other people or institutions if the parents are living in remote places. This also means identifying the issue(s) that caused the child to run away from his or her home, and preparing him or her for the reunion. There are follow-up visits after the children reintegrate with their families. However, this does not prevent the child from running away from his or her home after reintegration.

The Brother Yves Lescanne Home welcomes and shelters street children who are waiting for their reintegration.[23] The children are housed full-time and taken care of by the HoH. This level follows the same steps as the previous ones, but there are some differences. An educational psychologist also works with each child personally at the first step,[24] and religious education is added at the educational step. In addition, a certified primary school teacher comes every business day to improve the children's literacy and to give to some a refresher course. At the third level, one addition is the invitation to the family to visit the center. At the fourth level, one learns that the street child can be reintegrated within foster families or any other public or private structure.

There are also campaigns to sensitize the larger society to the condition of street children and young prison inmates.[25] The work with young inmates was the starting point of the endeavor, which was later expanded to the streets.[26] Indeed, most of the inmates were initially street children, and the initiators of the HoH thought that they could prevent these children from falling into the trap of criminality.[27]

Some Statistics and Discussion

Here are some statistics on the street children that are taken care of by the HoH:

From a gender perspective, the number of girls welcomed by the HoH appears to be lower than that of boys. The HoH confirms that a survey carried out in the months of July and August 2017 found that girls made up only 4 percent of the total of street children in the city of Yaoundé.[28] This confirms the scholarly literature, which states that "girls are fewer in numbers and more likely to be hidden on the streets."[29] In addition, given the possible violence they face on the streets, girls may take "a boyish appearance, such as dressing like boys and having short hair."[30] This could easily fool a researcher that rushes through the survey. Moreover, cultural norms may also explain the low figures. For instance, within Islamic settings "when a household becomes homeless, the woman and girls may be sent to live with relatives, [while] it is acceptable for the men and boys to live in the streets."[31] In addition, "young,

Table 1. The Action Street Projects' Achievements

Counseling Center and Orientation Center for Girls				
Year	Girls present	Newcomers	Reintegrated in family	Placed in a foster care family	
2015	966	86	08	02	
2016	1597	72	04	03	
Brother Antonio Counseling Center for Boys					
Year	Boys present	Newcomers	Placed in a foster care institution	Placed in families	Assisted in police station or in the court of law
2014	1794	149	32	30	
2015	2176	205	33	10	13
2016	2744	169	39	14	150

Source: Foyer de l'Espérance, 2018

Table 2. Brother Yves Lescanne Home's Achievements

Year	2014	2015	2016
Newcomers welcomed	70	79	82
Reintegrated in families	44	34	29
Returned to the streets	20	36	20
Enrolled in secondary education	5	4	6
Enrolled in primary education	11	11	27
Vocational training	1	3	2
Enrolled in primary education within families	3	2	4
Enrolled in secondary education within families	6	11	5
Vocational training within family	3	3	3
In refresher course	64	52	20

Source: Foyer de l'Espérance, 2018

Table 3. Brother Yves Lescanne Home's Reintegration Rate: 2000–2016

Year	Street children daily presence (cumulated)	Newcomers	Reintegration within families	Reintegration rate (percentage)
2000	3,539	77	48	62.3
2001	2,988	63	39	61.9
2002	3,377	69	37	53.6
2003	5,589	71	46	64.8
2004	7,860	77	37	48.1
2005	8,668	113	59	52.2
2006	9,364	119	56	47.1
2007	11,819	74	45	60.8
2008	10,471	103	38	38.8
2009	10,110	48	18	37.5
2010	9,996	39	11	28.2
2011	10,701	41	19	46.3
2012	10,797	41	38	92.6
2013	10,470	47	39	82.9
2014	10,250	70	44	62.9
2015	11,315	79	34	43.03
2016	9,062	82	29	35.4

Source: Foyer de l'Espérance, 2018

single, female rural migrants, arriving in the cities without any peer support, prior information about the area and skills, are most likely to survive through prostitution."[32] In that case, they tend not to be counted among the homeless population. Van Blerk confirms the fact that street girls have fewer earning options than boys and can be "drawn into sex work as a survival strategy."[33]

One other explanation of the lower number of girls on the streets is the issue of core places. The latter are understood as "particular niches in the city where young people carry out their daily activities."[34] They "may also be temporally located, only used at particular times of the day or night."[35] It is probable that, in Yaoundé, the researchers favored core places located in "busy central locations."[36] The HoH notices that girls were initially few on the streets, and presently can be seen mostly around markets.[37] This confirms that they look primarily for street children in the busy sections of the city. However, there are core places that can be in hidden or marginal locations.[38] There is a possibility that girls prefer such areas for their own safety. As I have learned from my own experience in Abidjan, Cote d'Ivoire, and which can be mutatis mutandis transferred to Cameroon, girls or young women who work as waitresses in local pubs would sometimes sleep in their place of work. This is because their low wages do not allow them to rent a place or go back every day to their homes. The same is true with domestic workers, cooks, and all types of workers who earn low salaries, and cannot afford to rent a place. They will generally sleep four or five days a week or even the whole week outside their homes in their workplace or shop. Some will make alternative arrangements by sleeping at a friend's place; such people will not be listed as homeless.

Another striking element is the lower reintegration rate for girls (see table 1). This seems to be more or less the same with boys at the Brother Antonio Counseling Center (see table 1). Even the Brother Yves Lescanne Home, which at times records higher reintegration rates, faces high rates of return to the streets (see table 2). The HoH follows an institutionalized model, which seeks to "remove young people from the streets for their own protection and to rehabilitate them as respectable citizens."[39] However, street children appear to respond differently to this program and are rarely successful in returning to their communities (see table 2).[40] Instead, they are using institutions like HoH as "places for making new street friends and learning new ways of becoming absorbed into street life."[41] This is why HoH has set up programs to empower street children through formal instruction and vocational training. The dimensions that have grown in importance for the HoH are following up on reintegrated children who continue their academic or vocational training, the transition from training to work and economic independence, and training in values.[42]

Another noticeable thing is the steady increase of the number of children welcomed into the various programs. In the Brother Yves Lescanne Home (table 3), the numbers have almost tripled between 2000 and 2015. Brother Antonio Counseling Center for Boys has seen an increase of 1,000 boys within two years (see table 1). Many factors account for this situation. These factors may be at the level of the individuals or structural, at the level of the community, or the larger society. The HoH has identified some, namely, the mass migration from rural to urban settings, the disintegration of traditional family support structures, a greater number of single mothers, and domestic violence.[43] These factors are confirmed by the literature.[44] In addition, there is the inability of the Cameroonian government to deal with the increased population and the socioeconomic demands that come with it. Between 1986 and 2018, the population has gone from 10 million to 25 million inhabitants. In the meantime, the population of Yaoundé has tripled.[45] This creates a situation of overcrowding or shared accommodations.[46] The other factor not mentioned by HoH is poverty, "coupled with a breakdown of family support"[47] or loss of a parent or both parents, or divorced/separated parents.[48] Another factor can be political instability[49] such as the war against terror in Northern Cameroon and the political crisis in English-speaking Cameroon, situations that have forcefully displaced hundreds of thousands of people (including children) from their homes.

Theological Insights

The Household of Hope does not clearly articulate its guiding spirituality. One can surmise that they are inspired—like many Catholic charitable works—by the parable of the last judgment (Mt 25:31–46) and/or the Good Samaritan parable (Lk 10:29–37). In the parable of the last judgment, Christ identifies with the most vulnerable: "Whatever you did for one of these least brothers of mine you did it for me" (Mt 25:40). The parable of the Good Samaritan emphasizes the model of a good neighbor by presenting a Samaritan attending to the man attacked by robbers on the road (Lk 10:29–37).

However, in the case of HoH, one needs to go a step further. I suggest mining the words "household" and "hope" in the phrase "household of God" to retrieve the unarticulated spirituality beyond the HoH, and to offer some ethical insights.

The Household

The concept of a home or household is critical in the church's teaching. Based on the parable of the last judgment, the magisterium indicates that "in each person or family lacking a basic good, and above all housing, the Christian must recognize Christ himself."[50] The sacred Scriptures show us that living in one's home is a sign of happiness and peace (Ps 128:3; Job 29:4; Jer 29:5; 28; 30:18, etc.).[51] The gospel of John tells us that the Word pitched his tent among us (Jn 1:14). Even the final destination of humans after death is labeled as home: "In my Father's house there are many rooms" (Jn 14:2).

Indeed, "our Christian religious tradition, inherited from Judaism, attributes a fundamental value to 'housing' which we can still recognize today."[52] In today's world, food, housing, education, and health care are perceived as human rights or at least as "basic needs of a person."[53]

We can see that the primary mission of the HoH is to help street children find a home. For the magisterium, "housing" is not limited to the physical; rather, "It is in direct relationship with the characteristics of the human person that are, at one and the same time, social, affective, cultural, and religious."[54] The HoH exhibits a complex understanding of household by providing a sense of community, of responsibility, of care, by imparting values and skills to street children. For street children, the notion of home is very fluid, and is "made up of particular social relations that are both spatially and temporally connected."[55]

The household is also tied to that of family. And the church in Africa defined itself after the first special synod on Africa as the Family-Church of God.[56] Although, the sense of family could be sometimes naïve, the idea of family remains important, especially for communitarian societies such as those in Africa.[57] The notion of family carries with it the ideas of "care for others, solidarity, warmth in human relationships, acceptance, dialogue, and trust."[58] Today, this ideal is in crisis or at least in transition in Africa. Street children must be seen as a symptom of a much more serious crisis that affects the whole society. Indeed, they are "the result of a whole series of economic, social, cultural, physical, emotional, and moral factors that specifically bear down on those who have never been integrated into the current social system."[59]

What is needed is structural change—this is why working in favor of marginalized groups like street children is understood as part of the preferential option for the poor. In addition, "action on behalf of justice and participation in the transformation of the world fully appear . . . as a constitutive dimension of the preaching of the Gospel."[60] Acting on behalf of street children is a matter of justice. In an environment where policymakers fail to act and to take homelessness seriously, the church as the body of Christ cannot remain silent.[61] In the church, there are initiatives from individuals and various institutions, but the hierarchical church has failed to take notice.[62] In a continent where many people are forced out of their homes for political or economic reasons, neither of the post-synodal apostolic exhortations— *Ecclesia in Africa* (1995) and *Africae Munus* (2011)—used the word "homeless." The phenomenon of street children in African urban settings calls for a robust apostolate for families, which must include advocacy for better laws protecting children and in particular female children from all kinds of abuses within family settings. It calls also for the creation of safe spaces within Christian groups and communities to especially welcome victims of domestic violence and abuse. It involves teaming up with counselors and psychotherapists to help families in crisis.

People of Hope: People on the Move

Along with the notion of the household, there is also the idea of hope in Household of Hope. Christian hope is grounded in God, "but not any god," warns Pope Benedict XVI, "but the God who has a human face and who has loved us to the end."[63] Hope is expressed through the Our Father: "thy Kingdom come." Jesus Christ and his Kingdom are the great hope of Christianity. This idea of hope permeates the action in favor of the homeless in two aspects. According to the first, "The witness that the Church seeks to give in collaborating in the search for a solution to the problems of the poor is a sign of the presence of the kingdom of salvation and liberation."[64] Like Jesus Christ, who through table fellowship welcomed the outcast people of his society, the HoH welcomes those who are rejected and criminalized by society. It exemplifies the radical inclusivity of the Reign of God, where all are welcomed regardless of their background. Hope works by pushing the limits of the larger society's imagination and by engendering in street children a sense that their situation can improve and that they can become better persons.

The second aspect of hope is a reminder that "the mission of the Church also consists in helping to make society more human."[65] Hope is about happiness understood as the good life. As the *Catechism of the Catholic Church* opines: "The virtue of hope responds to the aspiration to happiness which God has placed in the heart of every man."[66] Improving society is hope in action since [all serious and upright human action is hope in action."[67] The HoH tries to fight the marginalization and discrimination faced by street children.

Hope consists of the not-yet and the already. The Kingdom is an eschatological reality, but also something that can be felt here and now. The reality of hope reminds us that the present picture is not final, but transitory. Even the church is a pilgrim church. Indeed, the church "will attain its full perfection only in the glory of heaven, when there will come the time of the restoration of all things."[68] The church is on the move, just as the Lord who said, "The son of man has nowhere to lay his head" (Lk 9:57). In people left on the margins of the society, such as street children, the church sees the face of Jesus Christ. Jesus chose to be homeless because of his mission. He slept in "people's houses and inns without any home base to which he could return."[69] He adopted an itinerant lifestyle in order to be able to proclaim the Kingdom. By being homeless, he had to rely on people's generosity and kindness, and accept whatever he was given. Homelessness involves uncertainty and some form of dependence. Jesus was not constrained by biological bonds, but went beyond them since "anyone who does my father's will is my brother, sister, and mother" (Mk 3:34). This is probably the ultimate challenge that homelessness gives us: to think beyond spatial and blood ties. We must integrate fluidity of space and relationships—while guarding against abuse—and open ourselves to new horizons and experiences. A pilgrim church is a homeless church, nowhere at home, and feeling comfortable everywhere. However, homelessness is temporary, because, at the end, the believers must get to God's home.

Conclusion

The Household of Hope gives a sense of home and hope to street children in the city of Yaoundé. The phenomenon of street children is fueled by social dysfunctions within African societies that affect families and force children out of their families and onto the streets. Initiatives like the HoH are called to grow, and they must involve the whole church. They may also take different forms. The HoH chooses to work with street children and their families—it follows the Lord who, as a good shepherd, goes after the stray sheep (Lk 15:1–7), and who has come not for the healthy but for the sick (Mk 2:17). With the various problems faced by African societies today, the phenomenon of street children will not disappear any time soon. Street children as a phenomenon are just the tip of the iceberg alerting us to much deeper societal issues. This is why there is a need for a much more comprehensive approach that joins other types of initiatives to supplement the work of institutions like the Household of Hope.

Notes

1. L. Van Blerk, "Homeless People: Street Children in Africa," in *International Encyclopeida of Housing and Home*, ed. Susan J. Smith (Amsterdam-Boston: Elsevier, 2012), 127.
2. Ibid.
3. Ibid.
4. Ibid.
5. See for instance Suzanne Speak and Graham Tipple, "Housing and Homelessness in Developing Nations," in *Encyclopedia of Homelessness*, ed. David Levinson (Thousand Oaks, CA: SAGE, 2004), https://doi.org/10.4135/9781412952569.n76.
6. Human Rights Council, "Report of the Special Rapporteur on Adequate Housing as a Component of the Right to an Adequate Standard of Living, and on the Right to Non-Discrimination in This Context" (United Nations, December 30, 2015), para. 17.a; Catherine Cross et al., "Skeletons at the Feast: A Review of Street Homelessness in South Africa and Other World Regions," *Development Southern Africa* 27, no. 1 (March 2010): 7.
7. Social Policy Division, "Homeless Population" (OECD, July 24, 2017), https://www.oecd.org/els/family/HC3-1-Homeless-population.pdf.
8. Cross et al., "Skeletons at the Feast," 7.
9. Ibid.
10. Human Rights Council, "Report on Adequate Housing," para. 17.
11. Suzanne Speak, "Relationship between Children's Homelessness in Developing Countries and the Failure of Women's Rights Legislation," *Housing, Theory and Society* 22, no. 3 (October 2005): 131–32.
12. Ibid., 132.
13. Sophy Watson, "A Home Is Where the Heart Is: Engendering Notions of Homelessness," in *Homelessness: Exploring the New Terrain*, ed. Patricia Kennett and Alex Marsh (Bristol: Policy Press at the University of Bristol, 1999), 85–86.
14. Foyer de l'Espérance, "Réinsertion familiale et/ou sociale des enfants et jeunes, garçons et filles, de la rue et de la prison de Yaoundé, demande de projet pour 2018" (Foyer de l'Espérance, 2018), 2. See http://www.foyeresperance.net/organizacion_fr.html.
15. Ibid., 12.
16. In southern Cameroon, street children are called "nanga boko," a phrase that comes from two words in the Ewondo language meaning follow and go/depart/precede, which implies someone on the move, and also one who follows others. There is a pejorative meaning associated with being a *nanga boko*.
17. Foyer de l'Espérance, "Projet 2018," 4.
18. Ibid.
19. Ibid., 16.
20. Ibid., 2.
21. Ibid. The work with girls started only at the end of 2014.
22. From here onward see ibid., 13–14.
23. From here onward see ibid., 2.
24. From here onward see ibid., 14–15.
25. Ibid., 2.
26. Ibid., 4.
27. Ibid., 6.
28. Ibid., 4.

29. Van Blerk, "Homeless People," 129.

30. Ibid., 130.

31. Speak, "Children's Homelessness and Women's Rights," 132.

32. Ibid.

33. Van Blerk, "Homeless People," 129.

34. Ibid., 127.

35. Ibid.

36. Ibid., 128.

37. Foyer de l'Espérance, "Projet 2018," 6.

38. Van Blerk, "Homeless People," 128.

39. Ibid.

40. Ibid.

41. Ibid.

42. Foyer de l'Espérance, "Projet 2018," 7.

43. Ibid., 5.

44. Human Rights Council, "Report on Adequate Housing," para. 34; Speak and Tipple, "Housing and Homelessness in Developing Nations"; Speak, "Children's Homelessness and Women's Rights," 136–38.

45. Institut National de Statistique du Cameroun, *Annuaire statistique du Cameroun 2014* (Yaoundé: Institut National de Statistique, 2016), 59–62, http://www.stat.cm/downloads/2016/annuaire2016/.

46. Speak, "Children's Homelessness and Women's Rights," 136.

47. Speak and Tipple, "Housing and Homelessness in Developing Nations."

48. Ilesanmi Adetokunbo and Mgbemena Emeka, "Urbanization, Housing, Homelessness and Climate Change Adaptation in Lagos, Nigeria: Lessons from Asia," *Journal of Design and Built Development* 15, no. 2 (December 2015): 20.

49. Pontifical Commission Justice and Peace, *What Have You Done to Your Homeless Brother? The Church and the Housing Problem*, 1987, pt. II.2, http://theolibrary.shc.edu/resources/homeless.htm.

50. Ibid., pt. III.4.

51. From here onward see ibid., pt. III.4.

52. Ibid.

53. Ibid., pt. II.1.

54. Ibid., pt. III.4.

55. Van Blerk, "Homeless People," 127.

56. Proposition 8 in Maurice Cheza, ed., "Les 64 propositions," in *Le Synode Africain: Histoire et textes* (Paris: Karthala, 1996), 243.

57. *Ecclesia in Africa* recognizes the importance of family in the African context and adds: "Open to this sense of family, love, and respect for life, the African loves children who are joyfully welcomed as gifts of God." See John Paul II, *On the Church in Africa and Its Evangelizing Mission, Post-Synodal Apostolic Exhortation* Ecclesia in Africa (Yaoundé, Cameroon: Libreria Editrice Vaticana, 1995), para. 43, http://www.vatican.va/. Such a statement appears problematic in view of the family experience of street children when it is one of domestic violence, abuse, and neglect.

58. John Paul II, para. 63.

59. Pontifical Commission Justice and Peace, *The Church and the Housing Problem*, pt. II.2.

60. Synod of Bishops, "Justice in the World" (The Holy See, 1971), para. 6, http://www.shc.edu/theolibrary/resources/synodjw.htm.

61. The Household of Hope reveals that material and financial help from the state is minimal; they only received $500 from the government back in 2007. See Foyer de l'Espérance, "Projet 2018," 6.

62. Proposition 49 mentions in passing street children along other categories of children who are ill-treated. See Synode des évêques pour l'Afrique, "Les 57 propositions pour l'Afrique, document du synode des évêques," *La Documentation Catholique*, no. 2434 (November 15, 2009): 1052–53.

63. Benedict XVI, *Encyclical Letter on Christian Hope, Spe Salvi* (Rome: Libreria Editrice Vaticana, 2007), para. 31.

64. Pontifical Commission Justice and Peace, *The Church and the Housing Problem*, pt. IV.1. http://theolibrary.shc.edu/resources/homeless.htm.

65. Ibid.

66. Catholic Church, ed., *Catechism of the Catholic Church* (Vatican City: Libreria Editrice Vaticana; [distributed by] Loyola University Press, 1994), para. 1818.

67. Benedict XVI, *Spe Salvi*, para. 35.

68. Vatican II Council, *Dogmatic Constitution on the Church* Lumen Gentium (Vatican City, 1964), para. 48.

69. Samuel Oyin Abogunrin, "Luke," in *The International Bible Commentary: A Catholic and Ecumenical Commentary for the Twenty-First Century*, ed. William R. Farmer (Collegeville, MN: Liturgical Press, 1998), 1405.

Seeing the "Invisible"

Responses to Homelessness in India

Shaji George Kochuthara, CMI

On December 18, 2018, there was a newspaper report that a fourteen-year-old boy was crushed to death and three others, including a woman, were injured by a truck that had run over people sleeping on a footpath, at Nelamangala in the city of Bengaluru.[1] The report also said that those people, part of a larger group, had been living on the footpaths for nine months. Evidently, this is not the first time that we hear about people living on the footpaths being killed by negligent drivers. Often such news may not even be reported. Data from the police department reveal that 33,518 homeless people died in Delhi between January 2004 and October 2015.[2] No investigation is ever conducted into the cause of the death of a homeless person in India, and neither is anyone held responsible.[3]

In a general sense, homelessness can be defined as a condition of people lacking housing, because they cannot afford or are unable to maintain a regular, safe, and adequate shelter. However, homelessness is defined or understood in different ways in different countries, and each has its own approach to the topic. Homelessness is a growing phenomenon worldwide and also in India.

Article 25 of the Universal Declaration of Human Rights (December 10, 1948) states that adequate housing is a human right: "Everyone has the right to a standard of living adequate for the health and well-being of himself and of his family, including food, clothing, housing and medical care and necessary social services, and the right to security in the event of unemployment, sickness, disability, widowhood, old age or other lack of livelihood in circumstances beyond his control."[4] Also, the International Covenant on Economic, Social, and Cultural Rights includes housing among the rights of everyone: "The States Parties to the present Covenant recognize the right of everyone to an adequate standard of living for himself and his family, including adequate food, clothing and housing, and to the continuous improvement of living conditions. The States Parties will take appropriate steps to ensure the realization of this right, recognizing to this effect the essential importance of international co-operation based on free consent" (Article 11).[5] In many countries, various organizations have been advocating for the recognition of adequate housing as a basic human right of citizens, and to take proactive steps to solve the problem of homelessness, though these advocacy efforts have had limited success so far. Similarly, the Charter of the Rights of the Family

Presented by the Holy See to all Persons, Institutions, and Authorities Concerned with the Mission of the Family in Today's World (October 22, 1983) considers decent housing as a right of the family: "The family has the right to decent housing, fitting for family life and commensurate to the number of the members, in a physical environment that provides the basic services for the life of the family and the community" (Article 11).[6]

Understanding Homelessness

The United Nations, declaring 1987 as the International Year of Shelter for the Homeless, defined a homeless person as not only someone who lived on the street or in a shelter, but also someone whose shelter or housing failed to meet the basic criteria considered essential for health and social development.[7] However, the definition of homelessness may vary. For example, according to the Census of India, "Households which do not live in buildings or Census houses but live in the open or roadside, pavements, in Hume-pipes, under fly-overs and staircases, or in the open in places of worship, mandaps [= temple porch], railway platforms, etc. are to be treated as Houseless households."[8] This definition given by the Census of India is based on India's socioeconomic conditions, cultural norms, and the groups affected and the purpose for which homelessness is being defined.[9] However, many even in India would consider even this definition inadequate. They argue that the homeless people are

> those who lack fixed, regular, safe, and adequate night time shelter and also those who have night time residence at a publicly supervised or privately operated shelter designed to provide temporary living accommodation, or an institution that provides a temporary residence for individuals intended to be institutionalized, or a public or private place not designed for, or ordinarily used as, a regular sleeping accommodation for human beings.[10]

People living in substandard housing with inadequate facilities should also be included under homelessness. This would mean that the rise in the number of slum dwellers can be considered an indication of an increase in the number of the homeless.[11]

It is very difficult to obtain a clear idea of the actual number of the homeless, especially the urban homeless. One of the main difficulties is the difference in the understanding of homelessness itself, which I have just pointed out above. Another difficulty is that often official surveys are conducted during the daytime, when the homeless are not in the places where they spend the night. The homeless population is heterogeneous, in terms of age group, gender, livelihoods, religion, place of origin, and reasons for living on the streets. It is a group that we can meet only in the evenings and late into the nights.[12] Homeless persons also change places frequently, and hence trying to meet them just once or even a few times may not be sufficient. Moreover, many of them keep themselves away from officials because of fear, since many of the homeless are harassed by the police and other officials.

Street Homelessness: The Indian Scenario

According to the census of 2011, India has more than 1.7 million homeless residents, of which 938,384 are located in urban areas. But in general these figures are thought to be much lower than the real numbers of the homeless. According to many civil society organizations, at least 1 percent of the population of urban India is homeless. That would mean that the number of urban homeless is at least 3 million. We have to also remember that these figures are given according to the 2011 census, and the actual numbers at present (in 2019) must be much higher, especially because of growing urbanization. Add to this the often forgotten fact that India also has the highest number of street children in the world, although there is no official number, and there are no adequate schemes to respond to their special needs and concerns.[13] According to the Housing and Land Rights Network, an organization based in New Delhi, the number of homeless people in the major cities of India is as follows (as per the 2011 census):[14] Delhi: 150,000–200,000; Chennai: 40,000–50,000; Mumbai: 200,000; Indore: 10,000–12,000; Vishakhapatnam: 18,000; Bengaluru: 40,000–50,000; Hyderabad: 60,000; Ahmedabad: 100,000; Patna: 25,000; Kolkata: 150,000; Lucknow: 19,000.

Though there are homeless people in both urban and rural areas, the growth rate of the homeless population in rural areas has declined by 28.4 percent in 2001–2011, whereas the same group has increased by 20.5 percent in urban areas.[15] Such major forces as urban redevelopment, disasters, conflicts, rising property prices, and rental rates lead poor families into utter poverty, including homelessness.[16] The failure of agriculture, diminishing prices for crops, declining job opportunities, and so on drive more people from rural areas to urban areas, where many of them end up without stable employment or proper housing. The majority of the urban homeless belong to this group, that is, those who have escaped from rural destitution and oppression. They provide all forms of casual labor, especially in the unorganized sectors, and thus contribute to the urban economy without having any protection for their body or dignity.[17]

The homeless have to face multiple problems due to legal and administrative requirements, which are often unrealistic and even unattainable in their situation. For example, they have no legal access to sites for building houses or to establish temporary business activities. Thus, they are in a way criminalized in the very process of their survival. Even urban slum dwellers are not entitled to water or light connections unless they have a legal title of land. If they approach the authorities for any assistance, they will be considered encroachers and hence lawbreakers. Often, such areas of land may be controlled by local mafia that exploit these poor people even in their abject poverty. Without a permanent address, the homeless are denied ration cards and access to government welfare schemes.[18] They are not granted bank loans, since they do not have any valid identification cards or entitlement to land or other property to guarantee the loan. Thus, they are caught up in a vicious circle.

Homeless women, particularly young women, undergo the worst kinds of violence and insecurity, and are vulnerable to sexual exploitation and trafficking. Rape and molestation are common among homeless women. Many women spend sleepless nights trying to protect their young adolescent girls from being raped. Accessing health care is a tremendous challenge for homeless people, especially women.[19] "Homelessness constitutes the worst violation of the human right to adequate housing, and homeless people, especially women, are among the most marginalised, ignored, and discriminated against in the country."[20]

Considering some of the laws in the country, we may get the impression that homelessness itself is considered a crime in India. For example, under the Delhi Police Act of 1978, any person found under "suspicious circumstances between sunset and sunrise" can be detained by the police. Homeless people are often stigmatized as criminals. Their dwelling places are also targeted. Municipal laws of many towns consider bathing and living out in the open to be punishable offenses. Homeless people are rounded up routinely by the police to maintain "peace" under the Criminal Procedure Code; they are among the first to be questioned by the police or harassed by them when there is a crime; it is not rare that they are falsely implicated in crimes. Beggary prevention laws such as the Bombay Prevention of Begging Act of 1959, applicable in eighteen states in India, also punish vagrancy. All these laws allow the police to detain or arrest anyone who is poor or homeless.[21] Other laws that criminalize the urban homeless include the Tamil Nadu Prevention of Begging Act of 1945 and the Juvenile Justice Act of 2006, which allow officials to arrest and incarcerate people for sleeping or loitering on the streets. There is no law that prevents discrimination against homeless people in the country.

Responding to Homelessness

I shall first describe some of the initiatives taken by the government, the courts, and various organizations. Then, I shall mention some of the measures taken by the church. I should, however, make it clear that I could not come across many systematic works on the responses to homelessness in India. I had to depend on newspaper reports, reports published by civil organizations, personal interviews with a few people working in the field, and so on.[22] Another difficulty, as mentioned above, is that homelessness is defined in different ways. Thus, technically, those who are sleeping in night shelters may not be considered homeless in India.

Responses from the Civil Society

Here I refer to some of the court verdicts on the issue of homelessness and the right of the homeless to have adequate housing. I also particularly mention some of the initiatives taken in Delhi and Bengaluru. Article 21 of the Constitution of India, regarding the right to life, has been interpreted to recognize the right to shelter. However, the question is whether it has been put into practice.

In *PUCL v. Union of India and Others*, the Supreme Court ordered that sufficient shelters should be provided for the homeless. The court ordered that the essential needs of the urban homeless must be met such that there is at least one shelter per 100,000 people in every major urban area. The court also stated that the shelter homes should remain functional for 365 days (not just during the winter), and remain open twenty-four hours a day. The Delhi High Court has also recognized the human rights violations of homelessness in several orders.[23] In 2010, the High Courts of India passed two important judgments to address homelessness, upholding the right to adequate housing.[24]

There is an ongoing case in the Supreme Court of India regarding homelessness, namely, *E. R. Kumar & Others V. Union of India & Others*. This Public Interest Litigation was filed in the year 2003, but until 2014 the States and Union Territories failed to submit a status report. On November 11, 2016, the Supreme Court directed that a committee must be constituted which would be responsible for the physical verification of the available shelters for urban homeless and to verify whether the shelters are in compliance with the operational guidelines for the Scheme of Shelters for Urban Homeless under the National Urban Livelihoods Mission (NULM).[25] In fact, since 2013 the court has been monitoring measures to reduce/alleviate homelessness, and during a hearing in November 2017, the Supreme Court slammed the state governments for their apathy and insensitivity toward the plight of the homeless and appealed to them to show "sympathy and compassion" by constructing shelter homes for them.[26]

The National Urban Housing and Habitat Policy 2007, which was last revised in 2007, advocates public-private partnership for providing affordable housing for all and specifically to the urban poor. It was estimated that in 2006–07, the housing shortage in India was 24.7 million.[27] In 2015, the government announced the mission of "Housing for All" by 2022,[28] but its implementation so far is said to be much below what has been planned.[29]

Initiatives in Delhi

According to civil society estimates, in Delhi alone there are 150,000–200,000 homeless people, of which at least 10,000 are women and 50,000 are children. From January 1, 2016, to September 30, 2017, 5,578 unidentified dead bodies were recorded in Delhi. It is estimated that at least 4,184 (75 percent) of these belonged to homeless people.[30] Though Delhi currently has about 200 shelters for the homeless, they accommodate only about 10–15 percent of the city's homeless population. Besides, thousands of people live in slums, and the number of such people is increasing.

On December 25, 2009, a leading Delhi newspaper published on its front page a photo of people shivering in the cold, while the Municipal Corporation of Delhi (MCD) destroyed their temporary night shelter to "beautify" the place for the 2010 Commonwealth Games.[31] The eviction of homeless people in the winter and the ensuing deaths from the cold triggered a protest movement and the *suo moto* intervention of the judiciary in January 2010.[32] The High Court of Delhi ordered the Delhi City Corporation to provide the evicted families with temporary shelter until a permanent solution was found.[33] This court order gave momentum to the struggles for defending the rights of the homeless in Delhi. But, even before this—in September 2008—more than thirty organizations and individuals came together to work collaboratively on homelessness in Delhi. Thus, a network, namely, Shahri Adhikar Manch: Begharon Ke Saath (Urban Rights Forum: With the Homeless) was formed to develop a platform to work with and for the homeless people and ultimately to enable them to lead their own movement and advocate for their own rights.[34] Several initiatives have been taken by these organizations and by the Delhi government in addressing homelessness.

In May 2016, the Delhi government announced its plan to build 15,000 urban houses for the homeless, acknowledging that providing shelter is only a temporary solution. According to this plan, for individuals, a hostel-like facility with a common kitchen would be provided, and for families a single room with kitchen would be provided.[35]

Initiatives in Bengaluru

Bengaluru, the capital city of Karnataka state, is one of the largest metropolitan cities of India. Well known for its IT industry, often called the "Silicon Valley of India," Bengaluru has a population of over 13 million.[36] It ranks third among Indian cities in terms of population. Naturally, there are a number of homeless people in the city: the poor, the migrants who come to the city in search of work and more favorable living conditions, the slum dwellers, and so on. However, systematic studies on homeless people and attempts to solve the problem of homelessness had not been undertaken until recently. Following the Supreme Court ruling on homelessness, and taking inspiration from some of the initiatives in other cities such as Delhi, the Bengaluru city corporation (Bruhat Bengaluru Mahanagara Palike—BBMP), in collaboration with some of the NGOs, has recently initiated studies on street homelessness in Bengaluru and has taken various steps to respond to it. Two of the voluntary networks actively involved in the survey are Dream India Network and Impact India Consortium.

As a first step, a survey of homeless people in Bengaluru was conducted in December 2018. It was coordinated under the leadership of Fr. Edward Thomas, SDB, as a joint venture of fifty voluntary associations. It may be specially mentioned that Rev. Dr. Peter Machado, the archbishop of Bengaluru, joined as a volunteer for the survey during the night. The survey identified a few thousand people who sleep on the roadsides. Most of them sleep on the footpath, even without beds or mats, using newspaper or pieces of clothes as mats. They are sleeping in the most unhygienic conditions. They are exposed to mosquito bites; they are without warm clothes even during the night (in December 2018 and in the first half of January 2019, the temperature in Bengaluru during the night went down to 10 degrees Centigrade); there are no toilet facilities; and many of them are sick, but without receiving any medical care. The survey conducted in three zones of the city identified 3,991 homeless persons.[37] The survey is under way in other zones of the city, and the total number will undoubtedly be much higher. For example, a survey conducted eight years ago identified 18,000 homeless people in the city, and the indication is that the number has gone up considerably. D. Randeep, Special Commissioner of BBMP, explaining the findings of the survey, said that "it is a revelation for us that some have been sleeping on the streets for close to 20 years."[38] He also acknowledged, "We have never given priority to the homeless. . . . It is time that we took necessary action."[39] The BBMP is planning to address the issue in collaboration with voluntary organizations.

In a personal interview that I had with Fr. Edward Thomas, he explained some of the plans for constructing homes for the homeless in Bengaluru and the challenges ahead. The immediate plan was to provide forty homes/shelters by March 2019.[40] Each of these homes was to have sufficient space and facilities for 50–60 people. Various types of such homes are planned: (1) Night shelters: A good number of the homeless in the city are migrants who are working during the day. They need first of all a night shelter. There will be women-only night shelters as well. (2) Homes for the sick and elderly: They cannot work anymore, and they need medical care and a place to stay. At present they take recourse to begging for survival. Existing homes of this type also need to be upgraded. (3) Houses for families: In this case, the main challenge is the availability of the land, which is extremely expensive in the city. The city corporation and the government are working on finding the land for such houses. Also, the slums in the city are to be relocated. But if the houses are constructed far away from the city, people would not move to those houses, since it is only in the city that they can find work for their survival.

Church Responses to Street Homelessness

The church has been helping the homeless in various ways. This has been done as an important work of mercy or charity. Providing homes and constructing houses for the homeless and assistance for improving the condition of houses with inadequate facilities have been concerns of various dioceses, religious congregations, parishes, and voluntary organizations. However, detailed data and systematic studies of such initiatives are not available. Hundreds of houses were built for those who had lost them in natural calamities, so that those people would not be driven to the streets. For example, after the earthquakes in Latur in Maharashtra (1993) and in Gujarat (2001), and after the tsunami in 2004, various dioceses, congregations, and church organizations constructed hundreds of houses for those who lost their houses. Projects are under way to construct houses for those who lost them in the floods in Kerala (August 2018), Kodagu in Karnataka (August 2018), in the Ockhi Cyclone in Kerala and Tamil Nadu (November 2017), and in the Gaja Cyclone (November 2018).

However, such projects are undertaken mainly in village areas or small towns, where people own the land, or where the land price is affordable. In the cities and towns, assistance to the homeless has been mainly in providing shelter homes. In addition, this has been mainly to take care of the elderly and the sick abandoned on the streets. The ministry of taking care of the abandoned initiated by Mother Teresa and her congregation is well known. Tens of thousands of the homeless on the streets were given shelter and taken care of by Mother Teresa's institutions. There are other congregations and dioceses that have been giving shelter to those abandoned on the streets. A remarkable recent initiative is Akasa Paravakal (Birds of the Air), homes for the destitute and homeless, founded by Fr. George Kuttickal, MCBS.[41] Akasa Paravakal inspired many people, and within a short time a number of houses were founded in various parts of the country, especially in cities, giving shelter to the abandoned and the homeless. Many of these are managed by various religious congregations, while others are run by lay people.

There are also individual initiatives. For example, I have personally interacted with Joseph Das, who runs a home for the destitute and homeless in Kolkata (Calcutta). In his home founded in 2000, Ashabari (Home of Hope), he and his family, with the collaboration of others, take care of about one hundred destitute people and homeless.[42] There are many other people who are working like Joseph Das, but to get detailed data on such institutions is not an easy task.

There are various centers taking care of street children, apart from the traditional type of orphanages. A noteworthy initiative in taking care of the street children in the cities is BOSCO (also known as Bosco Mane) by the Salesians. Begun in 1980 as an initiative of Salesian students, it has grown into a network in the city of Bengaluru, and other cities, providing homes for thousands of children. BOSCO helps children receive basic education, vocational training, and job placement. When they become adults and employed, they also receive assistance finding affordable rooms.[43]

At the same time, it is difficult to say that street homelessness has been an important concern for the church. Working on this essay, I have been trying to collect some literature from the official pronouncements of the Indian church and from works by theologians. I could hardly find anything on this topic. Although I have been involved in organizing various conferences and seminars in the last few years, frankly speaking, I never thought of including a paper or discussion on street homelessness in such conferences or seminars, or in the curriculum where I teach Christian ethics. Besides, I haven't heard any of the participants of such conferences referring to the issue of street homelessness. I say this, above all as a self-criticism, to point out that street homelessness has not been an important theological concern so far; nor has it become an important social concern of the church in India. In light of my study and research for this essay, I agree with Fr. Edward Thomas, SDB, who told me during our discussion that the civil society is far ahead of the church in its work to respond to the issue of street homelessness and that we have a lot to learn from its example.

Conclusion

We have seen that various civil organizations in India have been working, especially in the last couple of decades, to respond to the issue of homelessness, particularly acknowledging it as a violation of human rights. They have succeeded to a great extent in gaining court judgments and policy decisions that recognize adequate housing as a human right.

Moreover, the church has also cared for the homeless, mainly as a work of mercy. That has to continue. However, it is also important to approach homelessness as an issue of justice, of human rights, and as a demand of the preferential option for the poor. As John Paul II has said, "Today, furthermore, given the worldwide dimension which the social question has assumed, this love of preference for the poor, and the decisions which it inspires in us, cannot but embrace the immense multitudes of the hungry, the needy, the homeless, those without health care, and, above all, those without hope of a better future."[44] However, it is doubtful whether street homelessness has been given sufficient attention in the social teaching of the church, especially as a justice issue. It is high time that we respond to it in solidarity as an expression of the preferential option for the poor.

The church has its limitations in providing homes for the homeless, especially in cities where land is not easily available and the land price or rents are very high. It is an area in which the church needs to collaborate with the civil society and organizations. But the church has to mobilize its own resources for ensuring justice to the homeless. In many of the cities in India, the church owns vast areas of land. Sharing its own resources with the homeless to ensure a dignified life for them and to guarantee their human rights should be recognized as an important area of practicing its preferential option for the poor and solidarity with the poor.

Therefore, we need to change society's perspectives on the homeless. They are often viewed as lazy, criminal, and a nuisance to social well-being. In fact, most of them are hardworking and thus contribute to the development of the society. They have to be seen as victims rather than as culprits.

Finally, we need to be mindful that the gap between the rich and the poor in India is widening at an alarming pace, especially due to the present model of development. As more people become poor, many are driven into homelessness. Failure of crops and declining prices for agricultural products are leading many farmers into destitution and debt, driving them into the streets of big cities. It is important to conceive an economic model that ensures more equitable distribution of wealth and job opportunities so that more people may not be forced into homelessness on the streets of the cities. Especially in a society like that of India, where people are divided into classes and human dignity is categorized based on caste, class, and wealth, it is important to advocate for and defend the equal dignity of all human beings, as everyone is created in the image and likeness of God, and to recognize that adequate housing is essential for ensuring human dignity.

Notes

1. "Truck Runs Over People Sleeping on Footpath, One Killed," *Hindu*, Tuesday, December 18, 2018.

2. "33,000 Homeless People Died on Delhi Streets since 2004: Government Report," *Times of India*, October 18, 2015, http://timesofindia.indiatimes.com/india/33000-homeless-people-died-on-Delhi-streets-since-2004-Government-report/articleshow/49442688.cms.

3. "The Human Rights to Adequate Housing and Land in India: Report for the United Nations Human Rights Council," *Housing and Land Rights Network*, September 2015, http://hlrn.org.in/documents/UPR_Recommendations_Housing_and_Land_India_HLRN_Sept_2015.pdf.

4. Universal Declaration of Human Rights, http://www.un.org/en/universal-declaration-human-rights/.

5. https://www.ohchr.org/en/professionalinterest/pages/cescr.aspx.

6. See Pontifical Council for the Family, *The Family and Human Rights* (Vatican City: Libreria Editrice Vaticana, 1999), 69.

7. As given in M. K. Jha and P. Kumar, "Homeless Migrants in Mumbai Life and Labour in Urban Space," *Economic & Political Weekly* 51 (2016): 69–77; Nishikant Singh, Priyanka Koiri, and Sudheer Kumar Shukla, "Signposting Invisibles: A Study of the Homeless Population in India," *Chinese Sociological Dialogue* 3, no. 3 (2018): 181.

8. Census of India, *Primary Census Abstract*, Office of the Registrar General of India, Ministry of Home Affairs, Government of India, 2011. The Census of India counted the homeless households on the night of February 28, 2011.

9. Singh, Koiri, and Shukla, "Signposting Invisibles," 182.

10. Sanjukta Sarkara, "Homelessness in India," *Shelter* 15, no. 1 (April 2014): 10.

11. Ibid.

12. Harsh Mander, *Living Rough: Surviving City Streets: A Study of Homeless Population in Delhi, Chennai, Patna and Madurai* (2013), http://planningcommission.nic.in/reports/sereport/ser/ser_rough.pdf, 5.

13. Housing and Land Rights Network, http://hlrn.org.in/homelessness.

14. Ibid.

15. Sarkara, "Homelessness in India," 9.

16. Singh, Koiri, and Shukla, "Signposting Invisibles," 191.

17. Ibid., 181.

18. N. C. Saxena, "National Strategy for Urban Poor Mid-Term Evaluation Report: a GOI-UNDP Project April 2007: A Study of Homeless Populations in Delhi, Chennai, Patna and Madurai for the Planning Commission of India," in *Living Rough: Surviving City Streets: A Study of Homeless Population in Delhi, Chennai, Patna and Madurai*, http://planningcommission.nic.in/reports/sereport/ser/ser_rough.pdf, 63.

19. For a study on homeless women, please see Shivani Chaudry, Amita Joseph, and Indu Prakash Singh, "Women and Homelessness," in *The Fear That Stalks: Gender-Based Violence in Public Space*, ed. Sara Pilot and Lora Prabhu (New Delhi: Zubaan, 2012), 263–300.

20. "The Human Rights to Adequate Housing and Land in India: Report for the United Nations Human Rights Council."

21. "The Trajectory of a Struggle, Shahri Adhikar Manch: Beharon Ke Saath," March 2014, http://hlrn.org.in/documents/SAM-BKS_The_Trajectory_of_a_Struggle.pdf.

22. I would like to specially acknowledge the help given by Prof. K. Hemalatha, MSW, PhD, Associate Professor in the Department of Social Work at Christ University Bengaluru, and Fr. Edward Thomas, SDB, Bengaluru. I am grateful to both of them for the time they spared for discussions and for providing helpful literature, especially on the Indian situation of homelessness and responses.

23. http://www.sccommissioners.org. As given in Special Rapporteur on the Right to Adequate Housing—Questionnaire on Homelessness Response from Housing and Land Rights Network, India, www.hlrn.org.in.

24. See *Reaffirming Justiciability: Judgements on the Human Right to Adequate Housing from the High Court of Delhi,* Housing and Land Rights Network, New Delhi, 2013, http://hlrn.org.in/documents/Reaffirming_Justiciability_Judgements_on_HRAH_from_High_Court_of_Delhi.pdf.

25. http://www.indiaenvironmentportal.org.in/content/437577/order-of-the-supreme-court-of-india-regarding-right-to-shelter-of-homeless-persons-in-urban-areas-11112016.

The Ministry of Housing and Urban Poverty Alleviation (MHUPA) has implemented a scheme which has been sponsored centrally, i.e., Swarna Jayanti Shahari Rozgar Yojana (SJSRY), since 1997, and which was reconstituted as Deendayal Antyodaya Yojana—National Urban Livelihoods Mission since September 2013.

26. Amit Anand Choudhary, "Show Some Compassion for Homeless, Construct Shelter Homes for Them: Supreme Court to States," *Times of India*, November 8, 2017, https://timesofindia.indiatimes.com/india/show-some-compassion-for-homeless-construct-shelter-homes-for-them-supreme-court-to-states/articleshow/61565212.cms.

27. Sarkara, "Homelessness in India," 14. In fact, there are various schemes introduced by the government. But the implementation of these schemes continues to be poor.

28. This mission, to be implemented during 2015–22, provides central assistance to Urban Local Bodies (ULBs) and other implementing agencies through States/Union Territories (UTs) for rehabilitation of existing slum dwellers using land as a resource through private participation, credit linked subsidy, affordable housing in partnership, and subsidy for beneficiary-led individual house construction/enhancement.

29. See, for example, https://www.downtoearth.org.in/news/governance/truth-about-pm-s-housing-for-all-scheme-it-is-far-off-target-56713.

30. http://hlrn.org.in/documents/Press_Release_SAM_BKS_World_Homeless_Day.pdf.

31. "Out in the Cold on Christmas Eve," *Times of India*, New Delhi, December 25, 2009.

32. High Court of Delhi, Writ Petition (Civil) No 29 of 2010, Court on Its Own Motion versus Government of National Capital Territory of Delhi [Govt. of NCT Delhi] and others.

33. See Véronique Dupont, "Which Place for the Homeless in Delhi? Scrutiny of a Mobilisation Campaign in the 2010 Commonwealth Games Context," *South Asia Multidisciplinary Academic Journal* [Online] 8 (2013), http://journals.openedition.org/samaj/3662; DOI: 10.4000/samaj.3662. See also http://hlrn.org.in/documents/SAM%20PR_HC%20order_7%20Jan%202010.pdf.

34. Vision Statement of Shahri Adhikar Manch: Begharon Ke Saath, http://www.hic-sarp.org/homelessness.html.

35. "Delhi Govt to Build 15,000 Houses for Homeless," *Hindustan Times*, May 11, 2016, https://www.hindustantimes.com/delhi-news/delhi-govt-to-build-15-000-houses-for-homeless/story-IazBwm2sWOir19xVK1TruM.html.

36. http://www.indiaonlinepages.com/population/bangalore-population.html.

37. "Survey Finds 3991 Homeless Persons in Three Zones," *Hindu*, December 30, 2018. See also "More Than 1500 Homeless Persons Found in West Zone Alone, Reveals Survey," *Hindu Metroplus*, December 18, 2018; "1255 Homeless in South Zone," *Deccan Herald*, December 27, 2018; "In Two Nights, BBMP Survey Identifies over 1400 Homeless," *Times of India*, Bengaluru, December 17, 2018.

38. "Survey Finds 3991 Homeless Persons in Three Zones," *Hindu*, December 30, 2018.

39. "Urban Homeless May be Highest in South B'luru," *Deccan Herald*, December 19, 2018.

40. "40 Urban Centres to Be Set Up for the Homeless by March Next Year," *Deccan Herald*, December 25, 2018.

41. "A Priest's Street Mission Takes Flight," *UCA NEWS* https://www.ucanews.com/news/a-priests-mission-takes-flight/5219; see also, https://sites.google.com/site/akashaparavakalfba.

42. Ashabari (Home of Hope), www.ashabari.org.in.

43. For more details, see http://boscoban.org.

44 John Paul II, *Sollicitudo Rei Socialis*, 42. http://w2.vatican.va/content/john-paul-ii/en/encyclicals/documents/hf_jp-ii_enc_30121987_sollicitudo-rei-socialis.html.

Moving *Again*

Women, Catholic Social Teaching, and Disguised Homelessness in Jamaica

Anna Kasafi Perkins

> Mi never live nowhere an mi always inna struggle fi sen mi children to school. Sometimes I can't even find food, so I'm thankful to Food For the Poor for the house, and to Pauline Fearon, owner of the Whitfield Bakery, for sponsoring my daughter, Kitanya Bruce, for the next three years she has in high school. I feel elated and my heart is more than happy.
>
> —Roxanne Williams, in Shanique Samuels,
> "Roof Over My Head — Mother Says Thanks
> for Support to Her and Family,"
> *The Gleaner*, January 14, 2017

Homelessness is everywhere evident in the urban centers of Jamaica: Kingston, Spanish Town, Montego Bay, and so on. Elderly men lie sleeping in the middle of the day in the plaza around the Supreme Court in Downtown Kingston; disabled and differently abled men and boys beg or wash windshields at traffic lights; a mentally ill woman conducts her daily ablutions in the busy Half Way Tree Square to the amusement of male taxi drivers and the indifference of passers-by. The public faces of such homeless people or, as we call them in Jamaica, "street people" or "mad people" (street boys, street children, men, and women), is a taken-for-granted part of the urban landscape only to be countenanced when one of them commits an egregious act[1] or, as in the case of the "Street People Saga," the presence of international visitors causes them to be transported across parish lines to ensure their invisibility.[2] In 2015, the visit by then-President Barack Obama was preceded by concerns that the homeless would again be mistreated and whisked away to prevent offending the sensibilities of the president. The eventual removal of almost two hundred persons from the route Obama traveled was presented as part of the routine response of the municipality to the problem.[3]

The numbers of street people are uncertain, but using data gleaned from Jamaica's *2011 Population and Housing Census* we arrive at a total of 934 persons, not including those who may be living in institutions.[4] More recent mappings suggest an even larger population of the homeless,[5] especially in metropolitan Kingston and St. Andrew. According to a 2015 point-in-time survey undertaken by the Board of Supervision, there was a 26 percent increase in the number of homeless persons between 2012 and March 2015 (1,418, up from 1,057). Yet only around 12 percent (less than 181) of those persons were on the Poor Relief Roll and therefore eligible for some kind of government support.[6]

In addition to the government activities geared at reducing homelessness—accommodation in shelters and drop-in centers, medical treatment, and reintegration with family[7]—the church as well as various philanthropic groups have responded in varying ways to the poverty and homelessness of these Jamaicans through providing low-cost housing, homes and shelters, feeding programs, and so on. However, as one homeless woman, who calls herself Miss Portia, complains, "The government needs to rise up now, man. People are disappointed in them; both sides have disappointed the people. Hats off to the private sector and the Catholics, 'cause a dem a run dis ting, nuh government' [because they are more effective in dealing with homelessness, not the government]."[8]

Not Counting the Women and Children

Homelessness in Jamaica has a gendered face, with more males being counted in the group. The Board of Supervision defines the homeless as anyone,

> who resides in places not meant for human habitation—cars, parks, sidewalks, abandoned buildings, and on the street; an emergency shelter; transitional and supportive homes for homeless persons who originally came from the streets or emergency shelters; in any of the above places, but is spending a short time (up to 30 consecutive days) in a hospital or other institution; has been evicted within a week from a private dwelling unit; has been discharged within a week from an institution, such as a mental health or substance abuse treatment facility or a jail/prison.[9]

This encompasses a broad range of persons and circumstances. One group of homeless persons that is even more difficult to count, and perhaps reach, are women with children who are in "residentially unstable situations." Many women and their children are forced to flee domestic violence and the effects of poverty such as eviction and job loss. "Aimee," an inmate at the Portland Rehabilitation Management homeless shelter, the only shelter for the homeless in the eastern part of Jamaica, became homeless due to a job loss:

> I was out there in Kingston, in the society living a normal life. I had work in the private sector, for seven years at a computer store. Then the global recession happened; it had a very adverse effect on my life. Job cut. Eviction. My life deteriorated rapidly. I couldn't compose myself materially or emotionally.[10]

Aimee's fellow resident, "Danna," fled domestic violence at home:

> Before coming to the shelter, I was at home. My brother was beating me
> up; early on this year he abused me with a machete and rope and so on. I
> had to go to the hospital, and they brought me to the shelter.[11]

Oftentimes, such women find themselves homeless for extended periods. This
existence is, however, disguised as the women enter further and various insecure
circumstances, eventually being forced to move *again*. Such homelessness has
numerous consequences such as child dispersal and insecurity, vulnerability to
sexual abuse, and truancy. It is possible to label such female homelessness in Jamaica
as "hidden," "disguised," or "concealed," especially since the figures for homelessness
show the homeless to be predominantly male and little account is taken of women
and their children.

   This chapter draws from official statistics of Jamaica, stories of homeless
women (with children), and the writings of the Antilles Episcopal Conference
(Roman Catholic Bishops of the Caribbean) to present a discourse around female
homelessness, which points to the resources from within the Caribbean Catholic
Social Teaching (CST) tradition that can address the particularly vulnerable existence of such women, whose plight may well be replicated across the Anglophone
Caribbean. Some of the responses that are called for include poverty reduction/
alleviation, sociocultural changes with regards to female dependence on males and
culturally sanctioned gender-based violence (GBV), and the provision of services
specific to the needs of such women and their offspring.

Disguised Homelessness

   Homelessness is one of the worst forms of urban poverty and social vulnerability. It is a glaring indicator of the failure of governance and the states'
commitment to the welfare of its citizens.[12]

   Women and children are to be found predominantly among the concealed
homeless. Concealed homelessness occurs when someone loses her home because
of a combination of various factors, including displacement due to gang/political
violence (e.g., as with recent events in Rockfort in St. Andrew), economic hardships, relationship loss/abandonment, mental illness, HIV/AIDS status, substance
abuse, or a fire or natural disasters such as hurricanes,[13] and may be forced to move
in with friends[14] or relatives (i.e., to "beg a kotch," as Jamaicans say). This idea of
a "kotch" is a very important one in Jamaica; it refers to the tenuous temporary
stay at someone's house. It also connotes a precarious posture or position such as
when someone is perched on a ledge or leans against an unstable object for support.
All these notions are clearly present in the actual circumstances of women who are
among the disguised homeless in Jamaica. In addition, children are often dispersed
across families and are vulnerable to exploitation and other harms. These tragic

stories are seen nightly on the evening news. The idea of "a kotch" presents the precariousness of the new living situation as usually the friends who have offered help are themselves already in cramped circumstances. It takes little for such concealed homelessness to tip over into direct homelessness. Nonetheless, these women and their children who are "kotching" are not visible and would not be counted as part of the homeless population. Essentially, such disguised homelessness is really family homelessness. (A case of not counting the women and children may be found in Matthew 14.21, which notes, "And those who ate were about five thousand men, besides women and children.")

Domestic Violence

One of the key causes of homelessness or residential instability for women and their children is domestic violence in a context where women are unable to find/afford appropriate housing options. Domestic violence increases a woman's vulnerability to homelessness, especially in a culture like Jamaica's where police are often reluctant to intervene in "domestic affairs," considered "man-woman business," and there are few options for crisis or transitional housing.[15] There are also the communal, societal, cultural, and religious beliefs that condone male violence toward women, especially intimate partners.[16] Additionally, the fear of homelessness prevents many women from leaving abusive situations, with several returning or asking for leniency for the abuser when he is brought before the courts. According to Joyce Hewitt, president of Woman's Inc., which runs the only official women's shelter in Jamaica, "Crisis never stops and domestic violence never stops, unfortunately." She questions further, as she speaks to the adequacy of the service provided, "Once they leave the shelter, for example, where do they go? If they have nowhere to go, they go back to their abusive situation. Our next thing is a transitional home, so that women can go and stay up to a year or if they need more than a year."[17] Currently, the refurbished shelter can only accommodate twelve women and their children.

The plight of such battered women and their children is captured in a poem by the Jamaican Juleus Ghunta called "Moving Again," from which this chapter takes its name.[18] The poet details the furtive actions of a woman fleeing with her children in the early hours of the morning. The central character of the poem is one of her children. The child is "eager to escape the afflictions of the parental wrangles of the nights before" and with mother and siblings falls "weeping in a huddle on the verandah of [their] *ninth* home" (emphasis added). This ninth escape indicates a pattern of constant fight, flight, and fear. Accompanied by the hastily gathered paraphernalia of the homeless—knapsacks and bulging plastic bags—this mother is able to take her children away to some safe haven . . . but for how long?[19] The unnamed mother may well have been supported by an informal "secret network" of former victims and other professionals who are committed to providing assistance for women in these situations.[20] Where possible these women are assisted with a place to live and new schools for their children outside of the parish where their abuser lives. Of course, the reach of this "secret network" is limited, as are the resources available through government and church agencies.

Although the number of women living in domestic violence situations in Jamaica is not known, statistics from the Jamaica Constabulary Force reveal that 116 female homicides were reported in 2015. Sexual violence against females remains very high. In fact, in 2014, young women twenty-four years and under accounted for 92 percent of all sexual-violence cases. The *2016 Jamaica Women's Health Report* (*WHSJ*), the first comprehensive study of the nature and prevalence of the experience of violence against women and girls in Jamaica, confirmed that violence against women was widespread in Jamaica. The *WHSJ* examined the factors associated with violence against women and girls, the impact of violence on women's physical and mental health, and the various coping strategies employed by women in response to violence. The report found that one in every four Jamaican women aged fifteen to sixty-four has experienced domestic and/or sexual violence during her lifetime. Pledges by successive governments to build three women's shelters across the island are yet to come to fruition.[21] Indeed, as in the case of the Women Inc. shelter and the "Secret Network," most of the initiatives toward women and their families come from the religious community, which offers short-term accommodation as discussed further below.

The Antilles Episcopal Conference

The Antilles Episcopal Conference pastors Catholics in the Anglophone, Francophone (except Haiti), and Netherlandophone Caribbean. As such, their pastorate is a subsection of the wider Caribbean. The population of the AEC pastorate is just over seven million. Since 1969, they have issued various encyclicals and other "statements" addressing issues affecting the people of the region. These statements represent a "rich but little-recognized source of pastoral and ethical reflection from within the region."[22]

They treat concerns such as poverty, broken family life, economic stagnation, cultural dependency, and increasing violence. From time to time they express particular concern with the status and treatment of women. Their expression of concern from their 1982 encyclical *True Freedom and Development* remains sadly relevant thirty-five years later:

> We are grieved to see that so many in our region are still living in degrading poverty, and in miserable housing conditions, uncertain where their next meal is to come from. Many children are still suffering from malnutrition while many women have to carry an appalling burden with little or no support from the fathers: they have to care for a house and children while at the same time having to go out to work in order to support themselves and those dependent upon them. (§8)

Perhaps given the number of social problems that are a part of the social fabric of the region, the bishops have not been able to reflect in a sustained way on the issue of homelessness or focus specifically on women's issues. This needs to be addressed soon if the AEC is to remain relevant. Both of these matters form a lacuna in the bishops' writings, especially as they—homelessness and the status of women—are closely linked in the Caribbean context, as this essay demonstrates.

Only two direct mentions are made of homelessness in the AEC documents: The first comes from *Caring for the Earth* (2005), the bishops' call to environmental stewardship that maintains the interconnectedness of all creation. In that statement they call upon St. Francis to intercede for all "who groaned" (§64) and specifically mention the displaced, refugees, *the homeless*, land perishing from drought, among others.[23] The pain of human beings directly affects the earth. They conclude by placing the Caribbean under the patronage of St. Francis of Assisi. In *The Gift of Life* (2008), they assert that "responding in practical ways to the needs of the destitute, drug addicts, *the homeless*, persons living with AIDS and their families, and all these whom Pope Paul VI described as the 'new poor,' e.g., the handicapped, should include material help, a welcome in the Church community, and a defence of their place and dignity in society" (§44, emphasis added).[24] Interestingly, any and all of these groups enumerated could be subsumed under the categories of the homeless since, as noted previously, destitution, drug addiction, disability, and HIV status, can all contribute to ending up on the streets. In addition, the bishops specifically commend those who are in ministry of serving life, including those who work in church homes for abandoned children and those who work at providing affordable housing for the poor.

Perhaps the bishops' most pertinent statement that treats with issues affecting women was written in 1994, the year the United Nations declared the Year of the Family. *Evangelising the Family* (*EFL* 1994) is perhaps the one document that takes the most focused account of the issues affecting Caribbean women in the family, which the bishops acknowledge as key to the development of the individual and of the society.[25] They take a very pastoral approach to the issues and outline specific pastoral directives for practical action at the level of dioceses, priests, parishes, families, private sector, and governments throughout.

The bishops early on acknowledged that they have become increasingly aware of the violence inflicted on women in the home (§4). They target specifically the economic dependency of women on men, which:

> For many . . . [leads to a] cycle of exploitation where women are used time and again by different partners in short term and irresponsible relationships. The cycle cultivates a condition of mistrust and insecurity. Women become dependent on visiting partners for financial help to survive and for companionship. They are demeaned and often subjected to physical and psychological abuse. Children in many such homes have the same

mother but different fathers. Infidelity and lack of commitment are rooted in this cycle. This, certainly, is not the Gospel value proclaimed by Jesus. (*EFL*, §3)

At the same time, they affirm "the increasing awareness of the dignity of women, the greater respect for family life, the heightening involvement of families in society" (§6). They call upon priests to be "particularly supportive of movements for the development of women in society, ensuring that their dignity is respected" (§9). In so doing, the priest/pastor witnesses to the positive understandings of women in society and offers his support. The priest is therefore called upon as one who ministers in the public sphere to uphold the responsibility of coming to the "defence of . . .[women's] place and dignity in society" against anything and anyone who would do otherwise.

Interestingly, the bishops call upon the governments of the region to make family a first priority. They say it is not enough for governments to draft policies to help families of the future. Rather, they state that families in the present are in need of "immediate care and protection" (§5). Furthermore, they call upon governments to provide adequate housing or to help with financing so that each family can have "its own dignified home" (§5). The bishops' urging the governments to take action calls to mind a poem by Helen-Ann Elizabeth Wilkinson, a Jamaican Roman Catholic poet, who challenges the church for delaying to respond to the social needs evident around them. In "Can't come, but love to say 'I'm coming,'" which plays on the way Jamaicans say, "I will be there shortly" but take an interminably long time to arrive or to act, Wilkinson says,

> Thanks God fi Jesus
> For the Master heal all ten ah we
> Not to mention "dose" dem "bedwardise"
> The mad, *homeless*, disregarded
> Douse wid flammable
> and en flame
> Fire
> set on fire.[26]

Wilkinson is aware of the many who in Caribbean society are disregarded and made outcasts like the ten lepers, whom Jesus healed willingly. She alludes to the framing of the homeless as mentally ill, as was done with Alexander Bedward (hence "bedwardise"), an iconic Jamaican preacher, who during colonial times preached against the injustices of a racist, colonialist system.[27] He started his native church in protest against the ways the colonial churches perpetuated the injustices against Black Jamaicans. He was eventually committed to an asylum to silence him. The incidents of the maltreatment of the homeless included some being doused with flammable liquid and set alight,[28] a different kind of fire than the one that should burn in Christians for the care of the poor and homeless, especially women with children.

Indeed, the bishops do speak of the ways the Catholic Church across the region continues to minister to the homeless in a variety of ways that often go unremarked. Individual pastors provide care and sustenance to street people, in religious groups such as the Missionaries of the Poor and Mustard Seed in Jamaica, Living Waters in Trinidad and Tobago, and street people ministries of St. Peter and Paul and St. Richard's Churches in Jamaica. Not to mention the individual efforts of other para-church groups like Food for the Poor, who assisted Roxanne Williams to "get a roof over her head" (FFP website). Williams had been unable to house or feed herself and her children after she came out of prison. The bishops call for dioceses, which it acknowledged have already established homes for abused women and children, to increase the number of such homes in order to provide spaces of refuge for the victims. Given the resource constraints of many dioceses, it is unclear how many additional homes have been provided. (Also, the impact of these pastorals is not measured.)

Conclusion

The causes of homelessness among women—disguised and visible—are myriad and complex. Owing to the impact on children, disguised female homelessness is also family homelessness, with all the attendant vulnerabilities. The AEC provides some insight into trajectories of homelessness for women, including the violence visited upon them in intimate partner relationships, their financial dependency on men, and the impact of natural or humanmade disasters. On the whole, the AEC is concerned about the dignity of women and how they are treated in ways that destroy this dignity, especially in the intimate relationships they enter or in the undignified way they are forced to live due to poverty and substandard housing. The importance of the dignity of women as divine creation can undergird and support various human rights approaches that call for a response to experiences of homelessness. A multilayered approach to homelessness in general and disguised homelessness in particular needs to be deployed. This account directly addresses the various stakeholders in the process, including the women "kotching."

First, part of that recognition is to find a way of including disguised homelessness in the definition of homelessness. As homeless is currently defined in the National Population and Housing Census or by the Board of Supervision,[29] it is wholly inadequate. The definition of a homeless person used by the Board of Supervision is "someone who resides in places not meant for human habitation—cars, parks, sidewalks, abandoned buildings, and on the street; an emergency shelter; transitional and supportive homes for homeless persons who originally came from the institution; has been evicted within a week from a private dwelling unit; has been discharged within a week from an institution, such as a mental health or substance abuse treatment facility or a jail/prison."[30] It is possible to include "living with someone in the hope of getting back on her feet." Without including such precariously tenured women and their children among the homeless, little provision can or will be made for their needs and to prevent them from eventually falling into direct homelessness. Therefore, ways need to be found to include such persons in the definition of homelessness and to contribute to the requisite responses.

Second, resources must be deployed to address the immediate needs of these women and their children, which often goes beyond just shelter but involves social services and skills training to address the immediate factors leading to homelessness in each specific case. Understanding the circumstances of life that have led to the experience of individual women being homeless can contribute to them "attaining and retaining stable housing."[31] If the circumstance which forced a woman into disguised homelessness includes dependency on an abusive male partner, then a particular set of resources and support needs to be deployed, including, resources permitting, the rehabilitation of the abusive partner.

Although the church across the region has been providing various services to such women, these efforts are insufficient. Moreover, the teaching tradition of the AEC has not treated homelessness (or women's issues) in a sustained or pointed fashion. Nonetheless, the church is equipped to continue to provide such services for women in a context of healing and support to build up and restore the dignity of the women involved. This may require continuing partnerships with NGOs, government, and private sectors. At the same time, the structural causes of homelessness among women with children need to be tackled. These include the cultural views of masculinity that make violence a characteristic of manhood, especially in the domestic sphere. Similarly, the agents of the state, like the police, with the mandate to serve and protect need to abandon perspectives that take reports of domestic violence less seriously than other kinds. Training with regard to the vulnerability of such women and the proneness of some women to return to their abusers is also necessary.

Importantly, in the process of designing the response to homelessness among women, the government should ensure that these women are counted and consulted. Members of civil society, including the church and NGOs already providing services for these women and their families, should also be a part of the conversation. A long-term plan to address homelessness generally, but homelessness among women specifically, needs to be drafted. There should be a plan to report periodically on the success of this plan. Those would be some initial steps to prevent one more woman from being forced to "move again."

Notes

1. Garfield Myers, "Cops Kill 'Ram Pus': Controversy over Shooting of Mentally Ill Man Accused of Beating Up 77-Year-Old," *Jamaica Observer*, Sunday, February 20, 2011, http://www.jamaicaobserver.com/news/Cops-kill-'Ram-Pus'.

2. See Letter to the Editor, Kenroy Williams, "No Mass Relocation of Street People for Obama's Visit," *Jamaica Observer*, Wednesday, April 8, 2015. The Board of Supervision, which functions under the auspices of the Poor Relief Act, has been "given additional duties to ensure the care and protection of Homeless and Street People island wide as mandated

by the Commission of Enquiry Act to enquire into the forced removal of Homeless Persons from Montego Bay to St. Elizabeth on the 15th Day of July, 1999" (https://www.localgov-jamaica.gov.jm/bos.aspx?c=duties),

http://www.jamaicaobserver.com/letters/No-mass-relocation-of-street-people-for-Obama-s-visit_18709294.

3. Daraine Luton, "Removal of Homeless before Obama Visit Was Start of Long-Term Solution—Mayor," *Jamaica Gleaner*, May 1, 2015, http://jamaica-gleaner.com/article/news/20150501/removal-homeless-obama-visit-was-start-long-term-solution-mayor.

4. Population and Housing Census, *Jamaica—General Report Vol. 1* (Statistical Institute of Jamaica, 2012). The census speaks of "persons on the street" (p. xxx). A group of persons who regularly swell the ranks of the homeless are members of the LGBT community. JFLAG, *Re-Presenting and Redressing LGBT Homelessness in Jamaica: Towards a Multifaceted Approach to Addressing Anti-Gay Related Displacement* J-FLAG (July 2014), http://jflag.org/wp-content/uploads/2014/07/rePresenting-and-Redressing-LGBT-Homelessness-in-Jamaica-JFLAG.pdf.

5. The 2012 Report of the Committee on Homelessness places the number at at least 1,160. See Sheryl Muir, "Dealing with Homelessness in Jamaica," *Jamaica Observer*, March 27, 2017, http://www.jamaicaobserver.com/columns/Dealing-with-homelessness-in-Jamaica_93757.

6. "Statistics Show Homelessness on the Rise," *Jamaica Observer*, January 13, 2016, http://www.jamaicaobserver.com/News/Statistics-show-homelessness-on-the-rise_48632.

7. Luton, "Removal of Homeless."

8. Jediael Carter, "Rugged Living on the Streets of Downtown Kingston: How Homeless Men and Women Struggle to Stay Alive," *Jamaica Observer*, April 30, 2017, http://www.jamaicaobserver.com/news/rugged-living-on-the-streets-rugged-living-on-the-streets-how-homeless-men-and-women-struggle-to-stay-alive_94936.

9. Ibid.

10. http://prmhomeless.org/resident-stories/.

11. Ibid.

12. Shivani Chaudhry, Amita Joseph, and Indu Prakash Singh, "Women and Homelessness," in *The Fear That Stalks: Gender-based Violence in Public Spaces*, ed. Sara Pilot and Lora Prabhu (New Delhi: Zubaan, 2014), 263.

13. It is believed that Hurricane Gilbert in 1988 contributed significantly to chronic homelessness in Jamaica.

14. It is noteworthy that the informal networks of care and support available to such women are often women-centered and are a feature of the helping practices of women who live in inner-city communities. Barry Chevannes, "Jamaican Diasporic Identity: The Metaphor of Yaad," in *Nation Dance: Religion, Identity, and Cultural Difference in the Caribbean*, ed. Patrick Taylor (Bloomington: Indiana University Press, 2001), 129–37.

15. See, for example, Maggie Schmeitz, "Two Steps Forward, One Step Backwards: Addressing Violence against Women in Suriname," *Caribbean Quarterly* 52, nos. 2 and 3 (June–September 2006): 66–83.

16. Ibid. See also Carol Watson Williams, *Women's Health Survey 2016: Jamaica*. (Statistical Institute of Jamaica, Inter-American Development Bank and the United Nations Entity for Gender Equality and the Empowerment of Women, 2018).

17. Nadine Wilson-Harris, "Women's Shelter Set to Reopen," *Sunday Gleaner*, September 17, 2017, http://jamaica-gleaner.com/article/news/20170917/battered-women-shelter-set-reopen.

18. Juleus Ghunta, "Moving Again," in *In This Breadfruit Kingdom: An Anthology of Jamaican Poetry*, ed. Mervyn Morris (Kingston: Blouse & Skirt Books, 2017), 60. Thanks to Juleus for permission to quote the poems.

19. My thanks to Juleus Ghunta for permission to reproduce the line from his poem. The poem is actually autobiographical as he notes in an email to this author (December 11, 2018): "Mother rented a place in Kendal. A year later, she returned to her partner in Pell River when the living costs became unbearable. She left me at our extended family home. Her partner expressed that there was no place for me in his house. Aunt X (see Part 2, Section B, 2.2.1), who lived in the family home, declared her wish to see me leave. After months of tension and arguments, my frustrated grandmother threw me onto the street. Having no place to go, I walked to Pell River, sought refuge with several families before an elderly man took me in. Shortly after that, mother left Pell River for Kendal. I was on my own." The excerpt is from Juleus Ghunta, "Adverse Childhood Experiences (ACE), the Performance of Wellness, and Storytelling as Victimisation, Therapy, and Defiance. An Autoethnography," unpublished MA dissertation, University of Bradford, 2018, 30.

20. Nadine Wilson-Harris, "Help from Underground—Secret Network Rescuing Abused Women from Life-Threatening Situations," *Sunday Gleaner*, September 4, 2016.

21. The minister of local government, Desmond McKenzie, in a news item on Television Jamaica (TVJ), December 20, 2018, 7:10PM, claimed that there were over three thousand homeless people in Jamaica with over one thousand in Kingston.

22. Anna Kasafi Perkins, introduction to *Justice and Peace in a Renewed Caribbean: Contemporary Catholic Reflections*, ed. Anna Kasafi Perkins, Donald Chambers, and Jacqueline Porter (New York: Palgrave Macmillan, 2012), 1.

23. Antilles Episcopal Conference, *Caring for the Earth* (AEC, 2005), https://www.archdioceseofnassau.org/index.php/archbishop/pastoral-letters/112-caring-for-the-earth.

24. Antilles Episcopal Conference, *The Gift of Life* (AEC, 2008), http://aecbishops.org/the-gift-of-life.

25. Antilles Episcopal Conference, *Evangelising Family Life* (AEC, 1994), http://www.archdioceseofkingston.org/Resources/EvangelizingFamilyLife.pdf.

26. This poem was originally published in the *Sunday Gleaner* (n.d.). Thanks to Helen Ann Elizabeth Wilkinson for permission to quote from her poem. Emphasis added.

27. Veront Satchell, "Early Stirrings of Black Nationalism in Colonial Jamaica: Alexander Bedward of the Jamaica Native Baptist Free Church 1889–1921," *Journal of Caribbean History* 38, no. 1 (January 1, 2004).

28. Shanice Watson, "Homeless Man Set on Fire in MoBay . . . Advocate Says Culprits Are Wicked," *Star*, September 3, 2016, http://jamaica-star.com/article/news/20160903/homeless-man-set-fire-mobay%E2%80%A6advocate-says-culprits-are-wicked.

29. The Board of Supervision is a statutory body operating under the portfolio of the Ministry of Local Government and Community Development, established under Jamaica's Poor Relief Act to supervise and monitor the delivery of the poor relief services performed by the parish councils and Kingston and St. Andrew Corporation (KSAC).

30. Jediael Carter, "Rugged Living on the Streets of Downtown Kingston," *Jamaica Observer*, April 30, 2017.

31. Priya Kissoon, "Before the Pavements: A Snapshot of the Housing Histories of Socially Displaced Persons," *UWI Today*, May 2015, https://sta.uwi.edu/uwitoday/archive/may_2015/article9.asp.

CONTRIBUTORS

Paul Houston Blankenship is a PhD candidate at the Graduate Theological Union in Berkeley. His dissertation is an ethnography on the spiritual lives of people experiencing homelessness in Seattle.

Dame Louise Casey, CBE, CB, is the co-founder and chair of the Institute of Global Homelessness and visiting professor at Kings College, London, the United Kingdom.

William T. Cavanaugh is professor of Catholic Studies and director of the Center for World Catholicism and Intercultural Theology at DePaul University.

Meghan J. Clark is an associate professor of moral theology at St. John's University (NY).

Alejandro Crosthwaite, OP, is dean and full professor of Catholic Social Teaching at the Faculty of Social Sciences at the Pontifical University of St. Thomas Aquinas (Rome).

Dennis P. Culhane is the Dana and Andrew Stone Professor of Social Policy at the University of Pennsylvania.

María Teresa (MT) Dávila is a lecturer in Religious and Theological Studies at Merrimack College. Her scholarly work focuses on various themes in Christian discipleship in the context of US civil society.

Julie George, SSpS, is a member of the Missionary Sisters Servants of the Holy Spirit. She is a women's rights lawyer and director of Streevani, a center for the empowerment of women in Pune, Maharashtra.

Rosanne Haggerty is the founder and president of Community Solutions, a not-for-profit organization working with communities to end homelessness and the conditions that create it.

Kat Johnson is the former executive director of the Institute of Global Homelessness. She is currently senior project manager for strategy at Community Solutions, whose mission is to end homelessness and the conditions that create it.

Kelly S. Johnson is the author of *The Fear of Beggars: Stewardship and Poverty in Christian Ethics* (Eerdmans, 2007) and an associate professor in the Department of Religious Studies at the University of Dayton.

265

Pat Jones recently completed PhD research focused on Catholic homelessness charities. She previously worked in senior roles in Depaul International, CAFOD, and the Catholic Bishops' Conference of England and Wales.

Toussaint Kafarhire, SJ, is a Congolese Jesuit and poet. He currently lives and teaches international relations and African cultures at Hekima Institute of Peace Studies and International Relations (HIPSIR) in Nairobi, Kenya.

James F. Keenan, SJ, is the Canisius Professor and director of the Jesuit Institute at Boston College and the founder of Catholic Theological Ethics in the World Church.

Shaji George Kochuthara, CMI, is an associate professor of moral theology at Dharmaram Vidya Kshetram, Bangalore, India. He is editor of *Asian Horizons* and *Dharmaram Journal of Theology*, and president of the Association of Moral Theologians of India.

Joseph L. Mben, SJ, is an assistant professor at the Jesuit Institute of Theology in Abidjan (Cote d'Ivoire) and editor-in-chief of *Kanien*, the scholarly journal of that same institute.

Joseph McCrave is a PhD candidate in theological ethics at Boston College. He received an MPhil in theology and a BA in philosophy and theology from the University of Oxford.

Mark McGreevy, OBE, is group chief executive of Depaul International, founder of the Institute of Global Homelessness based at DePaul University Chicago, and an Honorary Fellow of Leeds Trinity University.

Ann Elizabeth Montgomery is an investigator with the National Center on Homelessness among Veterans and an assistant professor at the University of Alabama at Birmingham School of Public Health.

Elias Opongo, SJ, is the director of Hekima Institute of Peace Studies and International Relations (HIPSIR), Hekima University College, and a senior lecturer and researcher in transitional justice, conflict resolution, democracy, and statebuilding.

Anna Kasafi Perkins is a Jamaican Roman Catholic theologian who works as a quality assurance officer at the University of the West Indies.

Daniel Franklin E. Pilario, CM, is a professor and the present dean of St. Vincent School of Theology, Adamson University in Manila. He is also a vice president of the theological journal *Concilium*.

Ethna Regan, chf, is an associate professor in theology and ethics and head of the School of Theology, Philosophy, and Music in Dublin City University. She worked in Trinidad and Samoa.

Carlo Santoro coordinates both the Sant'Egidio services for the homeless (North/West Rome) and the Villetta della Misericordia (residential unit—twenty homeless), visits the homeless at two Roman prisons, and works at the Italian Bioethics Committee.

Mary Scullion is a Sister of Mercy and a member of the Project HOME community in Philadelphia, Pennsylvania, which she co-founded in 1989.

Molly Seeley is program manager at the Institute of Global Homelessness.

Carol Elizabeth Thomas is a member of the Project HOME community, where she serves as director of homeless services, including street outreach.

Wilhelmina Uhai Tunu, LSOSF, is the regional coordinator of Strengthening the Capacity of Religious Women in Early Childhood Development Program in Eastern and Central Africa and an adjunct lecturer at the Catholic University of Eastern Africa and Tangaza University College.

Cardinal Peter Turkson is Prefect of the Dicastery for Promoting Integral Human Development.

Christopher Williams is a member of the Project HOME community in Philadelphia, Pennsylvania.

Tobias Winright is an associate professor of theological ethics in the Department of Theological Studies and an associate professor of Health Care Ethics in the Gnaegi Center for Health Care Ethics, both at Saint Louis University.

Mary Mee-Yin Yuen is the social ethics professor at the Holy Spirit Seminary of Theology and Philosophy, Hong Kong.

INDEX